Mikhail Bulgakov
Six Plays

**The White Guard, Madame Zoyka, Flight, Molière,
Adam and Eve, The Last Days**

'In the West, in the theatre and literature, he is relished as one of
the greatest of modern writers, perhaps *the* greatest.'

Independent

MIKHAIL AFANAS'EVICH BULGAKOV was born in Kiev
in 1891. After graduating from the Medical Faculty of Kiev
University in 1916 he served in the medical personnel, first in
World War One, then the Civil War, and in 1919 he was mobilized
as a doctor and posted to the Caucasus by the White Army. There
he embarked on a career as writer, and in 1921 he left for Moscow
to write articles and satiric short stories about the revolution and
the economic reconstruction in the young Soviet state. His first
substantial work was *The White Guard*, in which he drew on his
personal experiences as a White defending Kiev against the
Ukrainian Republic. He adapted it for the stage at the suggestion of
the Moscow Art Theatre, and he wrote *Madame Zoyka*, which cast
a sympathetic light on the private enterprises encouraged by the
New Economic Policy, for the Vakhtangov Studio. In 1926, the
year both these plays were premièred, his flat was searched by the
authorities and his diaries confiscated. In 1927 he wrote *Flight*, an
existential play set at a time of historic collapse: he chose as his
heroes Russians who opposed the revolution but found leaving
their country a moral impossibility. It was abandoned during
rehearsals in 1929, the year *Madame Zoyka* was removed from the
Vakhtangov's repertoire, and in which he wrote *Molière*, whose
hero's dependence on the patronage of the Sun King was to mirror
the author's on Stalin. In 1931 Bulgakov was commissioned to
write about a future war and *Adam and Eve* was the result.
Picturing a world on the brink of, and immediately after, a
catastrophic ideological conflict, Bulgakov nevertheless infuses the
play's moral questioning and horror with comedy. The final play in
this collection, *The Last Days*, shows the great poet Pushkin's death
in a duel engineered by the Tsar's secret police; as in *Molière*, the
artist's immortality is assured.

MIKHAIL BULGAKOV

Six Plays

Introduced by Lesley Milne

The White Guard
Translated by Michael Glenny

Madame Zoyka
Translated by Michael Glenny

Flight
Translated by Michael Glenny

Molière
Translated by Michael Glenny

Adam and Eve
Translated by Michael Glenny

The Last Days
Translated by William Powell and Michael Earley

Methuen Drama

METHUEN WORLD CLASSICS

This collection first published in Great Britain in 1991
by Methuen Drama
Reissued with a new cover in 1998
Methuen Publishing Ltd
215 Vauxhall Bridge Road
London SW1V 1EJ

www.methuen.co.uk

A CIP catalogue record for this book is available at the British Library

Methuen Publishing Ltd reg. number 3543167

ISBN 0 413 64530 4
(0052481851
Transferred to digital printing 2002

Contents

Chronology

At the end of the sixteenth century most of Europe adopted the Gregorian or New Style calendar. The Russians retained the Julian or Old Style calendar until February 1918. In the nineteenth century the difference between the dates was twelve days; in the twentieth century the difference was thirteen days. Dates before February 1918 are identified as either Old or New Style if this is necessary for the chronology of events. Dates after February 1918 are given according to the New Style calendar.

1891   Mikhail Afanas'evich Bulgakov born in Kiev (3 May Old Style, 15 May New Style), into a Russian family.

1901   Bulgakov entered the Alexander I High School, Kiev.

1909   Bulgakov entered the Medical Faculty of Kiev University.

1913   Bulgakov married Tat'yana Nikolaevna Lappa.

1914   *Outbreak of First World War.*

1916   Bulgakov graduated 'with distinction' from the Medical Faculty of Kiev University.
Bulgakov enlisted as Red Cross Volunteer, working in military hospitals on the south-west front.
In September Bulgakov was officially mobilized and posted to *zemstvo* (district) hospitals in the rear, in the province of Smolensk, where there was a shortage of medical personnel as a result of the call-up of experienced doctors to the front.

1917   *February/early March (Old Style): overthrow of tsarist autocracy; abdication of Tsar Nicholas II; establishment of Provincial Government.*
25 October (Old Style)/7 November (New Style): Bolshevik seizure of power in Petrograd.
The 'Triumphal March of Soviet Power', during which there was considerable fighting, particularly in the Ukraine, where Soviet power had been rejected.

1918   *February: first capture of Kiev by Bolshevik troops.*
        February: Bulgakov obtained his official discharge from
        the army and returned to Kiev.
        Civil War.
        December: Bulgakov joined in the defence of Kiev by the
        White Guard against the troops of the Ukrainian
        Republic.

1919   February: Bulgakov was mobilized as a doctor by the
        Ukrainian Republicans. He escaped and returned home,
        suffering from a high fever which appeared nervous in
        origin.
        Autumn: Bulgakov was mobilized as a doctor by the
        White Army and posted to the Caucasus.

1920   February: Mikhail Bulgakov abandoned his medical career
        and embarked upon a career in literature, starting with
        work as a journalist and dramatist in the Caucasus.

1921   *February: introduction of the New Economic Policy (NEP).*
        September: Bulgakov made his way to Moscow, where
        he subsisted as a journalist and sketch-writer and wrote
        his first mature works.

1924   Publication of the story *Diaboliada*.
        Bulgakov divorced Tat'yana Nikolaevna Lappa and
        married Lyubov' Evgen'evna Belozerskaya.

1925   Publication of the story *The Fatal Eggs*.
        Bulgakov wrote the novella *Heart of a Dog*.
        Journal publication of two parts of the novel *The White
        Guard*. The journal closed down before the final part
        appeared.
        The Moscow Art Theatre approached Bulgakov with the
        proposal that he adapt his novel for its stage.
        The Vakhtangov Studio approached Bulgakov with a
        similar suggestion.
        Bulgakov wrote the play *The White Guard* for the
        Moscow Art Theatre.
        For the Vakhtangov Studio he wrote *Madame Zoyka*.

1925–6 The stories of *A Country Doctor's Notebook* were published
        in the medical journal *Meditsinskiy rabotnik* (*The Medical
        Worker*).

1926   January: rehearsals of the play *The White Guard* began in
        the Moscow Art Theatre.
        Rehearsals of *Madame Zoyka* began in the Vakhtangov
        Studio.
        Heart of a Dog failed to pass the censor.

May: Bulgakov's flat was subjected to a house search. His diaries and a typescript of *Heart of a Dog* were confiscated.

June: the play *The White Guard* was performed for the body of theatrical censorship and was banned.

17 September: an ideologically revised text of the play *The White Guard* was performed for the theatrical censors; the ban on the play was maintained.

23 September: after further ideological revisions the play *The White Guard* was passed for public performance – but in the Moscow Art Theatre only.

5 October: première of *The White Guard* at the Moscow Art Theatre.

28 October: première of *Madame Zoyka* at the Vakhtangov Studio. *Madame Zoyka* permitted for other theatres in the Soviet Union.

1927   Bulgakov wrote the play *Crimson Island* on commission from the Kamerniy Theatre.

1927–8 Bulgakov wrote the play *Flight* for the Moscow Art Theatre.

1928   September: *Crimson Island* passed for performance in the Kamerniy Theatre.

October: rehearsals of *Flight* began in the Moscow Art Theatre.

11 December 1928: première of *Crimson Island* in the Kamerniy Theatre.

1928–9 Bulgakov began work on *The Master and Margarita*.

1929   January: rehearsals of *Flight* discontinued in the Moscow Art Theatre.

February: *Madame Zoyka* removed from the repertoire of the Vakhtangov Theatre.

April: formal adoption of the Five Five Year Plan, signalling the end of NEP.

June: *The White Guard* removed from the repertoire of the Moscow Art Theatre and *Crimson Island* removed from the repertoire of the Kamerniy Theatre.

October–December: Bulgakov wrote *Molière*.

1930   March: *Molière* banned.

28 March: Bulgakov wrote a letter to the Soviet Government.

18 April: Stalin telephoned Bulgakov.

Bulgakov appointed assistant director in the Moscow Art

Theatre and consultant to the Theatre of Working Youth (TRAM).

May–November: Bulgakov wrote a stage adaptation of Gogol's *Dead Souls*.

December: rehearsals of *Dead Souls* began in the Moscow Art Theatre.

1931 March: Bulgakov resigned from TRAM.

Spring: the Leningrad Krasniy Theatre commissioned from Bulgakov a play about a 'future war'.

August: *Adam and Eve* completed.

October: *Molière* passed for performance.

Bulgakov resumed work on *The Master and Margarita*.

1931–2 Bulgakov wrote a stage adaptation of *War and Peace*.

1932 February: *The White Guard* restored to the Moscow Art Theatre repertoire.

October: Bulgakov divorced Lyubov' Evgen'evna Belozerskaya and married Elena Sergeevna Shilovskaya (née Nurnberg).

Work on *The Master and Margarita*.

Bulgakov completed *The Follies of Jourdain*, a compilation of comic episodes from several of Molière's plays.

Rehearsals of *Molière* began in the Moscow Art Theatre (32 hours logged).

December: première of *Dead Souls*.

1932–3 Bulgakov wrote a biography of Molière, *The Life of Monsieur de Molière*.

1933 March–October: *Flight* in rehearsal at the Moscow Art Theatre.

Rehearsals of *Molière* continued in the Moscow Art Theatre (74 hours logged).

Work on *The Master and Margarita*.

1933–4 Bulgakov wrote the play *Bliss*.

1934 Rehearsals of *Molière* continued in the Moscow Art Theatre (266 hours logged).

Work on *The Master and Margarita*.

December: Bulgakov acted the role of the Judge in a Moscow Art Theatre adaptation of Dickens' *Pickwick Papers*.

1934–5 Bulgakov adapted the play *Bliss* into the comedy *Ivan Vasil'evich*.

Bulgakov wrote a film script of Gogol's *Dead Souls* and a film script of Gogol's *The Government Inspector*.

Bulgakov wrote the play *The Last Days*.

1935   Rehearsals of *Molière* continued in the Moscow Art
        Theatre (615 hours logged).
        Work on *The Master and Margarita*.
        September: *The Last Days* passed for production in the
        Vakhtangov Theatre.
        November: rehearsals of *Ivan Vasil'evich* began in the
        Moscow Satire Theatre.
1936   Rehearsals of *Molière* continued in Moscow Art Theatre
        (110 hours logged).
        Work on *The Master and Margarita*.
        Bulgakov conceived the idea of a play about Stalin.
        15 February: première of *Molière* at the Moscow Art
        Theatre.
        9 March: *Pravda* published a hostile review of *Molière*; the
        Moscow Art Theatre removed the play from its repertoire
        that same day.
        13 May: dress rehearsal of *Ivan Vasil'evich* in the Moscow
        Satire Theatre. Production abandoned.
        The Last Days dropped from repertory plans of
        Vakhtangov Theatre.
        September: Bulgakov resigned from the Moscow Art
        Theatre and transferred to the Bolshoi as librettist and
        consultant.
        November: Bulgakov began work on the novel *Black
        Snow*.
1936–8 Bulgakov wrote an opera libretto *Minin and Pozharsky*.
1937   Bulgakov wrote two opera libretti: *The Black Sea* and
        Peter the Great.
        Autumn: Bulgakov ceased work on *Black Snow* in order
        to concentrate energies on completing *The Master and
        Margarita*.
1937–8 Bulgakov adapted *Don Quixote* for the stage on a contract
        for the Vakhtangov Theatre (première: Pushkin Theatre,
        Leningrad, 13 March 1941).
1938   Bulgakov wrote an opera libretto *Rachel* (based on
        Maupassant's story *Mademoiselle Fifi*).
        June: *The Master and Margarita* substantially completed,
        apart from revisions.
1938–9 Bulgakov wrote for the Moscow Art Theatre a play about
        the young Stalin, *Batum*.
1939   May: revisions to *The Master and Margarita*.
        July: *Batum* accepted for production by the Moscow Art
        Theatre.

August: the production was cancelled after a negative
reception from Stalin of the play.

September: Bulgakov fell ill; onset of sclerosis of the
kidneys, the disease from which his father had died at the
same age.

1940   Last revisions to *The Master and Margarita*.

10 March: Bulgakov died.

Introduction

Imagine a non-existent year 1930. A new play, *Molière*, is opening at one of Moscow's leading theatres. For its author, Mikhail Bulgakov, this is his fifth major dramatic success since his début in October 1926. His plays have all been premièred at theatres of world class – the Moscow Art, the Vakhtangov, the Kamerniy – and are running at theatres all over the Soviet Union. Bulgakov is constantly dealing with enquiries about foreign translations. His status as a dramatist and the theatrical authority of his *œuvre* grow with each major production in each foreign capital. His plays are becoming part of the European cultural canon.

Now look at what really happened.

The theatrical press at the end of the 1920s in the Soviet Union was controlled by a group of ideological zealots who, on a platform of 'proletarian literature', conducted an unremitting campaign of vilification against Bulgakov and all that he represented as a member of the 'bourgeois intelligentsia'. In December 1928 Bulgakov had three plays running successfully in Moscow: *The White Guard* at the Art Theatre, *Madame Zoyka* at the Vakhtangov, and *Crimson Island* at the Kamerniy; a fourth play, *Flight*, was also in rehearsal at the Art Theatre. By June 1929, however, the campaign against Bulgakov had achieved its aim. The press triumphantly reported that all Bulgakov's plays had been removed from the repertoire and rehearsals of *Flight* had been abandoned. In March 1930 he received notification from the theatrical censors that his new play, *Molière*, had not been passed for public performance.

Meanwhile the tax demands had come in, based on the previous year's handsome royalties. Bulgakov was also in debt to the Moscow Art Theatre, for one of the more draconian clauses in the MAT contracts obliged authors, if their plays were banned before performance, to return any advance they had received: Bulgakov owed MAT the 1,000-rouble advance he had been paid for *Flight*. In acute financial distress, and as a publicly declared pariah unable

to find a source of income, Bulgakov on 28 March 1930 wrote a
letter to the Soviet Government:

> My name has been made so odious that offers of work from my
> side are greeted with *alarm* [emphasis in original], despite the fact
> that in Moscow there are plenty of actors and directors as well as
> theatre managers who are very well acquainted with my expert
> knowledge of the stage.

Bulgakov asked for permission to emigrate with his wife, Lyubov'
Evgen'evna Belozerskaya or, if that were not to be granted, to be
given work in the Moscow Art Theatre, any work: as an assistant
director, as an actor-extra or as a stage hand.·

> If that too is impossible, I ask the Soviet Government to deal
> with me as it sees fit, but to deal with me somehow, because I,
> the author of five plays, a dramatist well-known both in the
> USSR and abroad, am facing *at the present moment* [emphasis in
> original] destitution, the street and death.

The letter was delivered to seven addressees, but only one of them
responded: Stalin. On 18 April 1930 he telephoned Bulgakov. This
was four days after the suicide of Mayakovsky and may have been
an attempt to avert another literary suicide, which would have been
bad publicity. Bulgakov was not given permission to emigrate, but
as a result of Stalin's intervention he was given a post as assistant
director in the Moscow Art Theatre.

At first the dramatist was euphoric, but gradually came to
understand that he had been saved from 'destitution, the street and
death' only to be locked up inside a Soviet Union which offered no
outlet for his creativity. His play *Adam and Eve* (1931) was so out of
step with the demands of the day that no attempt was made to put
it into production. Several theatres were interested in *The Last Days*
(written 1934–5) in connection with the centenary of Pushkin's
death in 1937, and both Shostakovich and Prokofiev were
discussing with Bulgakov the idea of turning it into an opera
(Bulgakov's wife's diaries giving preference to Shostakovich). But
all such discussions were dropped when Shostakovich came under
attack for writing 'muddle instead of music', and when the play
Molière, finally produced in the Moscow Art Theatre in 1936, was
removed from the repertoire after only seven performances
following a critical blast from *Pravda*.

Molière has a special place in the annals of the Moscow Art
Theatre, for its rehearsals dragged on over a period of nearly four

years, from 1932 to 1936. Bulgakov came into conflict with
Stanislavski, who at the beginning of March 1935 took over the
rehearsals. Stanislavski demanded from Bulgakov a play showing
Molière's 'genius' in an obvious manner, and required of the actors,
who over three years had aged and grown out of love with their
roles, that they begin work on the play 'from scratch'. The
situation was impossible, and was ultimately resolved in a backstage *coup* by which Nemirovich-Danchenko in late May 1935 took
over responsibility for release of the production. The experiences
with *Molière*, in particular the Art Theatre's immediate capitulation
in face of that *Pravda* review, so alienated Bulgakov that in
September he severed his connections with the theatre that had first
brought him fame with his play *The White Guard*. His 'theatrical
novel' *Black Snow*, written 1936–37, is a brilliant parodic account of
his first encounter with the Art Theatre. It is a divorcee's account
of his honeymoon, full of love, pain, irony and comedy.

Between 1930 and his death in 1940 Bulgakov toiled
unremittingly, combining his work in the Moscow Art Theatre,
and later in the Bolshoi, with the writing of five plays, three stage
adaptations, two film scenarios, four opera libretti, a biography of
Molière and two novels. Of all these works only one, a stage
adaptation of Gogol's *Dead Souls*, reached an audience in its
author's lifetime. His reputation as a major dramatist and prose
writer is entirely posthumous.

In his own time he was known only as the author of one play,
The White Guard. Having been hounded from the Art Theatre in
1929, it was restored to the Art Theatre repertoire in 1932, because
Stalin liked the idea that Bolshevism had defeated such a strong
enemy as the Turbin family, and saw in this a convincing
demonstration of Bolshevik invincibility. *The White Guard* ran at the
Moscow Art Theatre until 1941, when the sets were destroyed while
on tour in Minsk. *The Last Days* eventually had its première in the
Moscow Art Theatre in 1943. The world was at war and theatres in
the Soviet Union, as in every combatant country, were seeking plays
that would appeal to patriotic spirit. *The Last Days* was directed by
Nemirovich-Danchenko, his last production before his death.

All the rest of Bulgakov's work remained under a ban, however.
Its scope and sweep, instead of impressing itself upon the theatre as
one creative surge, trickled on to the stage in widely separated
productions. *The White Guard* was revived in Moscow in 1954;
Flight had its première in 1957, in Volgograd; *Molière* was first
published in 1962 and had its second 'première' in Czechoslovakia
in 1963; *Madame Zoyka* was not published inside the Soviet Union

until 1982, opening the way for new productions; *Crimson Island* had to wait until 1987, the heyday of *glasnost'*, for its publication inside the Soviet Union and its restoration to the repertoire. In 1987 also *Adam and Eve* was published in the Soviet Union. Finally the Soviet publication in 1988 of Bulgakov's play *Batum*, about the young Stalin, completed the picture of the dramatist's work in the 1930s. All these plays had been available in the West since the mid 1970s, but the major productions, on which theatrical status is based, have to be rooted also in the dramatist's own country, in performances of world class in his native language, produced by directors steeped in the traditions of the dramatist himself. Piece by piece 'the theatre of Mikhail Bulgakov' has indeed been put together again, but his plays have been deprived of half a century of performance. The scenic authority which they would have acquired through major productions and revivals has still to be established. Bulgakov's true status as a dramatist can only be grasped through that imaginary construct of a non-existent year 1930.

One of the striking things about 'the theatre of Bulgakov' is its diversity in terms of genre and treatment combined with its clearly identifiable line of inner development. The two plays *The White Guard* and *Madame Zoyka* were written in the same year, 1925–6, and had their premières in the same month: *The White Guard* opened on 5 October 1926 at the Moscow Art Theatre and *Madame Zoyka* opened on 28 October at the Vakhtangov Studio (which became the Vakhtangov Theatre in November 1926). And yet these two plays, composed virtually simultaneously, are set in completely different worlds.

The White Guard dramatizes a moment of historical choice in the middle of the Civil War that followed the October Revolution of 1917. The February Revolution of 1917 overthrew the tsarist autocracy; the Provisional Government which took power based its policies on ideas of civil liberty. In areas such as the Ukraine these ideas merged with national liberation movements, although the Provisional Government itself, like the Bolshevik government that overthrew it in October 1917, was hostile to separatist movements and envisaged a unitary state to replace the former Russian Empire. The population of the Ukraine was itself divided on the matter of separatism. In 1917 the majority of the population in the large Ukrainian cities was of Russian stock or Russian culture, while the Ukrainians were a nation of peasantry and people from small towns. In November 1917 the Ukrainian Nationalists announced the creation of an Ukrainian Republic and in February 1918 concluded a separate peace treaty with Germany at Brest-Litovsk. The Republic could, however, defend its independence only with German support. The Germans for their part were concerned to see in the Ukraine a government that could ensure supplies and therefore in April 1918 supported a coup that replaced the Republic with a new form of government, a Hetmanate (from the traditional Ukrainian title of Hetman, military leader and head of government). The Hetman thus faced both the Bolsheviks in the north and the supporters of the Republic at home. As defeat of Germany in the First World War became imminent, the Hetman turned for assistance to the anti-Bolshevik, anti-separatist, Russian Volunteer Army, the White Guard, and in November 1918 published a declaration of a federative union with a future, non-Bolshevik Russia. This is the background to the play *The White Guard*, commissioned by the Moscow Art Theatre on the basis of Bulgakov's novel of the same name. The play is about the moral choices which have to be made at historical moments in which the situation is constantly changing and always confused.

The subject matter of the play, a positive treatment of the recently defeated enemy of Bolshevism, the White Guard, created problems with the theatrical censors and the text was altered several times before it was finally passed for production (and then it was passed for performance in the Moscow Art Theatre only). The present volume contains the text as passed by the theatrical censors of 1926, the text in which the play has become a theatrical legend. In the Soviet Union by the late 1980s, however, attention was beginning to focus on the earlier variants of Bulgakov's play, the text banned by the censors in 1926. The pre-censor text is pure Bulgakov, containing a characteristically strong comic element along with an inner intransigence: in the finale the Turbins do not so lightly 'convert' to Bolshevism. This text passed by the censors is a historical document showing the limits of the ideologically permissible in late 1926.

Even in its censored version, however, the play in 1926 provoked that campaign of vituperation that eventually drove all Bulgakov's plays off the stage in 1929. The decision to remove these plays from the repertoire had nothing to do with the box-office, it must be said. The name 'Bulgakov' was in the latter half of the 1920s a huge box-office draw, which of course made his plays all the more pernicious from the point of view of the self-appointed, and by 1929 government-supported, guardians of ideological orthodoxy.

Madame Zoyka is set in the period of NEP, the New Economic

Policy, which was introduced in 1921 and allowed a measure of
private trade in the interests of restoring an economy shattered by
Civil War. The play is in one of Bulgakov's favourite genres, the
'salon comedy', but the 'salon' is rather an interesting one: a high-
class brothel operating under the front of a dress-maker's *atelier*.
Bulgakov himself in 1926 defined the play's genre as 'tragic
buffonade' and identified its chief characteristics as 'piquant
situations, profound grotesque and elements of the crime thriller'.
In 1926, however, it was not ideologically respectable to be
indulgent toward the 'excesses of NEP' and the Vakhtangov
Theatre had, at least in its publicity, to stress the play's satirical
aspects. Only in the late 1980s, when Soviet economists were
permitted to re-assess NEP in a positive light as a perfectly
legitimate path of socialist development and one which ought never
to have been abandoned, did it become possible in the Soviet
Union to conceive of a non-satirical play set in the NEP period and
to play *Zoyka* as a *tragic* buffonade.

From the tragi-comic perspective, Zoyka's apartment offers a
little paradise for people like herself, seeking escape to live with a
loved-one in ideal surroundings. Of course the paradise is interim
and spurious, but the search for it does seem to be part of the
human condition, and much of *Zoyka*, with its fashion-orientated
whirl, its seduction of the *nouveaux riches* and its connection with
the drugs underworld, is not too dissimilar from some celebrity
lifestyles today.

In the last acts of both *The White Guard* and *Madame Zoyka* a
transformation-disguise is effected; by Shervinsky in *The White
Guard* and by Ametistov in *Madame Zoyka*. Two completely
disparate worlds are brought together by a theatrical device. In
Flight (1926–28) the two worlds are contained within the same
play: the historical path of moral choice and the carousel of money
and chance. General Khludov, a figure who has a historical
prototype, acts out his tragedy in the first; the invented character of
General Charnota is in his comic element in the second.

Flight was written for the young actors from the Moscow Art
Theatre Second Studio who had leapt into overnight fame with their
portrayals in *The White Guard*, and who subsequently formed the
core of the theatre's main troupe, its 'second generation'. The roles
of Khludov, Serafima and Golubkov were written for the actors
who had played Aleksei Turbin, Elena and Lariosik. Sub-titled 'a
play in dreams', *Flight* dramatizes the leaden nightmare of losing
and a wish-fulfilment dream of winning that is a comic *coup de
théâtre*. Although the play is set at a moment of historical collapse,

it is definitely not 'absurdist': it is about absolute moral values of conscience and atonement. The song sung by the choir at the 'cockroach races' is 'The Ballad of the Twelve Robbers', which tells the tale of the fierce robber leader Kudeyar who has 'spilt much blood of innocent Christians'. Suddenly, mid-way through a four-line stanza, God awakens the conscience of the fierce robber and the next, final, stanza brings his tale to a swift conclusion: 'Kudeyar left his comrades, gave up robbing and retired to a monastery to serve God and humankind.' The monastery, discredited in the first dream, is reasserted in the finale as a moral space. The *Flight* of the Russian title (*beg*) is likewise not a negative 'flight from' but simply the act of running and also 'a race'. *Flight* is to be interpreted in terms of 'running the race of life', as is indicated by its epigraph in Russian, three lines from Zhukovsky's poem 'The Bard in the Camp of the Russian Warriors':

> Immortality – a quiet, bright shore;
> Our path – a striving towards it.
> Rest, who his race has run! . . .

Charnota's 'race' is comically circular, in orbit round that parody of winning and losing, the cockroach races; the defeated Khludov's race is a tragically straight one. The author's own 'race' is towards 'immortality'.

The play *Molière* was written in the last quarter of 1929 and was a response to the situation in which Bulgakov found himself in that year. Molière had also been a victim of the ideological zealots of his day, but his case triumphantly proves the artist's immortality. The conflict in the play is not a simplistic one of 'talent versus the state', for in the play there are two centres of brilliance: Molière's theatre and the court of Louis XIV, the Sun King. But a black cabal manages to crush Molière with the complete connivance of the King. The 'incest theme' in the play is central to the plot, for it is used by Molière's enemies to trap the King. Connection with the 'incestuous' Molière besmirches the monarch who is trapped in the ideology of his own spotless supremacy.

Bulgakov defined the play's genre as a 'romantic drama' in which biographical accuracy, 'both impossible and unnecessary' is replaced by emblematic moment and heightened conflict. For example the irony that Molière was taken ill on stage during a performance of *Le malade imaginaire* and died at home a few hours later is sharpened by making him die on stage, surrounded by the characters of his creation and thus the pledge of his immortality. The culmination of the play's intrigue, the sudden, fatal removal of the King's patronage, was in reality a slow and gradual cooling of the King towards his *comédien*, who was replaced in the royal favour by the musician Lully. Molière in this play remains *comédien* to the end: he dies on stage because he will not abandon a performance; he welcomes back his betrayer, his talented young protégé Moirron, turning the Judas theme into that of the Prodigal Son, and even at the moment of supreme humiliation, rage and fear, his aesthetic sense does not desert him. Molière, actor-playwright-manager, is the epitome of Theatre, and in this realm it is he who is King.

Adam and Eve (1931) was commissioned by a Leningrad theatre, the Krasniy, as 'a play about a future war'. Explaining in a letter of 30 August 1931 to Stanislavsky why he had offered the play to the Vakhtangov Theatre in Moscow and not to the Art Theatre, Bulgakov cited that clause in the Art Theatre contracts about the return of the advance if the play was banned before production and mentioned that no such clause existed in the contracts with either of the theatres involved with *Adam and Eve*. Such an absence of financial pressure may explain the play's complete absence of self-censorship and refusal to engage with the mind-set of the censor.

Bulgakov had found his given theme of a 'future war' uncongenial, but he managed to make it thoroughly his own. The images of this future war are based on past experience: the gas of the First World War; the ideological hostilities of the Civil War transposed on to the international arena of the emergent 1930s. Despite the grimness of its warning, *Adam and Eve* contains an amount of comedy that would be surprising if the author were not Bulgakov. The main character, the brilliant scientist Yefrosimov is at moments a typical 'absent-minded professor'; the character Ponchik-Nepobeda is a richly malicious satire on the sold-out hack writer. The play is about intellectual integrity and Yefrosimov can be seen as a 'double' for the artist. His inner concentration is total and the apparatus that he invents is a metaphor for the beneficial ingenuity of the human mind. Having devised an antidote against the ultimate poison gas, Yefrosimov argues that 'in order to save mankind from destruction such an invention must be given to all countries simultaneously'. There was no chance of such a play being performed in the isolationist Soviet Union of the 1930s and the subsequent half-century. Only at the start of the 1990s can its theme of what might be termed 'intellectual internationalism' find broad international echo. Even today, however, in any country of the world, a scientist who threatened to act in this idealistic manner with an invention of military significance would be lucky to escape prosecution for treason. The play is still ahead of our time as well as of its own.

The name of Pushkin was always important to Bulgakov as a bench-mark for the 'Russian writer'. Like Molière, Pushkin is both an ethical model and an affirmation of the triumph of art. Pushkin's relationship to Tsar Nicholas I offers a paradigm of the artist's path, and his example protects the author from straying into the swamps of servility to an autocrat. The play *The Last Days* is an interesting counterpart to *Molière* in that it offers another idea of 'theatre'. Where *Molière* captures the swirl of the *commedia dell'arte*, there are elements in *The Last Days* that hint at an imitation of Greek tragedy. The cast-list in Russian is a single column of names and generic descriptions:

Pushkina
Goncharova
Vorontsova
Saltykova
Station-master's wife
Bitkov
Nikita
D'Anthès

The Russian audience does not need to be told the age of the beautiful Pushkina, Pushkin's wife, nor who Goncharova is, nor that D'Anthès was a young French officer in service of the Tsar. The audience, as in the Greek theatre, knows the whole story in advance: how Russia's greatest poet, a genius best described as Mozartian in the lightness of his profundity, was killed by D'Anthès in a duel that could perfectly well have been prevented, given that Pushkin's every step was being watched by agents of the Tsar. There is even a character in the play who equates to the Chorus, the spy Bitkov. He is the 'little man' of Russian history, implicated in the state's treacheries but accessible to Pushkin's poetic word.

It is only as poetic word that Pushkin is present in the play; his name is absent from the cast-list. Although this is always explained in terms of Bulgakov's aversion to the idea of an actor wearing a curly wig and stuck-on side-whiskers posturing on stage as he declaims Pushkin's verses, it works as an effective device. The moment of the poet's 'entrance' is infinitely deferred, but his physical absence emphasizes the powerful presence of his word, which touches all the other characters on stage, and they define themselves by their reception of this word. *The Last Days* ends on the image of an unquiet, unburied spirit. That plan for an opera by Shostakovich or Prokofiev haunts the imagination.

It was in the second half of the 1950s, in the post-Stalin 'thaw', that the name of Bulgakov began to return to Russian literature, first as a dramatist, with publication and productions of some of his plays, then as a prose writer. Publication of Bulgakov's prose culminated in 1966–67 with the first appearance of his great novel *The Master and Margarita*, which came as a literary revelation. Outside the Soviet Union Bulgakov is today more widely known as a prose writer than as a dramatist. One reason for this somewhat lop-sided appreciation of his art is that a novel needs only a competent reader for its adequate reception, whereas a play needs the full resources of the professional theatre.

The wonder is that Bulgakov did not choose the fame that was on offer in his time for literary and dramatic production on the topical themes of the day – industrialization, collectivization, idealization of the autocrat. Bulgakov remained stubbornly true to his own themes, at the price of non-publication and non-performance. Yet he always hoped to make that break-through to the audience and reader, never really reconciling himself to the idea that he could not reach his contemporaries, that he was writing *only* for posterity. It is in the context of this struggle to reach his contemporaries that the attempt to write a play about Stalin must be understood. It was a dangerous undertaking, but once the idea had been conceived and talked about in the Art Theatre, it was more dangerous to abandon the project than to proceed with it. In the event, this attempt to reach a contemporary audience failed. Stalin did not like the play. The stress associated with the composition of *Batum* is generally blamed for the onset of Bulgakov's terminal illness in 1939.

The inability to reach a contemporary audience is perhaps more painful for the dramatist than for the poet or prose writer. The poet and the prose writer can – and indeed must – write for some ideally imagined addressee in posterity, but a play, while also addressed to posterity, comes to life only on the stage. For a dramatist not to see that moment is a cruel deprivation. Bulgakov's buffoon double, the would-be dramatist Maksudov in his novel *Black Snow* (1936–7), gives voice to Bulgakov's own *cri-de-coeur*: 'To write plays and then not perform them is impossible!'.

Bulgakov, in a heroic act of theatrical abstinence, did do 'the impossible'. It is to be hoped that this volume of his plays will finally establish their theatrical authority on the English-speaking stage and reveal the full talent of this author who declared himself to use both the narrative and the dramatic genres 'as a pianist uses both hands'.

Lesley Milne
Nottingham, 1990

OTHER WORKS BY BULGAKOV IN ENGLISH TRANSLATION

Black Snow. A Theatrical Novel, tr. Michael Glenny (London, Hodder and Stoughton, 1967).

A Country Doctor's Notebook, tr. Michael Glenny (London, Collins, 1975).

Diaboliad and Other Stories, tr. Carl R. Proffer, ed. Ellendea Proffer and Carl R. Proffer (Bloomington–London, Indiana University Press, 1972).

The Early Plays of Mikhail Bulgakov, tr. Carl R. Proffer and Ellendea Proffer (Bloomington–London, Indiana University Press, 1972).

The Life of Monsieur de Molière, tr. Mirra Ginsburg (New York, Funk and Wagnalls, 1970).

The Master and Margarita, tr. Michael Glenny (London, The Harvill Press and New York, Harper and Row, 1967).

The White Guard [novel], tr. Michael Glenny (London, Collins and Harvill Press, 1971).

Secondary Literature

J. A. E. Curtis, *Bulgakov's Last Decade. The Writer as Hero* (Cambridge, Cambridge University Press, 1987).

Lesley Milne, *Mikhail Bulgakov. A Critical Biography* (Cambridge, Cambridge University Press, 1990).

Ellendea Proffer, *Bulgakov. Life and Work* (Ardis, Ann Arbor, 1984).

A. Colin Wright, *Mikhail Bulgakov. Life and Interpretations* (Toronto, University of Toronto Press, 1978).

The White Guard

A Play in Four Acts

Translated by Michael Glenny

Characters

ALEXÉI VASÍLIEVICH TURBÍN	colonel of artillery, aged 30
NIKOLÁI TURBÍN ('NIKÓLKA')	officer cadet, aged 18; ALEXÉI TURBÍN's brother
YELIÉNA VASÍLIEVNA TÁLBERG	their sister, aged 24
VLADÍMIR ROBÉRTOVICH TÁLBERG	colonel, General Staff, aged 38; YELIÉNA's husband
VÍKTOR VÍKTOROVICH MYSHLAÉVSKY	staff captain of artillery, aged 38
LEONÍD YÚRIEVICH SHERVINSKY	lieutenant, personal aide-de-camp to the HETMAN
ALEXÁNDER BRONISLÁVOVICH STUDZÍNSKY	captain, aged 29
LARIÓN LARIÓNOVICH SURZHÁNSKY ('LARIOSIK')	the TURBÍNS' cousin from Zhitómir, aged 21
HETMAN OF ALL THE UKRAINE	
BOLBOTÚN	colonel, commanding 1st Cavalry Division in Petlyura's army
GALANBÁ	squadron commander in Petlyura's cavalry; former captain of lancers
URAGÁN)	officers of Petlyura's army
KIRPÁTY)	
GENERAL VON SCHRATT	German army
MAJOR VON DUST	German army
DOCTOR	German army
DESERTER	from a Cossack regiment
MAN WITH A BASKET	
JEW	
FOOTMAN	
MAXIM	school porter, aged 60
TELEPHONIST	Ukrainian infantryman, Petlyura's army
FIRST OFFICER	
SECOND OFFICER	
FIRST OFFICER CADET	
SECOND OFFICER CADET	

The first, second and third acts take place in the winter of 1918, the fourth act early in 1919.
The place of the action is the city of Kiev.

This translation of *The White Guard* was first staged by the Royal Shakespeare Company at the Aldwych Theatre in May 1979. The cast was as follows:

ALEXÉI VASÍLIEVICH TURBÍN	John Nettles
NIKOLÁI TURBÍN ('NIKÓLKA')	Allan Hendrick
YELIÉNA VASÍLIEVNA TÁLBERG	Juliet Stevenson
VLADÍMIR ROBÉRTOVICH TÁLBERG	Geofrey Freshwater
VÍKTOR VÍKTOROVICH MYSHALAÉVSKY	Patrick Stewart
LEONÍD YÚRIEVICH SHERVÍNSKY	Michael Pennington
ALEXÁNDER BRONISLAVOVICH STUDZÍNSKY	John Bowe
LARIÓN LARIÓNOVICH SURZHÁNSKY ('LARIOSIK')	Richard Griffiths
HETMAN OF ALL THE UKRAINE	George Raistrick
BOLBOTÚN	Philip McGough
GALÁNBA	Malcolm Storry
URAGAN	Alan Barker
KIRPÁTY	James Griffin
GENERAL VON SCHRATT	Donald Douglas
MAJOR VON DUST	Dennis Edwards
DOCTOR	Dennis Clinton
DESERTER	Conrad Asquith
MAN WITH A BASKET	Michael Bertenshaw
JEW	Dennis Edwards
FOOTMAN	Bill Dean
MAXIM	Dennis Clinton
TELEPHONIST	Bill Buffery
FIRST OFFICER	Conrad Asquith
SECOND OFFICER	Michael Betenshaw
FIRST CADET	Ian Reddington
SECOND CADET	Bill Buffery
OFFICER CADETS	James Adams
	Sebastian Allen
	Danny Brooks
	Eric Carlson
	John Fortnum
	Simon Grigsby
	Philip Inman
	Adam Shaw
	Nicholas Turner
	James Wolfe
DIRECTOR	Barry Kyle
DESIGNER	Christopher Morley

ACT ONE

Scene One

The TURBINS' *apartment. Evening. A fire burning. As the curtain rises the clock strikes nine and gently plays a minuet by Boccherini.* ALEXEI *is bent over some papers.*

NIKOLKA (*plays the guitar and sings*).

Hey, little apple,
Where are you rolling?
Rolling to Petlyura
And won't come back again.

Hey, little apple,
Where are you rolling?
We've got the Maxim guns,
Petlyura can't win.

Hey, little apple,
Where are you rolling?
Away to Denikin
On the faraway Don . . .

ALEXEI. What is that nonsense you're singing? Errand-boys' stuff. Sing something decent.

NIKOLKA. What d'you mean — errand-boys' stuff? I made it up myself, Alyosha. (*Sings.*)

Sing away, I don't care,
But listen here my friend:
When your singing fills the air
My hair stands up on end . . .

ALEXEI. That's exactly what your voice does to me.

NIKOLKA. How can you say that, Alyosha? I know I haven't got a voice like Shervinsky's, but it's pretty good all the same. I've got a sort of dramatic tenor. Lena! Wouldn't you say I had a good voice?

YELIENA (*offstage*). Who? You? Certainly not.

NIKOLKA. She's worried, that's why she's so rude. I'll have you know, Alyosha, that my singing teacher said to me: 'You', he said, 'might have been an opera singer if it hadn't been for the revolution'.

ALEXEI. Your singing teacher's an idiot.

NIKOLKA. Why's everybody so jumpy in this house? My singing teacher's an idiot, my voice is no good even though it was perfectly all right yesterday, pessimism all round. Personally, I'm rather an optimist by nature. (*Strums guitar.*) All the same, Alyosha, I must admit I'm beginning to get a bit worried myself. It's nine o'clock and he said he'd arrive this morning. I suppose nothing can have happened to him, can it?

ALEXEI. Quiet. Think of Yeliena.

NIKOLKA. Oh God, who'd have a married sister.

YELIENA (*offstage*). What's the time?

NIKOLKA. Er . . . nine. The clock's fast, Lena.

YELIENA (*offstage*). Don't tell lies.

NIKOLKA. Oh, dear. Now I've upset her. (*Sings.*)
  Oh dark, oh dark and drear
  Is all the world around me . . .

ALEXEI. For heaven's sake — d'you want *me* to burst into tears too? Sing something cheerful.

NIKOLKA (*sings*).
  Hark, the sound of marching feet,
  Tramping, tramping down the street!
  See them come, a hundred strong,
  Hear their voices loud in song
        Run to the gate, girls . . .
        Don't you be late, girls!
  Hurrah! Hurrah! Hurrah!
  The guards . . . the guards . . . the guards . . .
  For the guards . . . are marching past!

  The electric light suddenly goes out. Outside a detachment of TROOPS *can be heard marching past and singing.*

ALEXEI. Damn thing. Keeps going out all the time. Bring us a candle, please, Lena.

YELIENA (*offstage*). Just coming . . .

ALEXEI. I wonder who those troops were?

As YELIENA *enters with a candle, she stops and listens. Rumble of distant gunfire.*

NIKOLKA. That was near. Sounded as if that firing came from round Svyatoshino. Interesting to know what's going on there. Alyosha, I suppose you couldn't send me down to Headquarters to find out what's happening? I'd be glad to go.

ALEXEI. They've got enough to do without you making a nuisance of yourself. Just stay where you are.

NIKOLKA. Yes, colonel . . . I only asked because, well, you know . . . sitting around and doing nothing . . . it is rather galling . . . other people are out there fighting . . . If only our regiment could be ready a bit sooner . . .

ALEXEI. When I need your advice about getting the regiment up to strength, I'll ask for it. Understand?

NIKOLKA. Of course. Sorry, colonel.

The electric light comes on again.

YELIENA. Alyosha, where *is* my husband?

ALEXEI. He'll come soon, Lena.

YELIENA. But why is he so late? He said he'd be here this morning, but it's nine p.m. and he still hasn't come. Do you suppose something can have happened to him? '

ALEXEI. No, of course not, Lena. You know the line to the west is guarded by the Germans.

YELIENA. In that case why hasn't he arrived yet?

ALEXEI. Well, obviously the train has been stopping at every station.

NIKOLKA. That's how trains move when there's a revolution. Go for one hour, stop for two.

Doorbell rings.

Talk of the devil, there he is! (*Runs to the door.*) Who's there?

VOICE OF VIKTOR MYSHLAEVSKY. Hurry up and open the door, for God's sake!

NIKOLKA (*lets* VIKTOR *into the hall*). Is it you, Viktor?

MYSHLAEVSKY. Of course it's me — or what's left of me! Take my rifle please, Nikolka . . . Bloody hell!

YELIENA. Where have you come from, Viktor?

MYSHLAEVSKY. From Krasny Traktir. Careful when you hang my coat up, Nikolka, there's a bottle of vodka in the pocket. Don't smash it. Lena, my dear, can I spend the night here? I'm frozen to the marrow.

YELIENA. God, of course you can. Come over to the fire.

ALL gather round the fire. MYSHLAEVSKY groans.

ALEXEI. Didn't they issue you with felt boots?

MYSHLAEVSKY. Huh! Felt boots! Not a hope — incompetent bastards. (*Crouches over the fire.*)

YELIENA. Look, the bath-water's just being heated. You two, undress him quickly, and I'll get some clean clothes. (*Exit.*)

MYSHLAEVSKY. Pull my boots off, there's a good fellow.

NIKOLKA. Yes, of course. (*Pulls off MYSHLAEVSKY's boots.*)

MYSHLAEVSKY. Easy does it, old boy, easy . . . ! I could do with some vodka now . . .

ALEXEI. Right away.

NIKOLKA. Alyosha, his toes are frostbitten.

MYSHLAEVSKY. My toes are done for, gone to blazes — I can see that.

ALEXEI. Nonsense. They'll thaw out. Nikolka, rub his feet with vodka.

MYSHLAEVSKY. You're not going to waste good vodka on my feet. (*Drinks.*) Rub them with your hands . . . Ow! That hurts . . . Ouch! . . . That's better.

NIKOLKA. You must have nearly died with cold.

YELIENA (*enter with dressing-gown and slippers*). Straight into the bath with him. Come along!

MYSHLAEVSKY. God bless you, Lena. Give us another vodka. (*Drinks.*)

Exit YELIENA.

NIKOLKA. Feeling a bit warmer, captain?

MYSHLAEVSKY. Yes, that's better. (*Lights a cigarette.*)

NIKOLKA. Tell us — what's going on at Krasny Traktir?

MYSHLAEVSKY. A blizzard, that's what's going on there. And
I say God damn and blast the snowstorm, the cold, Petlyura
and the bloody Germans . . .

ALEXEI. What I don't understand is — why did they send you
out there at all?

MYSHLAEVSKY. Because there are peasants at Krasny Traktir,
that's why. Mr Dostoyevsky's dear, simple, bloody God-
fearing peasants.

NIKOLKA. But surely — according to the newspapers, the
peasants are all on the Hetman's side, aren't they?

MYSHLAEVSKY. Don't mention 'newspapers' to me, Cadet
Turbin. I'd like to string up all those useless bloody
journalists. When I was out on reconnaissance this morning
I bumped into an old peasant and asked him where all the
lads in his village had gone. The place was completely dead.
He was so blind, he couldn't see the Russian officer's
epaulettes under the hood of my coat, and he said: 'They
be all gone off to join Petlyura . . .'

NIKOLKA. Oh, God . . .

MYSHLAEVSKY. 'Oh God' is right. I grabbed the old sod by his
shirtfront and I said: 'So they be gone to Petlyura, be they?
Well, I be a-going to blow your brains out, you old bugger . . .
I'll give you gone off to join Petlyura. You're going off to
join the next world. Right now.'

ALEXEI. How did you get back into town?

MYSHLAEVSKY. We were relieved today, thank the Lord. An
infantry detachment came and took over from us. Then I went
and made a scene at Headquarters. It was disgusting — there
they all were drinking brandy in a warm railway carriage.
You, I said, do nothing but lounge around here and the
Hetman sits in his palace, while you send artillery officers out
into the freezing cold in the wrong sort of boots to shoot it
out with the bloody peasants! They didn't know how to get
rid of me, so they said: 'Of course, captain, of course we'll
post you to your own arm of the service. Join any artillery
unit you like. Take the train into town . . . ' So here I am.
Alyosha. take me into your regiment.

ALEXEI. With pleasure. I was going to nominate you myself,
in any case. You can have No. 1 Battery.

MYSHLAEVSKY. You've saved my life . . .

NIKOLKA. Hurrah! We'll all be together. Studzinsky as adjutant
. . . Splendid!

MYSHLAEVSKY. Where are you stationed?

NIKOLKA. We've taken over the Alexander I High School.
Tomorrow or the day after we'll be ready to go into action.

MYSHLAEVSKY. You can't wait for Petlyura to put a bullet
through the back of your neck, can you?

NIKOLKA. Maybe we'll knock *him* out first!

YELIENA (*enters with towel*). Come along, Viktor, off with
you. Go and have a bath. Here's a towel.

MYSHLAEVSKY. Lena, Lena, let me give you a hug and a kiss
for all the trouble you've taken. Tell me, Lena, should I have
another vodka now or afterwards, at supper?

YELIENA. Better have it later with your supper. Viktor — have
you seen my husband? He's vanished.

MYSHLAEVSKY. Don't worry, my dear, he'll turn up. He'll be
back soon, you'll see. (*Exit.*)

The doorbell starts ringing and does not stop.

NIKOLKA. There he is now! (*Runs into the hall.*)

ALEXEI. Lord, what is wrong with the bell?

NIKOLKA *opens the front door to reveal* LARIOSIK
SURZHANSKY *with a suitcase and a bundle.*

LARIOSIK. Well, here I am. I seem to have done something to
your doorbell.

NIKOLKA. You've pressed the knob too hard. (*Runs out of the
door and downstairs.*)

LARIOSIK. Oh, my God! Please forgive me. (*Enters the living
room.*) Well, I've arrived. How do you do — you must be
Yeliena, I recognise you from your photographs. Mother
sends her warmest regards.

The doorbell stops ringing. Enter NIKOLKA.

And to you too, Alexei.

ALEXEI. Thank you very much.

LARIOSIK. Hello, Nikolka, I've heard so much about you.
(*Looks round at the* TURBINS.) I can see you're surprised to
see me. Let me give you this letter, it will explain everything.
Mother told me to give you this letter even before I took my
coat off.

YELIENA. What appalling handwriting!

LARIOSIK. Yes, it is awful, isn't it? Perhaps I'd better read it
for you, if you don't mind. Mother's handwriting is so bad
she sometimes can't even read it herself. Mine's just as bad,
too. It's hereditary. (*Reads:*) 'My dear, dear Lena! Since you
are related, I am sending my boy straight to you; shelter him
and care for him as only you can. You have such a large
flat . . . ' Mother loves and respects you and Alexei very much.
(*To* NIKOLKA.) And you too. (*Continues reading.*) 'My boy
is going to Kiev University. He is so gifted' . . . Oh, dear, the
things mother says! . . . '. . . he simply cannot just sit around
at home in Zhitomir wasting his time. I will send you the
money for his keep absolutely regularly. The boy is so used to
family life that I wouldn't care for him to lodge with strangers.
But I must stop now. The hospital train is leaving soon, and
he will tell you everything himself . . . ' H'mm . . . well, that's
all.

ALEXEI. Might I ask to whom I have the honour of speaking?

LARIOSIK. What? Do you mean you don't know who I am?

ALEXEI. I'm afraid not.

LARIOSIK. Oh, my God! Don't you know either, Yeliena?

YELIENA. No, I don't.

LARIOSIK. Oh dear, something seems to have gone terribly
wrong. I mean, mother sent you a telegram which was
supposed to explain everything. Mother's telegram was sixty-
three words long . . .

NIKOLKA. Sixty-three words! . . . Heavens above . . .

YELIENA. We've had no telegram.

LARIOSIK. You never got it? Oh my God, do forgive me. I
thought I was expected, that's why I came straight in and . . .
I do beg your pardon . . . I'm so sorry, I seem to have trodden
in something . . . I'm afraid I'm always putting my foot
in it . . . !

ALEXEI. Would you be kind enough to tell us your name.

LARIOSIK. Larion Surzhansky.

YELIENA. But you must be Lariosik — our cousin from Zhitomir!

LARIOSIK. That's right.

YELIENA. And you . . . you've come to stay here?

LARIOSIK. Yes. But you see, I thought you were expecting me. Please forgive me for bringing in this horrible stuff on to your carpet . . . I thought you were expecting me, but since you aren't, I'll go and find a room in some hotel . . .

YELIENA. A hotel? Nowadays? Impossible! Don't go yet, do at least take your things off.

ALEXEI. Come now, no one is going to throw you out on to the street. Please take your coat off.

LARIOSIK. Most extremely grateful.

NIKOLKA. Here you are — you can hang up your coat in the hall.

LARIOSIK. Most extremely grateful. What a lovely flat you have. (*Exiting to ball with* NIKOLKA.)

YELIENA (*whispers*). Alyosha, what are we going to do with him? He's rather sweet, shall we put him up in the library, the room's empty anyway.

ALEXEI. Of course. Go and tell him.

YELIENA. Larion, I suggest that first of all you should have a bath . . . Oh, there's somebody in the bathroom already . . . but I'm sure you must need one after your train journey . . .

LARIOSIK. Oh yes, it was awful . . . awful! You see it has taken me eleven days to come from Zhitomir to Kiev . . .

NIKOLKA. Eleven days! Good God!

LARIOSIK. Appalling . . . an absolute nightmare . . .

YELIENA. Off you go then.

LARIOSIK. Most extremely . . . Oh, I forgot — I'm sorry, Yeliena, but I can't have a bath.

ALEXEI. Why not?

LARIOSIK. I do apologise. You see, some wretch on that

hospital train stole my suitcase with all my clean clothes in it. They left me the suitcase with my books and manuscripts, but all my clothes are gone.

YELIENA. Well, that's one problem we *can* solve.

NIKOLKA. I can lend you some clothes.

LARIOSIK (*confidentially to* NIKOLKA). I think I have one shirt left. I wrapped my complete works of Chekhov in it. Could you lend me a pair of underpants, though?

NIKOLKA. Yes, of course. Though they might be a bit tight for you.

LARIOSIK. Most extremely grateful.

YELIENA. Larion, we're putting you in the library. Show him, Nikolka.

NIKOLKA. This way.

Exeunt LARIOSIK *and* NIKOLKA.

ALEXEI. What an extraordinary fellow! Personally I'd start by giving him a haircut. Light me a candle, in my room Lena, there's a dear. I've a mass of work to do and I keep getting interrupted. (*Exit.*)

Doorbell rings.

YELIENA. Who's there?

TALBERG (*offstage*). It's me. Open up.

YELIENA. Thank God! Where on earth have you been? I've been so worried.

TALBERG (*entering*). Don't kiss me, I'm freezing, you may catch a cold.

YELIENA. Where have you been?

TALBERG. I was delayed at the German headquarters. Important business.

YELIENA. Well, hurry on over to the fire and get warm. We'll have some tea in a moment.

TALBERG. Wait, Yeliena. I don't want any tea . . . Look here, whose tunic is this?

YELIENA. It's Viktor Myshlaevsky's. He's only just back from the front line frozen to death.

TALBERG. He might at least have hung it up.

YELIENA. I'll do it. (*Hangs tunic on a book behind the door.*) And there's some more news. My cousin from Zhitomir, the famous Lariosik, has descended on us unexpectedly. Alexei has said he can sleep in the library.

TALBERG. I might have known it! As if one Signor Myshlaevsky wasn't enough, we have to be invaded by the country cousins from Zhitomir as well. This isn't a home, it's a third class hotel. I simply don't understand Alexei.

YELIENA. Look, Volodya, you're just tired and bad tempered. Why don't you like Myshlaevsky? He's a very nice man.

TALBERG. Charming fellow. Spends all his time in cheap bars.

YELIENA. Volodya, really!

TALBERG. However, I can't waste time on Myshlaevsky now. Shut the door, Lena . . . A terrible thing has happened.

YELIENA. What?

TALBERG. The Germans are going to pull out and leave the Hetman to his fate.

YELIENA. What?! You don't mean it! How do you know?

TALBERG. I've just been told it, in strict secrecy, at the German Headquarters. Nobody knows yet, not even the Hetman himself.

YELIENA. What will happen now?

TALBERG. What will happen . . . h'mm . . . Half past nine. Ye-es . . . What will happen now? . . . Lena!

YELIENA. Well — Lena what?

TALBERG. Lena, I must get out of here at once.

YELIENA. Get out? Where to?

TALBERG. To Germany. To Berlin. Look, my dear, you surely realise what would happen to me if the Hetman's Russian loyalists, like Alexei and Nikolka, fail to beat off Petlyura and he takes Kiev.

YELIENA. We could hide you.

TALBERG. My dearest Lena, how could anyone hide me? I'm not a needle. There's not a soul in Kiev who wouldn't

recognise me. You can't hide the Deputy War Minister. I
can't go skulking about in other people's flats like Signor
Myshlaevsky. They'd find me in no time at all.

YELIENA. Wait a minute! I don't quite see . . . Do you mean
we must both leave?

TALBERG. That's just the point — we can't both leave. I've
just learned that the situation is catastrophic. The city's
surrounded on all sides and the only way out is on the German
headquarters train. They are not taking women. I only
managed to get one seat because of my connections.

YELIENA. In other words, you want to go alone?

TALBERG. My dear, I don't 'want to', I have no choice. You
must realise — this is disaster! The train's leaving in half an
hour. Make up your mind, and as fast as you can.

YELIENA. In half an hour? As fast as I can? Very well, I've
made up my mind — go.

TALBERG. Sensible woman. I always said you were.

YELIENA. How long are we going to be apart?

TALBERG. About a couple of months, I should think. I'll just
sit it out in Berlin until all this nonsense is over, and then
when the Hetman returns . . .

YELIENA. But supposing he doesn't return?

TALBERG. Impossible. Even if the Germans evacuate the
Ukraine, the Entente will occupy it and reinstate the Hetman.
Europe needs the Ukraine under the Hetman's rule as a
buffer-state against the Bolsheviks in Moscow. You'll see —
I've worked it all out.

YELIENA. Yes, I see. But there's just one thing: how is it that
the Hetman is still here and the officers are forming an army,
yet you are running away for everyone to see? Is that very
clever?

TALBERG. My dear, don't be naive. When I tell you that I'm
'getting out', I'm telling you that in secret, because I know
that you will never repeat it to anyone. Colonels of the
General Staff don't run away. They are posted away on
duty. I have a warrant in my pocket from the Hetman's War
Ministry ordering me to Berlin. Not bad, eh?

YELIENA. Not bad at all. And what's going to happen to all the others?

TALBERG. Thank you very much for lumping me in with the others. I am not 'all the others'.

YELIENA. You must warn my brothers.

TALBERG. Of course, of course. In a way I'm even glad that I'm going away alone for such a long time. You will make sure that you keep hold of our rooms in this flat, won't you?

YELIENA. My dear Vladimir, they are my *brothers!* You don't really think they'd push you out, do you?

TALBERG. No, no, no . . . of course not . . . But you know the proverb: 'Qui va a la chasse perd sa place'. Now one last favour. I presume that, er . . . person . . . Shervinsky, will be hanging around the place while I'm away . . .

YELIENA. He's been coming while you've been here.

TALBERG. Unfortunately, yes. You see, I don't like him.

YELIENA. Oh really, why not?

TALBERG. The attentions he pays to you are becoming too persistent, and I should prefer it if . . . h'mm . . .

YELIENA. What would you prefer?

TALBERG. I needn't tell you what I would prefer. You are an intelligent, well-bred young woman, and I know you won't disgrace the name of Talberg.

YELIENA. Very well . . . I shall not disgrace the name of Talberg.

TALBERG. Why do you answer me in that tone of voice? After all, I'm not suggesting that you would be unfaithful to me. I know that could not happen.

YELIENA. What makes you think it couldn't happen?

TALBERG. Yeliena, really! This is what comes of associating with Viktor Myshlaevsky! A married woman — deceiving her husband? Well, it's a quarter to ten, I shall be late.

YELIENA. I'll pack for you.

TALBERG. Don't bother, my dear — just an attache-case with a change of underwear. Only hurry, for God's sake. I give you just one minute.

YELIENA. You must say goodbye to my brothers.

TALBERG. Yes, of course I will. Only don't forget — I am going away temporarily on duty.

YELIENA (*runs off*). Alyosha! Alyosha!

ALEXEI (*entering*). Yes, what is it? . . . Oh, hullo, Vladimir.

TALBERG. Hullo, Alyosha.

ALEXEI. What's all the commotion?

TALBERG. Look, I have some important news for you. As from tonight the Hetman's position has become extremely grave.

ALEXEI. What do you mean?

TALBERG. Grave in the extreme.

ALEXEI. What's happening?

TALBERG. It is more than probable that the Germans will withdraw their support and we shall have to rely on our own forces to beat off Petlyura.

ALEXEI. You don't mean it!

TALBERG. It's highly likely.

ALEXEI. That's a fine state of affairs . . . Thanks for telling me.

TALBERG. The other thing I want to say is that since I've been ordered away on duty . . .

ALEXEI. Where to? . . . or is it a secret?

TALBERG. To Berlin.

ALEXEI. What? To *Berlin*?

TALBERG. Yes. Try as I might, I couldn't get out of it. It's the last thing in the world I wanted.

ALEXEI. Will it be for long, might I ask?

TALBERG. Two months.

ALEXEI. I see.

TALBERG. Well, all the best, old man. Look after Lena. (*Offers bis band.*)

ALEXEI *puts bis band bebind bis back.*

What does that mean?

ALEXEI. It means that I don't like the sound of your trip to Berlin.

TALBERG. Colonel Turbin!

ALEXEI. Yes, Colonel Talberg? I'm listening.

TALBERG. Kindly explain yourself!

ALEXEI. When would you like me to do that, Colonel Talberg?

TALBERG. When . . . Five to ten . . . When I get back.

ALEXEI. God knows what may happen when you get back.

TALBERG. You . . . You . . . I've wanted a talk with you for some time.

YELIENA (*entering*). What are you talking about?

ALEXEI. Oh nothing, Lena.

TALBERG. Nothing, my dear. Goodbye, Alyosha.

ALEXEI. Goodbye, Volodya.

YELIENA. Nikolka! Nikolka!

NIKOLKA. Here I am. Oh, he's arrived . . .

YELIENA. Volodya has been ordered abroad on duty for a while. Say goodbye to him.

TALBERG. Goodbye, Nikolka.

NIKOLKA. I hope you have a good trip, colonel.

TALBERG. There's some money for you, Lena. I'll send you some more as soon as I get there. Goodbye, everyone. (*Exit hastily towards the hall.*) Don't see me out, my dear, you'll catch cold. (*Exit, followed by* YELIENA.)

ALEXEI (*in a grating voice*). Yeliena, you'll catch cold!

Pause.

NIKOLKA. Why is he going away, Alyosha? Where's he going?

ALEXEI. To Berlin.

NIKOLKA. To Berlin? At a moment like this . . . ? (*Looks out of the window.*) He's haggling with the cab-driver. (*Philosophically.*) Do you know, Alyosha, I've just realised that he looks exactly like a rat . . .

ALEXEI (*dully*). You're absolutely right, Nikolka. And our house looks like a sinking ship. Come on, we have guests. Off you go.

Exit NIKOLKA.

That means that my regiment will be smashed to pieces. 'Extremely grave'. 'Grave in the extreme'. Rat!

YELIENA (*returning from the ball. Looks out of the window*). He's gone . . .

Scene Two

The table is laid for supper.

YELIENA (*at the piano, repeatedly playing the same chord*). He's gone. How could he . . .

SHERVINSKY (*suddenly appearing in the doorway*). Who's gone?

YELIENA. My God! What a fright you gave me, Shervinsky. How did you manage to come in without ringing the bell?

SHERVINSKY. Your front door was wide open. Good evening to you, Yeliena. (*Produces an enormous bouquet from its paper wrapping.*)

YELIENA. How many times have I asked you not to do this, Leonid? I don't like you spending money on me.

SHERVINSKY. Money exists to be spent, as Karl Marx said. May I take off my cloak?

YELIENA. And supposing I said that you may not?

SHERVINSKY. I would sit at your feet all night long, wearing my cloak.

YELIENA. A typically exaggerated army officer's gesture.

SHERVINSKY. I beg your pardon: a typically exaggerated *guards'* officer's gesture. (*Takes off his cloak in the hall, reppears in his magnificent Circassian tunic.*) I'm so glad to see you again! It's such a long time since I last saw you!

YELIENA. If my memory serves me right, you were here yesterday.

SHERVINSKY. Ah, Yeliena, in these terrible times 'Yesterday' was an age ago! Well, come on — who's gone away?

YELIENA. My husband, Vladimir.

SHERVINSKY. But . . . he was supposed to be coming *back* today!

YELIENA. Yes, he did come back and . . . went away again.

SHERVINSKY. Where to?

YELIENA. Berlin.

SHERVINSKY. To . . . Berlin? For how long, if you don't mind my asking?

YELIENA. About a couple of months.

SHERVINSKY. A couple of months! No! You don't say? . . . Oh dear, how very, very sad! . . . I'm really most upset!!

YELIENA. Shervinsky, that's the fifth time you've kissed my hand.

SHERVINSKY. It's because I'm so depressed! My God, and everyone's going to be here this evening! Hurrah!

NIKOLKA (*offstage*). Shervinsky!

YELIENA. Why are you so delighted?

SHERVINSKY. I'm delighted because . . . Oh really, Yeliena!

YELIENA. A well-bred man would know how to hide his feelings better.

SHERVINSKY. Why do you say that? No, I assure you I am extremely well-bred. It's just that I'm, well, er overwhelmed . . . So he's gone and you're left behind.

YELIENA. As you see. How's your voice?

SHERVINSKI (*at the piano*). Ma . . . ma . . . mi, mi, mi . . . He is far, far awa-ay . . . far away and will not know . . . Yes . . . I'm in splendid voice tonight. On my way in the cab I thought it had gone off somewhat but as soon as I get here, I find I'm in excellent voice.

YELIENA. Did you bring your music with you?

SHERVINSKY. Well, as it happens, I did . . . (*Sings.*) 'You are a goddess of the purest degree . . . '

YELIENA. The only good thing about you is your voice, and your real calling is to be an opera singer.

SHERVINSKY. I must admit the raw material is there. You know, Yeliena, one day at Zhmerinka I sang the 'Epithalamion', and the top note is a 'C', as you know — well I sang the 'E' above 'C' and held it for nine bars.

YELIENA. How many bars?

SHERVINSKY. Seven bars. Don't you believe me? Good God, why, Countess Hendrikov was there, and she fell in love with my high 'E'.

YELIENA. And what happened then?

SHERVINSKY. She poisoned herself. With potassium cyanide.

YELIENA. Oh Shervinsky, you're so vain, it's like a disease! Gentlemen, Shervinsky's here! Come to table!

Enter ALEXEI, STUDZINSKY *and* MYSHLAEVSKY.

ALEXEI. Evening, Leonid. Delighted to see you.

SHERVINSKY (*to* MYSHLAEVSKY). Viktor! You're alive! Thank God for that! Why are you wearing a turban?

MYSHLAEVSKY (*with a towel wrapped round his head*). Hullo, Leonid.

SHERVINSKY (*to* STUDZINSKY). Good evening, captain.

Enter LARIOSIK *and* NIKOLKA.

MYSHLAEVSKY. Allow me to introduce you. This is Captain Studzinsky, adjutant of our regiment; this is M'sieur Surzhansky. He and I have been having a bath together.

NIKOLKA. Our cousin from Zhitomir.

STUDZINSKY. How do you do.

LARIOSIK. Delighted to meet you.

SHERVINSKY. Shervinsky, lieutenant of Her Imperial Majesty's Own Regiment of Life Guards and personal aide-de-camp to the Hetman of the Ukraine.

LARIOSIK. Larion Surzhansky. Delighted to meet you.

MYSHLAEVSKY. Don't be too impressed by all that rigmarole. Ex-majesty, ex-life, ex-guards.

YELIENA. Supper is served, gentlemen.

ALEXEI. Yes, do come and sit down, or it will be midnight

before we know it, and we must all be up early tomorrow.

SHERVINSKY. What a magnificent spread! What is the occasion of this banquet, might I ask?

NIKOLKA. Our regiment's last dinner before we go into action tomorrow.

SHERVINSKY. Aha . . .

STUDZINSKY. Where would you like us to sit, colonel?

SHERVINSKY. Yes, where shall we sit?

ALEXEI. Where you like, where you like. Do sit down, Lena, you sit at the head of the table, as you're the hostess.

They all sit down.

SHERVINSKY. So he's gone away and left you behind, has he?

YELIENA. Be quiet, Shervinsky.

MYSHLAEVSKY. Lena, have some vodka?

YELIENA. Oh no, no!

MYSHLAEVSKY. Well, have some white wine then.

STUDZINSKY. May I pour you out a glass, colonel?

ALEXEI. Thanks — but please take some yourself.

MYSHLAEVSKY (*to* LARIOSIK). Your glass.

LARIOSIK. Well, actually I don't drink vodka.

MYSHLAEVSKY. My dear fellow, I don't drink either. But just one glass. How can you possibly eat pickled herring without vodka? The idea's absurd.

LARIOSIK. I'm most extremely grateful.

MYSHLAEVSKY. It's a very, very long time since I last drank vodka.

SHERVINSKY. Gentlemen! A toast to our hostess, Yeliena! Hurrah!

STUDZINSKY   )
LARIOSIK   ) Hurrah!
MYSHLAEVSKY)

YELIENA. Quiet! Really, gentlemen! You'll wake up the whole street. As it is, they're always complaining that we have wild parties every day.

MYSHLAEVSKY. Ah, that's good. Freshens you up, vodka, doesn't it?

LARIOSIK. Yes, it's remarkable!

MYSHLAEVSKY. One more round — please, colonel . . .

ALEXEI. Don't overdo it, Viktor. You may be going into action tomorrow.

NIKOLKA. And we *shall* go into action!

YELIENA (*to* SHERVINSKY). Tell me, how are things with the Hetman?

STUDZINSKY. Yes, what's the news from the Hetman?

SHERVINSKY. All's well. What a dinner he gave last night at the palace! Two hundred people. There was roast grouse . . . and the Hetman was wearing Ukrainian national costume.

YELIENA. But I hear the Germans are pulling out and abandoning us to our fate?

SHERVINSKY. Don't believe rumours, Yeliena.

LARIOSIK. Thank you, Captain Myshlaevsky. The fact is, as I said, I don't drink vodka.

MYSHLAEVSKY (*tossing back a glassful*). Shame on you, Larion!

SHERVINSKY)
NIKOLKA   ) Shame on you!

LARIOSIK. Thank you very much indeed.

ALEXEI. Don't hit the vodka too hard, Nikolka.

NIKOLKA. Yes, colonel! I'm sticking to white wine.

LARIOSIK. How neatly you toss it back, Viktor.

MYSHLAEVSKY. Comes with practice.

ALEXEI. Thanks, Studzinsky. Care for some salad?

STUDZINSKY. Thank you very much.

MYSHLAEVSKY. Lena, my sweet! Drink some white wine. Lovely auburn-headed Lena, I know why you're looking so moody. Forget it! It'll all be for the best.

SHERVINSKY. Yes, it will all turn out for the best.

MYSHLAEVSKY. No, not like that — the whole glass at one go, Lena.

NIKOLKA (*picks up his guitar and sings*).
Come fill the cup
Drink up, drink up . . .
Down in one . . .

ALL (*sing*). We look towards —
Yeliena!
Down in one, down in one!

YELIENA *drinks.*

Bravo! (ALL *applaud.*)

MYSHLAEVSKY. You look stunning tonight, Lena, by God you do. And that housecoat suits you, I swear it. Look at her housecoat, gentlemen, how the green suits her.

YELIENA. It's a dress, Viktor, and it's not green, it's grey.

MYSHLAEVSKY. Ah, well, who cares? Look at her all the same, gentlemen — wouldn't you say she was a beautiful woman?

STUDZINSKY. Indeed she is. Your health, ma'am!

MYSHLAEVSKY. My radiant Lena, let me embrace you and kiss you.

SHERVINSKY. Now then, Viktor, Viktor . . . !

MYSHLAEVSKY. Hands off, Leonid. Hands off another man's wife!

SHERVINSKY. Look here . . .

MYSHLAEVSKY. I'm allowed to because I'm an old friend of the family.

SHERVINSKY. You're not an old friend of the family, you're a swine . . .

NIKOLKA (*stands up*). Gentlemen, a toast to our regimental commander!

STUDZINSKY, SHERVINSKY *and* MYSHLAEVSKY *stand up.*

LARIOSIK. Hurrah! . . . Excuse me, gentlemen, I'm not a military man.

MYSHLAEVSKY. That's all right, Larion! You're doing fine!

LARIOSIK. My dear Yeliena! I can't tell you how pleasant it is to be in your home . . .

YELIENA. Thank you very much.

LARIOSIK. Dear Colonel Turbin! I can't tell you how much I like it here . . .

ALEXEI. Thank you.

LARIOSIK. Yeliena, gentlemen — these cream-coloured blinds . . . give one such a sense of peace and security . . . that one can forget all the horrors of civil war. And our wounded souls are so longing for tranquillity . . .

MYSHLAEVSKY. Do you write poetry, might I ask?

. LARIOSIK. Do I? Yes . . . I do.

MYSHLAEVSKY. I see. Sorry for interrupting. Do go on.

LARIOSIK. That's all right . . . These cream-coloured blinds . . . they cut us off from the rest of the world . . . I'm afraid I'm not a military man . . . dammit though, pour me out another glass.

MYSHLAEVSKY. Bravo, Larion! Crafty fellow — saying he didn't drink. I like you, Larion, but you're about as good at making speeches as an old boot.

LARIOSIK. Don't say that, Viktor — I've made speeches before, you know, quite a few in fact . . . at dinner parties with my late father's colleagues . . . in Zhitomir . . . All tax inspectors . . . and they were rude to me too . . .

MYSHLAEVSKY. Everyone knows that tax inspectors are monsters.

SHERVINSKY. Drink up, Lena, my dear!

YELIENA. Are you trying to get me drunk? Horrible man!

NIKOLKA (*at the piano, sings*).
   'Oh tell me, magician, beloved of the gods,
   What fate is in store for me lying?
   How soon in the fight 'gainst impossible odds
   Shall foemen rejoice at my dying? . . . '

LARIOSIK (*sings*).
   'So, let the music play the march of victory . . .'

ALL (*sing*).
  'The enemy is running away, away, away!
  And for the . . . '

LARIOSIK. 'Tsar! . . .'

ALEXEI. Oh, come now!

ALL (*sing the next line pianissimo*).
  'And for the tsar, the pride of Russia's history.'

  (*Aloud*.)

  'Let's raise the mighty cry: Hurrah! Hurrah! Hurrah!

NIKOLKA (*sings*).
  'Towards him there comes from the forest's dark shades.

ALL (*sing*).
  'Divinely inspired, the magician:
  "Oh, tell me, you dweller in whispering glades . . . " '

LARIOSIK. Ah, I can't tell you how delightful it is here, Yeliena.
  The lights, these people . . .

SHERVINSKY. Gentlemen! I propose the health of His Highness
  the Hetman of all the Ukraine. Hurrah!

  Pause.

STUDZINSKY. I'm sorry. Although I'm going out to fight
  tomorrow, I will not drink that toast and I advise other
  officers not to drink it either.

SHERVINSKY. Captain Studzinsky!

LARIOSIK. Oh dear, I don't like the sound of this . . .

MYSHLAEVSKY (*drunkenly*). He's the bastard who got my toes
  frost-bitten. (*Drinks.*)

STUDZINSKY. Colonel Turbin, do you approve this toast?

ALEXEI. No, I do not.

SHERVINSKY. Colonel, allow me to propose another toast!

STUDZINSKY. No, please let me do so.

LARIOSIK. No, let me. Yeliena Talberg, couple with the health
  of esteemed husband, who has been obliged to go to Berlin!

MYSHLAEVSKY. Well done, Larion. Very ingenious. Couldn't
  have said better myself.

NIKOLKA (*sings*).
  'Oh, tell me, you dweller in whispering glades . . . '

LARIOSIK. Forgive me, Yeliena, I'm not a military man and I
  don't know . . .

YELIENA. Don't worry, Larion. You're kind and sincere. Come
  over here and sit beside me.

LARIOSIK. Yeliena . . . Oh my God, I've spilled red wine on
  the tablecloth . . . !

NIKOLKA. Doesn't matter — we'll just sprinkle salt on it.

STUDZINSKY. That Hetman of yours!

ALEXEI. Just a moment, gentlemen! What is happening? Are
  we being made fools of, or what? If instead of putting on this
  absurd comedy of Ukrainisation your Hetman had begun
  forming officers' volunteer detachments in time, then you
  wouldn't have seen hide nor hair of Petlyura in the Ukraine.
  And not just that: we would have swatted those Bolsheviks
  in Moscow like flies. And now would be the time to do it, by
  all accounts: I hear they're eating cats in Moscow. And he
  could have saved Russia!

SHERVINSKY. The Germans wouldn't have allowed the Hetman
  to form an army, because they were afraid of it.

ALEXEI. I beg to differ. We should have made it clear to the
  Germans that we were no threat to them. That's all over.
  We've lost the war. What faces us now is something more
  terrible than the war or the Germans, more terrible than
  anything else in the world: the Bolsheviks. We ought to have
  said to the Germans: 'What do you need? Do you want wheat,
  sugar? Go on, take it, stuff yourself with it till you burst —
  only help us, help us to make sure our peasants don't catch
  the Moscow disease.' But now it's too late; by now our
  officers have degenerated into bar-flies. An army of bar-room
  spongers! Just try getting one of them to fight now. Like hell
  he'll fight! His pockets are stuffed with black market foreign
  currency, he spends all day sitting in a cafe on the Kreshchatik,
  surrounded by a parasitic horde of guards officers with cushy
  jobs at headquarters. Then one fine day they give Colonel
  Turbin an artillery regiment: panic, rush, hurry, form a unit
  from scratch, Petlyura's coming! . . . Oh, splendid! . . . I give
  you my word of honour that when I saw my recruits

yesterday, for the first time in my life my heart sank into my boots.

MYSHLAEVSKY. Alyosha, my favourite commanding officer! You're a soldier and a gunner to your fingertips. Here's to you, old man!

ALEXEI. My heart sank because for every hundred officer cadets I'd been given a hundred and twenty students, who didn't know one end of a rifle from the other. And yesterday on the parade ground . . . It was snowing, there was fog in the distance . . . I had a sudden feeling, you know, that I was going to a funeral . . .

YELIENA. Alyosha, why do you say such dreadful, gloomy things? Stop it!

NIKOLKA. Don't worry, colonel, we'll never give in.

ALEXEI. The fact is, as I sit here amongst you all, I'm obsessed by one thought: God, if only we could have foreseen all this earlier! Do you know what this Petlyura is? He's a myth, a black fog. He doesn't exist. Look out of the window and see what's there. A snow-storm, shadows, that's all . . . there are only two real forces in Russia, gentlemen: the Bolsheviks and us. And these two forces will clash before long. I see even blacker times ahead. I see . . . well, no matter. We shan't stop Petlyura. But he won't stay for long. And after him the Bolsheviks will come. That's why I shall go and fight. Against my will, but I shall fight! Because when we come face to face with them — then we shall see some fun. Either we shall bury them, or more likely, they will bury us. I drink to *that* meeting, gentlemen!

LARIOSIK (*at the piano, sings*).
   Urgent meetings,
   Pledges, speeches —
   All the world
   Is upside down . . .

NIKOLKA. Well done, Larion! (*Sings.*)
   Urgent meetings,
   Pledges, speeches —

   ALL *join in singing, slightly drunkenly.* LARIOSIK *suddenly bursts into tears.*

YELIENA. Lariosik, what's the matter?

NIKOLKA. Larion!

MYSHLAEVSKY. What is it, Larion, what's upset you?

LARION (*drunk*). I'm frightened.

MYSHLAEVSKY. What of? The Bolsheviks? We'll show 'em!
(*Draws his Mauser.*)

YELIENA. Viktor, what are you doing?

MYSHLAEVSKY. Going to shoot commissars. Which of you's a
commissar?

SHERVINSKY. That Mauser's loaded!

STUDZINSKY. Sit down this minute, captain!

YELIENA. Someone take it away from him!

The Mauser is removed from MYSHLAEVSKY's *grasp. Exit*
LARIOSIK.

ALEXEI. Look here, have you gone mad? Sit down, I tell you!
This is my fault, gentlemen.

MYSHLAEVSKY. I seem to have fallen among Bolsheviks.
Delightful. Greetings, comrades! Let's drink a toast to the
commissars — they're such charming people!

YELIENA. Viktor, you're not to drink any more.

MYSHLAEVSKY. Shut up, madam commissar!

SHERVINSKY. God, he's pretty far gone . . .

ALEXEI. It's my fault, gentlemen. Forget what I said just now.
It's just that my nerves are in pieces.

STUDZINSKY. No, colonel. Believe me, we understand you and
we agree with everything you said. We shall defend the
Russian Empire forever!

NIKOLKA. Long live Russia!

SHERVINSKY. Let me speak! You've misunderstood me. The
Hetman is in any case doing what you suggest. When we have
beaten off Petlyura and the Allies have helped us to smash
the Bolsheviks, then the Hetman will lay the Ukraine at the
feet of His Imperial Majesty, Tsar Nicholas II . . .

MYSHLAEVSKY. *What* tsar? And he says I'm far gone . . .

NIKOLKA. The tsar's dead . . .

SHERVINSKY. Gentlemen! The news of His Imperial Majesty's death . . .

MYSHLAEVSKY. Is slightly exaggerated.

STUDZINSKY. Viktor, how dare you! You're an officer . . .

YELIENA. Let him finish what he's saying.

SHERVINSKY. . . . was invented by the Bolsheviks. Do you know what happened at the court of Kaiser Wilhelm when the Hetman's staff was presented to him? The Kaiser said: 'And as for the future, it will be discussedwith you by . . . ' — the curtains parted and the tsar walked into the room.

Enter LARIOSIK.

He said: 'Gentlemen, go back to the Ukraine and form your regiments. When the time comes, I shall personally lead you to the heart of Russia, to Moscow.' And he burst into tears.

STUDZINSKY. But he was killed!

YELIENA. Shervinsky! Is that true?

SHERVINSKY. Yeliena!

ALEXEI. That is a myth, lieutenant. I've already heard that story myself.

NIKOLKA. I don't care. If the tsar is dead, long live the tsar! Hurrah! . . . The anthem! Shervinsky! The anthem!

(*Sings.*) 'God save the Tsar . . . '

SHERVINSKY)
STUDZINSKY) 'God save the Tsar . . .'
MYSHLAEVSKY)

LARIOSIK (*sings*). 'Mightiest ruler . . .'

NIKOLKA)
STUDZINSKY) 'Long to reign over . . . '
SHERVINSKY)

YELIENA)
ALEXEI) Gentlemen, what are you doing? Stop it!

MYSHLAEVSKY (*weeping*). Just look at the Russian people, Alyosha! They're just a band of thugs, a trades union of political assassins. Look at Tsar Peter III . . . what harm did he

do to them? They all yelled: 'Down with the war!' Fine . . .
he stopped the war. And then one of the very noblemen the
tsar had created smashed his face with a bottle! Tsar Paul
murdered by his own courtiers . . . And then that other
one . . . can't remember his name . . . the nice Tsar with the
side-whiskers, he thinks, let's do the peasants a good turn and
free them from serfdom. Ungrateful devils . . . what do they
do? Throw a bomb at him. They need flogging, the swine.
Alyosha! . . . Oh God, I feel terrible . . .

YELIENA. He's going to be sick!

NIKOLKA. He's unwell . . .

ALEXEI. Into the bathroom.

STUDZINSKY, NIKOLKA *and* ALEXEI *pick up*
MYSHLAEVSKY *and carry him out.*

YELIENA. I'll go and see what's the matter with him.

SHERVINSKY (*blocking the doorway*). Don't bother, Lena.

YELIENA. God, did they have to behave like this? . . . Chaos . . .
the room's thick with cigarette-smoke . . . Look, Lariosik's
still here!

SHERVINSKY. For heaven's sake, don't wake him up.

YELIENA. I'm half drunk myself, thanks to you. Oh, God, I
can't even walk straight.

SHERVINSKY. There now, sit down over there. May I sit
beside you?

YELIENA. Yes, do . . . What's to become of us, Shervinsky?
How is all this going to end? Mm? . . . I had a nightmare last
night. Everything around us is going from bad to worse.

SHERVINSKY. We'll be all right, Yeliena. You mustn't believe
in bad dreams . . .

YELIENA. No, no, my dream was prophetic. I dreamed we
were all sailing to America in a ship, sitting in the hold. Then
a storm blew up. The wind howled, it was freezing cold, rough
sea. And we were in the hold. The water rose up to our feet.
We clambered on to some bunks. Suddenly there were rats
everywhere — huge, repulsive rats. It was so awful that I woke
up.

SHERVINSKY. Do you know something, Yeliena? He's not going to come back.

YELIENA. Who?

SHERVINSKY. Your husband.

YELIENA. You're not supposed to say that. What business of . yours is it whether he comes back or not?

SHERVINSKY. It's very much my business. I love you.

YELIENA. Do you expect me to believe you?

SHERVINSKY. It's true, for God's sake — I love you.

YELIENA. Well, you can love me in silence.

SHERVINSKY. I won't. It's too boring.

YELIENA. Just a moment — what made you start talking about my husband just now?

SHERVINSKY. Because he's like a rat.

YELIENA. And you, Leonid, are like a pig! To start with, he doesn't look a bit like a rat.

SHERVINSKY. Oh yes, he does. The pince-nez on that long, sharp nose . . .

YELIENA. Charming! Slandering an absent man in front of his wife.

SHERVINSKY. You're completely the wrong person to be his wife.

YELIENA. What do you mean by that?

SHERVINSKY. Look at yourself in the mirror. You're beautiful, intelligent — emancipated as they say. Altogether, a magnificent woman. You're a splendid accompanist on the piano. Compared with you, he's nothing but a dummy. A careerist. A General Staff pen-pusher.

YELIENA. Brave boy — now that his back's turned! (*Closes his mouth.*)

SHERVINSKY. I would say all that to his face. Wanted to for a long time. I'd say it, and challenge him to a duel. You're not happy with him.

YELIENA. Is there anyone I *could* be happy with?

SHERVINSKY. With me.

YELIENA. No, you won't do.

SHERVINSKY. Why not?

YELIENA. What's good about you?

SHERVINSKY. Take a good look, and you'll see.

YELIENA. A pàir of gaudy aide-de-campe's tassels, a face like a pretty cherub. And a voice. That's all.

SHERVINSKY. I might have known it! Really it's too bad! Everyone says the same thing: either Shervinsky the aide-de-camp or Shervinsky the singer . . . but no one ever sees that Shervinsky's a human being with a soul, Shervinsky lives like a dog without a kennel. Shervinsky hath not where to lay his head.

YELIENA (*pushing his head away*). Ah Casanova — don't think I don't know your tricks! You tell the same sob-story to all your women. Including that long, thin one — with the painted mouth . . .

SHERVINSKY. She's not long and thin, she's a mezzo-soprano. I swear to you, Yeliena, I've never said anything of the kind to her and never shall. That was unkind of you, Lena, really unkind.

YELIENA. You may *not* call me Lena!

SHERVINSKY. All right — that was unkind of you, Yeliena Vassilievna. You are completely insensitive to my feelings.

YELIENA. The trouble is, I happen to like you very much.

SHERVINSKY. Aha! You like me. And you don't love your husband.

YELIENA. No, I do love him.

SHERVINSKY. Don't lie, Lena. A woman who loves her husband doesn't have your look in her eyes. I know women's eyes. They tell you everything.

YELIENA. I grant you've had plenty of experience.

SHERVINSKY. How could he run away like that?

YELIENA. You would have done the same, given the chance.

SHERVINSKY. Me? Never! It's shameful. Admit you don't love him!

YELIENA. Very well: I don't love him and I don't respect him. I don't respect him. Satisfied? But that doesn't mean you can jump to conclusions. Take your hands off.

SHERVINSKY. In that case why did you kiss me that time?

YELIENA. Liar! I've never kissed you. You're a gold-tasselled liar!

SHERVINSKY. Me — a liar? What about that time at the piano? I was singing 'All-powerful God', and we were on our own. I can even tell you the date — it was November the eighth. We were on our own and you kissed me on the lips.

YELIENA. I kissed you because of your voice. Do you see? It was a friendly kiss, because you have a remarkable voice. And that's all.

SHERVINSKY. Is that really all?

YELIENA. This is a nightmare, I swear it. All these dirty plates, everyone drunk . . . My husband's left me. And the light's so strong . . .

SHERVINSKY. We'll put that light out. (*Switches off the overhead light.*) That better? Listen, Lena, I love you very much. And I'm not going to let you go. You're going to be my wife.

YELIENA. You slide up like a snake . . . like a snake . . .

SHERVINSKY. Why am I like a snake?

YELIENA. Because you lead me into temptation. But I warn you — it won't do you any good. You'll get nowhere. Whatever his faults, I'm not going to ruin my life for your sake. You may even turn out to be worse.

SHERVINSKY. Lena, you're so beautiful!

YELIENA. Go away! I'm drunk. And *you* got me drunk on purpose. You're notorious. The whole of our life is collapsing. Everything's falling apart, Leonid.

SHERVINSKY. Don't be afraid, Yeliena, I won't abandon you at a time like this. I'll stay beside you, Lena.

YELIENA. Let me go. I'm afraid I might disgrace the name of Talberg.

SHERVINSKY. Lena, leave him altogether and marry me . . . Lena.

They kiss.

Will you divorce him?

YELIENA. Oh, to hell with everything!

They kiss.

LARIOSIK (*suddenly*). Stop kissing, or I shall be sick.

YELIENA. Let me go! Oh, my God! (*Runs off.*)

LARIOSIK *groans.*

SHERVINSKY. Young man — you haven't seen anything!

LARIOSIK (*vaguely*). No, I saw everything.

SHERVINSKY. Oh God, he's still plastered.

LARIOSIK. Wait and hear what my mother has to say to you when I die. I told you I wasn't a military man and shouldn't drink so much vodka. (*Collapses on top of* SHERVINSKY.)

SHERVINSKY. Christ, he really *has* overdone it!

The clock strikes three and plays a minuet.

Curtain

ACT TWO

Scene One

The HETMAN's *private office in the palace. A huge desk with several telephones. A field telephone on a side-table. On the wall a vast framed map. Night. The office is brilliantly lit. The door opens and a* FOOTMAN *admits* SHERVINSKY.

SHERVINSKY. Good evening, Fyodor.

FOOTMAN. Good evening, sir.

SHERVINSKY. What? Nobody here? Who is the officer on telephone duty?

FOOTMAN. His Highness Prince Novozhiltsev.

SHERVINSKY. And where is he?

FOOTMAN. Couldn't say, sir. He went out half an hour ago.

SHERVINSKY. What?! Do you mean to say there's been no duty officer here for half an hour?

FOOTMAN. But nobody's rung up, sir. I've been on the door all the time.

SHERVINSKY. That's not the point! Supposing somebody had rung up? And at a time like this!

FOOTMAN. I would have taken the message. They left instructions that I was to note down any telephone calls until you came.

SHERVINSKY. You? Take down military telephone messages?! What's the matter with him — has he gone soft in the head or what? . . . Ah, I see. I suppose he was taken ill, was he?

FOOTMAN. No sir. He left the palace.

SHERVINSKY. Left the palace? You must be joking, Fyodor. Left the palace without handing over to another duty officer?

Where did he go — to the madhouse?

FOOTMAN. Couldn't say, sir. All I know is he took his tooth-brush, soap and towel from the duty officer's room. I even gave him a newspaper.

SHERVINSKY. What newspaper?

FOOTMAN. Yesterday's newspaper, sir. He used it to wrap up his soap.

SHERVINSKY. Excuse me, but there's his sword over there!

FOOTMAN. Yes, he left in civilian clothes, sir.

SHERVINSKY. Either I'm out of my mind or you are. Surely he at least left me a note, or told you to give me a message?

FOOTMAN. He sent you his kind regards, sir.

SHERVINSKY. You may go, Fyodor.

FOOTMAN. Very good, sir. May I venture a remark, sir?

SHERVINSKY. Well, what is it?

FOOTMAN. I believe, sir, that Prince Novozhiltsev received some bad news.

SHERVINSKY. Bad news? What — from home?

FOOTMAN. No, sir. On the field telephone. It was then that he started to leave. And he had a funny look on his face, sir.

SHERVINSKY. I was not aware, Fyodor, that the facial expression of His Highness's aides-de-camp was any concern of yours. That remark was uncalled for.

FOOTMAN. I beg your pardon, sir. (*Exit.*)

SHERVINSKY (*picks up one of the telephones on the* HETMAN's *desk*). One, two, two, three, please . . . Thank you . . . Is that Prince Novozhiltsev's flat? . . . Would you mind asking him to speak . . . What? He's in the palace? No, he's not. I'm in the palace myself . . . Just a moment — Seryozha, that's you — I recognise your voice! . . . Seryo . . . Look here . . .

The telephone clicks and gives the calling tone.

Well, I'm damned — what a nerve! I could hear perfectly well that that was him speaking. Hullo, hullo. This is Shervinsky speaking. Hullo . . . (*Replaces the receiver. Picks up the field*

telephone and cranks the handle.) Svyatoshino Detachment
Headquarters, please . . . Chief of Staff, please . . . What?
He's not there? All right, give me the Deputy Chief of Staff . . .
Hullo, Svyatoshino Detachment Headquarters? . . . What
the hell's going on? (*Sits down at the desk, rings a bell.*)

Enter FOOTMAN.

SHERVINSKY (*writes a note*). Fyodor, give this note at once
to the messenger. Tell him to go to my flat on Lvov Street,
and they'll give him a parcel when he hands over this note.
Then he's to bring it straight back here. There's two roubles
for the cab-fare. And there's a pass to get him back into
headquarters.

FOOTMAN. Very good, sir. (*Exit.*)

SHERVINSKY (*strokes his sideburns; thoughtfully*). Christ, what
a mess!

A telephone rings on the desk.

Hullo . . . Yes . . . Lieutenant Shervinsky, personal aide-de-
camp to His Highness . . . Good evening, general . . . *What?*
(*Pause.*) Bolbotun?! . . . You mean . . . with the whole
headquarters? . . . Very good, sir. Yes, sir, I'll pass on the
message. Very good, sir . . . His Highness should be here at
midnight. (*Replaces receiver. Pause.*) And that, gentlemen,
means the end of me! (*Whistles.*)

*Distant command heard offstage: 'Guard! Attention! Present
arms!' Sound of rapidly approaching footsteps.*

FOOTMAN (*flinging open both wings of the double door*). His
Highness the Hetman of all the Ukraine!

Enter the HETMAN, *wearing a gorgeous Circassian tunic with
silver cartridge pockets, wide magenta-coloured trousers,
heel-less Caucasian boots without spurs; glittering General's
epaulettes on his shoulders. Clipped greying moustache, shaved
head. Aged about forty-five.*

HETMAN. Good evening, Lieutenant.

SHERVINSKY. Good evening, Your Highness.

HETMAN. Have they arrived?

SHERVINSKY. I beg your pardon, sir — have *who* arrived?

HETMAN. What d'you mean — who? I arranged a conference here for a quarter to twelve, to be attended by the commander of the Russian forces, the garrison commander and a representative of the German High Command. Where are they?

SHERVINSKY. I'm afraid I couldn't say, sir. No one has arrived yet.

HETMAN. Late as usual. Show me the duty officer's report for the past hour. Hurry up, man!

SHERVINSKY. I've just taken over, sir. Lieutenant Prince Novozhiltsev, who was on duty before me . . .

HETMAN. For a long time I've been meaning to remind you and the other officers of my staff that you are supposed to speak Ukrainian. It's disgraceful! Not a single one of my officers can speak the language of the country, and this makes the worst possible impression on the Ukrainian troops. Please speak Ukrainian.

SHERVINSKY. Very good, Your Highness. (*Aside.*) God, what is 'prince' in Ukrainian? (*Aloud.*) Er . . .

HETMAN. Oh, talk Russian, man!

SHERVINSKY. Yes, sir. Lieutenant Prince Novozhiltsev, who was on duty before me, was obviously taken unexpectedly ill and went home before I arrived . . .

HETMAN. What's that? Left his post? Listen — are you in your right mind? What do you mean — he went home? In other words, he left his post without orders. What in God's name is going on here? (*Picks up a telephone.*) Guardroom? Send a patrol at once to Lieutenant Novozhiltsev's quarters, arrest him and bring him back to the guardroom. At once.

SHERVINSKY (*aside*). Serve him right! That'll teach him to try and fool me with a fake voice on the telephone, the lout!

HETMAN (*on the telephone*). At once, d'you hear? (*To* SHERVINSKY.) Well, did he leave his report-sheet?

SHERVINSKY. Yes, sir, he did. But there's nothing on it.

HETMAN. Has he gone off his head, or what? I'll have him shot, right here on the palace ramparts. I'll show the lot of you! Get me the commander-in-chief's headquarters on the telephone, and ask him to come here at once. Also the

garrison commander and all regimental commanders. Look
sharp!

SHERVINSKY. I beg to report a message of extreme urgency,
Your Highness.

HETMAN. What message?

SHERVINSKY. Five minutes ago I was rung up from headquarters and informed that the general in command of the
Russian volunteer forces had been suddenly taken ill and had
left for Germany, along with his whole headquarters staff,
in a German train.

Pause.

HETMAN. Are you in your right mind? You look ill . . . Do you
realise what you're saying? What has happened? Some disaster?
Have they run away? . . . Why don't you say something? What
is it?

SHERVINSKY. You're right, sir. It is a disaster. At ten o'clock
this evening Petlyura's troops broke the city's defence line
and Bolbotun's cavalry has pushed through the gap . . .

HETMAN. Bolbotun's cavalry? Where?

SHERVINSKY. Six miles the other side of Slobodka.

HETMAN. Wait a minute . . . let's see . . . where? Ah yes, I see . . .
Well, you at least are a reliable, efficient and loyal officer. I've
noticed it for some time . . . Get through to the German
army headquarters and ask them to be kind enough and
send their representatives to me at once. Quickly, there's a
good fellow.

SHERVINSKY. Yes, sir. (*Picks up telephone receiver.*)
Extension three, please . . . Hallo — seien Sie bitte so liebenswürdig, Herrn Major von Dust an den Apparat zu bitten.

Knock at the door.

Ja . . . ja . . .

HETMAN. Come in.

FOOTMAN. The representatives of the German headquarters,
Genreal von Schratt and Major von Dust wish to see your Highness.

HETMAN. Ask them to come in at once. (*To* SHERVINSKY.)
Don't bother.

FOOTMAN *admits* VON SCHRATT *and* VON DUST. *Both are wearing field-grey uniform.* VON SCHRATT *has a long face and grey hair;* VON DUST *is red-faced. Both have monocles.*

VON SCHRATT. Wir haben die Ehre, Euer Durchlaucht zu begrüssen.

HETMAN. Sehr erfreut, Sie zu sehen, meine Herren. Bitte nehmen Sie platz.

The GERMANS *sit down.*

Ich habe eben die Nachricht von der schwierigen Lage unserer Armee erhalten.

VON SCHRATT. Das ist uns schon längere Zeit bekannt.

HETMAN (*to* SHERVINSKY). Please take the minutes of this meeting.

SHERVINSKY. May I write in Russian, Your Highness?

HETMAN. General, may I ask you to speak Russian?

VON SCHRATT (*with a strong accent*). Certainly. With pleasure.

HETMAN. I have just been informed that Petlyura's cavalry has broken through the city's line of defence.

SHERVINSKY *begins writing.*

Furthermore, I have received some utterly incredible news from the headquarters of the Russian volunteer forces. The Russian Commander and his staff have shamefully run away! Das ist ja unerhört! (*Pause.*) Through you, as intermediaries, I make the following appeal to the German government: The Ukraine is threatened by mortal danger. Petlyura's irregulars are about to occupy the capital. If this occurs, anarchy will ensue in the city. I therefore request the German High Command for an immediate allocation of forces to repel the advancing bands of irregulars and to restore order in the Ukraine, a country friendly to Germany.

VON SCHRATT. With regret, the German command cannot do such a thing.

HETMAN. What? Kindly inform me why not, general?

VON SCHRATT. Physisch unmöglich. Is physically impossible. Erstens, firstly, according to our informations, Petlyura has two hundred thousand men, excellently armed. Also, the German command concentrate their divisions and transport them back to Germany.

SHERVINSKY (*aside*). The swine!

VON SCHRATT. Therefore we do not have a disposal of sufficient forces. Zweitens, secondly, all Ukraine is on the side of Petlyura.

HETMAN. Lieutenant, underline that phrase in the minutes.

SHERVINSKY. Very good, sir.

VON SCHRATT. I have no objection to that. Underline. Consequently it is impossible to stop Petlyura.

HETMAN. So, without warning, the German High Command is leaving me, my army and my government to our fate?

VON SCHRATT. Nein. We have orders to take measures to save Your Highness.

HETMAN. What measures?

VON SCHRATT. Immediate evacuation of Your Highness. At once into railway wagon and off to Germany.

HETMAN. Excuse me, but I don't understand you . . . I beg your pardon . . . Wait a minute — was it the German High Command that arranged the evacuation of Prince Belorukov?

VON SCHRATT. Precisely.

HETMAN. Without my permission? (*Indignantly.*) I refuse. I hereby protest to the German government against their actions. I still have the ability to raise an army within the city and defend Kiev with my own forces. But responsibility for the destruction of the capital rests with the German High Command. And I am certain that the governments of Great Britain and France . . .

VON SCHRATT. What can the British and French governments do? The German government has sufficient strength to prevent the destruction of Kiev . . . if it wishes.

HETMAN. Is that a threat, General?

VON SCHRATT. A warning, Your Highness. Your Highness has no armed forces in his disposal. The situation is catastrophic . . .

VON DUST (*quietly, to* VON SCHRATT). Herr General, wir

haben Keine Zeit. (*Looks at watch.*)

VON SCHRATT. Ja — ja . . . Your Highness, permit that I tell you the latest news! We have just intercepted a message that the cavalry of Petlyura is eight kilometer from Kiev. And tomorrow evening it will enter . . .

HETMAN. And I am the last person to hear of this!

VON SCHRATT. Do you know what will happen to Your Highness if you are captured? On Your Highness a sentence has been pronounced. It is very sad.

HETMAN. What sentence?

VON SCHRATT. I must apologise to Your Highness . . . (*Pause.*) Hanging. (*Pause.*) I must ask Your Highness to give an answer at once. In my disposal are only ten little minutes, and after that time I take off from myself the responsibility for the life of Your Highness.

Long pause.

HETMAN. I'll go!

VON SCHRATT. Ach, you will go? (*To* VON DUST.) Kindly act in secret and without noise.

VON DUST. Of course — no noise. (*Fires two shots from his revolver into the ceiling.*)

SHERVINSKY *looks perplexed.*

HETMAN (*reaching for his revolver*). What does this mean?

VON SCHRATT. Do not be alarmed, Your Highness. (*Hides behind the curtain draped over the door stage right.*)

Noise and footsteps offstage, then a shouted order: 'Guard, stand to!'

VON DUST (*opening centre door*). Ruhig! Quiet! General von Schratt accidentally caught the hammer of his revolver in his breeches and has injured himself in the head.

VOICES OFF: The Hetman! Where is the Hetman?

VON DUST. The Hetman is very well. Kindly show yourself to the guard, Your Highness . . .

HETMAN (*facing offstage, through centre door*). All's well. No cause for alarm. Order the guard to stand down.

VON DUST (*through centre door*). Please allow the doctor to pass.

The noise stops. Enter a German Army doctor carrying a box, a folding stretcher and an instrument case. VON DUST shuts the centre door and locks it.

VON SCHRATT (*emerges from behind curtain*). Your Highness, please to change into German uniform, as if you am I and I am wounded. We will secretly bring you out of the city, so that no one shall know and so that we do not arouse the suspicion of the guards.

HETMAN. As you wish.

Field telephone rings.

Answer it, lieutenant!

SHERVINSKY. His Highness's private office . . . What? . . . How? (*To* HETMAN.) Your Highness, two regiments of your Ukrainian infantry have deserted to Petlyura . . . Enemy cavalry has appeared in the undefended sector. What orders shall I give, Your Highness?

HETMAN. What orders? Tell them to hold up the cavalry at all costs for at least half an hour. I must have time to leave. Tell them I'll send my armoured cars to support them.

SHERVINSKY (*on the telephone*). Can you hear me? Hold them off for half an hour. His Highness is sending you a detachment of armoured cars.

VON DUST (*taking a German uniform out of the box*). Where would Your Highness like to change?

HETMAN. In the bedroom.

SHERVINSKY (*downstage*). Shall I go too, or not? Would Yeliena go with me? (*To* VON SCHRATT, *firmly*.) I respectfully request your excellency to allow me to accompany the Hetman, as I am his personal aide-de-camp. Apart from myself there is also my, er . . . fiancée . . .

VON SCHRATT. Regret, lieutenant, that I not only cannot take your fiancée, but I cannot take you either. If you wish to try, go to our headquarters train, which is waiting at the station. But I warn you there are no places. A seat is already reserved for the personal aide-de-camp of his Highness.

SHERVINSKY. Who is that?

VON SCHRATT. Ah, what is his name . . . oh yes, Prince Novozhiltsev.

SHERVINSKY. Novozhiltsev! When did he find time to arrange that?

VON SCHRATT. When a catastrophe occurs, people take good care of themselves. A few hours ago he came to our headquarters.

SHERVINSKY. And will he continue to serve under the Hetman in Berlin?

VON SCHRATT. Oh no! Your Hetman will be alone. No staff. We shall only bring to the German frontier those who wish to save their skin from your revolting peasants. After that — every man for himself.

SHERVINSKY. I see. Thank you very much, but I think I can save my skin by staying here . . .

VON SCHRATT. You do right, lieutenant. A man should never leave his fatherland. Heimat ist Heimat.

Enter HETMAN *and* VON DUST. *The* HETMAN *is wearing a German General's uniform. He is smoking nervously.*

HETMAN. Lieutenant, burn all the papers in this room.

VON DUST. Herr Doktor, seien sie liebenswürdig . . . Sit down, please, Your Highness.

HETMAN *sits down. The* DOCTOR *bandages his head until the features are unrecognisable.*

DOCTOR. Fertig.

VON SCHRATT (*to* VON DUST). Ambulanz!

VON DUST. Sofort, Herr General.

VON SCHRATT. Lie down, please, Your Highness.

HETMAN (*in a muffled voice*). But the people must be told of this by a communiqué . . .

VON SCHRATT. A communiqué? At such a moment?

HETMAN. Write this down, lieutenant . . . God did not give me sufficient strength . . . and I therefore . . .

VON DUST. Please, there is no time for a communiqué . . . It can be sent from the train by telegram . . .

HETMAN. Let go of me!

VON DUST. Please lie down, Your Highness.

The HETMAN *is laid on the stretcher. Exit* VON SCHRATT.
The centre door is opened. Enter FOOTMAN. VON DUST,
DOCTOR *and* FOOTMAN *carry out the* HETMAN *through
a door stage left.* SHERVINSKY *helps to carry the stretcher
as far as the doorway, then returns. Re-enter* VON SCHRATT.

VON SCHRATT. Alles in Ordnung. (*Looks at his wrist watch.*)
One o'clock. (*Puts on his peaked cap and cloak.*) Goodbye,
lieutenant. I advise you not to stay here. You may dismiss
yourself. Take off your officer's shoulder-straps. (*Cocks his
head and listens.*) Do you hear?

SHERVINSKY. Running fire.

VON SCHRATT. Precisely. A joke! — 'running' fire — when they
are running away! Have you a pass to go out by the side
entrance?

SHERVINSKY. Yes, sir.

VON SCHRATT. Auf Wiedersehen! Und beeilen sie sich. Hurry,
lieutenant. (*Exit.*)

SHERVINSKY (*stunned*). German efficiency. (*Suddenly comes
to life.*) Well, there's no time to lose. (*Notices something on
the desk.*) Oh, his cigarette case. It's gold! The Hetman forgot
it. Should I leave it here? Certainly not, the servants would
pinch it. Oho! Weighs at least a pound. Historic relic. (*Puts the
cigarette case in his pocket.*) Well now, let's see . . . (*Sits at
the desk.*) We shan't burn any of these papers except the
aide-de-camp's duty roster. (*Burns a sheet of paper.*) Am I a
pig? I wonder? No, I am not. (*Picks up the telephone.*)
One, four, five, three, please . . . Yes . . . Is that the Mortar
Regiment headquarters? . . . Call the commanding officer to
the telephone. It's urgent . . . I don't care, wake him up.
(*Pause.*) Colonel Turbin? Shervinsky speaking. Listen very
carefully, Alexei. The Hetman has run away . . . Yes, run
away! . . . No, I'm quite serious . . . No, there's still time until
dawn . . . Send word to Yeliena not to leave the house
tomorrow on any account . . . I'll come in the morning
and hide myself. Goodbye. (*Rings off.*) Now my conscience
is clear. . . . Fyodor!

Enter FOOTMAN.

Did the messenger bring the package from my flat?

FOOTMAN. Yes, sir.

SHERVINSKY. Bring it here at once.

Exit FOOTMAN, *returns with a bundle.*

FOOTMAN (*anxiously*). May I ask, sir, what has become of his Highness?

SHERVINSKY. What business is it of yours? The Hetman has retired for the night. Now don't ask any more questions. You're a good fellow, Fyodor. There's something about you that is somehow . . . charming . . . Something, oh, proletarian . . .

FOOTMAN. As you say, sir.

SHERVINSKY. Fyodor, bring me my towel, soap and razor from the aide-de-camp's duty room.

FOOTMAN. Very good, sir. Would you like a copy of the newspaper as well, sir?

SHERVINSKY. Quite right. A newspaper too.

Exit FOOTMAN *stage left.* SHERVINSKY *puts on a civilian overcoat and hat, and removes his spurs. He wraps his own and* NOVOZHILTSEV's *sword in the bundle. Re-enter* FOOTMAN.

Does this hat suit me?

FOOTMAN. Oh yes, sir. Would you care to put the razor in your pocket, sir?

SHERVINSKY. Razor in my pocket . . . yes, good idea. My dear Fyodor, allow me to give you a parting gift of fifty roubles.

FOOTMAN. Thank you very much indeed, sir.

SHERVINSKY. And allow me to shake your honest working-man's hand. Don't be surprised, I've always been a democrat at heart. And Fyodor — I have never set foot in this palace and I never served as the Hetman's aide-de-camp.

FOOTMAN. I understand, sir.

SHERVINSKY. I don't know you. I am an opera-singer by profession . . .

FOOTMAN. Is it true that the Hetman has run away, sir?

SHERVINSKY. That's right. Cleared off.

FOOTMAN. The slimy devil.

SHERVINSKY. Cheap little crook.

FOOTMAN. Leaving all of us to our fate, I suppose?

SHERVINSKY. As you see. It's bad enough for you, but what about me?

Telephone rings.

Hello . . . Ah, it's you, Captain . . . Yes. My orders to you are to get the hell out of it and run for your lives . . . Yes, I do know what I'm saying. This is Shervinsky. . . Goodbye and good luck. (*Replaces receiver.*) My dear Fyodor, delightful though it is talking to you, you can see for yourself that I haven't another moment to spare . . . Oh yes, Fyodor — while I'm still in command, I hereby make you a present of this office. What's the matter? Don't be silly — think what a bedspread you could make out of that curtain. (*Exit.*)

Pause. Telephone rings.

FOOTMAN. Hello . . . Can I help you? . . . Shall I tell you? Get the hell out of it and run for your lives . . . this is Fyodor speaking . . . Fyodor.

Curtain

Scene Two

A gloomy hallway in an empty house. A sign reading in Ukrainian: 'Headquarters 1st Cavalry Division'. A standard in the blue and yellow colours of the Ukraine. A hurricane lamp by the doorway. Evening. From outside comes the occasional sound of horses' hooves and the faint sound of an accordion playing familiar tunes. A sentry is posted on either side of the door.

TELEPHONIST (*speaking into field telephone*). It's me, Franko. Just connecting up to the network again . . . Re-connecting, I said . . . Can you hear me? Headquarters cavalry division here. You don't understand? Listen — you're supposed to speak Ukrainian like the rest of us.

TELEPHONIST *rings off by cranking handle of field telephone. Noise offstage. Enter* URAGAN *and* KIRPATY, *leading in a Cossack deserter with a bloodstained face.*

BOLBOTUN. What's this?

URAGAN. We've captured a deserter, sir.

BOLBOTUN. What's your regiment?

Silence.

I'm asking you — what's your regiment?

Silence.

TELEPHONIST. It's me, I tell you! I'm calling from the cavalry division headquarters, re-connecting to the network . . . This is cavalry division headquarters! Can't you hear me? . . . What the hell? . . .

BOLBOTUN. What in God's name do you think you're doing, man? Eh? At a time when every decent cossack has gone to fight for the Ukrainian republic against the White Guards and communist Yids, at a time when every peasant has left his farm to join the Ukrainian army — you try and sneak off home! And do you know what the Hetman's officers are doing to our peasants — to say nothing of what the communists are doing? They're burying them alive in the ground! Do you hear? Well, I'm going to have you buried too! I shall personally see to it. Captain Galanba!

VOICE OFFSTAGE: Captain Galanba to see the Colonel! (*Noise and bustle.*)

BOLBOTUN. Where did you pick him up?

KIRPATY. Behind some stacks of timber. The dirty bastard was hiding and trying to get away.

BOLBOTUN. You scum!

Enter GALANBA, a cold dark man wearing a black Ukrainian fur cap.

Captain, interrogate this deserter . . . Franko, order all regiments to report location. Stop fooling around with that telephone.

TELEPHONIST. Yes, sir. At once, sir . . . 'stop fooling' he says — what the hell can I do with this bloody useless machine?

GALANBA (*grimly*) What regiment?

Silence.

What regiment?

DESERTER (*weeping*). I'm not a deserter! Don't be hard on me, captain, sir. I was trying to find the dressing station. My feet are frost-bitten.

TELEPHONIST (*into telephone receiver*). What's your location? . . . Yes, please. The commander of the cavalry division wants to know your location . . . Can you hear me? . . . How am I supposed to get through on this thing?

GALANBA. Feet frost-bitten, eh? So why haven't you got a chit from your regimental headquarters certifying you've reported sick? Eh? What's your regiment? (*Raises his arm threateningly.*)

Sound of horses crossing a wooden bridge offstage.

DESERTER. Second Cossack Cavalry.

GALANBA. Ah, we know you cossacks. You're all turncoats, traitors, Bolsheviks. Go on, take your boots off. If you're lying and your feet aren't frost-bitten, I'll shoot you on the spot. (*To* SENTRY.) Hey, you! Bring that hurricane lamp over here!

TELEPHONIST (*into receiver*). Send us a messenger with written confirmation of your positions . . . Where? To the big house by the bridge . . . Yes, that's right . . . Very good, sir. . . . Ah, is that you, Gritzko? Tell an orderly to collect the message giving your locations and bring it to our headquarters. Got that? Right . . . (*To* BOLBOTUN.) The location statement will be here right away, colonel.

BOLBOTUN. Good.

GALANBA (*drawing his Mauser automatic*). I promise you that if your feet aren't frost-bitten, I'll blow your head off. Move back, so that I don't hit anyone else by mistake.

The DESERTER *sits down on the floor and starts to pull off his boots. Silence.*

BOLBOTUN. Quite right, Galanba. Let him be an example to others.

The hurricane lamp shines on the DESERTER's *feet.*

KIRPATY (*sighs*). They're frost-bitten all right. He's telling the truth.

GALANBA. You should have asked for a chit, you fool, instead of just wandering off like that . . .

DESERTER. There was no one to give me a chit. We haven't got a doctor in our regiment. There was no one to ask. (*Bursts into tears.*)

GALANBA. Put him under arrest and take him to the dressing station under escort. As soon as the doctor has bandaged his feet, bring him back here and give him fifteen lashes just to remind him not to go running off from his regiment without proper documents.

URAGAN (*taking* DESERTER *out*). Go on, you.

Sound of accordion offstage and a mournful voice singing:

'Hey little apple,
Watch where you're rolling —
Roll to the haidamaks
And you'll never come back . . . '

SUDDEN EXCITED VOICES OUTSIDE THE WINDOW:
'Stop them, stop them!
Over there — past the bridge . . .
they're running across the ice . . . '

GALANBA (*calls out of the window*). Hey, what's going on over there?

VOICE OFF: It's a bunch of Yids, Captain. They're trying to get away across the river on the other side of the bridge.

GALANBA. Patrol, stand to! Stand to! Mount! Mount and move off! Kirpaty — take command! After them — at the gallop! Mind you bring them in alive — alive, d'you hear!

BOLBOTUN. Franko, keep in contact!

TELEPHONIST. Very good, Colonel! I'm keeping the line open.

Noise and footsteps offstage. Enter URAGAN, *leading in a man with a basket.*

MAN WITH BASKET. Hey, what d'you want me for? I'm nobody — just a tradesman . . .

GALANBA. What have you got in there?

MAN WITH A BASKET. Sorry, comrade, but . . .

GALANBA. What d'you mean — comrade? Who's your 'comrade'?

MAN WITH BASKET. Sorry, your honour.

GALANBA. And I'm not 'your honour' either. Give him one round the chops. Now d'you see there aren't any 'your honours' around here? All the White officers are with the Hetman in the city. And we're going to rip their guts out. See?

MAN WITH BASKET. I see.

GALANBA. Shine the light on him. Something tells me we've got a communist here.

MAN WITH BASKET. Look, you've got it wrong. I'm a cobbler, that's all.

BOLBOTUN. How come you speak Russian so well?

MAN WITH BASKET. We're from Kaluga province, sir. And I wish to God I'd never come down here to the Ukraine. I'm a cobbler.

GALANBA. Papers!

MAN WITH BASKET. Passport? Right away, sir. My passport's dead clean, as you might say.

GALANBA. What's in that basket? Where were you going?

MAN WITH BASKET. My basket's full of boots, your . . . hon . . . your . . . er, boots sir. We work for a shop in town. We live on this side of the Dnieper and take the boots into town ourselves.

GALANBA. Why are you taking them at night?

MAN WITH BASKET. So as they'll be ready for sale first thing in the morning.

BOLBOTUN. Boots, eh? Ha, that's good!

URAGAN *opens the basket.*

MAN WITH BASKET. Excuse me, sir, but they're not ours — they belong to our boss.

BOLBOTUN. Belong to your boss, do they? And very nice they are. He has good taste, has your boss. All right men, you can take a pair apiece of his boss's goods.

The boots are handed round.

MAN WITH BASKET. Mister War Minister sir! I'm done for

without those boots. I might as well lie down and die. Why there's two thousand roubles' worth there . . . and they belong to my boss . . .

BOLBOTUN. We'll give you a receipt.

MAN WITH BASKET. What good's a receipt to me? (*Pursues* BOLBOTUN, *who clouts him over the ear. Turns to* GALANBA.) Look, sir — those boots are worth two thousand roubles. I'd understand it if I was a bourgeois or, let's say, a bolshevik .˙. .

GALANBA *clouts him on the ear.*

MAN WITH BASKET (*sits down on the floor, confused*). What the hell's going on? All right, go on and take them for all I care. I suppose it's all right if they're needed to supply the army . . . But you might let me have a pair too, just to keep you company. (*Starts to take off his boots.*)

TELEPHONIST. Hey, look what he's doing, Colonel!

BOLBOTUN. Are you making fun of us, you scum? Get away from that basket. How much longer are you going to crawl around getting in our way? I've put up with you for too long. Out of the way, lads. (*Reaches for his revolver.*)

MAN WITH BASKET. What are you doing? I haven't done anything . . .

BOLBOTUN. Get out of here!

MAN WITH BASKET *runs for the door and exits.*

ALL. Thanks very much, Colonel! Thanks, sir!

TELEPHONIST (*into the receiver*). Hullo, yes . . . Cavalry Division Headquarters here . . . Hurrah! Colonel, Colonel — deserters from two Hetmanite regiments have come to one of our headquarters, and the regimental commander is talking to them about both regiments coming over to our side!

BOLBOTUN. Good news. İf those regiments join us, then Kiev is ours.

TELEPHONIST (*into the receiver*). Gritzko! And we've all got new boots here! Yes . . . Yes . . . Right you are . . . Colonel, please come to the telephone at once.

BOLBOTUN (*into the receiver*). First Cavalry Division commander Colonel Bolbotun speaking . . . Yes, I see . . . Yes, good . . . I'll move off at once. (*To* GALANBA.) Captain, order all four regiments to mount and move off immediately. The outskirts of the city are in our hands. Hurrah!

URAGAN)
KIRPATY) Hurrah! The attack!

Bustle and movement.

GALANBA.(*through the window*). Mount! All regiments mount and move off!

OFFSTAGE ROAR: 'Hurrah!'
GALANBA *runs out.*

BOLBOTUN (*to* TELEPHONIST). Disconnect the telephone. Bring my horse.

TELEPHONIST *disconnects telephone. All prepare to move.*

URAGAN. The colonel's horse!

VOICES OFF. No. 1. Squadron — at the trot — march!
              No. 2. Squadron — at the trot — march!

Offstage noise, clatter of hooves. Whistling. Exeunt all. Then an accordion strikes up, fading away into the distance.

Curtain

ACT THREE

Scene One

Hallway of the Alexander I High School. Rifles piled upright in threes. Ammunition boxes, machine guns. At the top of the vast staircase is a portrait of Tsar Alexander I. Dawn light in the windows. Music and tramp of feet offstage as the troops of the Mortar Regiment march along the corridors of the school to a band.

NIKOLKA (*offstage, sings the verse of a ridiculous popular song*).
'The night was full of throbbing passion
Of thoughts of love and mad desire.'
Whistle.

CADETS (*deafeningly burst into the chorus*).
'I waited for you by the window
I waited for you with a beating heart.'
Whistle.

NIKOLKA (*sings*).
'Our little room I decked with flowers . . . '

STUDZINSKY (*on the upper landing of the staircase*). Regiment — halt!

The REGIMENT *crashes to a halt offstage.*

Captain Myshlaevsky, take over and fall out the regiment.

MYSHLAEVSKY. No. 1. battery! Quick march!

The REGIMENT *marches.*

STUDZINSKY. Keep in step there!

MYSHLAEVSKY. Left, left, left, right, left! No. 1. Battery! Halt!

FIRST OFFICER. No. 2. Battery! Halt!

The REGIMENT *halts.*

MYSHLAEVSKY. On the command 'Fall out', you may break off and smoke. Battery! Fall out!

Talk and movement offstage.

FIRST OFFICER (*to* MYSHLAEVSKY). One of the troops of my battery is five men short. Obviously they've cleared off. What can you expect with students?

SECOND OFFICER. Riff-raff, if you ask me. Can't do a thing with them.

FIRST OFFICER. Why hasn't the colonel arrived yet? He was supposed to be here at six, and now it's a quarter to seven.

MYSHLAEVSKY. Quiet, lieutenant. He was called to the Hetman's palace by telephone. He'll be here any minute now. (*To the* CADETS). What's the matter — cold?

FIRST CADET. Yes, sir, it is a bit on the chilly side.

MYSHLAEVSKY. Why are you standing around, then? You look blue. Try stamping your feet or running on the spot. When you're told to fall out you don't have to stand there like a statue. Come along now — every man his own stove! Hey, you there in 'B' Troop — fetch some benches from the class-rooms, smash 'em up and light the stoves. Go on — look sharp!

CADETS (*shout*). Come on, lads, into the classrooms! Chop up the benches and let's get warm!

Noise and bustle.

MAXIM (*emerging, horrified from a cubby-hole under the stairs*). Look here, sir, you can't do that, you know. Burning the benches in the stoves?! It's vandalism! The headmaster's ordered me to . . .

MYSHLAEVSKY. Well, old man, what are we supposed to burn in the stoves?

MAXIM. Firewood, sir, firewood.

MYSHLAEVSKY. And where is your firewood?

MAXIM. We haven't got any.

MYSHLAEVSKY. Well then, sod off you old fool. Come on, 'B' Troop, what's the delay?

MAXIM. Lord God Almighty! Wonderful. He's yelling at them. I've never seen anything like it. Tartars! Vandals! We've had plenty of troops here before, but ... (*Exit. Shouts offstage.*) Look here, you can't do that!

CADETS (*smashing benches, sawing them up and lighting stoves. Singing*).
'In the sky hang the storm-clouds, heavy and low,
Whirling in circles the storm-driven snow;
The blizzard now howls like a beast in the wild,
Now softens its voice and sobs like a child ... '

MAXIM. Who d'you think you are — burning those in the stove?

CADETS (*singing*).
'Pile the logs and load the hay,
We are moving house to-day ... '
(OTHERS, *sadly*.)
'Have mercy, Lord, for one last time ... '
Sudden shellburst nearby. Pause. Confusion.

FIRST OFFICER. That was a shell.

MYSHLAEVSKY. A bit close, too.

FIRST CADET. I think they're firing at us, captain.

MYSHLAEVSKY. Rubbish! That was just Petlyura spitting.
The singing fades out.

FIRST OFFICER. I think we may be seeing Petlyura today. Interesting to know what he looks like.

SECOND OFFICER (*gloomily*). No need to hurry, you'll find out soon enough.

MYSHLAEVSKY. We're just a small cog in a big machine. If it happens to be our job, then we'll see him. (*To* CADETS.) What's the matter with you lot? Lost your voices? Keep singing!

CADETS (*sing*).
'And when the moment comes to climb
That long white staircase up to heaven ... '

SECOND CADET (*runs over to* STUDZINSKY). The colonel's coming, sir!

STUDZINSKY. Regiment — fall in! Regiment — attention! Dress by the centre! Fall in the officers!

MYSHLAEVSKY. No. 1. Battery — attention!

Enter ALEXEI TURBIN.

ALEXEI (*to* STUDZINSKY). The roll, please Captain Studzinsky. How many men absent?

STUDZINSKY (*quietly*). Twenty-two.

ALEXEI (*tears up the roll*). Is the road-block on Demiyorka Street manned by our troops?

STUDZINSKY. Yes, sir.

ALEXEI. Recall them.

STUDZINSKY (*to second* CADET). Bring back the men on the road-block.

SECOND CADET. Yes, sir. (*Runs off.*)

ALEXEI. I order all officers and men of the Mortar Regiment to listen carefully to what I am about to say. Listen and take good note of your orders; then go and carry them out.

Silence.

During the night a sudden and violent change has occurred in the situation for us, the White Russian army — in fact in the whole political situation of the Ukraine . . . I therefore have to inform you that our Regiment is hereby disbanded.

Dead silence.

The fight against Petlyura is over. I order all of you, including officers, immediately to remove your epaulettes and all other marks of rank and identification, to go home at once and conceal yourselves.

Pause.

That is all. Now go and do as I say.

STUDZINSKY. But colonel . . . but . . . Alexei . . .

FIRST OFFICER. Colonel Turbin . . . sir . . .

SECOND OFFICER. What does this mean?

ALEXEI. Be quiet and don't argue! Carry out your orders, and look sharp about it!

THIRD OFFICER. What does this mean, colonel. Arrest Colonel Turbin!

CADETS. Arrest him!
— What the hell's going on?
— What do you mean arrest him? Are you crazy?
— Petlyura's broken through!
— Christ, I might have known it.
— Quiet! Shut up!

FIRST OFFICER. Please explain yourself, colonel.

THIRD OFFICER. 'A' Troop — follow me!

Confused party of CADETS *march on stage with rifles at the ready.*

NIKOLKA. What in God's name are you doing?

SECOND OFFICER. Arrest him! He's gone over to Petlyura!

THIRD OFFICER. Colonel Turbin: you are under arrest, sir.

MYSHLAEVSKY (*restraining* THIRD OFFICER). Steady, lieutenant!

THIRD OFFICER. Hands off me, captain. Cadets — seize him!

MYSHLAEVSKY. Make your cadets stand back this minute.

FIRST OFFICER. Fall in! Attention!

CADETS. Fall in, lads. Stand to attention.

ALEXEI. Yes, indeed . . . I'd be a fine officer, I must say, if I went into battle with troops like these which the Lord God has seen fit to send me. However, gentlemen — what is excusable in an inexperienced young volunteer is unforgivable (*To* THIRD OFFICER.) in you, lieutenant. I thought every one of you would realise that a disaster has occurred, that your commanding officer was not the man to deceive you or betray you. It seems, though, that you haven't the sense to realise this. Now: whom are you proposing to defend? Answer me.

Silence.

Answer, when your commanding officer asks you a question! Whom do you mean to defend?

THIRD OFFICER. We have sworn to defend the Hetman.

ALEXEI. The Hetman? Excellent! Today, at three o'clock in the morning, the Hetman, abandoning his army to its fate, ran away to Germany in a German train, disguised in German uniform. Thus at the moment when the lieutenant here is preparing to defend the Hetman, that personage has long since left Kiev. He is safely on his way to Berlin.

CADETS. Berlin?!
  — What is he talking about?
  — We don't want to listen!

FIRST CADET. Why do you listen to him, for God's sake?

STUDZINSKY. Silence!

Uproar. The light in the windows is growing brighter.

ALEXEI. But that is by no means all. At the same time that one swine ran away, another scuttled away after him — His Highness, General Prince Belorukov, the Army Commander. Therefore, my friends, not only is there no one to defend, but there is not even anyone to give you orders, because Prince Belorukov's headquarters staff ran away with him too.

Uproar.

CADETS. It can't be!
  — It's impossible!
  — It's a lie!

ALEXEI. Who said it's a lie? Who said that? I have just come from headquarters and I have checked all my information. I take responsibility for every word I have said! . . . So, gentlemen: here we are, all two hundred of us. And there — is Petlyura. What am I saying — there? He's here! Petlyura's cavalry, my friends, is already on the outskirts of the city! He has two hundred thousand men, and as for us — well, there's this Mortar Regiment, two or three infantry detachments and three batteries of artillery. Now do you understand? Just now one of you pointed his revolver at me. I was absolutely terrified. Pathetic.

THIRD OFFICER. Colonel . . .

ALEXEI. Be quiet! Very well, then. If under these circumstances you were all to pass a resolution to defend . . . defend what?

Defend whom? . . . In short, if you decided to fight — then I would not lead you, because I refuse to take part in a farce, especially when every single one of you would pay for that farce — and absolutely pointlessly — with his own blood!

NIKOLKA. Those bastards at headquarters!

Noise and confusion.

CADETS. What are we supposed to do now?
    — Might as well lie down and die!
    — The shame of it!
    — Go to hell! What do you think this is — a political meeting?
    — Stand fast in the ranks!
    — We've been trapped.

THIRD CADET (*runs forward weeping*). One minute they shout — advance, and now it's — retreat. If I ever find the Hetman I'll kill him!

FIRST OFFICER. Shut up cry baby! Listen cadets — if what the colonel says is true, then fall in and follow me. We'll commandeer a train and go to the Don, to join General Denikin!

CADETS. To the Don! To Denikin!
    — Impossible — don't be a fool!
    — We could never reach the Don!

STUDZINSKY. They're right, Alexei. We must abandon everything and transfer the regiment to the Don.

ALEXEI. Captain Studzinsky, how dare you! I am in command of this regiment. I will give the orders and you will carry them out. To the Don, you say? Listen — there on the Don, if you manage to get there, you'll find exactly what you found here: the same generals and the same herd of idle, useless staff officers.

NIKOLKA. Yes, the same pack of headquarters swine.

ALEXEI. Precisely. And they'll make you fight against your own people. And when the Russian people fight back and split your heads open, those generals will run away abroad . . . I know that things in Rostov are exactly the same as in Kiev. Artillery regiments without any shells to fire, cadets without boots to wear, and the staff officers sitting around in cafés. Listen, my friends. I, a combatant officer, was ordered to make you fight. Fine — if there was anything to fight for. But there isn't. So I say to you that the White cause in the Ukraine is finished. And it's finished in Rostov-on-Don, finished everywhere! The people are not with us. The people are against us. Therefore — it's over. Into the coffin and screw down the lid. And I, Alexei Turbin, an officer of the Regular Army who fought through the entire war against the Germans, as Captains Studzinsky and Myshlaevsky here can witness, I take all my actions on my own conscience and responsibility — everything. I am warning you, and because I love you, I'm sending you all home. That is all I have to say.

Some stirring. Sudden shellburst.

Tear off your epaulettes, throw away your rifles and get home at once!

The CADETS *pull off their epaulettes and throw aside their rifles.*

MYSHLAEVSKY (*shouts*). Quiet! Colonel, permission to set fire to the school building?

ALEXEI. Permission not granted.

Gunfire. The windows rattle.

MYSHLAEVSKY. I'll take that machine-gun.

STUDZINSKY. Go home, cadets!

MYSHLAEVSKY. Cadets, sound the 'Retreat' and go home!

Offstage a trumpet sounds.
CADETS and OFFICERS *disperse, running, the lights go out as* NIKOLKA *smashes the switch-box with his rifle-butt. By the stove,* ALEXEI *tears up papers and burns them. Long pause.*

Enter SCHOOL PORTER.

ALEXEI. Who are you?

MAXIM. I'm Maxim, the school porter.

ALEXEI. Get out of here, or you'll be killed.

MAXIM. Where am I to go, sir? I can't leave the school — it's government property. They've wrecked all the benches in two of the classrooms and I can't tell you how much damage they've done. And now they've smashed the lights . . . We've had plenty of troops billeted here before now, but these ones — excuse me, but . . .

ALEXEI. Go away, old man.

MAXIM. You can cut me down with your sword if you like, sir, but I won't go. I was told by the headmaster . . .

ALEXEI. Well, what did the headmaster tell you?

MAXIM. Maxim, he said, Maxim — you will stay here on your own . . . you must see to it . . . And now look what you've done . . .

ALEXEI. Listen, you silly old man, can't you understand Russian? You'll be killed. Go away and hide somewhere in a cellar and don't let anyone catch sight of you.

MAXIM. But who will answer for all this? Maxim will have to answer for it. We've had all sorts here — some of them were for the tsar, some of them were against the tsar, terrible some of the soldiers were, but none of them smashed the benches . . .

ALEXEI. Where the hell are those lists of names? (*Kicks in the door of a cupboard.*)

MAXIM. Look here, sir, I've got a key to that cupboard. That cupboard's school property and you have to go and kick it . . . (*Moves off, crossing himself.*)

Gunfire.

Holy Mother of God . . . Jesus Christ . . .

ALEXEI. That's what I'd like to do with him! The music's starting — strike up the band . . . Christ, if I ever come across you, my lord Hetman, you reptile!

MYSHLAEVSKY *enters at the top of the staircase. Faint sunlight begins to shine in through the windows.*

MAXIM (*to* MYSHLAEVSKY). Won't you tell him to stop, sir? Look at him — he's kicked in the door of the cupboard!

MYSHLAEVSKY. Keep out of our way, old man. Get out.

MAXIM. Hooligans, that's all they are, hooligans . . . (*Exit.*)

MYSHLAEVSKY. Alyosha! I've set fire to the armoury and the stores. By the time Petlyura gets here there won't be so much as a brass button for him.

ALEXEI. For God's sake don't wait any longer, Viktor. Run home.

MYSHLAEVSKY. No hurry. I'll just chuck a couple of bombs into the hay-loft and then clear off. Anyhow, why are you still sitting around there?

ALEXEI. I must stay until that detachment from the road-block gets back.

MYSHLAEVSKY. Come on, now, Alyosha — must you?

ALEXEI. Of course I must — captain!

MYSHLAEVSKY. In that case I'm staying with you.

ALEXEI. What use are you here, Viktor? Go to Yeliena, at once and look after her — that's an order! I'll follow you. Has everyone gone crazy? Why doesn't anyone do as they're told?

MYSHLAEVSKY. All right, Alyosha. I'll go straight home to Lena.

ALEXEI. Have a look around to make sure Nikolka's gone too, and kick him up the behind if he hasn't.

MYSHLAEVSKY. Right. And look here, Alyosha — mind you don't take any stupid risks.

ALEXEI. Teach your grandmother!

Exit MYSHLAEVSKY.

ALEXEI. Grave. 'Grave in the extreme' . . . And when the moment comes to climb . . . the long white staircase up to heaven . . . If only the boys at the road-block haven't been overrun . . .

NIKOLKA (*appearing furtively at the top of the staircase*). Alyosha!

ALEXEI. Nikolka — what the hell are you doing? Is this meant to be a joke? Go home this instant and take off your epaulettes. Get out!

NIKOLKA. I shan't leave without you, colonel.

ALEXEI. What?! (*Draws his revolver.*)

NIKOLKA. Go on — shoot your own brother!

ALEXEI. You bloody clown.

NIKOLKA. Swear at me too, if you like. I know why you're staying here. You, the commanding officer, want to be killed because you can't bear the shame, can you? Well, I'm going to keep an eye on you. If I didn't Lena would murder me anyway.

ALEXEI. Hey, there, someone! Remove Cadet Turbin! Captain Myshlaevsky!

NIKOLKA. They've all gone.

ALEXEI. Just wait, you young devil — I'll speak to you at home!

Loud noises of approaching footsteps. THE ROAD-BLOCK DETACHMENT *enter at a run.*

CADETS (*running across the stage*). Petlyura's cavalry are right behind us . . .

ALEXEI. Cadets! Listen to my orders! Go through the cellars, out by the back door and head for the Lower City! Take off your epaulettes as you go. I'll cover you.

Exultant whistles and the sound of an accordion heard approaching offstage.

Run, run! I'll cover you! (*Runs upstairs to the window. To* NIKOLKA.) Run for it, I beg you, Nikolka! Think of Lena!

Shellburst nearby. Window-panes break. ALEXEI *falls.*

NIKOLKA. Colonel! Alyosha, Alyosha, what have you done?!

ALEXEI. Corporal Turbin, stop playing the hero. Get the hell out of here . . . (*Falls silent.*)

NIKOLKA. Colonel . . . you can't do this! Get up, Alyosha!

Uproar offstage. UKRAINIAN INFANTRY *burst in.*

URAGAN. There! Look! Look! Stop him, lads, stop him!

KIRPATY *fires at* NIKOLKA.

GALANBA (*running onstage*). We want him alive! Take him alive, lads!

His teeth bared, NIKOLKA *crawls up the staircase.*

KIRPATY. There he goes.

URAGAN. You won't get away!

Enter more TROOPS.

NIKOLKA. I won't surrender to you — scum. (*Jumps down from the staircase railings and vanishes.*)

KIRPATY. Fucking little acrobat! (*Fires.*) He's the last — there's no more of them.

GALANBA. Why the hell did you let him go?!

Accordion music swells. Cries of 'Hurrah! Hurrah!, and trumpet-calls offstage. Enter BOLBOTUN, *followed by* STANDARD BEARERS. *The* STANDARDS *float up the staircase. Offstage band strikes up a deafening march.*

Curtain.

Scene Two

The TURBINs' *apartment. Dawn. There is no electricity. A candle is burning on the card table.*

LARIOSIK. Yeliena, just tell me to do whatever you like. If you want me to, I'll put my coat on and go out and find them.

YELIENA. For heaven's sake,. Lariosik, don't do anything of the kind. You'll be killed on the street. We'll wait. Lord, I can see another fire burning. What a ghastly dawn it looks. What's happening out there? I only want to know one thing: where are they?

LARIOSIK. God, what a terrible thing civil war is.

YELIENA. Look — I'm a woman, they won't touch me. I'll go and see what's happening outside.

LARIOSIK. Yeliena, I won't let you go. I'll . . . well, I simply won't let you go, that's all! What would Alexei say to me if I did? He told me not to let you out of doors on any account, and I gave him my word.

YELIENA. I wouldn't go far . . .

LARIOSIK. No, Yeliena!

YELIENA. If only we could find out what's going on . . .

LARIOSIK. I'll go myself . . .

YELIENA. No, don't . . . we'll wait . . .

LARIOSIK. Your husband did the right thing by leaving. It was a very wise move. He'll be safe in Berlin while all this appalling upheaval goes on, and then he'll come back.

YELIENA. My husband? My husband? Don't mention my husband's name again in this house, do you hear?

LARIOSIK. Very well, Yeliena . . . I always manage to choose the wrong moment to say something . . . Would you like some tea, perhaps? I could put on the samovar . . .

YELIENA. No, don't bother . . .

Knock at the door.

LARIOSIK. Wait, wait. Don't open. We must make sure who it is . . . Who's there?

SHERVINSKY. It's me, me . . . Shervinsky . . .

YELIENA. Thank God! (*Opens the front door.*) What's happened? Some disaster?

SHERVINSKY. Petlyura has taken the city.

LARIOSIK. Taken Kiev? God, how terrible!

YELIENA. Where are they? Are they fighting?

SHERVINSKY. Don't worry, Yeliena. I warned Alexei several hours ago. Everything's going to be perfectly all right.

YELIENA. What d'you mean, all right? What about the Hetman? What about the army?

SHERVINSKY. The Hetman ran away last night.

YELIENA. Ran away? And left the army?

SHERVINSKY. Exactly. And so did Prince Belorukov. (*Takes off his greatcoat.*)

YELIENA. The miserable cowards!

SHERVINSKY. Unspeakable swine.

LARIOSIK. Why isn't the electric light working?

SHERVINSKY. They've been shelling the power-station.

LARIOSIK. Oh, lord . . .

SHERVINSKY. Yeliena, can I hide here? Any moment now they'll start looking for Russian officers.

YELIENA. But of course.

SHERVINSKY. If you knew, Yeliena, how happy I am that you are alive and well.

Knock at the door.

Larion, ask who it is . . .

LARIOSIK. Who's there?

MYSHLAEVSKY. Friends, friends . . .

LARIOSIK *opens the door.*
Enter MYSHLAEVSKY *and* STUDZINSKY.

YELIENA. Thank God! But where are Alyosha and Nikolai?

MYSHLAEVSKY. Don't worry, Lena, don't worry. They'll be here soon. There's no cause for alarm, it's still possible to move about in the streets. The guard detachment will escort them both. (*To* SHERVINSKY.) Ah, you're here already I see. Well, I suppose you know everything . . .

YELIENA. Yes, we do. God, the Germans . . .

STUDZINSKY. Nothing we can do about it now. The day of reckoning will come one day, though.

MYSHLAEVSKY. Hullo, Larion!

LARIOSIK. 'The times are out of joint'.

MYSHLAEVSKY. I couldn't have put it better myself.

YELIENA. You look terrible! Come and warm yourselves up, while I put on the samovar.

SHERVINSKY (*from the fireplace*). Shall I help you, Lena?

YELIENA. Don't bother. I'll do it. (*Exit.*)

MYSHLAEVSKY (*ironically, in Ukrainian*). Looking pretty good, aren't you, Mr Personal Assistant to the Hetman. Why — you're not wearing your special insignia, your aigullettes . . . I wonder why not? 'Go back to the Ukraine, gentlemen, and form you regiments' . . . And he burst into tears. Burst into tears, my arse . . .

SHERVINSKY. Why this farcical tone?

MYSHLAEVSKY. I am talking in a farcical tone because what happened was a farce, that's why. It was you who suggested that the Tsar was still alive and you who drank a toast to the Hetman. By the way, where is the Hetman at this moment?

SHERVINSKY. Why should that concern you?

MYSHLAEVSKY. I'll tell you why: Because if I happened to come across your Hetman right now I would pick him up by the feet and beat his head on the pavement until I felt completely satisfied. And your horde of staff officers should be drowned in the lavatory!

SHERVINSKY. You're forgetting yourself, Myshlaevsky!

MYSHLAEVSKY. Bastards!

SHERVINSKY. Wha-at?

LARIOSIK. Why must you quarrel?

STUDZINSKY. As senior officer, I must ask you to cease this conversation at once. It is completely senseless and will get us nowhere. Why do you have to pick on him, Viktor? Calm down, lieutenant.

SHERVINSKY. Captain Myshlaevsky's behaviour has been intolerable lately . . . You stupid boor — do you think I'm responsible for this disaster? On the contrary, it was I who warned you all. If it hadn't been for me, it's highly doubtful whether you would be standing here alive at this minute.

STUDZINSKY. Quite true, lieutenant. And we are extremely grateful to you.

YELIENA (*entering*). What is happening? What's going on?

STUDZINSKY. Keep calm, Yeliena, everything is going to be perfectly all right. I vouch for it. Better go back to your room.

Exit YELIENA.

Viktor, really, you have no right to say such things.

MYSHLAEVSKY. All right, I'm sorry, Leonid. My temper flared up, that's all. But the whole thing is so humiliating!

SHERVINSKY. Even so, it's a damned funny way to behave . . .

STUDZINSKY. Oh, shut up, you two. Things are far too serious . . . (*Sits down by the fire.*)

Pause.

MYSHLAEVSKY. Incidentally, where are Alyosha and Nikolka?

STUDZINSKY. I'm worried about them myself . . . I'll wait another five minutes, then I'll go back and try to find them . . .

Pause.

MYSHLAEVSKY. I suppose you were there when the Hetman scarpered were you?

SHERVINSKY. Yes, I was there up to the last moment.

MYSHLAEVSKY. That must have been a remarkable spectacle! I'd have given a great deal to have been there. Why didn't you kill him like a dog?

SHERVINSKY. I suppose you would have killed him if you'd been there!

MYSHLAEVSKY. Don't worry, I would have killed him all right. Didn't he say anything to you in farewell?

SHERVINSKY. Of course he did. He embraced me and thanked me for my loyal service . . .

MYSHLAEVSKY. And burst into tears, I suppose?

SHERVINSKY. Yes, he did, as a matter of fact . . .

LARIOSIK. He burst into tears? Well I'm damned!

MYSHLAEVSKY. And I suppose he also gave you a little keepsake? Like a monogrammed gold cigarette-case?

SHERVINSKY. Yes, he presented me with his cigarette-case.

MYSHLAEVSKY. Like hell he did! I'm sorry Leonid, I don't want to make you lose your temper again, and you're not a bad fellow really, but you have the most extraordinary habit . . .

SHERVINSKY. What do you mean by that?

MYSHLAEVSKY. Well, how shall I put it? . . . You should have been a writer . . . You have such a vivid imagination . . . 'He burst into tears' . . . Well, suppose I said: show me the cigarette-case!

Without a word SHERVINSKY *produces the cigarette-case.*

Well, I'm damned! It really is his monogram!

SHERVINSKY. What must you say now, Captain Myshlaevsky?

MYSHLAEVSKY. Of course, at once. In your presence, gentlemen, I apologise.

LARIOSIK. I've never seen such a beautiful thing in my life. I should think it weighs at least a pound, doesn't it?

SHERVINSKY. Twelve and a half ounces.

Knock at the window.

Gentlemen!

They stand up.

MYSHLAEVSKY. I don't like people playing tricks . . . Why can't they come in through the door?

SHERVINSKY. Better hide your revolvers, gentlemen. (*Hides the cigarette-case on the mantelpiece.*)

STUDZINSKY *and* MYSHLAEVSKY *go over to the window, move the blind cautiously aside and peer out.*

STUDZINSKY. God, I can't forgive myself . . .

MYSHLAEVSKY. What a ghastly business . . .

LARIOSIK. Oh my God! (*Runs to tell* YELIENA.) Yeliena . . .

MYSHLAEVSKY. Where the hell are you going? Are you crazy? How can you! (*Stops* LARIOSIK's *mouth.*)

All run off. Pause.
Re-enter, carrying NIKOLKA.

We must keep Lena out somehow . . . My God — but where's Alyosha? . . . Killing's too good for me . . . Put him down, put him down, straight on the floor . . .

STUDZINSKY. Better put him on the divan. Find his wound!

SHERVINSKY. His head's smashed in!

STUDZINSKY. There's blood in his boot . . . Take his boots off . . .

SHERVINSKY. Let's carry him over there. He's right, we can't leave him on the floor . . .

STUDZINSKY. Lariosik! Run and fetch a pillow and a blanket. Put him on the divan.

They carry NIKOLKA *to the divan.*

Cut his boot, cut his boot . . . There are some bandages in Alexei's study.

SHERVINSKY *runs off.*

Bring some iodine too! God Almighty, how did he manage to get here? What happened? Where's Alexei?

SHERVINSKY *runs on with iodine and bandages.* STUDZINSKY *bandages* NIKOLKA's *head.*

LARIOSIK. Is he dying?

NIKOLKA (*recovering consciousness*). Oh . . .

MYSHLAEVSKY. I shall go crazy . . . Nikolka, just one word: where's Alyosha?

STUDZINSKY. Where is Alexei?

NIKOLKA. Viktor . . .

MYSHLAEVSKY. What?

YELIENA *bursts in.*

Lena, you're not to worry. He fell and hit his head. It's nothing serious.

YELIENA. What are you talking about? He's wounded!

NIKOLKA. No, Lena, no . . .

YELIENA. But where's Alexei? Where's Alexei? (*Insistently.*) You were with him. Just tell me where's Alexei?

MYSHLAEVSKY. What can we do now?

STUDZINSKY (*to* MYSHLAEVSKY). It can't be! It can't . . .

YELIENA. Why don't you answer?

NIKOLKA. Lena . . . in a moment . . .

YELIENA. Don't lie to me! Whatever you do, don't lie to me!

MYSHLAEVSKY *signals to* NIKOLKA: *'Keep quiet'.*

STUDZINSKY. Yeliena . . .

SHERVINSKY. Lena, don't . . .

YELIENA. I see now! Alexei's dead!

MYSHLAEVSKY. What are you saying, Lena? How do you know?

YELIENA. Look at his face. Look at it. In any case, I don't need to see his face. I knew it, I felt it when he left here, I knew it would end like this!

STUDZINSKY (*to* NIKOLKA). Tell us what's happened to him!

YELIENA. Larion, Alyosha's dead. Yesterday you were sitting at table with him — remember? And now he's dead.

LARIOSIK. Yeliena . . .

SHERVINSKY. Lena, Lena . . .

YELIENA. And what about you?! You were his senior officers! His senior officers! You all came home, but your commanding officer was killed . . .

MYSHLAEVSKY. Lena, have pity on us, how can you say that? We all obeyed his orders. All of us!

STUDZINSKY. No, she's absolutely right. I am guilty! We should never have left him. I was the senior officer, and I shall make good my mistake. (*Draws his revolver and starts to exit.*)

MYSHLAEVSKY. What are you doing? No — stop! Stop!

STUDZINSKY. Let me go!

MYSHLAEVSKY. How could I stay alive if you kill yourself? Nothing was your fault! Nothing! I was the last to see him, I warned him and I carried out all his orders. Lena!

STUDZINSKY. Captain Myshlaevsky, let go of me this minute!

MYSHLAEVSKY. Hand over your revolver! Shervinsky!

SHERVINSKY. You haven't the right, Studzinsky. Do you want to make things even worse? You haven't the right. (*Holds* STUDZINSKY.)

MYSHLAEVSKY. Lena, order him — it's all because of what you said. Take away his revolver!

YELIENA. I didn't know what I was doing . . . I lost my head. Hand over your revolver.

STUDZINSKY (*hysterically*). Let no one dare reproach me! No one! No one! I obeyed all Colonel Turbin's orders!

YELIENA. No, no one . . . no one! I was out of my mind.

MYSHLAEVSKY. Nikolka, tell us . . . Lena, be brave. We'll find him . . . We'll find him . . . tell the plain truth . . .

NIKOLKA. The colonel is dead . . .

YELIENA *faints.*

Curtain

ACT FOUR

*Two months later. The eve of Twelfth Night, January, 1919.**
The apartment is brightly lit, the piano has been removed.
YELIENA *and* LARIOSIK *are decorating a Christmas tree.*

LARIOSIK (*standing on a step-ladder*). I think this star should go . . . (*Listens mysteriously.*)

YELIENA. What is it?

LARIOSIK. No, it must be my imagination . . . Yeliena, I'm absolutely certain this is the end. They are going to take the city.

YELIENA. Don't anticipate, Lariosik. Nothing's known for certain yet.

LARIOSIK. The shooting has stopped, and that's a sure sign. I frankly admit, Yeliena, that I've found all this shooting in the last two months extremely tedious. I don't like it.

YELIENA. I share your views.

LARIOSIK. I think this star will look very suitable just here.

YELIENA. Do get down, Lariosik, otherwise I'm afraid you'll fall off and crack your head open.

LARIOSIK. Oh Yeliena, whatever makes you think that? The Christmas tree is Al, as Viktor would say. I'd like to meet the

* Until February 1918, Russia observed the use of the Julian Calendar, which in the 20th century is thirteen days behind the Gregorian Calendar, used in the rest of the world. However, even after the change-over to the Gregorian Calendar, Russians continued (and the Russian Orthodox Church still continues) to observe religious festivals and holidays according to the Julian Calendar. Thus, although the Gregorian or 'New Style' dating of Act Four is 5th January, 1919 (i.e. the eve of Twelfth Night), the Turbins, in common with many Russians, celebrated the date as though it were Christmas Eve, i.e. 24th December, 1918 in the 'Old Style' of dating.

person who thinks a Christmas tree is an ugly thing. Oh
Yeliena, if only you knew how a Christmas tree reminds me
of those far-off days of my childhood in Zhitomir, now gone
forever . . . The lights . . . The green fir-branches . . . (*Pause.*)
Still, you know, I'm happier here, far happier, than I ever
was as a child. I never want to leave this house now . . . I
could spend the rest of my lifetime like this, sitting at your
feet under the Christmas tree and never going anywhere else . . .

YELIENA. You'd soon get bored. You're fearfully poetic,
Larion.

LARIOSIK. No, I'm a hopeless poet. Anyhow, what the hell . . .
oh, I beg your pardon, Yeliena.

YELIENA. Do read me something new that you've written.
Please. I like your poetry very much. You're very gifted.

LARIOSIK. Do you really mean that?

YELIENA. I really do.

LARIOSIK. All right . . . I'll read you something . . . it's a
poem dedicated . . . Well, in fact, it's dedicated to . . . No, I
won't read you my poem.

YELIENA. Why not?

LARIOSIK. What's the point?

YELIENA. At least tell me who it's dedicated to.

LARIOSIK. A woman.

YELIENA. Who? Is it a secret?

LARIOSIK. Yes, it's a secret. You.

YELIENA. Thank you, dear Lariosik . . .

LARIOSIK. What good is a 'thank you' to me? You can't sew
an overcoat out of thank-yous . . . Oh, I'm sorry Yeliena, I
got that from Viktor — his remarks are so catching. You know
how it is, one repeats them unthinkingly . . .

YELIENA. So I've noticed. I think you're in love with
Myshlaevsky.

LARIOSIK. No, I'm in love with you.

YELIENA. You mustn't fall in love with me, Larion, you
mustn't.

LARIOSIK. Do you know what? Marry me.

YELIENA. That is very touching. But it's impossible.

LARIOSIK. He won't come back! . . . And how can you manage alone? Alone, without support, without someone who cares for you? Well, I admit the support I could provide would be pretty lous . . er, poor, but to make up for it I would love you very much indeed. All my life. You are my ideal. He won't come back. Especially not now, when the Bolsheviks are advancing . . . He won't come back!

YELIENA. I know he won't come back. But that's not the point. Even if he were to come back, I could never live with him again.

LARIOSIK. So he's been cut off . . . I couldn't bear to look at you when he went away. My heart bled for you. God, it was awful to look at you . . .

YELIENA. Was I really so terrible?

LARIOSIK. Horrible! Nightmarish! You looked thin and drawn . . . and your face was a ghastly yellow . . .

YELIENA. You're making it up, Larion!

LARIOSIK. Oh, no . . . you really were, but . . . but now you look so much better . . . Now the roses are back in your cheeks again . . .

YELIENA. You're priceless, Lariosik. Come here, I'll kiss you on the forehead.

LARIOSIK. On the forehead? All right, then, on the forehead let it be!

YELIENA *kisses him on the forehead.*

In any case, how could anyone love me?

YELIENA. Very easily. But, you see, I'm already having a love affair.

LARIOSIK. What? An affair? Who? You? You — having an affair? You can't be!

YELIENA. Doesn't it suit me?

LARIOSIK. To me you're someone sacred. You . . . Who is it? Do I know him?

YELIENA. You know him very well.

LARIOSIK. I know him very well? . . . Wait, let's see — who can it be? Wait, wait, wait! . . . 'Young man — you haven't seen anything' . . . And I thought I had dreamt it. Some people are born lucky.

YELIENA. Lariosik! That's a bit mean.

LARIOSIK. I'm going out . . .

YELIENA. Out? Where to?

LARIOSIK. I'm going round to the Armenian shop for a bottle of vodka to drink myself insensible . . .

YELIENA. This is all my fault . . . Larion, I'll be your friend.

LARIOSIK. Oh yes, I've read that in novels . . . 'I'll be your friend' means it's over, finished, the end! (*Puts on his overcoat.*)

YELIENA. Lariosik! Come back quickly! The guests will be here soon!

As he opens the front door, LARIOSIK *bumps into* SHERVINSKY *coming in.* SHERVINSKY *is wearing a vile hat, a threadbare overcoat and a pair of blue spectacles.*

SHERVINSKY. Good evening, Yeliena. Hello, Larion.

LARIOSIK. Er, hello . . . hello. (*Exit.*)

YELIENA. My God! What a sight you are!

SHERVINSKY. Thanks, Yeliena. I've already put this outfit to the test. I was driving along in a cab this morning and there were already rather a lot of horny-handed proletarians walking up and down the pavements as if they owned the place. And one of them said in such a charming voice: 'Look at that posh bastard! Just you wait, wait till tomorrow. Then we'll pull all you lot out of your cabs soon enough!' As soon as I cast my observant eye on that gentleman, something told me it was time to go home and change clothes. I congratulate you. Petlyura's done for!

YELIENA. You don't mean it?!

SHERVINSKY. The reds will be here tonight. That means Soviet rule and the like!

YELIENA. Why are you so delighted? Anyone might think you were a Bolshevik!

SHERVINSKY. Let's say I'm a sympathiser. And I've hired this overcoat from the porter in our block. It's what you might call a politically neutral overcoat.

YELIENA. Kindly remove the disgusting thing at once!

SHERVINSKY. Very good, ma'am! (*Takes off overcoat, bat, galoshes and spectacles, to reveal himself wearing impeccable tails and white tie.*) You may now congratulate me: I have just made my debut. I sang and was accepted.

YELIENA. Congratulations.

SHERVINSKY. Is no one at home, Lena? How's Nikolka?

YELIENA. He's asleep.

SHERVINSKY. Lena, Lena . . .

YELIENA. Let me go . . . Just a minute: why have you shaved off your side-whiskers?

SHERVINSKY. It's more convenient for make-up.

YELIENA. More convenient for making yourself up to look like a Bolshevik, I suppose. You creep. Don't worry, no one's going to touch you.

SHERVINSKY. Just let them try touching a man with a range of two full octaves plus two tones above . . . Lena, my dear — may I speak my mind?

YELIENA. Speak away.

SHERVINSKY. Lena, this whole episode is over . . . Nikolka is recovering . . . Petlyura is being kicked out . . . I've made my debut as a singer . . . A new life is beginning now. There's no point in prolonging the agony. He won't come back. He's been cut off from Russia, Lena! I'm not such a bad catch, you know. Look at yourself. You're alone. You're pining away . . .

YELIENA. Will you reform, and turn over a new leaf?

SHERVINSKY. What is there about me that needs reforming?

YELIENA. Leonid, I'll marry you if you change. And first of all you must stop lying!

SHERVINSKY. Surely I'm not such a liar, am I, Lena?

YELIENA. No, you're not exactly a liar — God knows what you are, in fact: something hollow perhaps, like an empty nutshell . . . I mean, really! That story about the Tsar appearing through the curtains and bursting into tears . . . and all the time it was pure invention. And that tall, thin woman. You said she was a singer, a mezzo-soprano, and all the time it turns out she was a waitress in Semadini's cafe . . .

SHERVINSKY. Lena, she was only working as a waitress for a very short time while she couldn't get work as a singer.

YELIENA. It seems, though, that she had work of another sort. Hasn't she?

SHERVINSKY. Lena! I swear by the memory of my dear, dead mother, and of my father too — I'm an orphan, you see — that there was never anything between us.

YELIENA. I don't care if there was or not. I'm not interested in your shabby little secrets. What does matter to me is that you should stop bragging and lying. The only time you ever spoke the truth was about the Hetman's cigarette-case, and then nobody believed you — you had to produce the evidence. It's shameful Leonid.

SHERVINSKY. As it happens, that whole story about the cigarette-case was a lie from start to finish. The Hetman didn't give it to me as a keepsake, he didn't embrace me and he didn't burst into tears. He simply left it on the table, forgot it, and I removed it.

YELIENA. Pinched it.

SHERVINSKY. It is historically valuable.

YELIENA. My God, that is the absolute limit! Give it here! (*Snatches the cigarette-case and hides it.*)

SHERVINSKY. Lena, the cigarettes in that case are mine.

YELIENA. It's lucky for you that you had the sense to tell me how you really acquired it. Supposing I had found out for myself.

SHERVINSKY. And how would you have found out?

YELIENA. Monster!

SHERVINSKY. Not at all. Believe me, Lena, I have changed out of all belief. I don't recognise myself any longer, on my word of honour! I don't know whether it's this catastrophe of Alyosha's death that has affected me, but I'm a different person nowadays. And don't worry about money and so on,

Lena my dear, I am going to do very nicely . . . Today at my debut the director of the opera said to me: 'You', he said 'You, Leonid Yurevich, have enormous promise. One day you will have to go to Moscow, to the Bolshoi Theatre' . . . Then he came up to me, embraced me and . . .

YELIENA. And what?

SHERVINSKY. Er, nothing . . . he walked off down the corridor.

YELIENA. You're incorrigible!

SHERVINSKY. Lena!

YELIENA. What are we going to do about Talberg?

SHERVINSKY. Divorce. Divorce. Do you know his address? Send him a telegram and a letter telling him it's all over. Finished.

YELIENA. All right! I'm bored and I'm lonely. Miserable, in fact. Very well, I agree!

SHERVINSKY. Thou hast conquered, O Galilean! Lena! (*Sings.*) 'And thou shalt be-e the queen of all the wo-o-rld, . . . Hear that 'G'? Perfect! (*Points to* TALBERG's *photograph.*) I insist you throw that out; I can't bear looking at him.

YELIENA. Oho, listen to him!

SHERVINSKY (*tenderly*). I can't bear the sight of him, Lena! (*Rips the picture out of its frame and throws it into the fire.*) Rat! And my conscience is clear.

YELIENA. That white tie does suit you . . . I can't help it, you are so good-looking!

SHERVINSKY. We're going to survive, you and I.

YELIENA. Oh, I have no fears about you! *You* will survive all right!

SHERVINSKY. Let's go to your room, Lena . . . I'll sing and you can accompany me . . . After all, we haven't seen each other properly for two months. We're always surrounded by people.

YELIENA. Several people will be arriving soon.

SHERVINSKY. And then we'll come back in here and join them.

Exeunt, closing door. Sound of a piano offstage and of SHERVINSKY, *in magnificent voice, singing the epithalamion from Handel's 'Nero'.*

NIKOLKA (*enters on crutches, wearing a black peaked cap and student's uniform tunic. He is pale and weak*). Ah! They're rehearsing! . . . (*Notices the empty portrait frame.*) Aha! They've ripped it out. I see . . . I guessed long ago. (*Lies down on the divan.*)

LARIOSIK (*enters the ball*). Nikolka! You're up! Alone? Wait a moment, I'll bring you a cushion. (*Brings NIKOLKA a cushion.*)

NIKOLKA. Please don't bother, Larion. Thanks. It looks as if I am going to stay a cripple.

LARIOSIK. Oh nonsense, Nikolka! You ought to be ashamed of yourself, talking like that!

NIKOLKA. Haven't the others come yet?

LARIOSIK. Not yet, but they'll be here soon. I've just been walking down the street — endless trains of wagons, loaded with Petlyura's pigtailed troops getting out of the city as fast as they could go. Obviously the Bolsheviks have given them a terrible beating.

NIKOLKA. Serve them right!

LARIOSIK. But even so I managed to get a bottle of vodka! The only time in my life I've ever been lucky. I never thought I'd manage it — I'm that sort of person. The weather was magnificent when I left the house. Clear sky, the stars shining, no guns firing . . . everything in nature was perfect. But I only have to step out of doors for it automatically to start snowing. And it happened just like that — I went out and wet sleet started to pelt down. But I got a bottle! Now Myshlaevsky can see what I *can* do if I try. I fell down twice, hit myself an awful bang on the back of the head, but I held on to the bottle and kept it safe.

SHERVINSKY'S VOICE. 'Thou givst thy blessing to this love . . .'

NIKOLKA (*pointing to the portrait frame*). Hey, see that? Staggering news — Yeliena's going to divorce her husband! And she's going to marry Shervinsky.

LARIOSIK (*drops the bottle*). Already?

NIKOLKA. Oh, Lariosik, look what you've done! Really, Lariosik, what is the matter with you? Aha, I see now! You've fallen for her too, have you!

LARIOSIK. Nikolka, when you're talking about your sister Yeliena, expressions like 'fallen for her' are out of place. Do you see? She is pure and golden.

NIKOLKA. No, she's not, Larion, she's a red-head. It's her great misfortune. It's because she's red-headed that everyone falls for her. A man only has to catch sight of her to start bringing her the most enormous bunches of flowers. Our whole flat used to be full of bouquets standing around like . . . cauliflowers. And it made Talberg furious. Look, you'd better pick up the pieces of that bottle, or Myshlaevsky will be here any minute and he'll kill you.

LARIOSIK. Don't tell him, will you? (*Picks up the fragments of glass.*)

Doorbell rings. LARIOSIK *lets in* MYSHLAEVSKY *and* STUDZINSKY. *Both are in civilian clothes.*

MYSHLAEVSKY. The reds have smashed Petlyura! Petlyura's troops are leaving the city!

STUDZINSKY. Yes, it's true. The reds are already in Slobodka. In half an hour they'll be here.

MYSHLAEVSKY. So tomorrow we shall have a Soviet republic here . . . Just a minute — this place smells of vodka. Who's been drinking vodka before time? Come on, own up. What's going on in this blessed household? Are you polishing the floors with vodka, or what?! . . . I know whose work this is! Still smashing things? You're a one-man demolition squad. Whatever you touch — bang, fragments! If you must do it, try smashing crockery instead!

Piano heard offstage throughout.

LARIOSIK. How dare you lecture me! I won't have it!

MYSHLAEVSKY. Why is everybody shouting at me? They'll be assaulting me soon. However, I somehow feel in a good mood today. Pax, Larion. I'm not really cross with you.

NIKOLKA. Why isn't there any firing?

MYSHLAEVSKY. They're retreating silently, like good little boys. And without even putting up a fight.

LARIOSIK. And the most amazing thing of all is that absolutely everyone is glad to see them go, even the most dyed-in-the-wool bourgeois. It just shows how sick they all are of Petlyura.

NIKOLKA. I wonder what the Bolsheviks look like?

MYSHLAEVSKY. You'll soon see.

LARIOSIK. What's your opinion, captain?

STUDZINSKY. I don't know. I don't understand anything any more. The best thing for us would be to pack up and follow Petlyura. How we, the White Guard, can ever live alongside the Bolsheviks, I cannot imagine.

MYSHLAEVSKY. Where would we go if we followed Petlyura?

STUDZINSKY. Climb onto some baggage-wagon and make for Galicia.

MYSHLAEVSKY. And then where?

STUDZINSKY. Then to Denikin on the Don, and fight the Bolsheviks there.

MYSHLAEVSKY. You mean, go back to serving under the same old generals again? That's a very clever plan. A pity Alyosha's lying six feet under the ground, or he might tell you a few things about generals. Unfortunately the colonel has gone to his rest.

STUDZINSKY. Don't torture me by reminding me of it.

MYSHLAEVSKY. No, you're right, he's gone. So let *me* say something instead . . . Back to the army, back to fighting? . . . 'And he burst into tears?' No, don't bother to laugh; I've already done all the laughing I can stand. Especially when I saw Alyosha in the morgue.

NIKOLKA *weeps.*

LARIOSIK. Nikolka, don't — please don't!

MYSHLAEVSKY. Personally, I've had enough. I've been fighting since 1914. And what for? For my country? The country which treated me so shamefully? And now you want me to go back to those has-beens, the princes and generals and barons? No, thanks. Do you know what I think of them? (*Makes an obscene gesture.*) That's what I think of them.

STUDZINSKY. Try explaining yourself in words.

MYSHLAEVSKY. Very well, I will, if you'll hear me out. What do you think I am — an idiot? No. I, Viktor Myshlaevsky, hereby declare that I shall never have anything more to do with those swine the generals. That's all I have to say.

LARIOSIK. Viktor's turned Bolshevik.

MYSHLAEVSKY. Yes, if you like, I am for the Bolsheviks.

STUDZINSKY. Viktor, what are you saying?

MYSHLAEVSKY. I'm for the Bolsheviks, but against the communists.

STUDZINSKY. That's ridiculous. You obviously don't know what you're talking about.

LARIOSIK. You ought to know that they're one and the same thing — Bolshevism and Communism.

MYSHLAEVSKY (*mimicking* LARIOSIK). 'Bolshevism and Communism'. All right, then I'm for the Communists too . . .

STUDZINSKY. Listen — a moment ago you talked about your country. What sort of country is it, when the Bolsheviks are in power? Russia is finished. Remember what Alexei said, and he was right: 'There are only two real forces in Russia, gentlemen: the Bolsheviks and us . . . '

MYSHLAEVSKY. The Bolsheviks? Splendid! I welcome them.

STUDZINSKY. They'll mobilize you into the Red Army, you realise that?

MYSHLAEVSKY. I'll join up and serve. Yes, I will!

STUDZINSKY. Why?

MYSHLAEVSKY. I'll tell you why. Because . . . How many men did you say Petlyura had? Two hundred thousand. And now those two hundred thousand have turned tail and are running like hell at the very word 'Bolshevik'. You've seen them, haven't you? Total panic! And why? Because the peasants are behind the Bolsheviks in millions. . . . And what can I put up against them? A pair of well-cut riding-breeches with red piping? Unfortunately they can't see that piping, and anyway they'll just reach for a machine-gun. Don't you see? A solid wall of Red Guards in front of me, behind me the Hetman and a seedy pack of swindlers and profiteers — and myself in the middle. Thank you very much! No I'm tired of acting the part of a lump of shit between two cobblestones. Let them mobilize me! At least I'll know that I'm serving in a *Russian* army. The people aren't with us. They're against us. Alyosha was right!

STUDZINSKY. But what sort of a Russian army can it be, when they've destroyed Russia? In any case, they won't ask our opinion: they'll just shoot us.

MYSHLAEVSKY. And good for them! Take us to the Cheka, blindfold us and put us up against a wall. They'll feel better off for it, and so will we . . .

STUDZINSKY. I shall fight them!

MYSHLAEVSKY. All right, put your greatcoat on, and off you go! Stand up in front of the Bolsheviks and shout: you shall not pass! Nikolka's already been thrown from the top of a staircase. Have you seen his head? Well, they'll knock *your* block off altogether. But if I were you, I wouldn't try. Things have gone beyond the point where we can hope to do anything.

LARIOSIK. I'm against the horrors of civil war. What is the use of shedding blood after all?

MYSHLAEVSKY. Were you in the war?

LARIOSIK. No, Viktor. I was medically unfit. Weak lungs. Besides I was a 'sole breadwinner' — I am my mother's only son.

MYSHLAEVSKY. You did right, comrade breadwinner.

STUDZINSKY. In our day Russia was a great power!

MYSHLAEVSKY. And she will be again! She will be!

STUDZINSKY. Wait and see what sort of a power, though.

MYSHLAEVSKY. She won't be the old Russia, but a new one. Now you tell me something. When they beat the hell out of you on the Don — and I confidently predict they *will* beat the hell out of you — and when your Denikin runs away abroad — which I also predict — where will you go then?

STUDZINSKY. I'll go abroad too.

MYSHLAEVSKY. Where you'll be about as much use as a third wheel on a gun-carriage. Wherever you go, from Singapore to Paris, they'll spit in your face. I won't go; I shall stay here in Russia, come what may . . . Come on that's enough for now.

I declare this meeting closed.

STUDZINSKY. I see I'm alone.

SHERVINSKY (*runs on*). Wait, wait, don't close the meeting. I have an announcement that's not on the agenda. Yeliena Talberg is divorcing her husband, Colonel Talberg, formerly of the General Staff, and is marrying . . . (*Bows, pointing to himself.*)

Enter YELIENA.

LARIOSIK. Oh! . . .

MYSHLAEVSKY. Never mind, Larion. With looks like ours, you and I never had a chance anyway. Lena, my bright and beautiful Lena, let me embrace you and kiss you.

STUDZINSKY. I congratulate you, Yeliena.

MYSHLAEVSKY (*goes after* LARIOSIK, *who has gone into the hall*). Larion, come and congratulate them — or it'll look rude. Then you can come back in here.

LARIOSIK (*to* YELIENA). I congratulate you and hope you will be very happy. (*To* SHERVINSKY.) Congratulations . . . congratulations.

MYSHLAEVSKY. Well done, Leonid, well done indeed! What a woman! Speaks English, plays the piano and still knows how to put on a samovar. I wouldn't mind marrying you myself, Lena.

YELIENA. But I wouldn't marry you, Viktor.

MYSHLAEVSKY. You don't have to — I love you as it is. Anyway, I'm a military man and a bachelor by nature. I like my home to be comfortable, without any women or children, like in a barracks . . . Pour us out something, Larion. We must drink their health.

SHERVINSKY. Wait, don't drink that wine. I'll bring you some other stuff — and what wine! (*Kisses his fingers, then catching* YELIENA's *eye, he is deflated.*) Well, it's very ordinary stuff, really. Just local Russian champagne.

MYSHLAEVSKY. This is your doing, Lena! You may now marry her, Leonid. You are completely cured. Well, congratulations, and I wish you . . .

The front door opens. Enter TALBERG, *in civilian clothes and carrying a suitcase.*

STUDZINSKY. Gentlemen! Colonel Talberg . . .

TALBERG. Good evening.

Deathly pause.

MYSHLAEVSKY. What timing!

TALBERG. Hello, Lena! You look surprised.

Pause.

TALBERG. Well, this is all rather strange. One might think that *I'm* the one who should be surprised, coming home to find such a festive gathering in these hard times. Well, Lena, what's happening?

SHERVINSKY. What's happening is that . . .

YELIENA. Wait . . . Gentlemen, will you all please go out for a minute and leave me alone with Vladimir?

SHERVINSKY. I will not!

MYSHLAEVSKY. Just a moment, now . . . If we all keep calm, everything will be all right . . . Shall we make ourselves scarce, Lena?

YELIENA. Yes, please.

MYSHLAEVSKY. I know you're a clever woman. Just in case of anything, though, call for me. Personally. Come along, gentlemen, let's go to Larion's room and smoke a cigarette. Larion, bring a cushion and let's go.

Exeunt, LARIOSIK *for some reason walking on tip-toe.*

YELIENA. You were saying?

TALBERG. What does all this mean? Please explain.

Pause.

Is this some sort of joke? Where's Alexei?

YELIENA. Alexei was shot dead.

TALBERG. You don't mean it! . . . When?

YELIENA. Two months ago, two days after you left.

TALBERG. God, how terrible! But I warned him. Remember?

YELIENA. Yes, I remember. And Nikolka is a cripple.

TALBERG. Of course, it's appalling . . . But none of this is my fault . . . And you must agree it's not exactly a reason for putting on this, shall I say, absurd performance.

Pause.

YELIENA. Tell me — why have you come back? After all, the Bolsheviks are going to march in today . . .

TALBERG. I know exactly what is going on. The whole business of the Hetman turns out to have been a stupid farce. The Germans tricked us. But in Berlin I was able to get an order to travel to the Don, to General Krasnov. We must get out of Kiev at once . . . there's no time to spare . . . I've come to take you with me.

YELIENA. I must tell you that I'm going to divorce you and marry Shervinsky.

TALBERG (*after a long pause*). I see! Charming! Using my absence to indulge in a cheap affair . . .

YELIENA. Viktor!

Enter MYSHLAEVSKY.

MYSHLAEVSKY. Lena, will you allow me to explain everything?

YELIENA. Yes! (*Exit.*)

MYSHLAEVSKY. Right. (*Goes up to* TALBERG.) Well? Get out! (*Punches him.*)

TALBERG *staggers, then exit.*

MYSHLAEVSKY. That's from Lena — personally!

Enter YELIENA.

He's gone. He'll give you a divorce. We had a very nice talk!

YELIENA. Thanks, Viktor! (*Kisses him and runs off.*)

MYSHLAEVSKY. Larion!

LARIOSIK (*enters*). Has he gone?

MYSHLAEVSKY. Yes, he's gone.

LARIOSIK. You're a genius, Viktor!

MYSHLAEVSKY. In the words of the poet Igor Severyanin — 'I am a genius'. Put out the lights, light the lamps on the

Christmas tree and play a march.

LARIOSIK puts out the lights, switches on the ornamental lamps and runs off. A march is heard on the piano offstage.

Come in, everyone!

Enter SHERVINSKY, STUDZINSKY, NIKOLKA and YELIENA.

STUDZINSKY. Beautiful! And how cosy it makes the place suddenly.

MYSHLAEVSKY. That's Larion's doing. Now let's congratulate you properly. All right, Larion!

Enter LARION with a guitar, which he gives to NIKOLKA.

I congratulate you, my bright and beautiful Lena, now and forever. Forget about everything. And now — your very good health! (*Drinks.*)

NIKOLKA (*strums the guitar, sings*).
'Oh tell me magician, beloved of the gods,
What fate is in store for me lying?
How soon in the fight 'gainst impossible odds
Shall foe men rejoice at my dying.
No, let the music play the march of victory,
The enemy is running away, away, away!'

MYSHLAEVSKY (*sings*):
'And for the Council of People's Commissars . . . '

ALL *except* STUDZINSKY). 'Let's raise the mighty cry:
Hurrah! Hurrah! Hurrah!'

STUDZINSKY. Well, I'm damned! You ought to be ashamed of yourselves!

NIKOLKA (*sings*).
'Towards him there comes from the forest's dark shades,
Divinely inspired, the magician:
"Oh tell me, you dweller, in whispering glades" . . .

LARIOSIK. Wonderful! The lights . . . The Christmas tree . . .

MYSHLAEVSKY. Larion! Speech!

NIKOLKA. Yes, a speech . . .

LARIOSIK. Oh, I can't make speeches. Besides, I'm very shy.

MYSHLAEVSKY. Larion's going to make a speech.

LARIOSIK. Well, if the company insists on it, I will. Only please excuse me, because I haven't prepared it. Yeliena! Gentlemen! We are gathered at a difficult and terrible time and we have all been through a very great deal . . . myself included. I have suffered a private crisis . . .and for a long time my frail barque has been tossed upon the waves of civil war . . .

MYSHLAEVSKY. That's beautiful, about the 'frail barque' . . .

LARIOSIK. Yes, my frail barque . . . Until it sailed into this harbour with the cream-coloured blinds, the home of some people I've grown very fond of . . . And they, too, have lived through their drama . . . Well, it's no good dwelling on sorrows. Time has moved on. Petlyura has vanished . . . We're all alive . . . yes, we're all together again . . . and more than that: Yeliena too has also suffered a great deal and deserves happiness because she is a remarkable woman. And I want to say to her in the words of Chekhov: 'We shall rest, we shall rest . . .'

Distant gunfire.

MYSHLAEVSKY. That's right . . . They've come to rest too . . . five . . . six . . , nine!

YELIENA. Surely not more fighting?

SHERVINSKY. No. That's a salute!

MYSHLAEVSKY. Quite right: that's a six-inch battery firing a salute.

Offstage, far away but coming closer, a military band is heard playing the 'Internationale'.

Do you hear that, gentlemen? The Reds are coming.

All go to the window.

NIKOLKA. Gentlemen, this evening is a great prologue to a new historical play.

STUDZINSKY. For some a prologue; for others it's the epilogue.

Curtain

Madame Zoyka

A Comedy in Four Acts

Translated by Michael Glenny

The Characters

ZÓYA DENÍSOVNA	owner of an apartment and a fashion studio
MANYÚSHKA	her maid
BELTOFF	ex-sergeant major, chairman of the House committee
OBOLÓNSKY, Pavel Fyodorovich	former count
AMETÍSTOV, Alexander Tarasovich	Zoya's cousin
GOOSE, Boris Semyonovich	sales director
GA SO-LIN KO KA-IN }	Chinese landrymen
DRESSMAKER	
FIRST LADY	
SECOND LADY	
THIRD LADY	
SEAMSTRESS	
ÁLLA VADÍMOVNA	
MÁRYA NIKIFÓROVNA	
LIZÁNKA	
MADAME IVANÓVA	
FIRST STRANGER	
SECOND STRANGER	
DEAD BODY	
ROBBER	lawyer

ACT ONE

The action takes place in Moscow in 1927

We see the hall, sitting room and bedroom of ZOYA's *apartment, the sky through the windows aglow with a sunset in late May. Outside, the courtyard of the huge apartment house sounds like a musical-box gone mad. A gramophone is singing*: The human race in all the world . . .; *a voice is shouting*: We buy second-hand primus stoves!; *another*: Broken samovars soldered! ; *the gramophone*: . . . worships but one sacred idol . . .! *Tram-wheels grind, bells clang. Cars hoot. Cacophony. As the noise dies down slightly, an accordion plays a cheerful polka.*

ZOYA (*changing her clothes in front of a mirror-fronted wardrobe, sings to the accordion music*). '*You should see me dance the polka . . .* !' The papers! I've got them at last . . . permission to open the studio!

MANYUSHKA (*bursts in*). Zoya Denisovna! Beltoff's here!

ZOYA (*hisses*). Get rid of him! Tell him I'm not at home.

MANYUSHKA. He came straight in by the back door, damn him.

ZOYA. I don't care – see him off. Tell him I've gone out. (*Steps into the wardrobe and pulls the door shut behind her.*)

BELTOFF (*enters suddenly*). Are you at home, Zoya Denisovna?

MANYUSHKA. She's not in, I tell you. Anyway, comrade Beltoff, what do you mean by barging into a lady's bedroom?

BELTOFF. Separate bedrooms aren't allowed since the revolution. (*Leers.*) Maybe you'd like me to fix you up with a bedroom. When will she be back?

MANYUSHKA. How am I supposed to know? She doesn't tell me about her comings and goings.

BELTOFF. Expect she's off to see her fancy man, is she?

MANYUSHKA. Really, comrade Beltoff, what language! Just who are you talking about?

BELTOFF. Don't come the innocent with me. We know what you're up to in here. The House Committee knows everything about everybody in the building. The House Committee never sleeps – or rather we sleep with one eye and keep watch with the other. That's what we're here for.

MANYUSHKA. You really ought to go, Beltoff, you shouldn't be poking your nose into people's bedrooms.

BELTOFF. You know I'm the chairman of the House Committee, don't you? And you see I'm carrying my briefcase? That means I'm on Committee business and I can go anywhere I like. I'm wearing my official hat. (*Grabs* MANYUSHKA *and tries to embrace her.*)

MANYUSHKA. I'll tell your wife about you, and she'll pull your official hat down over your ears and scratch your eyes out.

BELTOFF. Don't you dare, you little devil!

ZOYA (*From the wardrobe*). Beltoff, you're a pig!

MANYUSHKA. Oh, my God! (*Runs off.*)

ZOYA (*Appearing from the wardrobe*). So this is how the chairman of the House Committee carries on! A nice way to behave!

BELTOFF. I thought you really weren't in . . . Why did she lie to me? You're a crafty one, Zoya Denisovna, and no mistake . . .

ZOYA. And you, Beltoff, are a tactless oaf. Firstly, you make rude and indecent remarks. What do you mean by 'fancy man'? Are you referring to Pavel Fyodorovich?

BELTOFF. I'm a plain-spoken man. I never went to no university.

ZOYA. Secondly, I'm not dressed and you burst into my bedroom. And thirdly, I'm not at home.

BELTOFF. What d'you mean, not at home? You *are* at home . . .

ZOYA. Why do you want to see me? Are you proposing to make me give up another room?

BELTOFF. Of course I am. You live alone here, and you've got six rooms.

ZOYA. I'm alone? And what about Manyushka?

BELTOFFF. Manyushka's a servant, so she's allowed fifteen square feet in the kitchen.

ZOYA (*Calls*). Manyushka!

MANYUSHKA (*Enters*). What is it, Zoya Denisovna?

ZOYA. What are you?

MANYUSHKA. Your niece.

BELTOFF. What do you call Zoya Denisovna?

MANYUSHKA. *Ma tante*.

BELTOFF. Little devil!

ZOYA. You may go, Manyushka.

Exit MANYUSHKA

BELTOFF. You can't carry on like this, Zoya Denisovna. Think
you can twist me round your little finger, don't you?
Manyushka's your niece, my foot! . . . If she's your niece, then
I'm your grandmother.

ZOYA. Beltoff, you are a rude, coarse man.

BELTOFF. And another of your bedrooms is empty, too.

ZOYA. It has a tenant, who happens to be away on official
business.

BELTOFF. Don't give me that fairy-story! He doesn't live in
Moscow at all. Let's be frank now: he gave you a piece of paper
from the china factory where he works and pushed off. He's a
mythical person, a ghost. All because of you, the tenants' general
meeting gave me such a belting I thought I wasn't going to get
away in one piece.

ZOYA. What does that rabble want?

BELTOFF. What are you talking about?

ZOYA. I'm talking about your tenants' general meeting.

BELTOFF. Now listen, Zoya Denisovna, if it was anyone but me
in this job . . .

ZOYA. That's the whole point – *you* are in this job and not
someone else.

BELTOFF. The meeting passed a resolution to make you give up
more of your rooms. And what's more, half of them were
yelling to have you thrown out altogether!

ZOYA. Have me thrown out? (*Shows him two fingers.*)

BELTOFF. What is that supposed to mean?

ZOYA. What it usually means!

BELTOFF. Right, then! May I drop dead if I don't put a worker into your empty room tomorrow. We'll see what happens if you try giving *him* the two-fingered salute! I'll be going now, *madam*. (*Starts to go.*)

ZOYA. Just tell me one thing, Beltoff: why is it that Monsieur Goose, who does live alone, is allowed to occupy eight rooms on the first floor?

BELTOFF. It's because Goose rented that apartment as part of a business arrangement. He's going to install central heating in the whole building.

ZOYA. Forgive a tactless question, but how much did he give you to evict Firsov from that apartment?

BELTOFF. Careful now, Zoya Denisovna – I'm here in my official capacity . . .

ZOYA. There is a quantity of ten-rouble notes in the inside pocket of your tunic. The serial number of the first one is VM 425900. Would you like to check that?

BELTOFF *unbuttons his tunic, pulls out a wad of banknotes, examines the first one and freezes in horror.*

ZOYA. What did I tell you?

BELTOFF. You, Zoya Denisovna, are in league with the devil, I've thought so for some time.

Pause.

ZOYA. So Manyushka and the mythical person can stay where they are.

BELTOFF. Honest to God, Zoya Denisovna, I can't swing it with Manyushka. The whole building knows she's a servant.

ZOYA. All right, I believe you. I'll bring in another tenant myself to fill up her space.

BELTOFF. And what about the other rooms?

ZOYA. Read that! (*Hands* BELTOFF *a document.*)

BELTOFF (*Reads*). 'Permission is hereby granted to citizeness
Smirnoff to open a dressmaking establishment and school of
needlework . . .' Oho! . . . '. . . to manufacture working clothes
for the wives of industrial workers and white-collar employees
. . . allocation of supplementary space . . .' Well I'm damned!
Did Goose fix this permit for you?

ZOYA. Does it matter? You, esteemed comrade, have only to
show a copy of this thing to your bunch of crooks on the House
Committee and the problem of my apartment is solved.

· BELTOFF. Well, yes, of course – this document does make the
whole situation a lot simpler.

ZOYA. By the way, I was given this fifty-rouble note in change at
Muir's today, and it's counterfeit. Take a look at it, you're an
expert on banknotes.

BELTOFF. Who, me? (*Examines the banknote.*) It's perfectly
genuine.

ZOYA. And I say it's counterfeit. Take the horrid thing and throw
it away.

BELTOFF. Very well, I'll . . . er . . . dispose of it.

ZOYA. Now, Beltoff – about turn! Quick march! I have to get
dressed.

BELTOFF (*Starts to go*). Only make sure you take in another tenant
today. I'll call back later to find out what arrangements you've
made.

ZOYA. Agreed.

*Somewhere a piano starts to play Tchaikovsky's setting of Pushkin's
poem:*
'Don't sing, my fairest one, to me
The melancholy songs of Georgia . . .'

BELTOFF (*Stopping in the doorway, in a strangled voice*). So does that
mean that Goose makes a note of the numbers whenever he
hands out ten-rouble notes?

ZOYA. What do you think?

Exit BELTOFF *through the sitting room and hall.* OBOLONSKY
enters the hall by the front door. He looks terrible

OBOLONSKY. May I come in, Zoya? (*Puts down his hat and stick.*)

ZOYA. Pavel! Of course you can . . . Not *again*, Pavel?

OBOLONSKY. I can't fight it . . . Send someone to the Chinamen, I implore you . . .

ZOYA. All right, all right . . . (*Shouts.*) Manyushka!

Enter MANYUSHKA.

Pavel Fyodorovich is unwell, run to the Chinamen – fly, Manyushka!

Blackout. ZOYA's *apartment vanishes.*
From the darkness emerges a squalid basement room, lit by a small paraffin lamp. Washing is strung out on ropes to dry. GA SO-LIN *crouches over a hissing oil stove;* KO KA-IN *stands in front of him.*

GA SO-LIN. You Chinese clook, bandit! You steal plates, you steal cocaine. Where you been? How I tlust you – ha?

KO KA-IN. Shut up, old maggot! Bandit yourself.

GA SO-LIN. Get out of my laundly, thief!

KO KA-IN. What you say? Chase out poor Chinaman? I was lobbed on Svetnoi Bouleva, thief take cocaine, almost kill me – look! (*Points to scar.*) I work for you but you chase me out. Then how poor Chinaman eat in Moscow? You bad comlade! I kill you!

GA SO-LIN. You kill me – communist police get you

Pause.

KO KA-IN. What? You chase out pa'tner? I hang you from lamp-post!

Pause.

GA SO-LIN. You go on stealing, lobbing?

KO KA-IN. No! No!

GA SO-LIN. Say: 'On glaves of my ancestors, I plomise no more steal.'

KO KA-IN. I plomise no more steal.

GA SO-LIN. Say again 'On glaves of my ancestors . . .'

KO KA-IN. On glaves of ancestors . . .

GA SO-LIN. Put on white coat and start work.

KO KA-IN. I hungly, Ga So-Lin, no eat two days, give me food.

GA SO-LIN. Blead in that sack – take some.

Knock at the door.

Who there?

MANYUSHKA (*outside the door*). Open up, Ga So-Lin, it's me!

GA SO-LIN. Ah, Manyuska! (*Opens door.*)

MANYUSHKA (*Enters*). Why do you lock the door? Funny sort of laundry where a customer can't get in.

GA SO-LIN. Gleetings, Manyuska.

MANYUSHKA. You must come over to the apartment, Ga So-Lin. Obolonsky is ill again.

GA SO-LIN. I no can come now, but I give you medicine.

MANYUSHKA. No, you must come yourself and prepare the stuff in front of them, otherwise they'll say you've been diluting it with water.

KO KA-IN. What that? Morphine?

GA SO-LIN *and* KO KA-IN *converse briefly in Chinese.*

GA SO-LIN. Manyuska, he go with you, he do all ploperly.

MANYUSHKA. Does he know how to?

GA SO-LIN. He know how, no ploblem. (*Fetches a box from a dark corner, hands it to* KO KA-IN *and gives him instructions in Chinese.*)

KO KA-IN. No need teach me – I know. Come on, missie.

GA SO-LIN. (*To* KO KA-IN). You behave better now, mind you bling back five loubles, bad boy.

MANYUSHKA. Don't scold him, he's as good as gold.

GA SO-LIN. Ha, gold! . . . Bandit!

MANYUSHKA. Goodbye, Ga So-Lin.

GA SO-LIN. Goodbye, Manyuska. When you going to mally me?

MANYUSHKA. When did I ever say I'd marry you?

GA SO-LIN. Ah, Manyuska, you say . . .

MANYUSHKA. I said 'You may kiss a lady's hand but not her lips!' Come on, we must go.

Exeunt MANYUSHKA *and* KO KA-IN.

GA SO-LIN. Good girl, Manyuska. Tasty girl, Manyuska. (*Sings a sad Chinese song.*)

Blackout.

ZOYA's *bedroom, sitting room and hall.* OBOLONSKY, KO KA-IN *and* ZOYA *are in the bedroom.* OBOLONSKY *is rolling down his sleeve, buttoning up his cuff. He is already feeling better and grows steadily more lively.*

OBOLONSKY. How much do I owe you, my dear Chinaman?

KO KA-IN. Seven loubles

ZOYA. Why seven and not five? Daylight robbery!

OBOLONSKY. No haggling, please, Zoya. It's worth it. (*Slaps his pockets.*)

ZOYA. Don't worry, Pavel, I'll pay. (*Gives money to* KO KA-IN).

KO KA-IN. Thanks, missie.

OBOLONSKY. See his lovely smile, Zoya! He's an angel. Such a clever Chinaman . . .

KO KA-IN. (*Confidentially, to* OBOLONSKY). You want I bling you evely day? You no tell Ga So-Lin . . . I have anything you want – morphine, stlong vodka . . . You want I give you beautiful tattoo? (*Exposes his chest, revealing a fearsome dragon tattooed in many colours.*)

OBOLONSKY. Amazing! Look, Zoya!

ZOYA. How appalling! Did you do that yourself?

KO KA-IN. Yes, I do myself, in Shanghai.

OBOLONSKY. Listen, Ko Ka-In, I'm ill and I have to be treated with morphine. Can you really come here every day – and will you prepare the solution here?

KO KA-IN. Agleed!

ZOYA. Be careful, Pavel. He may be just a tramp or a thief.

OBOLONSKY. Oh no, Zoya! He is a virtuous Chinaman, it's

written all over his face You're not a Party member, are you, Chinaman?

KO KA-IN. We laundly, wash clothes.

ZOYA. You work in a laundry? Come back in an hour's time and I'll offer you a job. I want you to do the ironing and pressing for my fashion studio.

KO KA-IN. OK, missie.

ZOYA. (*Calls*). Manyushka, see the Chinaman out.

MANYUSHKA (*Enters*). This way, please. (*Shows* KO KA-IN *into the hall.*)

OBOLONSKY *opens the curtains in the bedroom, revealing a vista of Moscow in early evening. The first lights are coming on, the city's daytime hum is quietening down. A voice strikes up the next line of the Tchaikovsky/Pushkin song: 'They call to mind another life, a distant shore . . .' and abruptly breaks off.*

KO KA-IN. (*In the hallway*). Bye-bye, Manyuska, I come back one hour. I come every day, Manyuska, now I work for Obolon.

MANYUSHKA. What sort of work?

KO KA-IN. I bling him medicine. Kiss me, Manyuska!

MANYUSHKA. We'll do without that, thank you . . . (*Opens front door.*)

KO KA-IN. When I'm lich man, you kiss me then? Lich, handsome . . .

MANYUSHKA. Go on, get away with you . . .

Exit KO KA-IN.

MANYUSHKA. What a funny man.

OBOLONSKY (*Standing by the bedroom window, sings*). 'They call to mind another life, a distant shore . . .'

ZOYA. Pavel, I've finally got official permission to open the studio. (*Pause.*) Count Obolonsky – why don't you answer when a lady speaks to you?

OBOLONSKY. I'm sorry, I was miles away. And please don't call me 'count'.

ZOYA. Why not?

OBOLONSKY. A man in jackboots came up to me today and said: 'You're a former count . . .'

ZOYA. Well?

OBOLONSKY. He spat his cigarette-end on to the floor . . . Then, when I was on my way here, the tram was passing the Zoological Gardens and I saw a placard that said 'Demonstration of Former Hen' . . . I got off and asked the gatekeeper what the hen was now and he replied: 'It's a cock now.' I just don't understand anything any more . . .

ZOYA. Oh Pavel, Pavel . . . (*Pause.*) Listen, my dear, you must make up your mind once and for all – do you agree to (*whispers.*) our plan?

OBOLONSKY. Nothing matters to me any more . . . yes, I agree. I can't face seeing former hens any longer! I want to get away from here at any price.

ZOYA. Yes, you poor thing, you're withering away in this awful country. So I'm going to take you to Paris! I promise you we'll have a million francs by Christmas.

OBOLONSKY. But how will we get out of Russia?

ZOYA. Goose is going to help us.

OBOLONSKY. A former goose! . . . I must say, he appears to be able to fix absolutely anything. I'm thirsty, Zoya. Have you got any beer?

ZOYA. Manyushka!

Enter MANYUSHKA.

Go and buy us some beer.

MANUSHKA. At once, Zoya Denisovna. (*Runs out through the sitting room and into the hall, where she puts on a headscarf and goes out by the front door, forgetting to close it behind her.*)

OBOLONSKY. I suddenly feel frightened . . . aren't you afraid they'll discover what we are doing?

ZOYA. If we're clever and careful, they won't find out. Come on, Pavel, let's go to the mythical person's room. I don't feel free to talk frankly in here.

ZOYA *and* OBOLONSKY *go through the sitting room into a*

bedroom, where she shuts the door behind her; through the door their voices can faintly be heard in conversation. Somewhere in the courtyard a thin, piping voice strikes up a song:
"'Twas evening and the stars were out,
A frosty night, so I am told . . .'

AMETISTOV (*Enters hall by the open door; picks up the words of the song*). '. . . Abandoned stood a poor young lad, All shivering (*sadly*) and blue with cold . . .' (*Puts down an extremely battered suitcase and looks around.*)

AMETISTOV *is wearing torn trousers, a greasy officer's tunic and peaked cap without badges; some kind of medallion is pinned to his chest.*

My God, four miles' slog from the Kursk Station lugging a suitcase is quite something . . . what wouldn't I give for a glass of beer! So here I am back on the old fifth floor. Wonder what I'll find here . . . (*Looks into the kitchen.*) Hey, comrades – anyone about. Is Zoya Denisovna at home? H'mm . . . (*Crosses the sitting-room, puts his ear to the door of the bedroom, hears the voices of* ZOYA *and* OBOLONSKY. *His face lights up, and he presses his ear closer.*) Oho! Seems I've come at just the right moment . . .

MANYUSHKA. (*Enters hall, carrying several bottles of beer*). Oh my God! I forgot to shut the front door.

AMETISTOV *comes back into the hall.*

Who are you? What are you doing here?

AMETISTOV. *Pardon, pardon!* Don't be alarmed, comrade . . . Beer! I *have* come at the right moment. I've been dreaming of a glass of beer all the way from the Kursk Station.

MANYUSHKA. Who do you want to see?

AMETISTOV. Zoya Denisovna. And with whom, ah . . . have I the pleasure . . . ?

MANYUSHKA. I am Zoya's niece.

AMETISTOV. Delighted to meet you! I had no idea Zoya had such a pretty niece. I am Zoya's cousin. (*Kisses* MANYUSHKA's *hand.*)

MANYUSHKA (*Runs into the sitting room, shrieks*). Zoya Denisovna! Zoya Denisovna!

AMETISTOV *picks up his suitcase and follows* MANYUSHKA

into the sitting room. ZOYA *and* OBOLONSKY, *alarmed by* MANYUSHKA's *shrieks, enter the sitting room from the bedroom.*

AMETISTOV. My dear, dear cousin Zoya! *Je vous salue!*

ZOYA *stops, astounded.*

AMETISTOV. Zoya dear, introduce me to this . . . citizen . . .

ZOYA. It can't be . . . it's you . . . it's you . . . (*To* OBOLONSKY.) Pavel Fyodorovich, this is my cousin Ametistov.

AMETISTOV. *Pardon* . . . (*To* OBOLONSKY.) Allow me to introduce myself: Sputnikov, no party affiliation, former gentleman.

OBOLONSKY (*Bewildered*). Er . . . delighted . . .

AMETISTOV. My dear cousin, allow me to beg a few words with you *à part.*

ZOYA. Please excuse me, Pavel, I must have a private word with Alexander . . .

AMETISTOV. *Pardon* . . . Vassily. Vassily Ivanovich. Such a short absence and you've already forgotten my name, Zoya . . . ah, that really hurts!

OBOLONSKY. Please don't let me disturb you. (*Exit.*)

ZOYA. Manyushka, go and pour out a glass of beer for Pavel Fyodorovich.

Exit MANYUSHKA. *Pause.*

ZOYA. But you were shot in Baku, weren't you?

AMETISTOV. What of it? Just because I was shot in Baku, that doesn't mean I can't come to Moscow. They shot me by mistake, I was completely innocent . . .

ZOYA. I'm feeling dizzy . . .

AMETISTOV. With joy?

ZOYA. Because it doesn't make sense . . . you were shot . . . you're in Moscow . . .

AMETISTOV. Ah, you see, I got away under the usual First of May amnesty of political prisoners . . . By the way, who is that niece of yours?

ZOYA. Niece? That's my maid, Manyushka.

AMETISTOV. I *see* . . . you call her a relative so you can keep her allocation of living-space . . . (*Shouts.*) Manyushka!

Enter MANYUSHKA, *flustered.*

AMETISTOV. Manyushka, go and get me a beer, I'm dying of thirst. Niece indeed! And I kissed her hand! The disgrace of it!

Exit MANYUSHKA, *crestfallen.*

ZOYA. Where are you planning to stay? Remember there's a housing crisis in Moscow.

AMETISTOV. I know there is. I'm staying here with you, of course.

ZOYA. And what if I say I can't have you?

AMETISTOV. Oh, so that's it, is it? Turning nasty! Go on then, be nasty! Throw out your own cousin when he's walked all the way here from the Kursk Station! And me an orphan! All right, throw me out. I know when I'm not wanted . . . (*Picks up suitcase.*) I won't even stay to drink your beer . . . (*Threateningly.*) You're going to regret this though, cousin *dear* . . .

ZOYA. Trying to frighten me? Sorry, that won't work.

AMETISTOV. Me? Try to frighten you? Come, come – I'm a gentleman. (*Whispers.*) And if I weren't such a decent fellow, damn me if I wouldn't go to the OGPU and denounce you for running a *so-called* fashion studio in your apartment. I know exactly what you're up to, Zoya, my sweet. (*Starts to go.*)

ZOYA. Wait a moment – how did you get in without ringing the bell?

AMETISTOV. Hell, let's stop playing games . . . and I haven't even kissed you yet, Zoya . . .

ZOYA (*Pushes him away*). God, it must be fate.

Enter MANYUSHKA *with a bottle of beer and a glass.*

ZOYA. Manyushka, was it you who left the front door unlocked? Oh, Manyushka, how could you? Go and apologise to Pavel Fyodorovich . . .

Exit MANYUSHKA.

AMETISTOV. (*Drinking the beer*). Ah, that's good. First class beer you have in Moscow. I see you've managed to hang on to the apartment, Zoya – well done!

ZOYA. There's nothing for it – I'm obviously doomed to have to put up with you.

AMETISTOV. Are you trying to make me take offence and go?

ZOYA. No. First of all – what do you want?

AMETISTOV. First of all – a pair of trousers.

ZOYA. Haven't you got any trousers? What's in that suitcase?

AMETISTOV. My suitcase contains six packs of cards and a booklet entitled 'Do Miracles Happen?' Thank God for those miracles, too – without them I'd have died of starvation. It's no joke, I can tell you, travelling from Baku to Moscow in a mixed goods and passenger train . . . The fact is, I grabbed a hundred of these brochures in the Cultural Department at Baku as a souvenir, and I sold them on the train at a rouble apiece . . . So miracles do happen, Zoya dear, and here I am! . . . Delicious beer . . . Buy a brochure, comrades, only a rouble apiece!

ZOYA. And I suppose the cards are marked, are they?

AMETISTOV. Really, madam, what do you take me for?

ZOYA. Chuck it, Ametistov! Tell me, where have you been these seven years?

AMETISTOV. Ah, my dear, it's quite a saga . . . In 1919 I was in charge of the Arts Department in Chernigov . . .

ZOYA *bursts into laughter*.

AMETISTOV. The Whites were advancing on the town, and the Reds gave me money so that I could be evacuated to Moscow, but instead I evacuated myself to the Whites in Rostov and went to work for them. Then the Whites paid the cost of my evacuation from Rostov and I went and joined the Reds in the Crimea, where I worked as the manager of a restaurant in Sebastopol . . . Bumped into a party of gamblers and they took me for fifty thousand in one evening at chemmy . . .

ZOYA. They took *you*? They must have been really top-class operators!

AMETISTOV. Sheer swindlers, I assure you . . . Well, then, as you know, after the Whites came the Reds, and I was sucked into the Soviet system. At Stavropol I was in the fire brigade, in Voronezh I was in charge of the food supply . . . But in the end I realised I wasn't going to make a career in ordinary jobs, so I decided to try my luck in the Party. I'll survive all that red tape, I thought, all that probationary membership stuff. Just then my roommate Karl Petrovich Chemodanov, lovely fellow, happened to die – and what's more he was a Party member . . .

ZOYA. Was this in Voronezh?

AMETISTOV. No, by then I was in Odessa. Well, I thought, what harm will it do the Party? One member dies and another immediately steps forward and takes his place in the ranks. I shed a few tears over his coffin, pocketed his Party card – and off to Baku. Nice quiet place, I said to myself, just the spot to set up a little game of chemin-de-fer. So I turned up there as Chemodanov. Then one day the door opens and in walks a friend of Chemodanov's – just like that. Tableau! He was holding a nine, you might say, and I was bust . . . so it was out of a first-floor window for me . . .

ZOYA. Good move!

AMETISTOV. Like hell – I was out of luck that day. You should have heard the speech I made at my trial. Believe me, it wasn't just the posh people in the public gallery – professors and suchlike – but even the *guards* were sobbing! Well, so they shot me . . . There was nothing for it – I had to get away to Moscow . . . You don't seem very sympathetic – I was at death's door! . . . Ah, Zoya, you've got hard over the years, hard as nails. You've lost the common touch, you've forgotten what it's like down there among the toiling masses.

ZOYA. All right, all right . . . So you know everything about me?

AMETISTOV. Just a piece of luck, Zoya, that's all.

ZOYA. You can stay.

AMETISTOV. Dear Zoya!

ZOYA. Shut up! I'll make you the manager of my firm. But watch your step, Ametistov: if you get up to any funny business, I won't care what the risks may be but I'll drop you in the shit. Take care, Ametistov, you've already told me too much about yourself.

AMETISTOV. So – I've been telling my tale of a poor vagabond to a snake, have I? *Mon dieu!*

ZOYA. Shut up, you fool! Where's the necklace you promised to keep safely for me just before you left?

AMETISTOV. Necklace . . . necklace? Wait a moment . . . was that the one with the little diamonds?

ZOYA. You swine!

AMETISTOV. *Merci, madame!* Just listen how Zoya treats her long-lost relatives!

ZOYA. Have you got any identity papers?

AMETISTOV. I have a whole pocket full of identity papers. It all depends on which one of them is, shall we say, the freshest . . . (*Takes out a handful of identity papers, fans them out like a hand of cards.*) H'mm . . . Karl Chemodanov – no, he's out of the question . . . Anton Siguradze, nationality Georgian . . . no, he won't do either – can't manage the accent.

ZOYA. But this is terrible . . . according to this one, your name's Sputnikov!

AMETISTOV. No, Zoya, I've got them mixed up, I'm afraid. Sputnikov is actually in Moscow himself, so that one's *out*. I really think the best thing is to use my own name. I haven't been in Moscow for eight years, so I'm sure they've forgotten about me. Go on, register me as Ametistov. Wait a moment – here's a certificate exempting me from military service because I've got a hernia . . . (*Produces a document*).

ZOYA. (*Takes a magnificent pair of trousers out of the wardrobe.*) Here, put these on.

AMETISTOV. Ah, God bless your kind heart. Turn the other way, Zoya.

ZOYA. Put them on behind that screen. (AMETISTOV *goes behind a screen.*) God, I need you like a dose of cholera! Kindly do your best to return those trousers, they belong to Pavel.

AMETISTOV. Your, er . . . common-law spouse?

ZOYA. You mind your manners when you talk to him – he's my husband.

AMETISTOV. What's his surname?

ZOYA. Obolonsky.

AMETISTOV. Not *Count* Obolonsky? Well now! . . .
Congratulations, Zoya! Though I don't suppose he has a bean
now, has he? Judging by the size of his waistline, he's a counter-
revolutionary . . . (*Comes out from behind the screen wearing the
trousers, which he admires in the mirror on the front of the wardrobe.*)
These trousers really do something for you. They make you feel
you're up on a platform making a speech . . . 'Comrades! In the
name of the revolution . . .'

ZOYA. Forget about the name of the revolution and make up your
mind what your *own* name is, otherwise you'll put me in an
embarrassing position. Pavel!

Enter OBOLONSKY.

ZOYA. I'm so sorry, Pavel, we were talking business.

AMETISTOV. We were carried away, reminiscing about our
childhood . . . Zoya and I grew up together, you know . . . I
was actually sobbing a moment ago . . . Look, I'm wearing your
trousers . . . do forgive me, I was robbed on the way here . . .
My other suitcase was pinched in Taganrog, it was positively
grotesque. I do hope you don't mind. We members of the
nobility don't bother about such things, do we . . .

OBOLONSKY. But of course . . . delighted to be of help . . .

ZOYA. Now, Pavel, Alexander is going to work for us as
manager. You don't object, do you?

OBOLONSKY. Of course not, delighted . . . if you vouch for M
Sputnikov, then . . .

AMETISTOV. *Pardon*, the name is Ametistov . . . You're
surprised? You see, Sputnikov is my stage name, but in real life
I'm Alexander Tarasovich Ametistov. It's a well known name,
many of my family were shot by the Bolsheviks . . . quite a
saga, really. You'll weep when I tell you . . .

OBOLONSKY. Delighted. And where, may I ask, do you come
from?

AMETISTOV. I? You ask where I've come from? Just now I've
come from Saratov. Quite a saga, really, you'll weep when I . . .

OBOLONSKY. May I enquire whether you belong to the Party?

AMETISTOV. *Quelle question!* Really!

OBOLONSKY. But you were wearing a badge of some sort on your chest . . . though it may have been my imagination . . .

AMETISTOV. Oh, that . . . no, no, I just wore that for the journey. It's a great help, you know, when one's travelling by train – one can get a reserved seat without queuing, and so on . . .

Enter MANYUSHKA.

MANYUSHKA. Beltoff is here.

ZOYA. Tell him to come in.

Exit MANYUSHKA.

(*To* AMETISTOV). He's the chairman of the House Committee, and don't forget it.

Enter BELFTOFF.

BELTOFF. Good evening, Zoya Denisovna. Good evening, citizen Obolonsky. Well, have you found a tenant, Zoya Denisovna?

ZOYA. Yes. Here are the papers. Register Alexander Tarasovich as a resident, please. He's going to be the manager of my fashion studio.

BELTOFF. Aha, thinking of working here, are you?

AMETISTOV. But of course . . . A glass of beer, comrade?

BELTOFF. Thanks, don't mind if I do. It's hot, and I'm on my feet all day . . .

AMETISTOV. Yes, terrible weather for the time of year. You have a huge house to run, comrade, huge . . .

BELTOFF. Don't tell me! It's murder. And do you have a hernia certificate that exempts you from military service?

AMETISTOV. Indeed I have. (*Hands him the document.*) Are you a Party member, comrade?

BELTOFF. I'm a sympathiser.

AMETISTOV. That's good to hear. (*Puts on his badge.*) I used to be a Party member myself. (*Whispers to* OBOLONSKY.) *Devant les domestiques, tu sais* . . . have to use a bit of cunning . . .

BELTOFF. Why did you leave the Party?

AMETISTOV. Petty disagreements about policy . . . There are a lot of things I don't approve of. I looked around me and I could see things weren't going right, so I said right to their faces . . .

BELTOFF. Right to their faces?

AMETISTOV. What did I have to lose but my chains? There was a time when I was very high up in the Party, you know . . . No, I said to them, no – this won't do! Firstly, we have deviated. Secondly – we have sullied the purity of our objectives. We have abandoned our principles. Oh, they said, so that's how it is, is it? Right, we'll get you! . . . Impetuous people, I'm afraid . . . Your very good health, comrade.

OBOLONSKY. I swear he's a genius!

ZOYA (*sotto voce*). He's a scoundrel! (*Aloud.*) All right, that's enough politics. And so, comrade Beltoff, as of tomorrow, I'm starting business.

AMETISTOV. Yes, we open tomorrow. I drink to the success of the fashion studio and the health of its owner – comrade Zoya Denisovna Smirnoff! Hurrah! (*Drinks beer.*) Now another toast – to the health of the esteemed chairman of our House Committee and Party sympathiser . . . (*Whispers to* ZOYA.) What's his name?

ZOYA (*Whispers*). Ex-Sergeant-Major Beltoff.

AMETISTOV. Just what I was going to say: Ex-Sergeant-Major Beltoff! Hurrah!

The sound of someone strumming a piano is heard from the courtyard and some little boys start singing: 'For he's a jolly good fellow . . .'

AMETISTOV. Quite right! How appropriate! 'For he's a jolly good fellow . . .'

Curtain

ACT TWO

The sitting room of ZOYA's *apartment has been turned into a dressmaker's workroom. Dummies with doll-like faces, swathes of material everywhere. The* SEAMSTRESS *is pedalling away at a sewing-machine, the* CUTTER *busy with a tape measure round her shoulders. Three* LADIES.

FIRST LADY. Oh no, my dear . . . You must take out the whole of this corner, take it out altogether, otherwise it will make me look as if I'm missing two ribs! For heaven's sake take it out!

CUTTER. Very well.

SECOND LADY (*Chatting to* THIRD LADY.) And just imagine – she said: 'First of all, madam, you need your head shaved bare'. Of course, I went straight to Jean in Kuznetsky Most, had my head shaved and ran back to her. She put a wig on me and just imagine – my whole face instantly looked like a kettle!

THIRD LADY. He, he, he!

SECOND LADY. Ah, my dear, you may laugh!

FIRST LADY. The pleats, my dear, the pleats!

CUTTER. Really, madam.

SECOND LADY. And then the impudence of her – 'That', she said, 'is because you've got such broad cheekbones!'

Bell rings.

AMETISTOV (*Dashes on*). Pardon, pardon, ladies – I won't look.

SECOND LADY. Monsieur Ametistov! What do you think? Have I got broad cheekbones?

AMETISTOV. You? *Qu'est-ce que vous dîtes, madame?* You haven't any cheekbones at all. (*Exit*).

FIRST LADY. Who was that?

CUTTER. The manager of our fashion studio.

FIRST LADY. A well-run business, this.

AMETISTOV (*re-enters*). *Pardon, pardon,* I won't look . . . your mantle is entrancing.

SECOND LADY. Entrancing? Have I really got such a big behind?

AMETISTOV. Your behind is entirely as it should be, madam.

Bell rings.

(*Aside.*) Oh, why don't you drop dead? (*Aloud.*) *Pardon, pardon!* (*Runs off.*)

FIRST LADY (*Takes off mantle*). Well, can you have it ready by Friday?

CUTTER. Impossible, madam, Varvara Nikolayevna won't have finished it in time.

FIRST LADY. But that's terrible! By Saturday, then?

CUTTER. By Wednesday, madam.

FIRST LADY. Goodbye. (*Exit.*)

SEAMSTRESS *hands a roll of material to* SECOND LADY.

SECOND LADY. Thank you.

AMETISTOV (*Rushing in*). *Au revoir, madame.*

Bell rings.

AMETISTOV. (*Aside*). What *is* going on? *Pardon, pardon* . . . (*Exit, running.*)

Exit SECOND LADY.

SEAMSTRESS (*Wraps up a roll of material in paper, hands it to* THIRD LADY). There is your stole.

THIRD LADY. *Merci.* (*Exit.*)

CUTTER (*Sits down exhausted*). Oof!

AMETISTOV. That's all for today, dear comrades. Time to shut up shop.

SEAMSTRESS *and* CUTTER *prepare to go.*

AMETISTOV. Time to rest and relax comrades, in accordance

with the labour regulations . . . Take a bus-ride to the Sparrow Hills, enjoy the golden autumn leaves . . .

SEAMSTRESS. Leaves, Mr Ametistov?! It'll be all I can do to drag myself home to bed!

AMETISTOV. Oh, I do know how you feel! All *I* long for is to lie down. Last thing at night I'll read a bit of the history of materialist philosophy and just drop off! Don't bother to tidy up, comrades. Comrade Manyushka will see to all that.

Exeunt SEAMSTRESS *and* CUTTER.

God, those women, they'll be the death of me. I shall be seeing bottoms, buttons and bodices in my sleep. (*Produces a bottle of brandy and a glass, takes several swigs.*) Ah, that's better!

Enter ZOYA.

AMETISTOV. Ah, Zoya my dear. . . . The burning question, *Madame la directrice*, is this: can you persuade Alla to perform – right away, if not sooner?

ZOYA. No, she won't play.

AMETISTOV. What? . . . Now listen to me. How much does she owe you?

ZOYA. Three thousand.

AMETISTOV. There's your trump card!

ZOYA. No. She'll pay.

AMETISTOV. She won't pay, I tell you. Her eyes don't look credit-worthy to me. You can always tell from a person's eyes whether they have any money or not. I know from my own experience: when I'm broke, I get all pensive, my thoughts take over and I even feel drawn to socialism. That woman has a thoughtful look: she needs money badly and she hasn't any. Just think: what an advertisement she'd be, what an ornament to the business. Listen to Ametistov! Ametistov is a great man!

Bell rings.

God, who can that be now?

Enter MANYUSHKA.

MANYUSHKA. Alla Vadimovna wants to know if she can see you.

AMETISTOV. There, what did I tell you? Squeeze her, twist her arm!

ZOYA. All right, all right, no need to fuss. (*To* MANYUSHKA.) Ask her to come in, please.

MANYUSHKA *opens door; enter* ALLA VADIMOVNA.

ALLA. Good evening, Zoya Denisovna.

ZOYA. Delighted to see you, Alla Vadimovna.

AMETISTOV. Allow me to kiss your hand, adorable Alla Vadimovna. Ah, wait till you see the new models that arrived today from Paris! You'll throw your dress out of the window – on my word of honour as an ex-guardsman.

ALLA. Were you in the Guards?

AMETISTOV. *Mais oui* . . . But alas, I must fly. (*Exit, winking at* ZOYA.)

ALLA. You have an excellent manager, Zoya Denisovna. Tell me, was he really in the Guards?

ZOYA. I'm afraid I can't tell you for certain . . . do sit down.

ALLA. I've come to see you about an important matter.

ZOYA. I'm listening.

ALLA. Oh, dear it's so unpleasant. . . . I should have paid you today. . . . I feel so ashamed, Zoya Denisovna, but I. . . . the fact is, my finances have been in a shocking state recently. . . .so I'm forced to ask you to wait a little. . . . (*Pause.*) Why don't you say something, Zoya Denisovna? I can't bear it!

ZOYA. What can I say, Alla Vadimovna? (*Pause.*)

ALLA. You're right, of course. . . . so I'll just say goodbye. Well, I'll make every possible effort to get the money and settle up with you. . . . Goodbye, Zoya Denisovna.

ZOYA. Goodbye, Alla Vadimovna.

ALLA *goes towards the door.*

ZOYA. Are things really so bad?

ALLA. Really. . . . I may owe you money, but that doesn't give you the right to speak to me in that tone of voice!

ZOYA. No, Alla my dear, that simply won't wash, I'm afraid! The tone of voice is what it's all about. It's not a question of who owes money to whom. If you had come to me and said simply and frankly that your affairs were in a bad way, we could have put our heads together and worked out a solution. . . . But you came in here with your nose in the air, as much as to say, 'I'm a lady of high society and you're just a dressmaker . . .' If that's the way you feel, why bother to ask favours of a mere dressmaker?

ALLA. Zoya Denisovna, that's all in your imagination, I assure you. I was simply so depressed at the thought of being in debt to you that I couldn't bring myself to look you in the eye.

ZOYA. That's enough about your debt! So – you haven't any money, is that it? Give me a straight answer as between friends. How much do you need?

ALLA. A lot. So much, in fact, that I get a cold feeling in the pit of my stomach just thinking about it.

ZOYA. But why so much?

Pause.

ALLA. I want to go abroad.

ZOYA. I see. So things aren't working out for you here?

ALLA. That's right.

ZOYA. Well, but he. . . . I don't want to know who he is, his name's not important. . . . In short, hasn't he enough money to make things easier for you here?

ALLA. Since my husband died, Zoya Denisovna, there has been no man in my life.

ZOYA. Oh!?

ALLA. It's true.

ZOYA. So you didn't manage to get away last time you tried, three months ago?

ALLA. No, I didn't.

ZOYA. I promise to arrange it for you.

ALLA. If you can do that, I'll be grateful to you for the rest of my life!

ZOYA. Don't worry, comrade! . . . And if you like, I'll give you the opportunity to earn enough money to pay off your debts too.

ALLA. There's simply no way that I can earn money in Moscow – at least, not by any remotely decent sort of work, as far as I can see.

ZOYA. Why not? Working in a fashion house is perfectly decent work. I'm offering you a job as a model.

ALLA. But Zoya. . . . that sort of work is paid chicken-feed!

ZOYA. Perhaps. . . . but chicken-feed is an elastic concept. . . . I'll pay you a salary of a thousand roubles a month, I'll cancel your debt and in addition I'll help you to get abroad. . . . The work will be evenings only, starting tomorrow. Well, what about it?

Pause.

ALLA. Starting tomorrow?. . . . Evenings?. . . . (*Suddenly realises what the 'work' involves.*) You must be joking!

ZOYA. It's only four months till Christmas. In four months time you'll be free, your debts will be paid and no one, d'you hear, no one will ever know that Alla worked as a model. By spring you'll be on the Grands Boulevards. . . . (*Whispers.*) The man you love is in Paris. . . .

ALLA. Yes. . . .

ZOYA. Next spring you'll be arm in arm with him and he'll never know.

ALLA. So that's what sort of fashion studio you're running! Evenings only. . . . Do you know what you are, Zoya? You're a she-devil! But not a word to anyone – ever!

ZOYA. I swear it!

Pause

Well, you might as well be hung for a sheep as for a lamb, eh? Allez-oop!

ALLA. All right, I agree. I'll start in three days' time.

ZOYA. Hey presto! (*Flings open a cupboard, in which a rack full of Paris dresses are lit up by a dazzling light.*) Choose one – it's my present to you, any one you like!

Blackout. ZOYA and ALLA vanish. Then a table-lamp is switched on, with AMETISTOV and ZOYA sitting beside it. Evening.

AMETISTOV. What did I tell you? Now do you see how useful I am?

ZOYA. You're not stupid, Alexander Ametistov.

AMETISTOV. Remember, Zoya, that half of all the money you make is due to my efforts. You won't abandon your cousin, will you? You'll take me with you, won't you? Ah, Nice, Nice – when shall I see it again? An azure sea and me strolling along the promenade in white trousers.

ZOYA. Let me beg of you just one thing – don't talk French, at least not when Alla's in the room. Every time you say something in French, she goggles at you in horror.

AMETISTOV. Why? Do I speak French badly, is that it?

ZOYA. You don't speak it badly – you speak it quite appallingly.

AMETISTOV. What impertinence, Zoya, *parole d'honneur*. I've been playing chemin-de-fer since I was ten and now, all of a sudden, I speak bad French!

ZOYA. And another thing – why do you have to tell such whopping lies the whole time? You – a Guards officer, for God's sake! What's the point of it, anyway?

AMETISTOV. Nothing gives you greater pleasure than saying something really nasty to somebody. If I were in the government, I'd send you to Siberia just for being such a horrid person.

ZOYA. Stop drivelling! Don't forget that Goose will be here soon. I'm going to change. (*Exit.*)

AMETISTOV. Goose? Why didn't you tell me? (*Seized by panic.*) Goose! Goose! And where's that pigtailed son of the Celestial Empire?! Cousin Manyushka!

MANYUSHKA (*Enters*). Here I am.

AMETISTOV. What on earth are you up to out there? Am I supposed to do everything myself?

MANYUSHKA. I was doing the washing-up.

AMETISTOV. You can finish the washing-up later. Come on, give me a hand in here.

They start to tidy up, re-arrange the furniture, and switch on lights. OBOLONSKY *enters, wearing white tie and tails.*

OBOLONSKY. Good evening.

AMETISTOV. Greetings, maestro!

OBOLONSKY. Excuse me, I've been meaning for a long time to ask you – kindly address me by my name.

AMETISTOV. Why are you offended? You are a funny chap. Between people of our class . . . Anyway, what's wrong with the word 'maestro'?

OBOLONSKY. Simply because it's unusual and it jars on my ear as much as the word 'comrade'.

AMETISTOV. Oh, *pardon, pardon*. There's a great difference between them. Talking of differences, do you happen to have a cigarette on you?

OBOLONSKY (*Proffers cigarette case*). Help yourself.

AMETISTOV. *Merci beaucoup.* (*Looks round the room.*) *Voilà!* Paradise! Come on, count, cheer up! Why are you sitting there like a lump of dough?

OBOLONSKY. What does that mean – 'dough'?

AMETISTOV. Oh dear, I see there's no cheering you up! What do you think of the apartment, by the way?

OBOLONSKY. Very comfortable. It reminds me distantly of my own former apartment.

AMETISTOV. Was it nice?

OBOLONSKY. Very nice. The only trouble is – it was confiscated!

AMETISTOV. No – really?

OBOLONSKY. Some men with red beards came and threw me out.

AMETISTOV. Incredible! You don't say! . . . What a sad story. . . .

ZOYA (*Enters*). Pavel! Good evening, my dear. Come on let's go to my room.

Exeunt ZOYA *and* OBOLONSKY. *A pre-arranged ring on the doorbell: three long and two short rings.*

AMETISTOV. Ah, there he is, damn him.

Exit MANYUSHKA. *After a short pause, enter* KO KA-IN.

AMETISTOV. Where have you been?

KO KA-IN. Plessing ladies skirts.

AMETISTOV. To hell with you and your skirts – have you brought the cocaine?

KO KA-IN. Yes.

AMETISTOV. Come in, then, let's have it! Listen, Ko-ko-nut, look me straight in the eyes.

KO KA-IN. I looking you in eyes.

AMETISTOV. Answer me truthfully: have you mixed ground-up aspirin in it?

KO KA-IN. No, no!

AMETISTOV. I know you, you Chinese bandit! If you have mixed in any aspirin, may God punish you!

KO KA-IN. God no punish Chinaman.

AMETISTOV. Oh yes He will, He'll strike you dead on the spot. He'll hit you on the back of the neck – and goodbye Chinaman! So don't try mixing aspirin in the cocaine, that's all. . . . (*Takes a trial sniff*) No, this is good, straight cocaine.

KO KA-IN *puts on a Chinese silk jacket and skullcap.*

That's much better. But why the hell do you Chinese shave your scalps? You'd look so much more authentic with a pigtail.

Secret signal (three long, two short rings) from doorbell. Enter MARYA NIKIFOROVNA.

MARYA. Good evening, Mr Ametistov. Good evening, Ko-Ko.

AMETISTOV. Go and get changed, Marya Nikiforovna, or you'll be late. We're going to show the new models.

MARYA. They've arrived, have they? Oh, how exciting! (*Exit*).

KO KA-IN *has lit a Chinese lantern in a niche, and is smoking a Chinese pipe.*

AMETISTOV. Don't try to push the stuff too hard.

KO KA-IN. I not push too hard. . . .(*Exit.*)

Secret signal from doorbell. Enter LIZANKA.

LIZANKA. Greetings to the Father Superior of this monastery!

AMETISTOV. *Bon soir, madame.*

Secret signal. Hearing it, AMETISTOV *runs over to mirror and hastily smartens himself up. Enter* MME. IVANOVA – *a very beautiful, haughty woman.*

AMETISTOV. Good evening, Madame Ivanova!

IVANOVA. Give me a cigarette.

AMETISTOV. Manyushka! Cigarette!

Enter MANYUSHKA *at speed, offers cigarettes to* IVANOVA.

Pause.

AMETISTOV. Is it cold outside?

IVANOVA. No.

AMETISTOV. We have a surprise tonight: the new models have arrived from Paris.

IVANOVA. Good.

AMETISTOV. They're astounding!

IVANOVA. Aha!

AMETISTOV. Did you come by tram?

IVANOVA. Yes.

AMETISTOV. I expect the tramcars were very crowded, weren't they?

IVANOVA. Yes.

Pause.

AMETISTOV. Oh, your cigarette has gone out. . . . allow me to light it again for you. . . .

IVANOVA. Thanks. (*Exit.*)

AMETISTOV. (*To* MANYUSHKA). Now *there's* a woman for you! You could spend a lifetime with her and never get bored. Not like you – chatter, chatter, chatter. . . .

Long, forceful ring at the doorbell.

It's him! That's a sales director's ring if ever there was one. *He* knows how to use a doorbell. Let him in! Then go and change. Ko Ka-In will help you.

KO KA-IN. (*Runs across stage*). Goose coming!

MANYUSHKA. Oh, heavens! Goose! (*Runs off.*)

AMETISTOV. Zoya, it's Goose! You meet him, I must vanish. (*Vanishes.*)

Enter Goose.

ZOYA. (*Enters, wearing an evening gown*). How glad I am to see you, Boris Semyonovich!

GOOSE. Good evening, Zoya Denisovna.

ZOYA. Do sit down here, it's more comfortable. . . . Dear me, what a naughty man you are! We're such near neighbours, you should at least have looked in to see me. . . .

GOOSE. Believe me, I would have done with pleasure, but. . . .

ZOYA. I'm only joking. I know what a busy man you are.

GOOSE. Don't tell me – I literally don't have time to sleep.

ZOYA. You poor thing, you're overdoing it. You need to relax and enjoy yourself.

GOOSE. No question of enjoying myself, I'm afraid. (*Glances round the room.*) You have a very nice place here.

ZOYA. My studio only exists thanks to you.

GOOSE. Oh, nonsense. By the way, talking of the studio: I've come to see you partly on business, but that's strictly between ourselves. I need a Paris outfit for a lady. You know, something that's positively *le dernier cri*, at about three hundred roubles or so.

ZOYA. I quite understand. A present?

GOOSE. Between ourselves – yes.

ZOYA. Don't worry, I won't tell your wife. Ah, you men! Very well, then: my manager will show you some of our very latest models in a few minutes, and you can choose whichever one you prefer. Then we'll have dinner. You're *mine* for this evening and I'm not going to let you go!

GOOSE. *Merci.* So you have a manager? Can one see what sort of a fellow he is?

ZOYA. You'll see him in a moment. (*Exit.*)

AMETISTOV (*Enters, attired in white tie and tails*). *Quand on parle du soleil, on voit ce rayon* – which translated into Russian means: 'Talk of the sun and lo! a shining ray'.

GOOSE. Sun. . . . ray. . . .? Do you mean me?

AMETISTOV. You, Boris Semyonovich – who else? Permit me to introduce myself – Ametistov's the name.

GOOSE. Goose.

AMETISTOV. Monsieur is looking for a little Paris outfit, I understand? You've come to the right place, sir, if I may say so. I can assure you that nowhere else in Moscow will you find such a selection to choose from. Ko Ka-In!

Enter KO KA-IN.

GOOSE. But, but. . . . he's a Chinaman!

AMETISTOV. Indeed, a Chinaman he is, Boris Semyonovich, as you so perceptively observe. Pay no attention to him, my dear sir. Just one of the *very* many sons of the Celestial Empire, who is distinguished from his innumerable compatriots by a single quality – his exemplary honesty.

GOOSE. But why a Chinaman?

AMETISTOV. He is my long-standing and devoted manservant, sir. I brought him here from Shanghai, where I once spent many years gathering material.

GOOSE. Remarkable. What sort of material?

AMETISTOV. Research material for a major work of ethnography – later, when we have time, I'll tell you all about my scientific peregrinations, my dear sir. You will simply weep when you hear about it. Ko Ka-In, bring the gentleman some cooling beverage.

KO KA-IN. Velly good, sir. (*Exit and re-enters immediately with a bottle of champagne and glasses.*)

AMETISTOV. Allow me, sir. (*Opens bottle and pours out champagne.*)

GOOSE. Is this champagne? You organise things very well here, citizen manager.

AMETISTOV. *Je pense!* Having worked for Paquin in Paris, one picks up these little refinements, you know.

GOOSE. You've worked in Paris?

AMETISTOV. Five years, my dear sir. Ko Ka-In, you may go, my little angel.

Exit KO KA-IN.

GOOSE. Do you know, if I believed in an after-life I might say he really was an angel.

AMETISTOV. Yes, to look at him one can't help thinking it! Your astoundingly good health, sir! And to the health of your Refractory Metals Trust! Hurrah! Hurrah! Hurrah!. . . . No, no, sir – no heel-taps! Drain your glass, please! Anything less would be an insult to our firm!

GOOSE. You certainly do things properly here.

AMETISTOV. *Mille merci*!. . . . So – what is she? A blonde? Or a brunette?

GOOSE. Who?

AMETISTOV. *Pardon, pardon.* . . . I refer, of course, to the charming personage for whom the outfit is intended.

GOOSE. Strictly between ourselves, she is a light brunette.

AMETISTOV. I knew it at once – you have taste, sir. Pray have another glass. . . . and may I also beg you to be so kind as to stand up for a moment? Thank you. . . . yes, yes. . . . this elegant morning coat of yours demands precisely a light brunette to set it off. You have staggeringly good taste, my dear sir. Ko Ka-In!

Enter KO KA-IN.

AMETISTOV. Ask the maestro to come in, also mademoiselle Liza.

KO KA-IN. Velly good, sir (*Exit.*)

Enter OBOLONSKY, who sits down at the piano.

AMETISTOV. Please settle yourself comfortably, Boris Semyonovich. Would you care for an almond? (*Claps his hands.*) *Défilez, s'il vous plait!*

OBOLONSKY *starts to play. A curtain is flung open and LIZANKA advances on to the floodlit catwalk wearing a luxurious and distinctly revealing evening gown. GOOSE stares at the apparition in amazement.*

LIZANKA (*Whispers to AMETISTOV*). Shall I shake my tits out?

AMETISTOV. Shake 'em, Lizanka, shake 'em!

LIZANKA *retreats seductively to the curtain, which closes behind her.*

What do you say to that one, my dear Boris Semyonovich?

GOOSE (*In a strangled voice*). H'mm, well, yes. . . .

AMETISTOV. *Encore un petit verre?* (*Refills GOOSE's glass.*)

GOOSE. Were you at court?

AMETISTOV. Ah, Boris Semyonovich! One day I'll tell you a few secrets, it'll reduce you to tears, I assure you. . . . *Défilez, s'il vous plait!*

The curtain opens and MARYA NIKIFOROVNA appears on the catwalk wearing a dress even more daringly open than the previous model. OBOLONSKY plays, while MARYA NIKIFOROVNA shimmies along the catwalk in time to the music.

AMETISTOV. (*To OBOLONSKY*). Something a little livelier, please. (*Whispers to MARYA NIKIFOROVNA.*) Let's see your legs!

MARYA. (*Hisses*). Pig!

AMETISTOV. *Vous êtes très aimable.*

MARYA NIKIFOROVNA *skips back down the catwalk and the curtain closes behind her.*

AMETISTOV. *Défilez!*

OBOLONSKY *plays 'The Moon is shining', a lively Russian folktune. MANYUSHKA prances through the curtain, dressed in a very skimply approximation to a Russian peasant costume, and dances along the catwalk.*

KO KA-IN (*Suddenly pops out and whispers to* MANYUSHKA). Manyushka, look at me when you dance, not at old guest. . . .

MANYUSHKA (*Aside, to* KO KA-IN). Go away, you jealous devil!

OBOLONSKY (*Bursts out*). Here am I playing while a housemaid prances across the stage in a state of undress! What on earth is happening?

AMETISTOV. Sshh!. . . . (*Whispers to* MANYUSHKA.) Manyushka, off you go now and lay the table for dinner! Look sharp!

MANYUSHKA *dances off behind the curtain.*

GOOSE (*Suddenly*). Défilez!

AMETISTOV. Quite right, Boris Semyonovich. Défilez, s'il vous plait!

The curtain opens. OBOLONSKY *plays a slow, languorous waltz.* MME. IVANOVA *glides on the catwalk, wearing a two-piece dress that is stunning but barely decent.* AMETISTOV *jumps up on to the stage, waltzes with* IVANOVA *and whispers to her:*

AMETISTOV. I am really a deeply unhappy man, Mme. Ivanova. . . . I long to get away from all this and go to Nice with the woman I love. . . .

IVANOVA (*Whispers*). What rubbish you talk!

The waltz ends.

AMETISTOV. And now, mademoiselle, show off the dress to monsieur . . . (*Exit.*)

MME. IVANOVA *steps down from the catwalk like a statue descending from its pedestal and twirls herself provocatively in front of* GOOSE.

GOOSE (*Bewildered*). Thank you very . . . very . . . much indeed, from the bottom of my heart. . . .

IVANOVA (*Half-coquettishly*). How dare you look at me like that! What impudence!

GOOSE (*Confused*). Who said I was looking at you?

IVANOVA. No, you are bold and impudent, there's something. . . .(*huskily*) *African* about you. I like men like you. (*Exit suddenly behind the curtain.*)

GOOSE (*Ecstatically*). *Défilez!*

AMETISTOV (*Dashes on, switching on all the lights*). *Pardon, monsieur.* . . . there will now be an intermission!

Curtain

ACT THREE

A grey, dull day. AMETISTOV *is sitting glumly by the telephone in the sitting room.*

AMETISTOV (*Hiccups*). God, they won't stop – damned hiccups.

Pause.

Enter OBOLONSKY, *tired and limp.*

AMETISTOV (*Hiccups*). Pardon!

Telephone rings.

Ko Ka-In, telephone!

KO KA-IN (*Runs on, picks up telephone receiver*). Hullo, please. . . . ah. . . . Goose for you. (*Exit*).

AMETISTOV (*Into telephone*). Comrade Goose? A very good morning to you, sir. I trust you are in good health?. . . . Oh yes, very well, thank you. . . . We're waiting, waiting. . . . (*Suddenly hiccups.*) *Pardon*, someone is thinking of me. . . . What? A secret, a secret, there's a surprise waiting for you; Boris Semyonovich. . . . goodbye, my dear sir. (*Hiccups.*)

OBOLONSKY. Astonishingly vulgar man, that Goose, don't you think?

AMETISTOV. No, I don't. A man who earns five thousand roubles a month can't be vulgar (*hiccups.*). . . . Who can be thinking of me, I'd like to know? Who on earth needs me?. . . . Yes, I respect Goose. . . . Who has to hoof it around Moscow? You do.

OBOLONSKY. Excuse me, Monsieur Ametistov, I do not 'hoof it' – I walk.

AMETISTOV. God, how you do take offence! All right, you walk – but *he* drives around by car. You live in one room – oh, I beg your pardon, perhaps 'live' is a rude word in high society – you *reside* in one room, but Goose has seven rooms. You knock out –

sorry, you *earn* – a hundred roubles a month on your piano, but Goose makes five thousand. You play – but Goose dances!

OBOLONSKY. Because this government has created a system in which it is impossible for a gentleman to exist.

AMETISTOV. *Pardon*, but I don't agree. A gentleman can survive under any circumstances. I am a gentleman, therefore I survive. Listen, old man – I arrived in Moscow without so much as a pair of trousers, and now. . . .

OBOLONSKY. I object to you addressing me as 'old man'.

AMETISTOV. Oh, don't be so touchy! What does it matter, between us members of the nobility?

OBOLONSKY. Forgive me for asking, but are you really from the nobility?

AMETISTOV. What a question? Can't you see for yourself? (*Hiccups.*) Oh, hell. . . .

OBOLONSKY. You see, I've never come across your surname before.

AMETISTOV. Much that proves! It's a well-known name from the province of Penza. Ah, *signore*! If you knew what I suffered from the Bolsheviks. . . . the family estate ransacked, the house burned to the ground. . . .

OBOLONSKY. In which province was your estate?

AMETISTOV. Mine? It depends on which one you mean. . . .

OBOLONSKY. Well, the one that was burned down.

AMETISTOV. Oh, that one. . . . I don't want to talk about it, it's too painful. . . . A white colonnade along the front of the house, as I recall. . . . seven columns, each one more beautiful than the next. . . . But that's nothing – what about the pedigree herd of cattle, the brick-works. . . .

OBOLONSKY. My aunt, Varvara Nikolayevna, had a splendid stud farm.

AMETISTOV. What if she did? I had one myself. But why are we letting ourselves sink into this gloomy mood, old man? Come on, cheer up!

OBOLONSKY. I feel so depressed.

AMETISTOV. Funny, but so do I. Why, I wonder? God knows. Some presentiment, perhaps. . . . Now there's nothing like a game of cards to buck you up when you're feeling low.

OBOLONSKY. I don't like cards, I like horses. I had a horse called Pharaoh. . . .

A voice from the courtyard can be heard faintly singing: 'They call to mind another life. . . .'

AMETISTOV. I used to love playing faro, too. . . .

OBOLONSKY. . . . my racing colours were red with yellow sleeves and a black sash. . . . ah, Pharaoh. . . .

AMETISTOV.. . . . and when you noticed your opponent starting to bend down the corners of the cards, you'd break out in a cold sweat, I can tell you! Wait a bit, though, and later, when you trumped his ace with a nifty deal off the bottom of the pack – bang! – you had him by the short and curlies!. . . . But why upset ourselves by talking of old times? God, what wouldn't I give to get away from Moscow right now!

OBOLONSKY. Yes! Yes! Right now! Get away. . . . I can't stand living here a moment longer!

AMETISTOV. Don't let it upset you, old chap. Another three months and we'll all be off to Nice. Were you ever in Nice, Count?

OBOLONSKY. Many times.

AMETISTOV. So was I, of course, but only as a small child. Ah, me. . . . my late mother, God rest her soul, used to take me there. . . . two governesses and our nanny went with us. My hair was a mass of golden curls in those days. . . . Tell me, are there any card-sharpers in Monte Carlo?

OBOLONSKY. I don't know. . . . Oh, I don't know anything. . . .

AMETISTOV. I've got it! We need a change of air. . . . Look here, Count, while we're waiting for Zoya to come, why don't you and I nip out to the 'Bavaria'?

OBOLONSKY. You really amaze me with your suggestions. A beer bar?! The noise, the dirt, the people. . . .!

AMETISTOV. You obviously haven't seen the fresh crayfish they

delivered to the 'Bavaria' yesterday! Each one is at least *that*
big. . . . I'm not lying – as big as a guitar! Ko Ka-In!

Enter KO KA-IN.

AMETISTOV. Listen, my dear major–domo of the yellow race,
when Zoya Denisovna comes tell her that the count and I have
gone to the Tretyakov Gallery for a minute or two to look at the
pictures. Come on, old man! Look out, crayfish – here we come!
(*Exit with* OBOLONSKY.)

KO KA-IN. Manyuska! They gone out!

MANYUSHKA (*Runs on, kisses* KO KA-IN). Why I like you so
much I'll never know! You're as yellow as a lemon, but I fancy
you. Are you Chinamen Lutherans?

KO KA-IN. Some luthelans, some wash laundly. . . . Listen,
Manyuska, big news. You and I leave here, soon. I take you
Shanghai!

MANYUSHKA. I am not going to Shanghai.

KO KA-IN. You will go.

MANYUSHKA. Who are you giving orders to? What d'you think
I am – your wife?

KO KA-IN. I mally you in Shanghai, Manyuska.

MANYUSHKA. You have to ask me if I'll marry you first. Have I
signed a marriage contract yet? And what did I sign it with, eh?
Your pigtail?

KO KA-IN. Maybe you want mally Ga So-Lin?

MANYUSHKA. I might at that. I'm a free woman – and it's no
good staring at me like that with your Chinese eyes, I'm not
afraid of you.

KO KA-IN. Ga So-Lin?

MANYUSHKA. Who know?

KO KA-IN (*His features suddenly contorted into a look of terrifying
fury*). Ga So-Lin?

MANYUSHKA (*Alarmed*). What's the matter with you?

KO KA-IN (*Grips* MANYUSHKA *by the throat, draws a knife*). I kill you now. (*Starts to throttle* MANYUSHKA) Tell me tluth – you kiss Ga So–Lin?

MANYUSHKA. Oh, let go of my throat. . . . Lord have mercy on me. . . .

KO KA–IN. You kiss him? You kiss him?

MANYUSHKA. Ko-Ko, angel. . . . never kissed him – don't kill a poor orphan girl. . . . spare my young life. . . .

KO KA–IN (*Puts away his knife*). You mally Ga So–Lin?

MANYUSHKA. No, no, never!. . . .

KO KA–IN. You mally me?

MANYUSHKA. No . . . Oh, yes, yes, I will. . . .(*To audience*.) Tell me, comrades, what is he doing?

KO KA–IN. I make you ploposal.

MANYUSHKA. Funny sort of proposal! A fiancé who goes for you with a knife!. . . . You're nothing but a bandit, Ko Ka–In!

KO KA–IN. No. . . . me no bandit, me sad – evlyone chase me. . . . they want put Chinaman in plison for selling cocaine. . . . Ga So–Lin blackmail me. . . . make me wash laundly all night. . . . he takes all money, give me only forty kopecks . . . I starve with hunger. . . . Chinaman can't live in Moscow, too cold. . . . Chinaman like live in Shanghai. . . . listen, Manyuska, you collect your things, we soon go away, I plan get many loubles. . . .

MANYUSHKA. Oh, Ko-ko, what have you been planning? I'm afraid for you – you'll only land in trouble!

Doorbell rings.

Run into the kitchen! (*Exit* KO KA–IN. MANYUSHKA *opens the front door.*) Oh my God!

Enter GA SO–LIN.

GA SO–LIN. Gleetings, Manyuska.

MANYUSHKA. Oh, go away, Ga So–Lin!

GA SO–LIN. No! Why I go away? I not go away. You alone, Manyuska? I come make you ploposal.

MANYUSHKA. Get out, Ga So–Lin!

GA SO-LIN. No, why? What you told me, eh? You told me you love me. You cheat Ga So-Lin?

MANYUSHKA. That's a lie! I never told you anything of the sort. I'll call Zoya Denisovna. . . .

GA SO-LIN. You not call her. She not home. You tell many lies, Manyuska. I love you!

MANYUSHKA. Have you got a knife? Tell me now, if you've got a knife. . . .

GA SO-LIN. I have knife. To make ploposal.

KO KA-IN (*Bursts in*). Who make ploposal?

GA SO-LIN. Ah! My young fliend! Why you here?

KO KA-IN. You go away from apartment! This my apartment, Zoya's and mine!

MANYUSHKA. Oh God, what's going to happen?

GA SO-LIN. Yours? Bandit! You steal apartment. You no better than dog. . . . I come make ploposal Manyuska!

KO KA-IN. I alleady make. She my wife. She love me.

GA SO-LIN. Fool! Lobber! She *my* wife, she love *me*!

MANYUSHKA. He's lying, Ko-ko, he's lying!

KO KA-IN. Get out my apartment!

GA SO-LIN. You get out! At police-station I tell all, tell how you Chinese bandit!

KO KA-IN. Police. . . . (*hisses something in Chinese.*)

GA SO-LIN (*Hisses in Chinese*).

MANYUSHKA. Stop it, you two! For God's sake don't start fighting, you yellow devils!

KO KA-IN *screams, draws his knife and lunges at* GA SO-LIN.

MANYUSHKA. Help! Help! Help!

GA SO-LIN *jumps into the mirror-fronted wardrobe and pulls the door shut behind him.*

Doorbell rings.

MANYUSHKA. Help! Put that knife away, you madman!

Doorbell rings.

KO KA-IN. I kill him later. (*Locks the wardrobe door and pockets the key. Exit.*)

MANYUSHKA *opens the front door, to admit two* STRANGERS *in plain clothes, both carrying briefcases.*

1ST STRANGER. Good Morning, comrades. Was somebody in here shouting for help just now?

MANYUSHKA. Shouting for help? Of course not. That was me singing. . . .

2ND STRANGER. Aaah!

MANYUSHKA. What do you want, comrades?

1ST STRANGER. We, comrades, are an official commission. We've come to inspect your dressmaking workshop.

MANYUSHKA. I'm afraid the manager's out at the moment.' . . . we're not working today. . . .

1ST STRANGER. And who might you be?

MANYUSHKA. I'm a trainee model.

2ND STRANGER. Well, you can show us round. Otherwise we'll only have to come again.

MANYUSHKA. All right, then. . . .

1ST STRANGER. What goes on in this room, for instance?

2ND STRANGER. Nice room. (*Points to dummies.*) And what are those for?

MANYUSHKA. Dummies, of course – for fitting the clothes.

1ST STRANGER. In that case, what are models for?

MANYUSHKA. When they want to fit the clothes on something that moves, they fit them on us trainees.

1ST STRANGER. Aha.

2ND STRANGER (*Pulls aside a curtain, to reveal* KO KA-IN *holding an iron*). H'mm. A Chinaman.

MANYUSHKA. He comes in from the laundry to press skirts.

1ST STRANGER. Aha.

KO KA-IN *spits on the iron and exit.*

1ST STRANGER. Well, let's see the rest of the place. (*Exit, followed by* MANYUSHKA.)

2ND STRANGER (*Stays behind; takes out a bunch of keys, opens one wardrobe, looks inside, shuts it, opens the other and jumps back in amazement. Crouched inside is* GA SO-LIN, *clutching a knife*). Another one! What are you doing in there?

GA SO-LIN. I sitting here.

2ND STRANGER (*Whispers*). What for?

GA SO-LIN (*Plaintively*). I hide. . . . Bandit Ko Ka-in going to kill me. . . . save me, please. . . .

2ND STRANGER. Quiet! We'll save you, don't worry. And who might you be?

GA SO-LIN. Me Ga So-Lin, honest Chinaman. I come here make ploposal housemaid and he tly kill me! He bling opium to sell here.

2ND STRANGER. I see, I see. . . . well, come on out of that wardrobe. Go down to the police station and wait for me there. And don't think you can run away, because I'll find you even if I have to go to the bottom of the sea.

GA SO-LIN. I not lun away! Only you catch Ko Ka-In, he Chinese bandit. (*Jumps out of wardrobe and exit through hallway.*)

SECOND STRANGER *follows* MANYUSHKA *and* FIRST STRANGER. *After a short pause, all three return.*

1ST STRANGER. Well, everything seems to be in first-class shape. The workshop is very well set out and organised.

2ND STRANGER. You don't say!

1ST STRANGER (*To* MANYUSHKA). Now, comrade, please give our compliments to the manageress and tell her that the commission inspected her premises and found the workshop to be in exemplary order. We'll send you our official certificate shortly.

2ND STRANGER. My respects to the manageress.

Exeunt STRANGERS; MANYUSHKA *shuts the front door behind them.*

KO KA-IN (*Bursts in, furious, brandishing his knife.*) Ah, they gone? You tell police? I give you police! (*Flings himself at the mirror-fronted wardrobe.*)

MANYUSHKA. You devil! Help! Help! Help!

KO KA-IN (*Wrenches open wardrobe door, freezes in amazement*). Chinese pig! He had another key!

Curtain

ACT FOUR

Night. ZOYA's *sitting room, lit by shaded lamps. In a niche is a lighted Chinese lantern, beneath which sits* KO KA-IN, *wearing his exotic costume, in an inscrutable pose reminiscent of a Chinese statuette of Buddha. From offstage come the sounds of two guitarists singing* 'Two Guitars'. *Draped dummies are standing around in attitudes that make it impossible to tell whether they are alive or dead. A profusion of flowers in vases.*

AMETISTOV (*Puts his head round a door, calls to* KO KA-IN). Ko Ka-In! Champagne!

KO KA-IN. Velly good, sir! (*Exit; after a short pause, returns and resumes his pose in the niche*).

The sound of the guitars fades away, to be replaced by a foxtrot played on a piano. DEAD BODY *emerges from one of the doors, gazes disconsolately around and makes his way unsteadily towards* KO KA-IN.

DEAD BODY. May I have this dance, madame?

KO KA-IN. I not madam. . . .

DEAD BODY. Good God! What on earth are you?. . . . (*Approaches one of the dummies.*) Shall we take a turn on the floor, madame?. . . . You'd rather not? Very well, as you wish. . . . Please smile – only make sure your smile doesn't turn into tears. . . . (*Goes up to another dummy.*) Madame. . . . (*clasps the dummy round the waist and dances with it.*) Never in my life have I held such a waist as yours. . . . (*stares at the dummy, pushes it away from him and bursts into tears.*)

AMETISTOV (*Rushes on stage*). Ivan Vasilievich! There, there. . . . what has upset you? What are you missing in your life? What is the matter?

DEAD BODY. You blackguard! It's your fault. . . .

AMETISTOV. Ivan Vasilievich, I'm going to give you a few
  drops of spirit of ammonia.

DEAD BODY. More insults! Everyone else gets champagne – but
  you make *me* drink ammonia. . . .

AMETISTOV. Ivan Vasilievich, my dear fellow. . . . please. . . .

*During this scene, a door opens at the far end of ZOYA's half-lit
bedroom, through which BELTOFF silently enters. He hides himself
behind a curtain and watches the proceedings. ROBBER enters the
sitting room.*

ROBBER. Ivan Vasilievich – what on earth is the matter with you?

DEAD BODY. They're making me drink spirit of ammonia!

MARYA (*Enters sitting room*). Dear, dear Ivan Vasilievich!

DEAD BODY. Go away! Everybody leave me alone!

Enter ZOYA.

ROBBER. Zoya Denisovna, please accept my deepest apologies on
  behalf of Ivan Vasilievich and myself.

ZOYA. Oh, don't worry – these things happen.

AMETISTOV (*To MARYA NIKIFOROVNA*). Go on, do
  something – take him away and dance with him.

MARYA NIKIFOROVNA *entices the weeping DEAD BODY out
of the room, followed by AMETISTOV.*

ROBBER. Your party is quite delightful, Zoya Denisovna. By the
  way, before I forget – how much do I owe you?

ZOYA. You're too kind. . . . two hundred roubles.

ROBBER. Very good. . . . I'll pay for Ivan Vasilievich too, so two
  hundred plus two hundred makes. . . .

ZOYA. Four hundred. . . .

ROBBER. Of course. . . . (*Hands her the money.*) *Merci.* May I have
  this dance, Zoya Denisovna?

ZOYA. I'm so sorry – I don't dance.

ROBBER. Oh, why not? What a shame! (*Exit.*)

*Suddenly MANYUSHKA puts her head round the door from the hall
and makes a signal to KO KA-IN, who leaps to his feet. ZOYA nods*

to MANYUSHKA, *who opens the door to admit* ALLA
VADIMOVNA, *dressed in a long coat and a veil.*

ZOYA (*Whispers*). Good evening, Alla. (*To* MANYUSHKA.)
Take Alla Vadimovna to your room and help her into her dress.

Exeunt MANYUSHKA *and* ALLA *through* ZOYA'S *bedroom.*
KO KA-IN *slips away noiselessly.* BELTOFF *enters from behind the
curtain where he has been hiding.*

ZOYA (*Staggers, appalled*). Beltoff?! What the hell are you doing
here? How did you get in?

BELTOFF (*Whispers*). Through the back door. I have keys to all
the apartments. Well, well, Zoya Denisovna . . . Funny sort of
fashion studio you've got here! Now I see what you've been up
to!

ZOYA (*Gives* BELTOFF *money*). Get out and keep your mouth
shut! When they've all gone, you can come back and we'll talk
again. . . .

BELTOFF. I'm warning you, Zoya Denisovna, take care. . . .

ZOYA. Get out. . . .

Exit BELTOFF *through the bedroom, followed by* ZOYA. *Sounds of
a foxtrot heard offstage. Enter* GOOSE, *in a state of maudlin gloom.*

GOOSE. Goose, you're drunk. . . . You, the stale. . . scales. . .
sales director of the Reflat. . . Refractory Metals Bust. . . Trust,
are ink. . . ink. . . incredibly drunk. . . Only you, Goose, know
why you're sunk. . . drunk. . .! But you'll never tell anyone the
season. . . reason, will you, Goose? And for why? Because
you're too proud!. . . Lovely women are whirling . . .
twirling. . . swirling around you and men are abusing. . .
amusing themselves, but you're not happy, Goose. . . . your
soul is miserable. . . (*To a dummy.*) Ah, dummy, if only. . . .

ZOYA *silently enters the bedroom from the rear.*

GOOSE. To you alone, you dumb mummy. . . .dummy, will I
tell my secret: I am. `. . .

ZOYA. In love!

GOOSE. Zoya! Have you been heaves. . . eavesdropping on
me?. . . Well, I don't mind – you're Zoya. . . . Zoya, a serpent

has coiled itself round my heart. . . . Oh, Zoya, instinct tells me she's worthless. . . . but I'm her slave!

ZOYA. Dear Goose, she can't be worth so much agony. You'll find another one.

GOOSE. Oh no, never. Even so, Zoya, please show me someone else, so that I can forget about her, even for a while, and stop myself from eating my heart out. . . . She doesn't love me, Zoya!

ZOYA. Dear Goose, my old friend, just wait a few minutes and you'll see a woman who'll make you forget everyone else in the world. And she'll be yours, because what woman can resist you, Goose?

GOOSE. Thank you, Zoya, for those kind words!

Enter OBOLONSKY *and* AMETISTOV, *both in white tie and tails.*

GOOSE. I want to show my appreciation, Zoya – how much do I owe you?

ZOYA. I don't want to take any money from you, Goose.

GOOSE. You may not want to take it, but I want to give it. Go on – there's five hundred roubles.

ZOYA. *Merci.*

GOOSE (*To* AMETISTOV). Aha! The manager! You have created a paradise, in which the tortured soul can find rest and peace. There you are – (*Hands him money.*)

AMETISTOV. *Danke sehr.*

GOOSE (*To* OBOLONSKY). Count! Your piano-playing is superb! Kindly accept this. . . . (*Hands him money.*)

OBOLONSKY. *Merci.* When the times have changed for the better, I will send you my seconds.

GOOSE. Please do – I'll give them something too.

AMETISTOV. Bravo!. . . . *Monsieur Goose, attention s'il vous plait!* There will be a short pause for a change of scene, and then we will show you our newest and most stunning creation – direct from Paris. Lights! (*Switches off lights.*)

For a few moments the whole apartment is in total darkness, then the lights are gradually turned on until the scene is lit by a soft glow. The catwalk is in position, chairs have been set out and on them are seated ZOYA, GOOSE, ROBBER, DEAD BODY, MARYA NIKIFOROVNA, LIZANKA *and* MME. IVANOVA. OBOLONSKY *is at the piano.* AMETISTOV *emerges from behind the curtain drawn across the niche.*

AMETISTOV. *Attention, Messieurs 'dames, s'il vous plait! Le nouveau modèle en couleur de lilas!* Shown at the Paris collection only last week! Price – six thousand francs! *Défilez, s'il vous plait!*

OBOLONSKY *strikes up a waltz.* ALLA *glides on to the catwalk in time to the music.*

ALL. Bravo! Bravo! (*Applause.*)

GOOSE (*Instantly sober*). What is this?!

ALLA. Oh, it's you! How did you get here?

GOOSE. How do you like that?! *She* asks *me* how I got here – when I should be asking *her* how *she* got here!

ALLA. I work here as a model.

GOOSE. A model! The woman I love! Here am I, proposing to leave my wife and children so that I can marry this creature – and she goes to work as a model! Have you any idea, you wretched woman, what this place is?

ALLA. Yes, it's a fashion house.

GOOSE. It may be written 'fashion house', but it's pronounced 'whorehouse'!

ROBBER. What's that? What did you say?

GOOSE. My dear comrades, have you ever seen a fashion house where the collection is only shown in the middle of the night, launched on an ocean of champagne and to the strains of suggestive music?

DEAD BODY. Quite right. . . . Why on earth should there be music? I ask you. . . .

AMETISTOV. *Pardon, pardon,* but. . . .

ZOYA. Ah, *now* I see! (*Mimics* ALLA's *voice.*) 'Since my husband died, Zoya Denisovna, there has been no man in my life. . . .'

Why, you little fraud! To think that I warned you, tried to help and protect you – and you pay me back by creating a scandal!

GOOSE. Zoya Denisovna, you have procured me a whore, disguised as a fashion model, who turns out to be the woman I'm going to marry. . . .

ALLA. I'm not marrying you!

GOOSE. And who is, what's more, my mistress!

DEAD BODY. Oh thank God – now I'm beginning to enjoy myself. . . .

OBOLONSKY (*To* GOOSE). Sir, will you kindly cease insulting this lady?

GOOSE. Oh, shut up! Go away and play the piano.

ZOYA. Gentlemen – there has been a slight misunderstanding which will all be cleared up in a moment. Do, please, go back into the dining – er, the ballroom . . . Monsieur Ametistov, please take over!

AMETISTOV. Of course, of course. This way, please, ladies and gentlemen. Take your partners for the foxtrot. Meanwhile in here everything will be resolved as between friends. . . . This sort of thing quite often happens in high society. . . . Lizanka! Ivan Vasilievich! Will you lead the way?

The men and women pair off and exeunt, followed by AMETISTOV *and* OBOLONSKY. ZOYA *remains in the niche, concealed behind the curtain.*

GOOSE. You – in this so-called 'fashion studio'?!

ALLA. And what are you doing here, for that matter?

GOOSE. Me? I'm a man. I wear trousers – and not a dress that's open down the front to below your navel! I came here because you're driving me to despair. And what's your reason?

ALLA. Money.

GOOSE. What do you want money for?

ALLA. To go abroad.

GOOSE. I won't give you money for that.

ALLA. That's exactly why I took this job.

GOOSE. But you have everything you could possibly want here in Moscow! I've proposed to you seven times! And you want to go abroad. . . . I suppose they're all waiting for you there – no doubt the president of France is getting worried because Alla Vadimovna hasn't arrived yet!

ALLA. Yes, someone in Paris is getting worried about me, though it's not the president – it's my fiancé.

GOOSE. Who?. . . . Your *fiancé*?!. . . . If that's true, then you're nothing but a . . . a . . . little slut!

ALLA. How dare you insult me. I admit I kept you in the dark about it, but then I never imagined you were going to fall in love with me. I wanted to get enough money from you so that I could buy a ticket to Paris – and then off I would go!

GOOSE. Take as much money as you want, only stay. . . .

ALLA. No, I will not stay at any price.

GOOSE. I see. . . . Now that you're wearing my rings, it's 'not at any price', is it? Look at your fingers.

ALLA (*Pulls rings off fingers and throws them to the floor*). There! There! There! You can have them all back!

GOOSE. Who cares about rings? Answer my question: will you marry me or not?

ALLA. No, I will not!

GOOSE. I'll count to three. One. Two. . . . I'll count to ten. . . .

ALLA. Stop counting, Boris, you're wasting your time. I'm not going to marry you. I don't love you.

GOOSE. You whore!

ALLA. How dare you. . . .

ZOYA (*Appearing from the niche*). Oh, don't be such a damned fool, Alla!

AMETISTOV (*Enters suddenly*). *Pardon*, Monsieur Goose. . . .

GOOSE. Get out!

AMETISTOV. *Pardon*, Boris Semyonovich. . . . Alla Vadimovna, do come with me, you need to rest. . . . and compose yourself. . . .

ALLA (*Starts to go*). Zoya Denisovna, I apologise for causing such a scene. . . . I'll return the dress to you. . . .

ZOYA. You're so stupid you'd better keep it, you little idiot!

GOOSE (*To* ALLA). Stop! Where are you going? Abroad?

ALLA. Yes – even if I die in the attempt!

AMETISTOV throws ALLA's *coat over her shoulders, and she runs off.*

GOOSE (*Shouts after* ALLA). I won't let you do it!

ZOYA. Calm him down, for God's sake.

AMETISTOV. All right, I will. You go and join the guests.

Exit ZOYA, *closing the door behind her.*

GOOSE (*Into space*). You'll sell your things one by one in the flea market, you'll end up in the V.D. ward. . . . And I'll watch you walking the streets in your lilac dress. . . . (*Falls to the ground in a fit of anguish.*)

AMETISTOV. Oh, Boris Semyonovich, do be careful – the carpet's so dirty. . . . Don't worry, everything will be all right in the end. She's not the only woman in the world, is she? Forget her! She's not even pretty, *entre nous soît dit*, she's really rather . . . *ordinaire* . . .

GOOSE. Go away and leave me to my misery.

AMETISTOV. Excellent! The first sign of recovery. Have a good moan all by yourself. . . . There are drinks and cigarettes, just help yourself. . . . (*Exit.*)

A foxtrot is heard offstage.

GOOSE. Goose is grieving. . . . Why do you grieve, poor man? Because you have suffered a tragedy. . . . Oh, wretched Goose! I achieve everything a man could want – only to be infected by the virulent poison of love and now I'm lying on the carpet. And where? In a brothel!. . . . Alla! Come back! (*Loudly.*) Alla! Come back!

AMETISTOV (*Enters*). A little quieter please, Boris Semyonovich, or the proletariat downstairs may hear us. . . . (*Exit, closing the door behind him.*)

KO KA-IN *enters silently, looks round and approaches the prostrate* GOOSE.

GOOSE. Go away, I'm grieving. . . .

KO KA-IN. Why you glieve?

GOOSE. I don't want to see a single human being, except, perhaps, you, because you have a kind face. . . . Ko Ka-In, my little Chinaman. . . . I am torn by grief and that is why I'm lying on the carpet.

KO KA-IN. Glief. . . . I too have glief. . . .

GOOSE. Ah, Chinaman. . . . What have you to grieve about? You're young, the future is all yours. . . .

KO KA-IN. Madam cheat you? All madams velly, velly bad. . . . But not to wolly! You find another madam. . . . In Moscow many, many madams. . . .

GOOSE. I'll never find another madam!

KO KA-IN. Why not? You got no money?

GOOSE. My dear Chinaman, getting money was never my problem. No, my brain has never been able to solve a different problem: how to turn money into love. Look! (*Pulls several thick wads of banknotes out of his pockets.*) I made five thousand this morning. And now this evening I'm struck by a blow that has felled me to the ground, leaving me lying by the roadside, where everyone can spit on the stricken Goose just as I spit on all this money.

KO KA-IN. Spit on money? Funny man! You have money and no madam. . . .I have madam, but where is money? Let me take money and iron it smooth for you.

GOOSE. Take it and iron it if you like.

KO KA-IN. Ah, loubles, loubles, lovely loubles. (*Suddenly draws a knife and stabs GOOSE under the left shoulderblade. GOOSE expires without a sound.*) Loubles. . . . now for warm Shanghai. (*Puts money away, removes GOOSE's gold watch and chain, pulls the rings from his fingers, wipes the blade of his knife on GOOSE's jacket, lifts* up the body and puts it into an armchair as if asleep. He turns down the light and says in a loud whisper.) Manyuska!

MANYUSHKA (*Puts her head round the door*). What do you want?

KO KA-IN. Sshhh. . . . Now we go away Shanghai. . . . go to station and catch tlain. . . .

MANYUSHKA. What have you done, you devil?

KO KA-IN. I kill the goose.

MANYUSHKA. Oh, horrors. . . . you monster!. . . .

KO KA-IN. Go, or I kill you too! In a moment soon be plenty tlouble!

MANYUSHKA. Oh, my God! (*Exeunt* MANYUSHKA *and* KO KA-IN).

AMETISTOV (*Enters on tiptoe*). I've just come in for a moment, Boris Semyonovich, to find out how you're feeling. . . . Well, how are you? Ah, you've over-excited yourself, I can see that. Your hand is so cold. . . . (*Suddenly stares hard at* GOOSE.) What? Hell's bells! Some bandit's done him in!. . . . This, comrades, was *not* on the programme. What happens now? This is it. . . . curtains. . . . Of course – Ko Ka-In! Robbed him and scarpered. . . . But what about *me*? Goodbye France, goodbye Nice! (*Pauses. Starts to sing in a dull voice:*) 'Twas evening and the stars were shining. . . .' Hell! What am I doing sitting here? Action! (*Pulls off his tail coat and white tie, runs into* ZOYA's *bedroom, opens the desk and extracts money and papers, which he stuffs into his pockets. Pulls out his old suitcase from under the bed, takes out his old army tunic and cap and puts them on*). Ah, my faithful old Comrade Suitcase – it's you and me on our own again. But where do I go now? Kindly tell me, comrades – where in God's name can I go this time? Ah, well no time left. Merciless fate strikes again. . . . Goodbye, Zoya, and forgive me. I had no choice. Farewell, Mme. Zoya's apartment – it was fun while it lasted! (*Exit with suitcase.*)

Pause.

The door into the bedroom is opened quietly and into the room creep the FIRST *and* SECOND STRANGERS, *followed by two more* STRANGERS.

ZOYA (*Enters sitting room*). Are you alone, Boris

Semyonovich?. . . .But where's Ametistov? (*Stares at the body.*) Oh my God, my God! We're finished, ruined! Oh, my God! (*Whispers loudly through the doorway.*) Pavel!

Enter OBOLONSKY.

ZOYA. Pavel, something quite terrible has happened! Look! (*Points at* GOOSE.)

OBOLONSKY (*Peering at the body*). What's happened!

ZOYA. It's disaster! It was that Chinaman – he and Ametistov. We must run, Pavel! We must escape!

OBOLONSKY. Escape? Why? How?

ZOYA. Come to your senses, Pavel! Don't you see? It's murder – here in the apartment! But why am I just standing here. . . . The money's in the bedroom. We must get it and go. . . .

1ST STRANGER (*Entering from bedroom*). Steady on, citizeness, you're not going anywhere.

ZOYA. Who are you?

1ST STRANGER. Calm down. We have a warrant.

OBOLONSKY. Zoya, what is happening.

ZOYA. Ah, I see now. . . . This is the end, Pavel. Be a man. Remember – we're innocent.

2ND STRANGER. Who is dancing in there?

ZOYA. My guests. Kindly note that we have nothing – absolutely nothing – to do with this murder. It was the Chinaman and Ametistov.

1ST STRANGER. Quiet, citizeness. (*Goes over to the main double doors, flings them open.*) Your papers, please, citizens!

Blackout

Flight

A Play in Eight Dreams

Translated by Michael Glenny

Characters

SERAFÍMA KORZÚKHIN	A young lady of Petersburg
SERGÉI GOLUBKÓV	Son of a professor of philosophy from Petersburg
ATHANASIUS	Archbishop of Simferopol, chaplain-general to the White Russian forces, alias MAKHROV, a chemist
PAÍSIOS	A monk
AGED ABBOT	
BÁYEV	Regimental commander in Budyonny's cavalry army
TROOPER	In Budyonny's cavalry army
GRIGÓRY CHARNÓTA	A Zaporozhets cossack, major-general in the White army
BARABÁNCHIKOVA	A lady existing entirely in General Charnota's imagination
LYÚSKA	General Charnota's mistress
KRAPÍLIN	Charnota's orderly
DE BRISARD	Commander of a White Hussar regiment
ROMÁN KHLÚDOV	
GOLOVÁN	Cossack captain, Khludov's aide-de-camp
STATION COMMANDANT	
STATION MASTER	
NIKOLÁYEVNA	Stationmaster's wife
ÓLGA	Stationmaster's 4-year-old daughter
PARAMÓN KORZÚKHIN	Serafima's husband
TÍKHII	Chief of counter-intelligence
SKÚNSKY	
GÚRIN	Counter-intelligence officials
COMMANDER-IN-CHIEF OF THE WHITE RUSSIAN ARMY	
GIRL CASHIER	
YÁNKO YÁNKOVICH	The cockroach king
FIGURE	in bowler hat and quartermaster's epaulettes
TURKISH WOMAN	
BEAUTIFUL PROSTITUTE	
AMOROUS GREEK	
ANTOINE GRÍSHCHENKO	Korzukhin's manservant

MONKS; WHITE STAFF OFFICERS; COSSACKS OF THE
WHITE C-in-C's BODYGUARD; COUNTER-INTELLIGENCE
OFFICIALS; BRITISH, FRENCH AND ITALIAN SAILORS;
TURKISH AND ITALIAN POLICEMEN; GREEK AND TURKISH
BOYS; ARMENIAN AND GREEK FACES AT WINDOWS;
ISTANBUL MOB

The first dream takes place in Southern Russia, October 1920.
The second, third and fourth dreams take place in the Crimea,
November 1920.
The fifth and sixth dreams take place in the summer of 1921 in
Constantinople.
The seventh dream occurs in Paris, Autumn 1921.
The eighth dream takes place in Constantinople, Autumn 1921.

FIRST DREAM

The abbey church of St. Nicholas.

The sound of a choir of monks chanting the Orthodox liturgy is faintly heard rising from below.

Gradually the shadowy interior is revealed by the light of a few votive candles in front of ikons. Their unsteady flicker shows up the desk where candles are sold, a wide bench beside it, a barred window, the brown face of a saint in a fresco, the faded wings of seraphim, gilded candelabra. Outside, a cheerless October evening, sleet. On the bench, swathed in a horse-blanket, lies BARABANCHIKOVA.

MAKHROV, in sheepskin jerkin and fur hat on his long hair, is leaning on the window-sill and straining to discern something in the murk outside.

SERAFIMA, dressed in a fur coat, is seated on the abbot's high-backed throne. To judge from her face she is ill. Beside her, on the abbot's footstool, is GOLUBKOV, a young man with a Petersburg look to him, wearing gloves and a long, black astrakhan-collared overcoat.

GOLUBKOV (*listening to the chanting*). Can you hear it, Serafima? I've just realised that they must be in a crypt underneath us . . . How weird this all is! Do you know there are moments when I honestly believe I'm dreaming? We've been on the run right across Russia for a month now, Serafima, and the further we go the more incredible it seems . . . Look – we've even landed up in church! When all that terrible fighting was going on this morning I actually felt homesick for Petersburg – I did, you know! Suddenly, quite clearly, I saw the green-shaded lamp in my study . . .

SERAFIMA. Moods like that are fatal, Sergei. Beware of nostalgia when you're running away from something. Wouldn't you have done better to have stayed?

GOLUBKOV. Oh no, there's no turning back now, whatever happens. Anyway, *you* know what it is that keeps me going on this ghastly journey . . . since that day we bumped into each other in the guard's van, under the lamplight – remember? In fact it wasn't so very long ago, but I feel I've known you for years. *You* make our nightmare escape in this filthy autumn weather bearable, Serafima, and I shall feel proud and happy when we reach the Crimea and I can deliver you safe and sound to your husband. I shall miss you, but I shall be happy because you'll be happy . . .

SERAFIMA *silently puts her hand on* GOLUBKOV's *shoulder and he caresses it*

Your hand's very hot. Have you got a temperature?

SERAFIMA. No, it's nothing.

GOLUBKOV. What d'you mean – nothing? You're feverish!

SERAFIMA. Nonsense, Sergei, it'll go . . .

Dull thump of distant gunfire. BARABANCHIKOVA *twitches and groans.*

My dear, you need help. Look, one of us must try and get through to the village, there's sure to be a midwife there.

GOLUBKOV. I'll go.

BARABANCHIKOVA *stops him from going by grabbing the hem of his coat.*

SERAFIMA. Why don't you want him to go?

BARABANCHIKOVA (*coyly*). Don't bother.

SERAFIMA *and* GOLUBKOV *are mystified.*

MAKHROV (*quietly to* GOLUBKOV). A most peculiar person!

GOLUBKOV (*in a whisper*). Do you think . . .

MAKHROV. I don't think anything, but . . . in these troubled times, my dear sir, one is apt to find some strange bedfellows! A mysterious woman . . . lying in a church . . .

The subterranean chanting stops.

PAISIOS (*appearing silently from the crypt, black-clad, terrified*). Papers, papers, have your papers ready, good people! (*Blows out all the candles except one.*)

SERAFIMA, GOLUBKOV *and* MAKHROV *produce their papers.* BARABANCHIKOVA *thrusts out a hand and puts her passport on top of the blanket.*

BAYEV (*in a short fur-lined coat, spattered with mud, bursts in. Behind him is a trooper with a lantern*). God damn all monks! Ugh, the place is infested with them. Hey, you, father superior or whatever you call yourself – where's the spiral staircase up to the belfry?

PAISIOS. Here, here . . .

BAYEV (*to* TROOPER). Go and have a look.

TROOPER *disappears through iron doorway.*

BAYEV (*to* PAISIOS). Was there a light in the belfry?

PAISIOS. Light? Light? What light? No one . . .

BAYEV. There was a flashing light up there! Now if I find anybody up in that belfry I'll put every last one of you up against a wall – including you, you old black devil. You've been signalling to the Whites with a lantern.

PAISIOS. Lord have mercy on us!

BAYEV. Who are these people? You said there were no strangers in this monastery.

PAISIOS. They are refugees, ref . . .

SERAFIMA. Comrade, we were caught in the village when the firing started this morning and we ran to the monastery for safety. (*Points to* BARABANCHIKOVA.) This woman is going to give birth at any moment . . .

BAYEV (*walks over to* BARABANCHIKOVA, *picks up her passport and reads it*). Barabanchikova, married woman . . .

PAISIOS (*petrified with terror, whispers*). Oh Lord, oh Lord above, preserve us! (*Starts to creep away.*) Holy Demetrius, blessed martyr, preserve . . .

BAYEV. Where's your husband? (*Grabs* PAISIOS).

BARABANCHIKOVA *groans.*

You've chosen a fine time and place to have a baby, haven't you. (*To* MAKHROV.) Papers!

MAKHROV. Here you are. I'm a chemist from Mariupol.

BAYEV. Rather a lot of you 'chemists' in a front-line area, aren't there?

MAKHROV. I was out buying food, cucumbers and . . .

BAYEV. Cucumbers!

TROOPER (*bursts in*). Comrade Bayev! There was nobody up in the belfry but I saw something else . . . (*whispers in* BAYEV's *ear*.)

BAYEV. Did you, by God. Where were they coming from?

TROOPER. It was pitch dark, but I saw them all right, comrade commander.

BAYEV. All right, let's go. (*To* GOLUBKOV, *who is offering his papers*). No time now, later. (*To* PAISIOS.) You monks wouldn't get mixed up in a civil war, would you?

PAISIOS. Oh no, no, no . . .

BAYEV. You just pray, I suppose? But I wonder – who do you pray for? For the black barons or for the Soviets? All right, I'll be back soon and I'll sort you out tomorrow. (*Exit, with* TROOPER.)

Words of command heard outside, then complete silence. PAISIOS *crosses himself feverishly, lights the candles again and disappears.*

MAKHROV. They've drawn a blank . . . It is truly written: thou shalt brand them with a mark on their hand and on their brow . . . did you see their five-pointed stars?

GOLUBKOV (*in a whisper to* SERAFIMA). I can't make it out – I thought this locality was occupied by the Whites. What were those Reds doing here? Have they suddenly broken through? How could this happen?

BARABANCHIKOVA. It happened because General Krapchikov is no general – he's an arsehole. (*To* SERAFIMA.) Pardon, madame.

GOLUBKOV (*dully*). Well?

BARABANCHIKOVA. Well – well what? He was sent a signal that the Red cavalry had outflanked him and he, God rot his soul, put off deciphering the signal until next morning and sat down to play whist instead.

GOLUBKOV. Well?

BARABANCHIKOVA. He's nothing but a stuffed dummy in red breeches.

MAKHROV. Oho, oho, *what* a curious person!

GOLUBKOV. Excuse me, but you seem very well informed: I was told that General Charnota's headquarters was supposed to be here in Kurchulan . . .

BARABANCHIKOVA. You were told right. The headquarters certainly was here. Only now it's gone.

GOLUBKOV. And where's it gone to?

BARABANCHIKOVA. I can tell you that all right – to hell.

MAKHROV. How do you happen to know all this, madame?

BARABANCHIKOVA. You're very inquisitive for an archbishop, aren't you?

MAKHROV. What do you mean by calling me an archbishop?

BARABANCHIKOVA. Oh, shut up and go away – you bore me.

PAISIOS *rushes in again, extinguishes all the candles except one and peers out of the window.*

GOLUBKOV. What is it now?

PAISIOS. Ah, sir, how are we to know who the Lord has sent us now? We may all be dead by morning! (*Vanishes as though swallowed up by the floor.*)

Clatter of horses hooves, flickering lights.

SERAFIMA. Is it a fire?

GOLUBKOV. No, those are torches. I simply don't understand it, Serafima! They're White troops, I swear it, they're Whites! We're saved! Thank God, Serafima, the Whites are back! The officers are wearing epaulettes!

BARABANCHIKOVA (*sitting up, still wrapped in the horse-blanket*). Be quiet, you bloody little intellectual, and shut your trap! Epaulettes! This isn't Petersburg, this is the Ukraine and funny things can happen. Just because they're wearing epaulettes it doesn't mean they're Whites! Supposing it was a detachment disguised in White uniforms? What then?

Suddenly a muffled bell begins to peal.

Christ, they've started ringing the bells! That means those idiotic monks have seen them too. (*To* GOLUBKOV.) What colour are their breeches?

GOLUBKOV. Red! . . . Some more have just ridden into the courtyard and they're wearing blue breeches with red down the sides . . .

BARABANCHIKOVA. Red down the sides! God help us all. Do you mean they have red stripes?

DE BRISARD's *word of command is heard:* 'No. 1 Squadron – dismount!'

What's that? It can't be! It's his voice! (*To* GOLUBKOV.) Now you can shout! You have my full permission to yell your head off! (*Throws off rags and horse-blanket and jumps up dressed as* GENERAL CHARNOTA, *in cossack uniform with grey persian-lamb fur hat, crumpled silver epaulettes. He stuffs the revolver he was holding into his pocket, runs to the window, flings it open, shouts.*) Hullo there, hussars! Hullo there, Don Cossacks! Colonel De Brisard – report to me!

Door opens. First to run in is LYUSKA, *wearing nurse's headdress, leather jerkin, riding boots and spurs. Behind her enters the heavily bearded* DE BRISARD *and the orderly* KRAPILIN, *carrying a torch.*

LYUSKA. Grisha! (*Flings herself at* CHARNOTA *and embraces him.*) I can't believe my eyes! You're alive! You escaped! (*Shouts out of the window.*) Listen, men! General Charnota's escaped from the Reds!

Noise and shouting outside.

And we were going to hold a memorial service for you!

CHARNOTA. I was as near death as I am to you now. I'd ridden over to Krapchikov's headquarters and the son of a bitch sat me down to play whist . . . the stuffed dummy . . . suddenly there was a burst of machine-gun fire – Budyonny had dropped on us like a bolt from the blue! Shot the whole headquarters to pieces! I had to shoot my way out, jumped through a window and over the back gardens till I landed up in the village schoolmaster's house – man called Barabanchikov. Quick, I said, give me your papers in case they catch me! He was in such a panic he picked up the wrong papers, so that when I crept into this monastery I looked at them and they were his wife's papers – Madame

Barabanchikova – and what's more there was a doctor's certificate saying she was pregnant! Well, what could I do? The place was crawling with Reds, so I had to creep into church as I was – I lay down and pretended I was having a baby, then I heard a pair of spurs clinking . . .

LYUSKA. Who was it?

CHARNOTA. One of Budyonny's regimental commanders.

LYUSKA. God!

CHARNOTA. Just you watch your step, you bolshevik, I thought to myself. I had a loaded revolver under my blanket. Go on, lift it up! They'll give you a lovely funeral! He took my passport but he never touched the blanket!

LYUSKA *whistles.*

CHARNOTA (*runs out of the doorway, shouting.*) Bravo, Cossacks! Well done, lads!

Shouts in reply. LYUSKA *runs out after* CHARNOTA.

DE BRISARD. Well, I'm going to lift up a few blankets! Damn me if I don't hang somebody in this monastery just for fun! Obviously the Reds were in such a hurry that they overlooked this bunch. (*To* MAKHROV.) Well, l needn't ask you for your papers. I can tell your sort from the length of your hair. Krapilin, bring some light over here.

PAISIOS (*Rushing up to* DE BRISARD). What are you doing! Don't you know who this is? His grace – his grace the Right Reverend Archbishop Athanasius!

DE BRISARD. What the hell are you gibbering about, you black devil?

MAKHROV *throws off his fur hat and sheepskin jerkin.* DE BRISARD *stares into his face.*

What?! Is it really you, archbishop? How on earth did you come to be here?

ATHANASIUS. I came to Kurchulan to bless the Don Cossack corps and the Reds captured me during a raid. The monks provided me with identity papers, thank God.

DE BRISARD. Well, I'm damned! (*To* SERAFIMA.) Papers, woman.

SERAFIMA. I am the wife of the deputy minister for trade. I was stranded in Petersburg. My husband has already reached the Crimea, and I'm on my way to join him. These are false papers and this is my real passport. My name is Korzukhin.

DE BRISARD. Mille excuses, madame! And what about you there, you great long caterpillar, I suppose you are the . Prosecutor of the Holy Synod?

GOLUBKOV. Excuse me but I am not a caterpillar and I am certainly not the Procurator of the Holy Synod! I am the son of Professor Golubkov the famous philosopher and I am a university teacher. I have escaped from Petersburg to join the Whites because it has become impossible for me to go on working in Petersburg.

DE BRISARD. Charming! I see this isn't a monastery at all – it's Noah's ark!

A trap-door in the floor opens and from it rises the aged, decrepit ABBOT followed by a choir of monks, all holding candles.

ABBOT (*to* ATHANASIUS). His Grace the Archbishop! (*To* MONKS.) Brethren! We have snatched our lord archbishop from the sinful clutches of the socialists!

MONKS enrobe the nervous ATHANASIUS in a cope and hand him a crozier.

My lord. Receive again thy pastoral staff and with it comfort and succour thy flock. . . .

ATHANASIUS. Look down from heaven, oh God, behold this Thy vineyard and stretch out Thy right hand over it!

MONKS suddenly begin intoning Greek hymn, CHARNOTA appears in the doorway, followed by LYUSKA.

CHARNOTA. Have you all gone mad? This is no time to hold a service! Singing – at a moment like this! Clear off! (*Gestures to the choir to go away.*)

ATHANASIUS. Hence, brethren!

ABBOT and MONKS vanish underground.

CHARNOTA (*To* ATHANASIUS). Archbishop, why in God's name did you have to start a service now of all times? We've got to cut and run! The Reds are on our heels and if we don't get

moving they'll catch us. Budyonny is pushing us into the sea.
We must go to the Crimea and join up with Roman Khludov.

ATHANASIUS. This is terrible! (*Grabs his sheepskin jerkin.*) Have
you a wagon I could ride on? (*Disappears.*)

CHARNOTA. Give me a map. Light, Krapilin. (*Studies the map.*)
We're cut off. Hopeless.

LYUSKA. Damn that fool Krapchikov . . .

CHARNOTA. Wait a minute! I've found a loophole! (*To* DE
BRISARD.) Take your regiment and head straight for the
Almanaika river. Draw the Reds after you for a bit, then
disengage, turn *here*, double back and ford the river at Babii Gai,
even if you have to swim for it. I'll follow you with the Don
Cossacks after a short interval and make for this Dukhobor
settlement *here*. Then I'll wheel south-west to the railway line at
Arabat and meet you there. Move off in five minutes from now.

DE BRISARD. Very good, sir.

CHARNOTA. Phew!. . . .Give me a swig from your flask,
colonel.

GOLUBKOV. Did you hear that, Serafima? The Whites are
leaving! We must go with them, or we'll be caught by the Reds
again . . . Serafima, why don't you answer me? What's the
matter with you?

LYUSKA. Give me a drop too.

DE BRISARD *hands the flask to* LYUSKA.

GOLUBKOV (*to* CHARNOTA). General, I beg of you – take us
with you. Mrs. Korzukhin is sick . . . We're trying to get
through to the Crimea . . . Have you got a field hospital?

CHARNOTA. Did you go to a university?

GOLUBKOV. Yes, of course . . .

CHARNOTA. Funny – you strike me as being completely
uneducated. What the hell good is a field hospital going to be to
you if you get a bullet through your head at Babii Gai? Why
didn't you ask if we had an X-ray machine as well? Christ, you
intellectuals . . . Give me some more of that brandy!

LYUSKA. We must take her. She's pretty and if the Reds get her
you know what they'll do to her . . .

GOLUBKOV. Serafima, get up! We're going!

SERAFIMA (*dully*). You know, Sergei, I really think I *am* ill . . . you go on alone, I'll find a bed here in the monastery . . . I feel terribly hot . . .

GOLUBKOV. You can't stay here, Serafima! You must get up!

SERAFIMA. I want a drink . . . and I want to go home . . . to Petersburg . . .

GOLUBKOV. What's the matter with her?

LYUSKA. Typhus, that's what's the matter with her.

DE BRISARD. You must leave this place, madame, or the Reds will get you. Hell, I'm no good at talking to people. Krapilin, you're a great talker, persuade the lady!

KRAPILIN. Yes, sir. You must go.

DE BRISARD (*looking at his wristwatch*). Come on! Time to go. (*Runs out.*)

From outside, words of command: 'Regiment! Prepare to mount!' *Pause, clink of spurs, stamping feet.* 'Regiment! Mount! . . . Regiment! At the trot – march!' *Clatter of hooves as hussars move off.*

LYUSKA. Krapilin! Pick her up, we'll have to move her by force.

KRAPILIN. Very good, ma'am. (KRAPILIN *and* GOLUBKOV *lift* SERAFIMA *to her feet, help her to walk.*)

LYUSKA. Put her in one of the wagons.

Exeunt.

CHARNOTA (*alone, looks at his watch, drinks the rest of the brandy, looks at his watch again*). Time to go.

ABBOT *emerges through the trap-door.*

ABBOT. White General! Where are you going? You cannot abandon us now . . . How can you leave this monastery to its fate when it has given you aid and succour?!

CHARNOTA. Out of my way, father. Tie up the clappers of your bells and hide in the cellar! I must go. Goodbye! (*Exit.*)

Commands offstage: 'Cossacks – mount! At the gallop – march!'

Deafening thunder of hooves, then silence. PAISIOS enters from the crypt.

PAISIOS. Father Abbot! Oh, father Abbot! What are we to do? The Reds will be upon us soon! And we used our bells to signal to the Whites. Must we earn a martyr's crown?

ABBOT. But the archbishop – where is he?

PAISIOS. Gone – gone in a wagon with the baggage-train!

ABBOT. Oh unworthy shepherd, thus to leave his flock! (*Shouts down to the crypt.*) Pray, brethren, pray!

From the crypt rises the muffled chanting of an invocation: 'Holy Father Nicholas, martyr and saint, pray for us . . .'

Darkness settles on the monastery.

The End of the First Dream

SECOND DREAM

From the dark materialises the waiting-room of a large railway station somewhere in the Northern Crimea. Upstage, large windows on to the platform, in darkness lit only by faint blue electric lights. There is a savage frost, completely unexpected for early November in the Crimea. Sivash, Chongar, Perekop and this station are frozen solid. The windows are iced up; beyond them flicker the occasional serpentine lights of passing trams. The room is heated by a number of small, portable cast-iron stoves and kerosene lamps on the tables. In the far corner, over the door leading to the platform, is a notice in the old pre-revolutionary spelling: Operations Section. A glass partition, behind it a government-issue desk lamp with a green shade and two monstrous green eyes – railway guards' lanterns. Beside them, against a dark and peeling background a young horseman in white is spearing a scaly dragon. The young man is St. George, Bringer of Victory, and there burns before him a coloured cut-glass ikon-lamp. The waiting room is in use by WHITE STAFF OFFICERS, most of them wearing fur caps with ear-flaps tied across the top. Innumerable field telephone sets, maps stuck with little flags, typewriters. Now and again a coloured bulb glows on a telephone as it gives a subdued ring.

The headquarters staff of the White Army Group has been installed in this station for the past three days and for three days it has not slept, working like a machine. Only an experienced and attentive observer would notice the film of anxiety clouding the eyes of these men. And there is another look in their eyes – a compound of fear and hope – that can be detected whenever they glance towards what used to be the first class buffet.

There, divided from the rest of the headquarters staff by a tall, glass-fronted dresser, sitting on a high stool at the counter, is ROMAN KHLUDOV. *The man has a bone-white face, black hair neatly parted and cut to regulation length.* KHLUDOV *is snub-nosed, with a clean-shaven, actorish face, seems younger than all the others, but his eyes are old. He is wearing a soldier's greatcoat, belted nonchalantly like a country gentleman wearing a dressing-gown. He has field-service epaulettes of cloth, on which are carelessly sewn the black zig-zag of general's rank. Khaki field-service peaked cap, dirty, tarnished badge. Mittens on his hands.* KHLUDOV *is unarmed. He is ill, this man, sick from head to foot. He frowns, his face twitches and he constantly changes his tone of voice when he speaks. He asks himself questions and answers them. When he wants to manufacture a smile, he bares his teeth. He is a man who arouses fear.* ROMAN KHLUDOV *is sick.*

Beside KHLUDOV, *at a table with several telephones, sits* KHLUDOV's *obedient and completely devoted Cossack aide-de-camp,* CAPTAIN GOLOVAN. *He is typing.*

KHLUDOV (*dictating to* GOLOVAN). '. . . comma. But the Red army commander Frunze did not feel inclined to act the part of a simulated enemy as if we were on manoeuvres. Full Stop. This is not a game of chess nor is it Tsarskoye bloody Selo. Full stop. Signed – Khludov. Full stop.'

GOLOVAN (*hands the typed signal to an orderly*). Encode this signal and send it to the Commander-in-chief.

FIRST STAFF OFFICER (*his face is lit up as the warning light flashes on his telephone, groans*). Yes, Operations . . . yes . . . Budyonny? . . . Budyonny?

SECOND STAFF OFFICER (*wearily picks up telephone*). Hello, Operations . . . where? . . . Taganash? . . . Taganash?

THIRD STAFF OFFICER (*croaking*). No, no, at Karpov Gorge . . . when? how far? . . .

GOLOVAN (*as his warning light glows, handing receiver to* KHLUDOV). It's for you, general . . .

KHLUDOV (*into receiver*). Yes. Yes. Yes. No. Yes. (*Hands receiver back to* GOLOVAN.) Send the station commandant to me.

GOLOVAN. Commandant!

Voices offstage echoing away 'Commandant! Commandant!' *The* COMMANDANT, *a pale officer with a squint, in a peaked cap with a red band, comes trotting anxiously between the tables to* KHLUDOV, *salutes.*

KHLUDOV. I've been waiting an hour for the armoured train on the Taganash line. What's wrong, man? What's wrong? What's wrong?

COMMANDANT (*expressionlessly*). The station master has just reported, sir, that the armoured train can't get through.

KHLUDOV. Send the station master to me.

COMMANDANT (*as he trots away, to a* STAFF OFFICER, *in a hoarse voice*). What does he expect me to do about it?

KHLUDOV. Troubles are starting, I see. An armoured train is suddenly stricken with paralysis. The armoured train has been steaming down the line at full speed as far as here but now it somehow can't get through. (*Rings a bell.*)

Spotlight picks out another sign on the wall in the waiting-room, counter-intelligence section.

As the bell rings TIKHII *emerges from behind partition screening off the counter-intelligence section, walks over to* KHLUDOV *and awaits instructions.*

KHLUDOV (*turning to* TIKHII). Nobody loves us. And because of that our troubles are starting. And nobody cares. They might as well be watching a play for all they care.

TIKHII *says nothing.*

KHLUDOV (*furiously*). I smell something. That stove is giving off fumes. It's dangerous.

GOLOVAN. No, sir. I can't smell any fumes, sir.

The COMMANDANT *returns, followed by* THE STATION MASTER.

KHLUDOV (*to* STATION MASTER). Did you report that the armoured train can't get through.

STATION MASTER (*moves and talks, but he is dead with fear and exhaustion*). Yes, general. It's physically impossible. We've tried to shunt it by hand, but the points are frozen solid.

KHLUDOV. I knew I could smell fumes. Aren't they coming from that stove over there?

GOLGOVAN. I'll see to it, sir. (*To a* STATION OFFICER.) Put that stove out!

STATION MASTER. That's fumes all right.

KHLUDOV (*To* STATION MASTER.) I don't know why, but I somehow feel you're on good terms with the Bolsheviks. Don't be afraid, you can speak frankly. Everyone has his convictions and he shouldn't hide them. There's a cunning look about you.

STATION MASTER (*babbling with terror*). Why ever should you suspect me, general? I've got little children . . . served for years under the emperor Nicholas . . . Olga and Paul, my little babies . . . I haven't slept for thirty hours – God's truth, sir, I haven't – the Speaker of the Duma, Mr. Rodzyanko, sir, knows me personally, if only he was here, sir . . . although I don't agree with his politics . . . my children.

KHLUDOV. You're an honest man, aren't you? And you love your family. Good. Love works wonders, especially in war. (*To* TIKHII *reproachfully*.) But nobody loves *me*. (*Curtly*.) Detail a squad of sappers to help shunt that train. I give you fifteen minutes to have that armoured train on the main line with the signal at green. If within that time my order has not been carried out, arrest the Commandant. And hang the stationmaster from the signal-gantry with a spotlight on the sign above him which will read 'Sabotage'.

Distant sound of a brass band playing a waltz.

STATION MASTER (*limply*). General, sir, my kids don't even go to school yet . . . They're only babies . . .

TIKHII *takes the station master by the arm and leads him away, followed by the* COMMANDANT.

KHLUDOV. What's that – a waltz?

GOLOVAN. It's Charnota, general. He's due to arrive now.

STATION MASTER (*behind a glass partition, shouting desperately into a telephone*). Christopher Fyodorich! This is urgent – for Christ's sake get all the rolling-stock from tracks four and five shunted on to the Taganash line. There'll be a squad of sappers to help you. I don't care how you do it, but for God's sake get it done!

NIKOLAYEVNA (*enters, sidles up to the* STATION MASTER). What's the matter, Vasya?

STATION MASTER. I'm in real trouble this time. The whole family's in trouble! Look – go and get little Olga, bring her here as fast as you can – run!

NIKOLAYEVNA. Olga? Why? (*Runs out.*)

The waltz stops. The door from the platform opens. Enter CHARNOTA *in cossack cloak and fur hat, walks up to* KHLUDOV. LYUSKA *enters with him, but stays by the door.*

CHARNOTA. Composite cavalry division reporting, General, from the Chongar defile.

KHLUDOV *says nothing, stares at* CHARNOTA.

CHARNOTA. *General*! (*points to the distance.*) What's going on here? (*Suddenly pulls off his fur hat.*) Roman! You're the chief of staff – what the hell's going on? Roman, stop staring at me like that and say something!

KHLUDOV. Shut up!

CHARNOTA *puts his hat on again.*

Leave your baggage-train here and take your men to Karpov gorge. Hold the line there for as long as you can.

CHARNOTA. Very good. (*Walks away.*)

LYUSKA. Where to?

CHARNOTA (*grimly*). Karpov gorge.

LYUSKA. I'm coming with you. Just let me get rid of the wounded and the woman with typhus.

CHARNOTA (*glumly*). It'll be dangerous. You may get killed.

LYUSKA. What if I do? (*Exit with* CHARNOTA.)

Sounds of clanking and banging, then the hoarse, martyred shriek of the armoured train's whistle. NIKOLAYEVNA *enters from behind a glass partition, dragging* OLGA *swathed in a shawl.*

NIKOLAYEVNA. Here she is – here's Olga.

STATION MASTER (*into telephone*). You made it, Christopher Fyodorich?! Oh, thank you, thank you! (*Grabs* OLGA *by the hand, runs to* KHLUDOV, *followed by* TIKHII *and* COMMANDANT.)

KHLUDOV (*To* STATION MASTER). Well, my dear fellow, you seem to have done it. Is the train on the main line?

STATION MASTER. Yes, general, we did it! The train's ready to move.

KHLUDOV. What's the child doing here?

STATION MASTER. My little girl, Olga . . . she's a good girl, sir, clever too. Twenty years service, sir . . . Haven't slept for nearly three days, sir . . .

KHLUDOV. Hello, little girl. Can you bowl a hoop yet? Can you? (*Takes a sweet out of his pocket.*) There you are, little girl. My doctors tell me I mustn't smoke, bad for my nerves, so they give me sweets to suck instead. But sweets don't help. I still go on smoking.

STATION MASTER. Take it, Olga darling, take it . . . Say 'thank you' to the kind general, Olga, there's a good girl. (*Picks up OLGA, carries her behind the partition. NIKOLAYEVNA takes the little girl away.*)

Waltz strikes up again, slowly fades into the distance. From a door leading from the station yard enters PARAMON KORZUKHIN, a very sophisticated-looking man in spectacles, wearing an extremely expensive fur coat and carrying a briefcase. Walks up to GOLOVAN, hands him a visiting-card. GOLOVAN passes the card to KHLUDOV.

KHLUDOV. I'm listening.

KORZUKHIN (*To KHLUDOV*). Allow me to introduce myself. Korzukhin, deputy minister of trade. The council of ministers has instructed me, general, to put three questions to you. I have just arrived from Sebastopol. Firstly, they have ordered me to find out what has happened to five workmen who were arrested in Simferopol and brought here to Headquarters on your orders.

KHLUDOV. I see. Oh yes, of course, you must have arrived on the other platform and crossed over. Captain, show the prisoners to the deputy minister.

GOLOVAN. This way please, sir.

Tension. GOLOVAN leads KORZUKHIN to the door on to the platform, opens it and points up into the air. KORZUKHIN shudders, walks back with GOLOVAN to KHLUDOV.

KHLUDOV. Does that answer your first question? Next question please.

KORZUKHIN (*nervously*). The second directly concerns my own ministry. A particularly important consignment of goods has gone astray at this station. I should like to request your permission – and your cooperation, general – to move this consignment to Sebastopol as a matter of urgency.

KHLUDOV (*softly*). What does this consignment consist of?

KORZUKHIN. Furs, for export abroad.

KHLUDOV (*smiling*). Ah, furs for export! How many truckloads?

KORZUKHIN (*handing over a sheet of paper*). This is the waybill, with full details.

KHLUDOV. Captain Golovan! Shunt all the trucks on this waybill on to a siding, douse them with petrol and set fire to them.

GOLOVAN *takes paper, exit.*

(*Quietly.*) Third question – briefly, please.

KORZUKHIN (*almost speechless*). What . . . what is the situation at the front?

KHLUDOV (*yawning*). What do you expect? Chaos. Gunfire. Someone is trying to gas me with a stove that gives off poisonous fumes, the commander-in-chief has sent me a present of some Kuban cossacks, but they can't fight because they haven't got any boots. There's no food and no women. We're all bored stiff with sitting here on these stools like a row of tin parrots in a shooting-gallery. (*Changes his tone, whispers.*) Do you really want to know what the situation is? Go straight back to Sebastopol, Mr Korzukhin, and tell those yellow weevils in your so-called government to start packing their trunks. The Reds will be here tomorrow. And you can tell them something else – a few whores in Paris are going to have to do without their sable coats. So much for your furs.

KORZUKHIN. This is monstrous! (*Stares round desperately.*) I shall regard it as my duty to report you personally to the commander-in-chief.

KHLUDOV (*politely*). Please do.

KORZUKHIN (*staggering, makes for the door, asks as he goes*). When is the next train for Sebastopol?

No one answers. Sounds of train pulling into station.

STATION MASTER (*deathly pale, saluting* KHLUDOV). Special just in from Kerman Kemalchi, sir.

KHLUDOV. Gentlemen! Atten-tion!

The whole headquarters staff jump to attention. Enter two COSSACKS *of the Commander-in-Chief's bodyguard in magenta cloaks, who take up position on either side of the door. Enter* WHITE

COMMANDER-IN-CHIEF, *in white fur hat pushed to the back of his head, wearing long, wide-skirted greatcoat and curved cossack sword. He is followed by* ARCHBISHOP ATHANASIUS, *who bestows a blessing on the headquarters staff, crossing himself and bowing to the ikon.*

C-in-C. Good evening, gentlemen!

ALL OFFICERS (*in chorus*). Good evening, your excellency!

KHLUDOV. Permission to report to your excellency in private, sir.

C-in-C. Very good. Everybody leave the room. (*To* ATHANASIUS.) Archbishop, I must talk to the chief of staff in confidence.

ATHANASIUS. Of course. I trust all is well.

Exeunt all except KHLUDOV *and* C-in-C.

KHLUDOV. Three hours ago the enemy took Yushun. The Bolsheviks are in the Crimea.

C-in-C. Is this the end?

KHUDLOV. Yes.

Silence.

C-in-C (*shouts through the door*). Archbishop!

Enter ATHANSIUS, *nervous and pale.*

Archbishop – abandoned by the Western European powers, stabbed in the back by the treacherous Poles, there is nothing left to us in this fearful hour but to call on the mercy of God.

ATHANASIUS (*realising that disaster has come*). Lord have mercy!

C-in-C. Pray, Archbishop!

ATHANASIUS (*in front of the ikon of St. George*). Why, almighty God, why? Why dost Thou send ever new tribulations upon Thy children, upon these warriors dedicated to Thy Son, our Lord Jesus Christ? The power of the Lord is with us, He blesseth the sword that smiteth the hosts of Midian . . .

The STATION MASTER's *face, distorted with fear, peers from behind the glass partition.*

KHLUDOV. Excuse me for interrupting you, your Grace, but

why bother God now? It's quite obvious that He gave us up long ago. Anyway, why should He be on our side? If you ask me He never was. Our sand has run out, that's all, and now it's the Bolsheviks' turn. Look – St. George is laughing at you!

ATHANASIUS. General – this is blasphemy!

C-in-C. I categorically forbid you to talk in this tone, Khludov. You are obviously ill and I'm only sorry that you didn't go abroad this summer for a cure, as I advised you.

KHLUDOV. Oh, for God's sake! And if I'd gone, then who, might I ask your Excellency, would have made your troops hold the Isthmus of Perekop? Who would have sent Charnota tonight from Chongar to delay the Reds at Karpov gorge? Who would have done your hanging for you? I ask you, your excellency – who would have been your hangman?

C-in-C (grimly). General – be careful . . .

ATHANASIUS. Oh Lord, look down upon them, give them light and strengthen them! For Holy Russia is divided against herself and her hour of travail is come . . .

C-in-C. However, there's no time now to . . .

KHLUDOV. No, there's no time. You must go back to Sebastopol immediately.

C-in-C. Yes. (He takes a sealed envelope from his tunic pocket, hands it to KHLUDOV.) Please read this, then destroy it at once.

KHLUDOV. Ah, I see you came prepared. So you knew in advance? Good. Lord, now lettest Thou Thy servant depart in peace . . . Very good, sir. (Shouts.) His Excellency's train! Escort! Staff!

STATION MASTER (behind partition, rushes to telephone). Clear the line to Kerman Kemalchi! Clear the line!

Enter COSSACKS of the bodyguard and STAFF OFFICERS.

C-in-C. Gentlemen! (STAFF OFFICERS snap to attention.) The chief of staff will give you my orders. May the Lord God send you strength and good fortune to survive our country's terrible fate. I tell you honestly, one and all, that we no longer hold any territory besides the Crimea.

Suddenly the door is flung open and DE BRISARD *appears, his head bandaged. He stand to attention in front of the C-in-C.*

DE BRISARD. Good evening your imperial majesty! (*To* STAFF OFFICERS, *mysteriously*)
'Countess, for one rendezvous
with you,
I'll tell the secrets of my heart . . .'

C-in-C. What is this?

GOLOVAN. Colonel Count de Brisard, sir, commanding the White Hussars. Head wounds and concussion, sir.

KHLUDOV (*to himself*). Chongar . . . Chongar . . .

C-in-C. Put him on my train and send him to Sebastopol. (*Strides out accompanied by his cossack escort.*)

ATHANASIUS Lord have mercy on you! (*Blesses the* STAFF OFFICERS *and exit hastily.*)

DE BRISARD (*as he is helped out by two* STAFF OFFICERS). Sorry . . . 'Countess, for one rendezvous . . .'

STAFF OFFICERS (*struggling with* DE BRISARD). Come on, Colonel, you're going to Sebastopol . . .

DE BRISARD. Sorry . . . didn't mean . . . (*He is removed.*)

KHLUDOV (*opens envelope, reads it, grins mirthlessly. To* GOLOVAN). Send a despatch-rider to General Barbovich at Karpov gorge. Order: disengage from the enemy, make for Yalta at the gallop and embark!

Someone mutters amen. Then silence.

Send another despatch-rider to General Kutyepov: disengage, head for Sebastopol and embark. Fostikov and his Kuban cossacks to Theodosia. Kalinin and the Don cossacks to Kerch. Charnota – to Sebastopol. All troops to embark. This headquarters is to be moved immediately to Sebastopol. The Crimea has surrendered.

GOLOVAN (*running out*). Despatch-riders! Despatch-riders!

STAFF OFFICERS *start to pack up. Maps are rolled up. Telephones disconnected, papers burned in the stoves. Shriek of a locomotive whistle, a train is heard pulling out. Activity grows more feverish and disordered.*

The door on to the platform is thrown open. In walks CHARNOTA followed by SERAFIMA in a cossack cloak. GOLUBKOV and KRAPILIN are trying to hold her back.

GOLUBKOV. Serafima, please, you can't come in here! (*To the astonished* STAFF OFFICERS.) This woman's got typhus!

KRAPILIN. That's right. Typhus.

SERAFIMA (*loudly and piercingly*). Which of you is Roman Khludov?

This stupid question produces total silence.

KHLUDOV. It's all right, let her talk to me. I am Khludov.

GOLUBKOV. Don't listen to her, she's a sick woman.

SERAFIMA. We've been running away ever since we left Petersburg . . . Where have we been running to? To Roman Khludov – he'll take care of us, they said! Everybody keeps saying Khludov, Khludov, Khludov . . . I even dream about Khludov! (*Smiles.*) So now I'm allowed to see him – sitting on a stool, surrounded by men dangling in the air with sacks over their heads . . . Rows and rows of hanged men . . . Beast! Jackal!

GOLUBKOV (*in desperation*). She's got typhus! She's delirious! . . . We've just arrived in General Charnota's wagon-train!

KHLUDOV *rings a bell,* TIKHII *and* GURIN *emerge from behind their partition.*

SERAFIMA. Look out! They're coming for us!

Whispering among the STAFF OFFICERS 'She's a communist . . . . . . communist . . .'

GOLUBKOV. Are you crazy? She's the wife of Korzukhin, deputy minister of trade! She's out of her mind, she doesn't know what she's saying!

KHLUDOV. Good. As far as I can see, when people here *do* know what they're saying, you can't get a word of truth out of them.

GOLUBKOV. She's Korzukhin's wife!

KHLUDOV. Wait a minute! Who, did you say? Korzukhin? The man with the furs? So he's not only a swine, he has a wife who's a communist, has he? What a piece of luck. Now I can really settle accounts with him. If he hasn't managed to get away, send him here at once.

TIKHII *gestures to* GURIN, *who vanishes.*

TIKHII (*quietly to* SERAFIMA). What is your name?

GOLUBKOV. Serafima . . . Serafima Korzukhin . . .

GURIN *brings in* KORZUKHIN. *He is deathly pale.*

Are you Paramon Korzukhin?

KORZUKHIN. Yes, I am.

GOLUBKOV. Thank God! You were coming here to meet us! At last!

TIKHII (*kindly, to* KORZUKHIN). Your wife Serafima has arrived from Petersburg to see you.

KORZUKHIN (*glancing at* TIKHII *and* KHLUDOV, *sensing some kind of trap*). I know no one called Serafima. I have never see this woman before in my life, I'm not expecting to meet anyone from Petersburg. This is a trick.

SERAFIMA (*staring dully at* KORZUKHIN). You . . . you daren't acknowledge me, you loathsome brute!

KORZUKHIN. This is blackmail!

GOLUBKOV (*desperately*). Korzukhin – for God's sake! What are you saying, man? You can't do this!

KHLUDOV. Are you telling the truth? Well, that's your affair, Mr. Korzukhin, and I wish you luck of it. You and your furs. Get out!

Exit KORZUKHIN.

GOLUBKOV. Please – interrogate us! I can prove she's his wife!

KHLUDOV (*To* TIKHII). Take them both out and interrogate them.

TIKHII (*To* GURIN). Take them to Sebastopol.

GURIN *takes* SERAFIMA *by the arm.*

GOLUBKOV. You're not fools – I can see that. I can prove it . . .

SERAFIMA. He's the only real man I've met since I left Petersburg

. . . Oh, Krapilin, they told me you were so good at talking, why don't you say something?

SERAFIMA *and* GOLUBKOV *are led out.*

KRAPILIN (*walks up to* KHLUDOV). Very well. Like she says – jackal! But you can't win a war just by tying hangman's knots. Weren't you satisfied, you swine, when you sent my regiment to be slaughtered at Perekop? Wasn't that enough? Now you've caught a woman. All she did was take pity on the men you'd hanged. But no one can get away from you, can they? If you see someone – it's into the sack with them and hoist them up! What do you feed on – dead men's flesh?

TIKHII. Permission to remove him, sir?

KHLUDOV. No. There's some sense in what he says about winning a war. Go on, soldier, go on.

TIKHII (*signals with his index finger.* TWO MEN *emerge from the counter-intelligence section. Whispers to a* THIRD MAN). Get me a board. (*The men slip out.*)

KHLUDOV. What's your name, soldier?

THIRD COUNTER-INTELLIGENCE MAN *returns with a plywood board.*

KRAPILIN (*with the eloquence of despair*). What does it matter what my name is? Nobody knows who I am – I'm just private Krapilin. But your time's coming, you butcher, when you'll finish up stiff and dead in the gutter! Just you wait – sitting there on your stool. (*Smiles.*) You won't wait, of course, you're running away now – all the way to Constantinople! Coward – all you can do is hang women and civilians!

KHLUDOV. You're wrong, soldier. At Chongar I led my troops into action and I was wounded twice. I went in to action with bands playing.

KRAPILIN. Yes – if your bands hadn't played, you madman, half those men would be alive now! (*Suddenly looks round, shudders, stares, drops to knees, whines pitifully.*) Oh, sir, forgive me sir, I'm nobody sir, just private Krapilin! I don't know what I've been saying, sir!

KHLUDOV. No! Too late. You began well, but you finished badly – on your knees. Hang him! I can't bear the sight of him.

In a moment two COUNTER–INTELLIGENCE MEN *throw a black hood over* KRAPILIN *and hustle him out.*

GOLOVAN (*enters*). Orders carried out, sir. All despatch-riders have left.

KHLUDOV. Everybody on board the train. Captain, have my escort fall in on the platform.

Exeunt.

KHLUDOV (*alone, picks up the telephone*). Chief of staff speaking. Tell the commander of the armoured train to proceed up the line as far as he can go and fire at random all the way. When he gets to Taganash, halt and bombard the town till it's flat. We'll give them something to remember us by. Then full steam back to Sebastopol and rip up the track behind him! (*Replaces receiver, sits alone, hunched up on his stool.*)

Distant wail of armoured train.

What's the matter with me? Am I sick?

Salvo of gunfire from the armoured train. The shock is so violent that the station lights go out and all the frost-covered windows are shattered. The platform is now visible. A row of lamp-standards, giving a weak blue light. Hanging from the nearest is a hooded man with a board tied to his chest marked: 'Private Krapilin – Bolshevik'. Another hooded body dangles from the next lamp-standard, then blackness.

KHLUDOV (*in semi-darkness, staring at* KRAPILIN's *body*). I'm sick, But what with? I don't know . . .

OLGA, *forgotten in the panic, enters, blunders about between the tables and overturned chairs.*

STATION MASTER (*groping in the half-light, whispering urgently*). Oh that woman . . . Olga – Olga, where are you? Olga darling, where are you? (*Grabs her by the hand.*) Come on, you silly little girl, hold daddy's hand . . . Don't look over there, darling . . . (*Picks her up, hugs her to stop her seeing through the window, gropes his way out.*)

The End of the Second Dream

THIRD DREAM

Dim lighting. Autumn twilight. An office of the White Counter-Intelligence in Sebastopol. A single window, a desk, and a divan. A heap of newspapers on a table in the corner. A cupboard. Heavy curtaining over the door. TIKHII, in civilian clothes, is sitting at the desk. The door opens and GURIN shows GOLUBKOV into the room.

GURIN. In here . . . (*Exit.*)

TIKHII. Sit down, please.

GOLUBKOV (*wearing overcoat, holding his hat*). Thank you. (*Sits down.*)

TIKHII. You, I take it, are a reasonably intelligent person?

GOLUBKOV *coughs modestly.*

So I am sure you realise how important it is for us, and for the army Command, to find out the truth. The Reds have been spreading disgusting rumours about the counter-intelligence service. In reality we are doing an honest and extremely difficult job in safeguarding the state against the Bolsheviks. Do you agree?

GOLUBKOV. Well, I . . . you see . . .

TIKHII. Are you afraid of me?

GOLUBKOV. Yes.

TIKHII. But why? Did anyone do you any harm while you were being brought here to Sebastopol?

GOLUBKOV. Oh, no.

TIKHII. Smoke? (*Offers cigarettes.*)

GOLUBKOV. Thank you, I don't smoke. Please tell me, I beg of you – how is she?

TIKHII. Who?

GOLUBKOV. The woman who . . . Serafima Korzukhin, who was arrested with me. I swear the whole thing was just a ridiculous misunderstanding. She had a fit of delirium, she's seriously ill.

TIKHII. Now don't get excited. Calm down. We shall talk about her in a moment of two.

Silence.

Right – now you can stop playing the absent-minded professor! I'm bored with this play-acting, you filthy little traitor. Don't you know who I am? Stand up! Stand to attention! Hands to your sides!

GOLUBKOV (*standing up*). My God! What . . .

TIKHII. What's your real name? Answer me!

GOLUBKOV. But . . . my real name is Golubkov!

TIKHII (*draws a revolver and aims it at* GOLUBKOV, *who covers his face with his hands*). Do you realise that you're completely in my hands? No one is going to help you now – understand?

GOLUBKOV. Yes, I understand.

TIKHII. Right. So we can agree on one thing: you are going to tell me the absolute truth. Look at this. The moment you start lying I shall switch on this electric needle (*switches on needle, which begins to glow*) and touch you with it. (*Switches off needle.*)

GOLUBKOV. I swear my name really is . . .

TIKHII. Shut up! Just answer my questions. (*Puts away revolver, picks up a pen, says in a bored voice.*) Sit down, please. What is your name, patronymic and surname?

GOLUBKOV. Sergei Pavlovich Golubkov.

TIKHII (*writing wearily*). Permanent residence?

GOLUBKOV. Petrograd.

TIKHII. Why did you leave Soviet Russia and enter territory under White control?

GOLUBKOV. I've been trying to reach the Crimea for a long time, because conditions in Petrograd are so bad that I find it impossible to go on working there. In the train I met Serafima

Korzukhin, who was also trying to escape, and together she and I joined the Whites.

TIKHII. Why did this woman who calls herself Serafima Korzukhin, come to White territory?

GOLUBKOV. I firmly . . . I *know* that she really is Serafima Korzukhin!

TIKHII. You were there at that railway station when Korzukhin said she was lying.

GOLUBKOV. *He* was the one who was lying – I swear it!

TIKHII. Why should he lie?

GOLUBKOV. He was frightened, because he realised that he was in danger.

TIKHII *puts down his pen, reaches for the needle.*

What are you doing? I'm telling the truth!

TIKHII. Your nerves are upset, Mr Golubkov. I am writing down your statement – that's all. How long has she been in the Communist Party?

GOLUBKOV. That's impossible! She can't be!

TIKHII. Well, she is. (*Pushes sheet of paper towards* GOLUBKOV, *hands him the pen.*) Write down everything you have just said. I'll dictate it, to make it easier for you. I warn you that if you stop I shall touch you with this needle. You have nothing to fear as long as you go on writing. (*Switches on the needle, dictates.*) 'I, the undersigned . . .

GOLUBKOV *starts writing.*

. . . Golubkov, Sergei Pavlovich, when questioned at the Counter-Intelligence Section of the Southern Front Headquarters on 31 October 1920 made the following statement – colon – Serafima Vladimirovna Korzukhin, wife of Paramon Ilyich Korzukhin . . .' don't stop! '. . . a member of the Communist Party, left Petrograd and entered the territory occupied by the Armed Forces of Southern Russia for the purposes of spreading communist propaganda and establishing contact with the communist underground movement in the town of Sebastopol full stop. Signed, Golubkov, Lecturer, Petrograd University.' (*Takes sheet of paper from* GOLUBKOV, *switches off needle.*)

Thank you for your frank and honest statement, Mr Golubkov. I have no doubt of your complete innocence. I'm sorry I had to be a little sharp with you. You may go. (*Rings a bell.*)

GURIN. Sir!

TIKHII. Take the prisoner outside and release him. He is free to go.

GURIN (*To* GOLUBKOV). Come on.

GOLUBKOV, *forgetting his hat, goes out with* GURIN.

TIKHII. Lieutenant Skunsky!

Enter SKUNSKY, *very morose.*

TIKHII (*lighting the lamp on his desk*). Take a look at this statement. How much do you think Korzukhin will pay to buy it off us?

SKUNSKY. Here, on the quayside? Ten thousand dollars. Less in Constantinople. I advise you to get a confession out of his wife, as well.

TIKHII. I agree. Find some excuse to stop Korzukhin going on board ship for half an hour or so.

SKUNSKY. What's my share?

TIKHII *holds up two fingers.*

SKUNSKY. Right. I'll send a man at once. Hurry up with the woman. It's getting late, the cavalry will start embarking soon.

TIKHII *rings bell. Enter* GURIN.

TIKHII. The Korzukhin woman – is she conscious?

GURIN. She seems to be making sense now.

TIKHII. Bring her in.

Exit GURIN; *after a short pause he returns with* SERAFIMA, *who has a high fever. Exit* GURIN.

TIKHII. Are you ill? I won't keep you long, sit down there on the divan.

SERAFIMA *sits down on the divan.*

Admit that you came here to spread propaganda and I'll let you go.

SERAFIMA. What? . . . Me? . . . What propaganda. Oh God, why did I ever come here.

Sound of a brass band playing a waltz, faint at first, grows nearer, with it the clatter of hooves.

Why are they playing a waltz?

TIKHII. It's Charnota's cavalry on the way to the quayside. Don't try and change the subject. Your accomplice Golubkov has stated that you came here to spread communist propaganda.

SERAFIMA (*breathing hard, lies back on the divan*). Will you please leave the room, I want to sleep . . .

TIKHII. No. Wake up. Read this. (*Shows SERAFIMA, GOLUBKOV's signed statement.*)

SERAFIMA (*frowning, reads it*). Petersburg . . . he's gone out of his mind. (*Suddenly grabs the sheet of paper, crumples it up, runs to the window, smashes the glass with her elbow, shouts.*) Help! Help! It's a plot! Charnota! Help – here!

TIKHII. Gurin!

GURIN *rushes in, seizes* SERAFIMA.

Take that document away from her! Damn and blast her!

Waltz breaks off. Fur-hatted face appears at window. Voice: 'What's going on in there?' More voices, noise, knocking at the door, which bursts open to admit CHARNOTA *in cossack cloak, followed by two more* COSSACKS. *Enter* SKUNSKY. GURIN *tries to push* SERAFIMA *out by another door.*

SERAFIMA. Charnota! Thank God, it's you. Charnota! Do something! Look what they're trying to do to me! Look what they've forced him to sign!

CHARNOTA *takes the document.*

TIKHII. Kindly leave the Counter–Intelligence offices at once! Get out!

CHARNOTA. Who are you telling to get out? What are you doing with this woman?

TIKHII. Lieutenant Skunsky, call the guard!

CHARNOTA. I'll give you guard! (*Draws revolver.*) What are you doing to this woman?

TIKHII. Put the lights out, Skunsky!

Lights go out.

(*In darkness.*) You're going to regret this, General Charnota!

The End of the Third Dream

FOURTH DREAM

*Twilight. A room in what was once the governor's palace in Sebastopol.
Confusion. The curtain over one window is half torn, there is a large
whitish square on the wall where a map used to hang. A wooden chest on
the floor, half filled with papers, other papers piled round it. Fire burning
in the fireplace; DE BRISARD is sitting in front of it, his head bandaged.
Enter the* WHITE COMMANDER-IN-CHIEF.

C-in-C. Well, how's your head now?

DE BRISARD. It's stopped aching, thank you sir. The doctor gave
me some aspirin.

C-in-C. I see. Aspirin. (*Vaguely.*) Tell me, do you think I look like
Alexander the Great?

DE BRISARD (*showing no surprise*). I'm afraid I haven't seen any
pictures of his majesty for a long time.

C-in-C. Who are you talking about?

DE BRISARD. Alexander the Great, sir.

C-in-C. His *majesty*? . . . H'mm . . . Look, Colonel, you need a
rest. I've been glad to put you up here for as long as I could, you
deserved it as an officer who has done his duty to his country.
But now it's time for you to go.

DE BRISARD. Where am I to go, sir?

C-in-C. On board ship. Once we're safe abroad I shall see that you
are taken care of.

DE BRISARD. Yes, sir. When the Reds are finally beaten, I shall
be happy to be the first to report to your majesty in the Kremlin!

C-in-C. I think your views are somewhat extreme, Colonel. You
must learn to control yourself. Thank you for all you have done
and now – take your men on board.

DE BRISARD. Yes, sir. (*As he goes he hums a mysterious tune. Exit.*)

C-in-C (*To an invisible orderly offstage*). I will see the others now. Send them in to me at three-minute intervals without waiting to be told. I will see as many as I can. Send a cossack to escort Colonel de Brisard to a cabin in my quarters on the ship. And write a note to the ship's doctor that he won't cure that man by giving him aspirin – he is obviously not normal. (*Walks back to the fireplace, reflectively*.) Alexander the Great! . . . The fools!

Enter KORZUKHIN.

What do you want?

KORZUKHIN. Korzukhin, deputy minister of trade.

C-in-C. Ah, yes! You're just in time. I was meaning to send for you, even though we are somewhat pressed for time. Mr Korzukhin, do you think I look like Alexander the Great?

KORZUKHIN *looks at him in amazement.*

I'm asking you seriously: do I look like him? (*Snatches a newspaper from the mantlepiece, thrusts it at* KORKUKHIN.) You're the editor of this newspaper, aren't you? So you're responsible for everything that's printed in it. Look, there's your name – 'Editor: Paramon Korzukhin' (*Reads.*) 'The Commander-in-Chief, like Alexander the Great, walks up and down the platform . . .' What is this ridiculous trash supposed to mean? There weren't any railway platforms in Alexander the Great's time! As for me looking like him! And it goes on: 'One look at his cheerful face and every worm of doubt is bound to melt away . . .' Really, man, I could write better myself. Since when have worms melted away? And you call me cheerful! Cheerful, am I? If I'm cheerful, think yourself lucky you haven't seen me when I'm angry! How dare you print this cheap, sycophantic drivel, Korzukhin, a mere two days before I'm forced to flee from Russian soil in ignominious defeat! When we get to Constantinople I shall have you court-martialled! If your head's aching – which I hope it is – take an aspirin!

Deafening peal of a telephone bell from the next room. Exit C-in-C, *slamming the door behind him.*

KORZUKHIN (*gasping for breath*). Well, it serves me right! What in God's name induced me to come here? To complain to one madman about another? They've got Serafima – but what can I do? Put my own head in the noose to save her? . . . If that swine thinks he can court-martial me . . . I shall go to Paris. Paris isn't

Constantinople, he can't touch me there. Damn you – damn you all, now, henceforth and for ever and ever . . . (*Rushes towards the door.*)

ATHANASIUS (*entering*). Amen. Are you leaving, Mr Korkukhin?

KORZUKHIN. Yes, I am. (*Slips out without the* ARCHBISHOP *noticing.*)

ATHANASIUS (*seeing the chest*). Lord have mercy on us! And the children of Israel journeyed from Rameses to Succoth, about six hundred thousand on foot that were men, beside children . . . Ah, Russia . . . And a mixed multitude went up also with them . . .

KHLUDOV *strides in.*

You General? How strange – Mr Korzukhin was here a moment ago . . .

KHLUDOV. Was it you who sent a bible to headquarters as a present for me?

ATHANASIUS. Well, General, I thought . . .

KHLUDOV. I can even remember some of it. I read it in the train at night when I was bored. 'Thou didst blow with thy wind, the sea covered them: they sank as lead in the mighty waters.' Exodus, isn't it? 'The enemy said I will pursue, I will overtake, I will divide the spoil; my lust shall be satisfied upon them.' How's that for a man the Commander-in-Chief thinks is off his head? And what are you hanging around here for?

ATHANASIUS. General – I protest! I am not 'hanging around'. I am waiting for the Commander-in-Chief.

KHLUDOV. To him who waits shall be given. Sounds like a quotation from your bible, doesn't it? Do you know what you will get if you wait here any longer?

ATHANASIUS. What?

KHLUDOV. The Reds.

ATHANASIUS. Will they really be here so soon?

KHLUDOV. Anything can happen now. Here are you and I, sitting here and calmly swapping quotations from the bible and at this very moment the Red cavalry is galloping down on

Sebastopol from the north . . . (*Leads* ATHANASIUS *over to the window*.) Look . . .

ATHANASIUS. Dawn! Oh, Lord have mercy on us!

KHLUDOV. Yes, dawn. Run, Archbishop, and board that ship while you still can.

Exit ATHANASIUS, *feverishly crossing himself.*

C-in-C (*entering*). Ah, thank God! I've been waiting for you. Well, are they all embarked?

KHLUDOV. The Ukrainian irregulars gave the cavalry a bad mauling on the way here, but on the whole I think we can say that they've all managed to get away. Personally I had a comfortable journey. I pushed my way to a corner seat in the train, so nobody trod on my toes and nobody tripped over me. I felt I was back in the kitchen, in the dark . . .

C-in-C. What was that? I don't understand.

KHLUDOV. It was something that happened when I was a boy. I once went into the kitchen when it was dark – there were cockroaches on the stove. I lit a match – it spluttered – and they all ran away. The match went out. I listened and I could hear their feet pattering – rustle, rustle . . . It was just like that on the retreat – darkness and rustling. I watched them and I wondered: where are they running away to? Just like the cockroaches – straight into a bucket of water. Off the edge of the kitchen table and – plop!

C-in-C. Thank you, general, for all you have done for the Crimean front with your great strategic skill. I shall not keep you any longer. I myself am moving into a hotel for tonight.

KHLUDOV. Nearer to the quayside?

C-in-C. If you do not change your tone, general, I shall have you arrested.

KHLUDOV. I thought you might try that. My bodyguard is outside in the hall. There would be a great scandal. I am a popular man.

C-in-C. No, I was wrong, you're not ill. You've been putting on this clownish performance for the past year now to conceal the fact that you hate me.

(handwritten in left margin: Drawn out of control)

KHLUDOV. I admit I hate you.

C-in-C. Jealous? Longing for power?

KHLUDOV. Oh, no. I hate you for dragging me into this shambles. Where are the Allied troops that we were promised? What has become of the Russian Empire? Why did you try and fight the Soviets when you were so weak? Can't you understand the hatred a man must feel when he is forced to act, yet knows that whatever he does is hopeless? You were right before. I am sick – and you're the cause of it. (*Calming down.*) However, all this is pointless. We're both heading for oblivion now.

C-in-C. I advise you to stay here in this palace – that will be your quickest route to oblivion.

KHLUDOV. It's a thought, I agree. But I haven't had time yet to make up my mind.

C-in-C. I shall not keep you, general.

KHLUDOV. Dismissing your faithful servant? 'For thee have I shed my blood like water in ceaseless fight . . .'

C-in-C (*picking up a chair and banging it on the floor*). You clown!

KHLUDOV. Alexander the Great is supposed to be a hero. Heroes don't go about smashing chairs.

C-in-C (*furious at the words 'Alexander the Great'*). If you say one more word . . . If you . . .

COSSACK OF C-in-C'S ESCORT (*entering silently*). Your Excellency, the cavalry training school from Simferopol has arrived. Everything is ready.

C-in-C. Very good. Let us go. (*To* KHLUDOV.) We shall meet again. (*Exit.*)

KHLUDOV (*alone, sits down by the fireplace, his back to the door*). Empty. And a good thing too. (*Jumps up restlessly and opens a door, revealing a perspective of dark, abandoned rooms with chandeliers wrapped in muslin bags.*) Hello – anybody there? Nobody. (*Sits down.*) Well, shall I stay here and wait for the Reds? No, that won't solve my problem. (*Turns round, talks to someone.*) Will you go away or not? This is ridiculous. I could walk through you just as I drove in the train through the fog last night. (*Walks forward as if passing through something.*) There – I've swept you away. (*Sits down.*)

Silence. Then the door opens stealthily and GOLUBKOV *enters, wearing overcoat but hatless.*

GOLUBKOV. For God's sake let me come in just for one minute!

KHLUDOV (*without turning round*). Come in, come in, by all means.

GOLUBKOV. I know it's a terrible impertinence, but I was promised I could see you personally. Now everyone seems to have vanished, so I've come without being announced.

KHLUDOV. What do you want from me?

GOLUBKOV. I was bold enough to come here, your excellency, because I must report an act of criminal violence perpetrated by the Counter-Intelligence section. I want to lodge a complaint about a brutal crime instigated by General Khludov.

KHLUDOV *turns round.*

GOLUBKOV (*recognises* KHLUDOV, *screams*). Aaah! . . .

KHLUDOV. Interesting. You are alive aren't you? You haven't been hanged, have you? What is your complaint?

Silence.

I somehow like the look of you. I've seen you somewhere. Please tell me – what's your complaint? Come on, don't be cowardly. You came to say something – well, go on, say it.

GOLUBKOV. All right, I will. The day before yesterday at the railway station you ordered a woman to be arrested . . .

KHLUDOV. I remember, yes. Of course, I remember. I recognise you now. Who were you coming to complain to about me?'

GOLUBKOV. To the Commander-in-Chief.

KHLUDOV. Too late. He's gone. (*Points to the window.*)

Distant lights, the first signs of dawn.

Straight into a bucket of water. He has just disappeared into oblivion. You can't complain about General Khludov, because there's no one to complain to any longer. (*Walks over to the desk, picks up one of the telephone receivers.*) Main entrance? . . . Captain Golovan, please . . . Listen, captain, I want you to take an escort and go over to the Counter-Intelligence Section, there's a woman being held there on my orders . . . (*To* GOLUBKOV.) Her name's Korzukhin, isn't it?

GOLUBKOV. Yes, Serafima Korzukhin.

KHLUDOV (*into telephone*). Serafima Korzukhin. If she hasn't been shot, bring her here to me at once. (*Replaces receiver.*) Let's wait and see.

GOLUBKOV. Did you say: 'if she hasn't been shot'? If she hasn't been shot? . . . Were they planning to shoot her . . . If they've done that, I . . . (*Breaks down, weeps.*)

KHLUDOV. Come on, pull yourself together and behave like a man.

GOLUBKOV. Still shouting at people! All right, I'll pull myself . . . If she's dead, I shall kill you.

KHLUDOV (*wearily*). Perhaps it would be the best way out if you did. No, on second thoughts, you could never kill anybody, I'm afraid. Be quiet.

GOLUBKOV *sits down in silence.*

(*Turning away from* GOLUBKOV, *speaking to someone else.*) If you are going to haunt me, soldier, then at least talk to me. I can't bear your silence, though I might be able to bear what you have to say. Or leave me. I'm a man with a strong will and I'm not going to collapse at the sight of my first ghost. People get over it. Don't you see, you were just one of many who fell under the wheels and they simply crushed you? Why follow me? Look where your obstinacy has brought you.

GOLUBKOV. Who are you talking to?

KHLUDOV. What? Who was I talking to? We'll soon know. (*Slashes the air with his hand.*) Nobody. I was talking to myself. Yes. Who is she – your mistress?

GOLUBKOV. Certainly not! She's just someone I met by chance, but I love her. God, what a miserable fool I am! Why, why did I have to carry her away from that monastery when she was ill and persuade her to come here, to this jungle . . . I'm a miserable fool!

KHLUDOV. Yes – why did you have to come and get under my feet? What made you come here? And now that the mechanism has been smashed you march in and demand something I can't give you. She's gone, I tell you. She's been shot.

GOLUBKOV. You monster!

KHLUDOV. Now they're attacking me from both sides – one of them's a live, talking fool and the other a soldier who never speaks. What's the matter with me? My mind's split in two, I hear words dimly as if I were under water and sinking like a piece of lead. They're both hanging onto my legs, damn them, dragging me down into the dark and the dark is beckoning me.

GOLUBKOV. Now I see it! You're mad! I understand everything – the ice on the Chongar river, the black hoods, and the frost! What have I done to deserve this? Why couldn't I save Serafima? There's the man who murdered her, standing there. And what use is he now that he's gone out of his mind?

KHLUDOV. There, you fool – catch! (*Throws* GOLUBKOV *his revolver.*) Do me a favour and shoot. (*Into space.*) Now will you go away? He may decide to shoot.

GOLUBKOV. No, I can't shoot you, you sicken me. I even pity you.

KHLUDOV. Yes, you're right. What is all this play-acting?

Distant footsteps along the palace corridor.

Wait, someone's coming! Perhaps that's him. We'll know in a moment.

Enter GOLOVAN.

Has she been shot?

GOLOVAN. No, sir.

GOLUBKOV. She's alive? Where is she, where?

KHLUDOV. Quiet. (*To* GOLOVAN.) In that case why didn't you bring her here?

GOLOVAN *nods uncomfortably towards* GOLUBKOV.

You can talk in front of him.

GOLOVAN. Very good, sir. This afternoon at four o'clock Major-General Charnota forced his way into the Counter-Intelligence offices, removed the prisoner Korzukhin by armed force and took her away.

GOLUBKOV. Where to? Where to?

KHLUDOV. Quiet. (*To* GOLOVAN.) Where to?

GOLOVAN. On board the *S.S. Vityaz*. The *Vityaz* cast off at five o'clock and half an hour later she was in the open sea.

KHLUDOV. I see. Thank you. Well, there you are, she's alive. Your woman Serafima is alive.

GOLUBKOV. She's alive . . .

KHLUDOV. Captain, take the standard, fall in the escort, march them to the quayside and embark on the *St George*. I'll join you shortly.

GOLOVAN. May I suggest, sir, that you come with us . . .

KHLUDOV. I'm in my right mind, thank you, captain. I shall come when I'm ready, don't worry.

GOLOVAN. Very good, sir. (*Exit.*)

KHLUDOV. So now she's on her way to Constantinople.

GOLUBKOV (*vaguely*). Yes, Constantinople . . . But I'm not going to leave you. Look at the lights out there in the harbour. Take me to Constantinople. ·

KHLUDOV. Oh, hell, hell, hell . . .

GOLUBKOV. Come on, Khludov, let's go while we still can . . .

KHLUDOV. Shut up. (*Mutters.*) Well, that's one of them dealt with, now I'm free to talk to you. (*Into space.*) What do you want? Do you want me to stay? No reply. Growing paler, moves away, mist . . .

GOLUBKOV (*wearily*). Khludov, you're sick. You're delirious. Stop it! We've got to hurry! The ship's leaving, we'll miss it.

KHLUDOV. Christ . . . What's her name – Serafima? . . . Come on – we're going to Constantinople . . . (*Exit quietly, followed by* GOLUBKOV.)

Darkness. The End of the Fourth Dream.

FIFTH DREAM

Strange symphony of Turkish songs, the Russian tune 'Parting' played on a barrel-organ, street-hawkers' cries, grinding of streetcars.
Lights go up on Constantinople in late afternoon sunshine. A towering minaret, roofs. In the foreground is a weird structure something like a fairground booth, crowned by an enormous placard lettered in French, English and Russian:

> Sensation de Constantinople!
> Courses des cafards
> <u>Races of cockroaches!</u>
> Licensed by Police

The structure is decorated with the flags of various countries. Betting windows labelled 'Win' and 'Win and Place', over them a sign reading:

> Commencement à 5 heures du soir
> Begins at 5 pm

To one side, an open-air restaurant; surrounded by a gilded wreath of laurels the sign reads:

> Russian delicacies. Per portion – 50 piastres

Above this, cut out of plywood and painted, is a cockroach in a tailcoat offering a foaming tankard of beer. Laconic sign:

> Bière
> Beer

Behind the booth, running uphill, a narrow, sleepy little alley. Veiled Turkish women, Turks in fezzes, foreign sailors in white summer rig. An occasional overloaded, blinkered donkey. A stall selling coconuts. A few White Russian troops in tattered uniforms. Monotonous cry of a lemonade-vendor. A boy squeaking urgently 'Presse du soir!'

At the end of the alleyway, near the booth, stands CHARNOTA *in cossack uniform minus epaulettes, in black fur cap despite the heat, grimly trying to sell rubber dolls on strings that are piled on a tray slung round his neck.*

CHARNOTA. Unbreakable! Harmless! – Watch them jump! Buy a Red commissar for the kids! Madame! Madame! Achêtez pour votre enfant!

TURKISH WOMAN. Bunin fiya ty nadyr? Combien?

CHARNOTA. Cinquante piastres, madame, cinquante!

TURKISH WOMAN. Oh, yokh! Bu pakhali dyr! (*Passes on.*)

CHARNOTA. Madame! Forty! Quarante! Oh, go to hell then, stupid bitch. Don't suppose you ever had any kids, anyway . . . Gehen Sie! . . . Gehen Sie! . . . Back to the harem. My God, what a cesspit this town is!

The tenor voice of the lemonade-vendor warbles enticingly: 'Ambulasi! Ambulasi!' A bass voice cries: 'Kaimaki, Kaimaki!'
A girl's face appears at the betting window. Charnota walks over to her.

CHARNOTA. Ah, Maria Konstantinovna!

GIRL'S FACE. What is it, Grigory Lukyanich?

CHARNOTA. Look, please do me a favour . . . will you give me credit to put a bet on Jannissary tonight?

GIRL'S FACE. Grigory Lukyanich, you *know* I can't.

CHARNOTA. I'm not a swindler, am I? I'm not some Stamboul crook . . . you know me. Can't you trust a general – especially a general with a pitch right next to your miserable racecourse?

GIRL'S FACE. We'll see . . . You'll have to ask Yanko Yankovich yourself.

CHARNOTA. Yanko Yankovich!

YANKO (*pops out on to booth steps like a puppet from behind a screen, painfully buttoning up the collar of his dress shirt*). What's the matter? Who wants me? Ah! . . . What can I do for you?

CHARNOTA. Look, I just wondered if you could possibly . . .

YANKO. No! (*Vanishes.*)

CHARNOTA. Hey – where's your manners? You've gone before I even asked you.

YANKO (*re-appears*). Because I know perfectly well what you're going to ask.

CHARNOTA. Oh, really? How interesting. What was I going to say?

YANKO. What *I'm* going to say is much more interesting. No credit – to anybody!

CHARNOTA. Swine!

Two French soldiers enter the restaurant, shouting 'un bock! un bock!'
Waiter serves them beer.

GIRL'S FACE. There's a bug crawling on you, Grigory Lukyanich, pick it off.

CHARNOTA. To hell with it, why should I pick it off, what's the use? Let it crawl, I don't mind. God, this town . . . I've seen some places in my time, but this . . . I've been everywhere, seen the most beautiful cities in the world.

GIRL'S FACE. What towns have you seen, Grigory Lukyanich?

CHARNOTA. Lord! I've seen Kharkov! Rostov! Kiev! Now Kiev – there's a beautiful city, Maria Konstantinovna! The monastery glittering on the hilltop – and the Dnieper – ah, the Dnieper. The air, the light – indescribable. The grass, the smell of hay, the hills and dales, the barges on the Dnieper! Ah, what a magnificent fight that was at Kiev – a beautiful fight! It was warm, sunny, but not too hot, Maria Konstantinovna. And the lice – there were plenty of them too . . . The louse – now there's an insect for you!

GIRL'S FACE. Oh, you are disgusting, Grigory Lukyanich!

CHARNOTA. Disgusting? Why? You've got to be able to tell one insect from another. Your louse is a soldier, he fights, but your bug's just a parasite. Your louse comes in squadrons, in cavalry formation, and when your louse gets to work you know you've really got a fight on your hands! (*Miserably.*) Yanko!

YANKO (*looks out in tails and white tie*). What's the matter with you now?

CHARNOTA. You're a sight for sore eyes, Yanko! Look at you in your tails! You're not a man, you're a force of nature – the cockroach king. Good luck to you! You're a born financier, too – like all your race.

YANKO. If you're going to start spreading anti-semitism again I shall cease this conversation.

CHARNOTA. Why should you care? You told me you were Hungarian.

YANKO. All the same I don't like it.

CHARNOTA. So I say good luck to all Hungarians! Now I'll make you a proposition, Yanko Yankovich: I want to liquidate my business. (*Points to his tray.*)

YANKO. Fifty.

CHARNOTA. Fifty what?

YANKO. Piastres.

CHARNOTA. You're joking of course. I sell these at fifty piastres apiece!

YANKO. All right, carry on selling them!

CHARNOTA. Bloodsucker.

YANKO. You don't have to take my offer if you don't want to.

CHARNOTA. It's lucky for you, Yanko Yankovich, that I didn't get my hands on you when I was fighting the Reds in the Crimea!

YANKO. Well we're not in the Crimea now, thank God.

CHARNOTA. Take the cartridge-pockets from my tunic. They're silver.

YANKO. I'll give you two pounds fifty piastres for your cartridge-pockets and the trayful of rubber dolls.

CHARNOTA. All right, they're yours. (*Removes his silver cartridge-pockets and toy-tray, hands them to* YANKO.)

YANKO. It's a deal. (*Gives* CHARNOTA *money.*)

Two men walk up to the booth dressed in caps with peacocks' feathers, singlets; one has an accordion.

YANKO (*disappears, then looks out again and shouts*). Five o'clock! We're open! This way, gentlemen!

The Russian imperial tricolour flag is hoisted over the booth. A steam organ strikes up a rollicking march. CHARNOTA *is the first to rush to the betting window.*

CHARNOTA. Maria Konstantinovna – two pounds fifty piastres on Janissary to win!

A crowd starts to form at the windows. A group of Italian sailors strolls up, followed by some English sailors with a prostitute. Various pick-pockets, touts and con-men mix with the crowd, a negro appears. The march blares. A waiter darts about the restaurant serving beer. YANKO in top hat and tails appears at the top of the steps leading into the booth. The march stops.

YANKO. Messieurs – dames! Les Courses commencent! The races are open! A game never before played outside the walls of the Tsar's palace! Course de cafards! Corso di piatelli! Race of cockroaches! The favourite pastime of her late majesty the tsarina at Tsarskoye Selo! L'amusement préféré de la défunte impératrice à Tsarskoie Selo!

Two policemen, an Italian and a Turk, enter.

Place your bets now, ladies and gentlemen, for the first race! The runners in the first race on tonight's card are: No. 1 – Black Pearl; No. 2 – the favourite – Janissary!

ITALIAN SAILORS (*clapping, shouting*). Evviva, evviva!

ENGLISH SAILORS (*booing*). Shut up, go to hell!

A sweating, excited figure rushes on, wearing Russian uniform with quartermaster's epaulettes and a bowler hat.

FIGURE. Am I too late? Have they started?

VOICE. You're just in time.

YANKO. No. 3 – Baba Yaga. No. 4 – Don't Cry, Baby, a grey cockroach with black spots.

Shouts of: 'Hurrah! Two pounds on Don't Cry Baby to win! It's a bloody swindle!'

YANKO. No. 6 – Hooligan. No. 7 – Buttons.

Whistles. Shouts of 'It's a racket!'

I beg your pardon! This is a fair race! The cockroaches run on open planks with paper jockeys. The cockroaches live in a sealed box under the supervision of a professor of entomology from

Kazan Imperial University, just escaped from the Bolsheviks. No more bets now, gentlemen – they're under starter's orders! (*Disappears inside the booth.*)

The crowd surges into the booth. Boys climb on to the stone wall for a free look. Shouting, then dead silence. The accordion strikes up a fast Russian song, the player imitating the pattering of cockroaches' feet. Desperate shout: 'They're off!'
A Greek boy looking like a little demon, dances up and down on the stone wall shouting: 'Theyov! Theyov!' Shout from the booth: 'Janissary's run out!'

CHARNOTA (*at the betting window*). What – run out? He can't have!!

Voice from the booth: 'Don't Cry Baby!'
Another voice: 'Come on Black Pearl!'

CHARNOTA. I'll kill Yanko!

Girl's face looks anxiously out of the window. The policemen look worried, peer into the booth.

FIGURE (*rushing out of the booth*). It's a swindle! It's rigged! Yanko got Janissary drunk on beer!

YANKO *bursts·out of the booth. Both the tails of his coat have been torn off, his top hat has been squashed flat, his collar torn off. His face is covered in blood. A crowd of bettors chase him out.*

YANKO (*desperately*). Maria Konstantinovna, call the police!

Girl's face vanishes. Policemen whistle.

ITALIAN SAILORS (*shouting*). Ladro! Scroccone! Truffatore!

PROSTITUTE. Giovanni – kill Yanko! (*To* YANKO.) Ingannatore!

ENGLISH SAILORS. Hurrah! Well done Buttons!

PROSTITUTE. Brothers! Fratelli! Someone bribed Yanko to make Janissary lose and Buttons win! The favourite's lying on its back and waving its legs in the air completely pissed! When has Janissary ever run off the course before?

YANKO (*desperate*). Cockroaches can't get drunk. When have you ever seen a drunken cockroach? Je vous démande un peu – où est-ce que vous avez vu un cafard sôul? Police! Au secours! Police! Help!

PROSTITUTE. Mensonge! It's all lies! Everybody had a bet on Janissary! Beat him up, the crook!

ITALIAN SAILOR (*seizing* YANKO *by the gullet and throttling him*). A, marmalia!

OTHER ITALIANS. Canalia!

YANKO (*faintly*). They're killing me . . .

ENGLISH PETTY OFFICER (*to the* ITALIAN SAILOR). Stop it! Let go, you stinking little Wop! Leave him alone! (*Makes a grab at the Italian.*)

FIGURE. Punch him one on the ear!

PROSTITUTE (*to the Englishman*). Oh, so that's the way you carry on, is it?

An English sailor punches the Italian sailor in the face and knocks him down.

PROSTITUTE. A soccorso, fratelli! Help! Beat up the English! Come on you Italians – smash their faces! Avanti, Italiani! Avanti!

English and Italian sailors fight. Italians draw knives. At the sight of the knives the crowd draws back to either side with a roar of terror. Greek boy, dancing on the wall, shouts: 'Kill Englis! Kill Englis!' A squad of Turkish and Italian police charge out of the alley, blowing whistles and waving revolvers. CHARNOTA *ducks out of sight.*

The dream dissolves. Mist. Silence.
The next dream slowly materialises.

SIXTH DREAM

Courtyard of a two-storied Turkish house, a gallery running all round the first floor, a cypress tree. On one wall is an ornamental water-pipe, from which water drips slowly into a large stone basin. A marble bench beside the gateway. A steep, narrow street curves away uphill past the gate. The setting sun picks out the balustrade of a minaret. Shadows of approaching evening; silence.

CHARNOTA (*entering from street*). Bloody cockroaches! Still, I suppose it's not their fault I'm broke, finished . . . God, she'll skin me alive. Should I run away? And where, Grigory Charnota, do you think you're going to run to? This isn't the Crimea, running away won't help now. Christ . . .

A door in the gallery opens, enter LYUSKA. She is dirty, untidy and starving. Her glittering wolfish eyes give her a look of unearthly, ephemeral beauty.

LYUSKA. Ah, good evening, General! Bonjour, Madame Barabanchikova!

CHARNOTA. Hello, Lyuska.

LYUSKA. Why are you back so early? If I were you I'd find any excuse to stay out as late as you could, things at home being what they are – no food, no money. But I can see good news written all over your expressive features. No rubber dolls. And no silver cartridge-pockets either. I'm beginning to understand. Come on, hand over the money – Serafima and I haven't eaten since yesterday morning. Please.

CHARNOTA. Where's Serafima?

LYUSKA. That doesn't matter. She's doing the washing. Now let's have the money.

CHARNOTA. There's been a disaster, Lyuska.

LYUSKA. What d'you mean? Where are your cartridge-pockets?

CHARNOTA. I was going to sell them, Lyuska, and I put them in a box. I took it out for a moment in the Grand Bazaar and . . .

LYUSKA. It was stolen?

CHARNOTA. Mm'hh . . .

LYUSKA. By a man with a black beard, I suppose?

CHARNOTA (*weakly*). What are you talking about?

LYUSKA. It's always a man with a black beard who steals things from thickheaded fools in the Grand Bazaar. Tell the truth – were they really stolen?

CHARNOTA *hangs his head.*

I see. Do you know what you are, Grigory Charnota?

CHARNOTA. What am I?

LYUSKA You're a miserable, stupid bastard!

CHARNOTA. Lyuska – how can you?

Enter SERAFIMA *with a bucket. She stops.* CHARNOTA *and* LYUSKA *do not notice her.*

LYUSKA. I've a right to say it – that box and those rubber dolls were bought with my money.

CHARNOTA. We're as good as man and wife, the money belongs to both of us.

LYUSKA. Does it? You earn it from selling dolls, but I earn it selling a different sort of goods!

CHARNOTA. What d'you mean?

LYUSKA. Stop playing the fool! Where do you think I went with that Frenchman last week? To church? Did any of you ask me how I suddenly had five pounds? And you and I and Serafima lived off those five pounds for a week! But that's not all! You didn't lose that box and your cartridge-pockets at the Grand Bazaar, either – you lost them at the cockroach races! So where does that leave us? The gallant General Charnota smashed up the Counter-Intelligence section so he was drummed out of the army. Now he's flat broke in Constantinople and I, fool that I am, am living with him!

CHARNOTA. But you can't blame me for saving a woman from being shot! I saved Serafima's life and you blame me!

LYUSKA. No, I don't. But I can say what I think about Serafima! (*Taking the bit between her teeth.*) All right – let dear, pure Serafima go on living, and sighing for her long-lost Golubkov, and let gallant General Charnota go on living! Let them both go on living off the earnings of Lyuska the whore!

SERAFIMA. Lyuska!

LYUSKA. You shouldn't eavesdrop, Serafima – it doesn't suit you.

SERAFIMA. I wasn't eavesdropping. It was pure chance that I overheard you and a good thing I did, too. Why didn't you tell me about those five pounds before?

LYUSKA. Oh, really, Serafima, why bother to pretend? You're not blind.

SERAFIMA. I swear to you I had no idea. I thought he'd brought you the five pounds. But don't worry, Lyuska, I'll pay it back to you.

LYUSKA. Spare me the high-minded stuff, for God's sake!

SERAFIMA. Don't lose your temper, Lyuska, let's not quarrel. Let's talk it over reasonably.

LYUSKA. There's nothing to talk over. It's all too plain – tomorrow the Greeks are going to kick us out of this house, there's absolutely nothing to eat and we can't raise a single piastre – we've sold everything. (*Getting angry again.*) No, I refuse to keep calm! It's all his fault that we're in this state! (*To* CHARNOTA.) Come on, out with it – you gambled and lost, didn't you?

CHARNOTA. Yes, I did.

LYUSKA. Oh, you . . .

CHARNOTA. But put yourself in my place, Lyuska! I can't sell rubber dolls! I'm a soldier!

SERAFIMA. Oh, stop it, Lyuska . . . Stop it, what difference would two or three pounds have made to us, anyway?

Silence.

It really does seem as though some evil fate is pursuing us!

LYUSKA. Oh, how very poetic.

CHARNOTA (*suddenly, to* LYUSKA). Did you really sleep with the Frenchman?

LYUSKA. Shut up and go to hell!

SERAFIMA. For God's sake be quiet, you two! Stop quarrelling, I'm going to see what I can get for supper.

LYUSKA. Leave us alone, Serafima, and mind your own business. Don't upset yourself on my account. I'm a whore and I'm not going to stop now. I just refuse to sit here and starve. I haven't got any principles.

SERAFIMA. I refuse to sit and starve too, but I also refuse to eat at someone else's expense. I'm not such a hypocrite that I can sit here knowing that you're out earning the rent on the streets. I haven't sunk as low as that yet. You should have told me, Lyuska! If we're really in the gutter, then at least let's be in it together!

LYUSKA. Charnota could sell his revolver.

CHARNOTA. Lyuska, I'll sell my trousers, I'll sell anything, only not my revolver! I can't live without a revolver!

LYUSKA. Well, I suppose it is more use than your head. All right, live off us women then!

CHARNOTA. Don't push me too far!

LYUSKA. If you so much as touch me, I'll poison you.

SERAFIMA. Stop it! Why do you two have to bicker the whole time? What good does it do us? I'm going out to earn the supper, since you say you're starving.

LYUSKA. What are you up to now, you little fool?

SERAFIMA. I'm not a fool – at least, I'm not any longer. What does it matter what we sell? It's all the same in the end. (*Goes back into her room, then appears again in a hat.*) Wait for me (*At the gate.*) but, please, no more quarrelling.

A distant barrel organ plays Parting.

LYUSKA. Serafima, I didn't . . .

CHARNOTA. Serafima!

Silence.

Lyuska. Ugh, this revolting place! Ugh, the bed-bugs! Ugh, the Bosphorus . . . And to top it all – you . . .

CHARNOTA. Shut up, you miserable bitch!

LYUSKA. I hate you, I hate myself, and I hate all Russians! We're rotten to the core! (*Climbs up to the gallery, exit.*)

CHARNOTA (*alone*). Where can I go? Paris? Berlin? Madrid, maybe? Never been to Spain before . . . But I bet it's a filthy hole. (*Squats down, scrapes around in the dust under the cypress tree, finds a cigarette-end.*) Christ, those Greeks are so mean. He smokes them down till there's nothing left, the son of a bitch. No, she's wrong, we Russians *are* better – at least we're not mean. (*Lights the butt-end, clambers up the gallery steps.*)

Enter GOLUBKOV, wearing a British army tunic, puttees and a Turkish fez. He is carrying a portable barrel organ. He puts it down, starts to play it, first Parting, then a march.

CHARNOTA (*shouts down from the gallery*). Shut up, you Turkish wog, stop that filthy noise!

GOLUBKOV. What? Gri . . . Grigory Charnota! They told me I'd find you if I went on looking – and I have!

CHARNOTA. Who's that? . . . Christ, it's the professor!

GOLUBKOV (*excited he sits down on the edge of the water basin*). I found you.

CHARNOTA (*runs down to him*). You mean you were really looking for *me*? . . . And I thought you were a Turk. You see, I . . . (*kisses GOLUBKOV.*) Sergei! But look at you . . . you've aged! We thought you'd stayed with the Bolsheviks. Where the hell have you been for the last six months?

GOLUBKOV. First of all I landed up in an internment camp, then I caught typhus and spent two months in hospital, and when they let me out I walked all the way to Constantinople. Khludov put me up in his flat. I suppose you know he was dismissed from the army.

CHARNOTA. Yes, so I heard. I'm a civilian now, too. I had a slight difference of opinion with the Commander-in-Chief. We

get all sorts here, Sergei – but we've never had anyone with a barrel-organ yet . . .

GOLUBKOV. A barrel-organ has its uses. I go from courtyard to courtyard and that way I can look for her. Tell me, is she dead? Don't be afraid to tell me. I can take anything now.

CHARNOTA. Serafima, dead? Not a bit of it. She got well and now she's fine.

GOLUBKOV. She's alive! (*Embraces* CHARNOTA.)

CHARNOTA. Of course she's alive. But I warn you, professor, we're in a bad way here. We've just about hit rock-bottom, Sergei.

GOLUBKOV. But where is Serafima?

CHARNOTA. She's here. She'll be back any time now. She's gone to pick up a man on the Pera.

GOLUBKOV. What?!

CHARNOTA. It's not my fault! We're dying of hunger. I've even sold my cartridge-pockets. We're broke.

GOLUBKOV. You don't really mean she's gone to the Pera, do you? You're lying!

CHARNOTA. What's the point in lying any more? I haven't even had a cigarette all day. Maybe I ought to go to Madrid . . . I dreamed about Madrid all last night . . .

Voices. Enter SERAFIMA, *followed by* AMOROUS GREEK, *loaded with bags of shopping, a bottle under one arm.*

SERAFIMA. Oh no, we'll be very comfortable, we'll sit down and have a nice talk, just the two of us . . . We live like gypsies here, anyway . . .

AMOROUS GREEK (*with heavy accent*). How nice! Of course I don't want to be in the way . . .

SERAFIMA. Let me introduce you to General . . .

CHARNOTA *turns his back on her.*

Don't be so rude, Grigory!

AMOROUS GREEK. Delighted, I'm sure!

SERAFIMA (*recognises* GOLUBKOV). Oh, my God!

Frowning hard, GOLUBKOV *get up, walks over to the Greek and punches him on the ear. The Greek drops his parcels and staggers. Anxious Greek and Armenian faces pop out of the windows.* LYUSKA *comes out on to the gallery.*

AMOROUS GREEK. What . . . what are you doing?

SERAFIMA. God, the shame!

CHARNOTA (*to* GREEK). Look here, you . . .

AMOROUS GREEK (*miserably*). I see it – it is a trap! Robbers!

SERAFIMA. Forgive me, monsieur, please, for God's sake! This is terrible, they don't understand!

CHARNOTA (*drawing his revolver and pointing it up to the windows*). Get inside and mind your own business!

Faces vanish, windows slam.

AMOROUS GREEK (*in sing-song moan*). Oh God, oh God . . .

GOLUBKOV (*threatening the* GREEK). If you don't . . .

AMOROUS GREEK (*pulling out his wallet and watch*). Take my money and take my watch, sir! I'm a poor merchant but I give you all for my life – I have wife, shop, children . . . I say nothing to police . . . take it, good man, and thanks to almighty God . . .

GOLUBKOV. Get out!

AMOROUS GREEK. Ai, Stamboul, what a place it's become . . .

GOLUBKOV. Take your parcels with you!

The GREEK *starts to pick up his shopping, but gives a terrified look at* GOLUBKOV's *face and runs for his life.*

LYUSKA. Ah, Mr Golubkov! We were just talking about you. We thought you were still in Russia with the Bolsheviks. Congratulations! You chose a brilliant moment to turn up.

GOLUBKOV. What's happened to you, Serafima? I've walked half-way through the Balkans, I've been in hospital, look (*Pulls off fez.*) they shaved my head . . . All that, just to find you! And look what you've become!

SERAFIMA. What right have you to blame me?

GOLUBKOV. I love you – I've been hunting for you for six months just to tell you that.

SERAFIMA. Let me go. Get out! I don't want to hear any more, d'you understand? You bore me with all this drivel. Why the hell did you have to come sniffing after me as if I was a bitch on heat? We're finished, broke, done for! I never want to see you again – any of you . . . I just want to creep into a hole in the ground by myself and die of shame! My God, the humiliation! Goodbye!

GOLUBKOV. Don't – please don't go!

SERAFIMA. Nothing will ever make me come back now! (*Exit.*)

GOLUBKOV. Oh, no . . . ! (*Suddenly grabs* CHARNOTA's *dagger from its sheath and rushes after* SERAFIMA.)

CHARNOTA (*grabs him, removes dagger*). Have you gone mad! D'you want to go to prison?

GOLUBKOV. Let me go! I don't care – I shall find her and I shall make her come back! You'll see. (*Sits down on the edge of the stone basin.*)

LYUSKA. Great performance. The Greeks are defeated. Fine. Now open one of those parcels, Charnota, I'm hungry.

GOLUBKOV. I won't let you touch a single one of them!

CHARNOTA. No, he's right, I refuse to open them!

LYUSKA. Oh, you won't, won't you? Right. I've no more patience with you. I've had more of Constantinople than I can take. (*Runs upstairs, picks up a hat and a bundle.*) Well, Grigory Charnota, goodbye and good luck. This is the end of us. Lyuska knows somebody who works on the Orient Express and Lyuska was a fool to waste six months in this stinking city. Goodbye!

CHARNOTA. Where are you going?

LYUSKA. To Paris! Paris! For the last time – goodbye! (*Exit to street.*)

CHARNOTA *and* GOLUBKOV *sit in silence. Water drips. Turkish boy slips in, looks round, turns, beckons someone in, says:* 'Here, effendi, here!' *Enter* KHLUDOV *in civilian clothes. He looks old and grey.*

CHARNOTA. It's Roman Khludov. So you've turned up too. I

can see you're looking at where my cartridge-pockets used to be. I'm a civilian now, like you.

KHLUDOV. So I see. How are you, Grigory? Yes, we do seem to follow one another about, don't we? (*Pointing at* GOLUBKOV.) First I cured him of typhus, now he's playing with the idea of curing *me*. In his spare time he plays the barrel-organ. (*To* GOLUBKOV.) Well, had any luck with the barrel-organ?

GOLUBKOV. Yes, I have. I've found her. Only please don't ask me any more. Don't ask me about anything.

KHLUDOV. I wasn't going to. That's your affair. I only want to know whether you've found her – that's all I care about.

GOLUBKOV. Khludov! I've only one more favour to ask you and you're the only person who can do it. Go after her, she's left me. Stop her, keep her from going on the streets.

KHLUDOV. Why can't you do that yourself?

GOLUBKOV. Just now, sitting here by this water-pipe, I made up my mind. I'm going to Paris. I'm going to find Korzukhin, her husband. He's a rich man. He ruined her. He *must* help her.

KHLUDOV. How will you go? They'll never let you into France.

GOLUBKOV. I shall go illegally. I was playing my barrel-organ on the dockside today. I made friends with a ship's captain, he took a liking to me and said he'd help me. He's promised to let me stow away in his hold and take me to Marseille.

KHLUDOV. I see. How long must I be this woman's watchdog?

GOLUBKOV. I'll be back soon and I give you my oath that I'll never ask you to do anything for me again.

KHLUDOV. That episode on the railway-station is costing me dear. (*Turns away.*) No, no, I tell you.

CHARNOTA (*in a whisper*). Fine sort of guardian he is! He won't do it.

GOLUBKOV (*whispering back*). Don't look at him. He's trying to convince himself.

KHLUDOV. Where did she go just now?

CHARNOTA. Not hard to guess. She's gone back to that Greek's shop to say she's sorry. I know the place.

KHLUDOV. Good.

GOLUBKOV. If you can only keep her off the streets!

KHLUDOV. Keep her at my place? Don't worry, I won't let her get away. As a certain soldier rightly said – no one gets away from me. (*Unhooks a medallion from his watch-chain.*) There, take this medallion. As a last resort you can sell it. (*Exit.*)

The evening shadows have lengthened. The sweet, thin voice of the muezzin floats out from the minaret: 'La illah illa illah . . .'

GOLUBKOV. It's nearly night . . . This terrible, unbearable city – it's stifling me! Anyway, why am I wasting my time here? I've got to be on board that ship tonight.

CHARNOTA. I'm coming with you. I don't believe we'll get any money out of that bastard, but I've simply got to go somewhere. I told you I was thinking of going to Madrid, but Paris – well, it's somehow more the place for me. Come on. Our Greek landlord will be glad to see the back of me anyway!

GOLUBKOV (*going*). This filthy hothouse never cools down – not even at night.

CHARNOTA (*exit with GOLUBKOV*). Paris it is then!

Turkish boy runs up to the barrel-organ, turns the handle. Plays a march. The muezzin's voice dies away from the minaret. Darkness. Lights flicker on. A pale gold crescent appears in the sky.

The Dream Ends

SEVENTH DREAM

An autumn evening in Paris. KORZUKHIN's *study in his elegant house. The room is imposingly furnished; among the fittings is a large safe. A desk, telephones, and a card table laid ready for a game with cards, scoring-pads, pencils and two unlit candles.*

KORZUKHIN. Antoine!

Enter a handsome, French-looking manservant in a green baize apron.

Monsieur Marchand m'avait averti qu'il ne viendra pas aujourd'hui. Ne remuez pas la table. Je m'en servirai plus tard.

Silence.

Répondez–donc quelque chose! Don't you understand me?

ANTOINE. No sir, I don't.

KORZUKHIN. How do you say that in French?

ANTOINE. I don't know, sir.

KORZUKHIN. Antoine, you're an idle Russian blockhead. When will you learn that when you live in Paris Russian is only any use for swearing, or worse still, for shouting revolutionary slogans? And it's rude to do either of those in Paris. You must learn French, Antoine, otherwise it makes life so difficult. Que faites-vous à ce moment? What are you doing at the moment?

ANTOINE. Je . . . I'm cleaning the knives, sir.

KORZUKHIN. What's the French for 'knives', Antoine?

ANTOINE. Les couteaux, sir.

KORZUKHIN. Correct. You must learn, Antoine.

Bell rings.

KORZUKHIN (*goes out, unbuttoning his pyjama-jacket*). Show them in. Whoever it is might like a game of cards and I can play with them instead of Marchand. Je suis à la maison. (*Exit.*)

Exit ANTOINE, *returns with* GOLUBKOV, *who is wearing seaman's bell-bottom trousers and a crumpled grey jacket. He is clutching a peaked cap.*

GOLUBKOV. Je voudrais parler à Monsieur Korzukhin.

ANTOINE. Your card, please . . . votre carte, monsieur.

GOLUBKOV. You're a Russian! And I thought you were a Frenchman. I'm so glad!

ANTOINE. Yes, I'm Russian. The name is Grishchenko.

GOLUBKOV *shakes* ANTOINE *by the hand.*

GOLUBKOV. Look, the fact is I haven't got any visiting cards. Just say its Golubkov – Golubkov from Constantinople.

ANTOINE. Very good, sir. (*Exit.*)

KORZUKHIN (*enters, straightening his tie and buttoning his jacket*). Who on earth is Golubkov? . . . Golubkov? . . . Well now, what can I do for you?

GOLUBKOV. I don't expect you recognise me. We met a year ago, that terrible night on a railway station in the Crimea when your wife was arrested. She is now in Constantinople and on the verge of ruin.

KORZUKHIN. On the verge of what? I'm sorry, but firstly, I have no wife, and secondly, I remember nothing about a railway station.

GOLUBKOV. What? It was night-time . . . there was a bitter frost . . . surely you remember that frost when the Crimea was taken by the Reds?

KORZUKHIN. I'm afraid I remember no such thing. You must be mistaken.

GOLUBKOV. But you're Paramon Korzukhin, aren't you? I recognise you! You *were* in the Crimea!

KORZUKHIN. Well, it's true I did spend some time in the Crimea when those lunatic White generals were running wild. But I've left it forever now, I have nothing more to do with Russia. I have become a naturalised French citizen. I was never married and although it's no business of yours, I should mention that a Russian emigrée lady has been living here for the past three months in the capacity of my private secretary who has also taken French citizenship and a French surname – Fréjol. This charming creature has so touched my heart, that, entre nous, I intend to marry her shortly. You will realise, therefore, that I find any remarks about a woman alleged to be my wife both painful and tactless.

GOLUBKOV. Fréjol . . . That means you're disowning her, abandoning a human being . . . your own wife! She was escaping, across Bolshevik Russia to join you! Don't you remember, she was arrested? Think back – the frost, the ice-covered windows, the dim lighting on the platform . . . .

KORZUKHIN. Yes, the frost . . . it was freezing cold . . . What if it was? What does that prove? The White Counter-Intelligence people have already tried to blackmail me more than once with some trumped-up story about a woman who was supposed to be my wife – and a Communist into the bargain. Monsieur Golubkov, I regret to say that I find this conversation extremely unpleasant.

GOLUBKOV. Oh, God. Have I dreamed it all?

KORZUKHIN. Obviously.

GOLUBKOV. I see. She's an embarrassment to you, so she doesn't exist. Good. So she isn't your wife. Just as well. I love her, d'you realise? And I'll do anything to save her. But I beg you to help me – at least temporarily. Everybody knows you're a very rich man, you invested all your money abroad. Lend me a thousand dollars and as soon as we're on our feet again I swear to you on my oath that I'll pay it back. Every last cent – I'll make it my life's work to see that you're paid back.

KORZUKHIN. Forgive me for being a cynic, monsieur Golubkov, but I somehow guessed that this conversation about a mythical wife was leading towards the subject of money. A thousand dollars, you said? I must have mis-heard you.

GOLUBKOV. Yes, a thousand. I swear I'll pay them back to you.

KORZUKHIN. Ah, young man, before you start talking so casually about a thousand dollars, let me tell you, what *one* dollar means. A dollar! The almighty god! It's everywhere! Far away over there on a roof-top there burns a golden ray and beside it, high in the air, a black cat with its back arched – it's there, the dollar's there! (*Points mysteriously at the ground.*) A vague tremor, no sound, nothing more perhaps than a rumbling in the bowels of the earth – there are trains running down there and there are dollars in them. Now shut your eyes and imagine – darkness and waves as high as mountains. Darkness and roaring water – the ocean! It is a hungry wild beast that swallows men. But on that ocean, with a hissing of boilers, thrusting aside millions of tons of water, sails a monster – roaring, crashing and spitting fire! It has to fight to cleave the water, but down there among the naked, sweating stokers, is the monster's golden cargo, its gold-like heart – the dollar!

Outside, the sound of a distant military band.

Suddenly there is tension in the world. There they go! Marching away, their heads welded into steel helmets. They're on the march. Now they're running! Now they throw themselves with a roar on to rows of barbed wire! Why do they do it? Because somewhere, someone has offended the almighty dollar! But the trouble is over now and everyone is blowing trumpets and shouting for joy! The war is over! The dollar is avenged! Long live the dollar!

The military band fades away.

So, monsieur Golubkov, are you still going to insist on my handing over a thousand dollars to a total stranger?

GOLUBKOV. No, I won't insist. But just before I go, Korzukhin, I should like to tell you something else. You are the most inhuman, corrupt, the most revolting creature I have ever been unlucky enough to set eyes on. One day retribution will catch up with you – it must. Goodbye. (*Starts to go.*)

Bell rings. Enter ANTOINE.

ANTOINE. General Charnota.

KORZUKHIN. Hmm . . . Today seems to be Russian day. All right, show him in.

Exit ANTOINE. *Enter* CHARNOTA. *He still wears his cossack fur hat, but has no silver belt and no dagger. He is wearing bright yellow underpants. His face shows that he has nothing more to lose.*

CHARNOTA. Ha, Paramon! How are you?

KORZUKHIN. I don't believe I have had the pleasure . . .

CHARNOTA. What a thing to say – come now, Paramon, have you forgotten Sebastopol?

KORZUKHIN. Oh yes, of course . . . delighted . . . But, forgive . . . you seem to be wearing . . . underpants . . .

CHARNOTA. And why not? If I were a woman it would be indecent, but I'm not so it's not.

KORZUKHIN. D'you mean to say, er . . . general . . . that you've been walking around the streets of Paris dressed like that?

CHARNOTA. No, of course not. In the street I was wearing trousers, but I took them off in your hall . . . What an idiotic question!

KORZUKHIN. Pardon, monsieur.

CHARNOTA (*quietly, to* GOLUBKOV). Did he give you the money?

GOLUBKOV. No, I'm going. Come on, I can't bear it here.

CHARNOTA. Go? Where have we got to go *to*? (*To* KORZUKHIN.) Look here, Paramon, is this any way to behave? Here are two of your fellow countrymen who risked their lives for you fighting the Bolsheviks and you refuse them some trifling sum of money. Don't you understand? Serafima is starving in Constantinople.

GOLUBKOV. Shut up. Come on, Grigory, let's go.

CHARNOTA. Do you know, Paramon, I never thought I could live to say such a thing, but I would have volunteered for the Bolsheviks just to have the chance of shooting you. I would have shot you, then deserted and joined the Whites again. I see you've had the cards put out. Do you play?

KORZUKHIN. I see nothing odd in that. I'm very fond of a game of cards.

CHARNOTA. You're a card-player! What's your game?

KORZUKHIN. Well, I like playing 'Nines'.

CHARNOTA. All right – play with me.

KORZUKHIN. I'd love to – but I'm afraid I only play for cash.

GOLUBKOV. Grigory – stop humiliating yourself! Come on – let's go.

CHARNOTA. I'm not humiliating myself. (*Whispers.*) Remember what Khludov said? As a last resort. If ever I saw a last resort this is it. Give me Khludov's medallion!

GOLUBKOV. All right. I'm past caring now, anyway. And I'm going.

CHARNOTA. No, we'll go together. I'm not going to let you out on the street with a face like that. I can see you're still pining for Serafima. (*Shows medallion to* KORZUKIN.) How much?

KORZUKHIN. H'mm . . . nice thing . . . Let's see . . . ten dollars.

CHARNOTA. Oh, really Paramon! It's worth much more than that but you're obviously ignorant about these things . . . All right, done! (*Hands medallion to* KORZUKHIN, *who gives him ten dollars. Sits down at card table, rolls up his sleeves, shuffles pack of cards.*) What's the name of that slave of yours?

KORZUKHIN. H'mmm . . . Antoine.

CHARNOTA (*loudly*). Antoine!

Enter ANTOINE.

Antoine, be a good fellow and bring me a bite to eat, will you?

ANTOINE (*smiling in polite astonishment*). Er . . . very good, sir . . . A l'instant! (*Exit.*)

CHARNOTA. What stake shall we play for?

KORZUKHIN. Those ten dollars. Card, please.

CHARNOTA. Nine.

KORZUKHIN (*pays*). Quits, please.

CHARNOTA (*throws down card*). Nine again.

KORZUKHIN. And quits again.

CHARNOTA. Want another card?

KORZUKHIN. Yes. Thank you. Seven.

CHARNOTA. And I've got an eight.

KORZUKHIN (*smiling*). Very well – quits.

GOLUBKOV (*suddenly*). Charnota! Are you crazy? He'll double, and then he'll take it all back from you!

CHARNOTA. If you think you can play this game better than I can, you'd better sit behind me.

GOLUBKOV. I don't know how to play!

CHARNOTA. Then keep out of my light! Card?

KORZUKHIN. Yes, please. Hell, bust!

CHARNOTA. I have a three.

KORZUKHIN. Won't you buy on a three?

CHARNOTA. Sometimes, when I feel I should.

ANTOINE *brings in a tray.*

(*Drinks.*) Have a glass, Golubkov?

GOLUBKOV. No thanks.

CHARNOTA. What about you, Paramon?

KORZUKHIN. Merci. I've just had dinner.

CHARNOTA. Aha . . . Card?

KORZUKHIN. Yes. A hundred and sixty dollars.

CHARNOTA. A hundred and sixty it is. (*Hums a tune.*) Nine.

KORZUKHIN. Incredible! I've never had such bad luck. Three hundred and twenty, then!

CHARNOTA. I'll have it in cash, please.

GOLUBKOV. Charnota – I beg you – stop it! Stop it now!

CHARNOTA. Be a good fellow and find something to do. There, go and look at his album. (*To* KORZUKHIN.) Cash, please.

KORZUKHIN. Just a moment. (*Opens safe. Immediately bells start ringing all over the house.*)

The lights go out and come on again. Enter ANTOINE *holding a revolver.*

GOLUBKOV. What's happening?

KORZUKHIN. It's an anti-burglar device. It's all right, Antoine, you can go, I opened it.

Exit ANTOINE.

CHARNOTA. Splendid trick. Another hand! Eight!

KORZUKHIN. Will you play it for six hundred and forty dollars?

CHARNOTA. No. The bank won't accept that stake.

KORZUKHIN. You're a good player. How much will you accept?

CHARNOTA. Fifty.

KORZUKHIN. Done. Nine!

CHARNOTA. I'm bust.

KORZUKHIN. Hand it over.

CHARNOTA. There you are.

KORZUKHIN. Five hundred and ninety!

CHARNOTA. You're a gambler, Paramon! It's your weakness!

GOLUBKOV. Charnota, for God's sake let's go!

KORZUKHIN. Card! I have a seven!

CHARNOTA. Seven and a half! I'm joking – eight.

With a groan GOLUBKOV *covers his ears and lies down on the divan.* KORZUKHIN *unlocks the safe. Bells, darkness, light again. It is night. Candles in pink shades are burning on the card table.* KORZUKHIN *has his jacket off, his hair tousled. Outside are the lights of Paris, vague sounds of music. Piles of money in front of* KORZUKHIN *and* CHARNOTA. GOLUBKOV *lying on the divan asleep.*

CHARNOTA (*humming to himself*). Bust.

KORZUKHIN. Four hundred, please! I stake three thousand. Seven!

CHARNOTA. Nine. Cash, please!

KORZUKHIN *goes to safe. The same performance with the burglar alarm. Pale dawn breaking over Paris. Silence.* KORZUKHIN, CHARNOTA *and* GOLUBKOV *look like shadows. Empty champagne bottles scattered about the floor.*
GOLUBKOV *starts to stuff banknotes into his pocket.*

CHARNOTA (*to* KORZUKHIN). Have you got a newspaper we could wrap it in?

KORZUKHIN. No. I tell you what – give me back the cash and I'll give you a cheque instead.

CHARNOTA. What, Paramon? You don't suppose any bank would pay out twenty thousand dollars to a man in his underpants, do you? No thanks!

GOLUBKOV. Charnota, buy back my medallion, I want to give it back.

KORZUKHIN. Three hundred dollars.

GOLUBKOV. There you are! (*Throws him the money.*)

In exchange KORZUKHIN tosses him the medallion.

CHARNOTA. Well, au revoir, Paramon. We've had a good game, now it's time to go.

KORZUKHIN (*blocking the door*). No, stop! I'm not well – I must be going out of my mind . . . You wouldn't take advantage of me in this condition, would you? Look – give me back the money, and I'll give you five hundred dollars to clear off and keep your mouths shut.

CHARNOTA. You're joking.

KORZUKHIN. Very well, in that case I shall immediately ring the police and tell them you've robbed me. You won't have a chance. Look at you – a couple of tramps.

CHARNOTA (*to GOLUBKOV*). D'you hear that? (*Draws his revolver*). Right, Paramon – start praying to Notre Dame de Paris. You are just about to die.

KORZUKHIN. Help! Murder!

In runs ANTOINE, in his underwear.

The whole house is asleep! Nobody can hear me – I'm being robbed! Help! Police!

A curtain over a doorway is pushed aside. Enter LYUSKA, wearing pyjamas. At the sight of CHARNOTA and GOLUBKOV, she freezes.

Lucie, while you're asleep I'm being robbed by a couple of Russian thugs!

LYUSKA. Oh, my God! I see my purgatory isn't over yet . . . I thought I had a right to some peace by now, but apparently not

. . . No wonder, when I dreamed of cockroaches last night! I'd just like to know one thing – how did you two get here?

CHARNOTA (*amazed*). It can't be!

KORZUKHIN (*to* CHARNOTA). Do you know Mademoiselle Fréjol?

Behind KORZUKHIN's *back* LYUSKA *kneels down and clasps her hands in entreaty.*

CHARNOTA. How should I know her? Never seen her in my life.

LYUSKA. Let me introduce myself, then. Lucie Fréjol.

CHARNOTA (*bows*). Major-General Charnota.

LYUSKA. Well, what seems to be wrong, gentlemen? (*To* KORZUKHIN.) Why were you screaming like that, Ratty, what have they done to you?

KORZUKHIN. He's won twenty thousand dollars off me! And I want him to give them back!

GOLUBKOV. I've never heard of such disgusting behaviour!

LYUSKA. No, really, Ratty, it simply isn't done. You've lost and that's that. Don't be so childish.

KORZUKHIN. Where did Antoine buy those cards?!

ANTOINE. You bought them yourself, sir.

LYUSKA. Go to hell, Antoine! What do you mean by appearing in front of me in that state?

Exit ANTOINE.

Gentlemen! The money is yours and there is no misunderstanding. (*To* KORZUKHIN.) Go on, little boy, run away to bed. You've got bags under your eyes.

KORZUKHIN. I'll sack that fool, Antoine! I don't want to see any more Russians in this house! (*Exit spluttering.*)

LYUSKA. Well, I was delighted to see some of my fellow-countrymen and I'm only sorry I shan't see you again. (*In a whisper.*) All right, you've won – now get out! (*Aloud.*) Antoine!

ANTOINE *appears in the doorway.*

These gentlemen are going. Please show them out.

CHARNOTA. Au revoir, mademoiselle.

LYUSKA. Adieu!

Exeunt CHARNOTA *and* GOLUBKOV.

Thank God they've gone. Lord! Let's hope to God I've seen the last of them!

Steps heard in the street outside.

LYUSKA (*looks furtively around, runs to the window, opens it, shouts hoarsely*). Goodbye! Golubkov – look after Serafima! Charnota! Buy yourself a pair of trousers!

Darkness.

The Dream Ends

EIGHTH AND LAST DREAM

A room furnished with carpets, low divans, a hookah. Upstage a huge studio window, with French windows opening in the middle of it. Through them are seen a minaret, the domes of Constantinople and the top of YANKO's *booth. Sunset.* KHLUDOV *is sitting on a carpet, his legs crossed Turkish-fashion, talking to someone.*

KHLUDOV. You've tortured me enough. But I know now what I have to do. You mustn't forget, though, that you're not the only one. There are living people who are clinging to me too, and demanding my help. Don't you see. Fate has tied them to me and I can't throw them off now. I accept it. But one thing I can't understand – you. How did you escape from that long line of faint blue lights, those lampposts? Why *you*? You see, you weren't the only one. Oh no, there were many of you . . . (*Mutters.*) How many were there, how many . . . I'll never remember. (*Reflects ages, hangs his head.*) Yes. And it was all to no purpose. If I'd not hanged them the Bolsheviks would still have beaten us. And then what? Darkness. Oblivion. Then this stifling heat and the roundabout turning all day. But how – how did you come so far and catch me, how did you do it, how did you throw a hood over *my* head? Leave me alone now, stop tormenting me. I've made up my mind – I swear it. As soon as Golubkov comes back I'm leaving. Set my mind at rest, nod to me if you mean to leave me. Just a nod, Krapilin! You were a great talker once – at least spare me a nod now! There, you've nodded. I'll go.

Enter SERAFIMA.

SERAFIMA. Are you doing it again, Roman?

KHLUDOV. What?

SERAFIMA. Who were you talking to? There was nobody in the room except you.

KHLUDOV. You must have been hearing things. Anyway, I have a habit of muttering to myself. I hope it doesn't disturb anybody?

SERAFIMA (*sits down beside* KHLUDOV *on the carpet*). For four months I've been hearing the sound of your voice through the wall. Do you think I like it? It keeps me awake. And now you're doing it in the daytime. You poor man.

KHLUDOV. All right, I'll get you another room, only nearby, so that I can still keep an eye on you. I've sold a ring, so there's some money. I know another room – it's clean and light, windows on the Bosphorus. But I can't pretend it's very comfortable. What can you expect? We lost, we were thrown out, we must take the consequences. And do you know why we lost? (*Points mysteriously over his shoulder.*) He and I know. I feel uncomfortable, too, with you next door, but I must keep my word.

SERAFIMA. Roman, you remember the day Golubkov left? You ran after me and dragged me back by force, remember?

KHLUDOV. When a person goes out of their mind you have to use force. None of you are normal.

SERAFIMA. I started to feel sorry for you, Roman, and that's the only reason why I stayed.

KHLUDOV. I don't need a nanny, but you do!

SERAFIMA. Don't get angry, you only hurt yourself when you do.

KHLUDOV. Yes, you're right . . . I can't hurt other people any longer. Remember that night at the headquarters . . . Khludov the beast, Khludov the jackal – remember?

SERAFIMA. All that's in the past. I've forgotten it and you're not to remind me.

KHLUDOV (*mutters*). Yes, yes . . . No, I *must* not forget . . . I shall remember.

SERAFIMA. You know, Roman, I was thinking all last night . . . We must make up our minds to do *something*. How long are we going to sit here?

KHLUDOV. As soon as Golubkov comes back this little club of ours is going to break up. I'll hand him over to you and then it's every man for himself. Goodbye to this stinking place.

SERAFIMA. We must have been crazy to let him go! I'll never forgive myself for it. God, how I miss him! It was all Lyuska's fault . . . I lost my head when she goaded me . . . Now I'm like you, I can't sleep either, because he's probably lost and may be dead.

KHLUDOV. This town is stifling – it's unbearable! And as for that degrading farce, the cockroach races! Everybody says I'm mad, but look at *them*. But why did you let him go? Has that husband of yours really got any money?

SERAFIMA. I have no husband. I've forgotten him, God rot him!

KHLUDOV. So what are we going to do?

SERAFIMA. We've just got to face the truth – Sergei has gone for good. I made up my mind last night: the Reds are letting the cossacks go back to Russia. So I'm going to go back to Petersburg. Why did I ever leave, fool that I was?

KHLUDOV. Very sensible. You're right, Serafima. You did nothing against the Bolsheviks, there's no reason why you shouldn't go back.

SERAFIMA. Yet, I'm still not sure – there's one thing only that holds me back. What's going to become of you?

KHLUDOV (*beckons her mysteriously. She moves closer and he whispers into her ear*). The only things is . . . (*Whispers.*) . . . you're safe, but the White counter-intelligence people never let me out of their sight, they have a nose for things like this . . . (*Whispers.*) I'm going back to Russia too, I may even go tonight. There's a steamer leaving tonight for Odessa.

SERAFIMA. Are you going back secretly, under a false name?

KHLUDOV. Under my own name. I shall turn up and say: I've arrived – I'm Khludov.

SERAFIMA. But you'll be shot out of hand!

KHLUDOV. Instantly. (*Smiles.*) On the spot. Cotton shirt, down to the cellar, snow outside . . . Take aim! Fire! All my troubles are over. Look, he has moved away.

SERAFIMA. Ah, so that's what you've been muttering about! Do you want to die? You must be mad! Stay here, you may recover in time.

KHLUDOV. I recovered today. I'm completely well now. I'm not a cockroach, I'm not going to scuttle around in the dark till I fall off the edge and drown in a bucket of water. I can't forget our army, the fighting, the lampposts, those men with sacks over their heads . . . that's why I've got to go back.

Loud knock at the door. Enter GOLUBKOV *and* CHARNOTA. *Both dressed in elegant suits.* CHARNOTA *is carrying a small suitcase. Silence.*

SERAFIMA. Sergei! . . . Sergei!

CHARNOTA. Roman, we're back – aren't you going to say something?

KHLUDOV. So here they are. Didn't I tell you . . .

GOLUBKOV. Serafima, darling . . .

In tears, SERAFIMA *embraces* GOLUBKOV.

KHLUDOV (*frowning*). Come out on to the balcony, Charnota, I want a word with you. (KHLUDOV *and* CHARNOTA *go out by the french windows.*)

GOLUBKOV. Now don't cry, don't cry. What are you crying for, Serafima! Look – I'm back . . .

SERAFIMA. I thought you were dead! Oh, if you only knew how I've missed you! . . . I realise now . . . And I waited for you, didn't I! You're never to leave me again, I shan't let you go!

GOLUBKOV. Of course I won't! That's all over. Now we've got to think what we're going to do next. How have you managed here without me, Serafima? Say something!

SERAFIMA. I was so worried I couldn't sleep. As soon as you went I came to my senses and I couldn't forgive myself for having let you go. I used to sit up all night watching the lights out there and I had visions of you wandering round Paris, ragged and hungry . . . And there's something the matter with Khludov – he frightens me.

GOLUBKOV. Don't, Serafima, don't!

SERAFIMA. Did you see my husband?

GOLUBKOV. Yes, I saw him. He has completely given you up, found himself another wife . . . and . . . Well, it's better that way, you're free now! (*Shouts.*) Thanks, Khludov!

Enter KHLUDOV *and* CHARNOTA.

KHLUDOV. So everything's all right now, is it? (*To* GOLUBKOV.) Do you love her? Eh? Do you, honestly? I advise you to go where she tells you. I'm off. Goodbye, everybody. (*Picks up his overcoat, hat and suitcase.*)

CHARNOTA. Where are you going?

KHLUDOV. There's a steamer leaving tonight and I'm going with it. Only don't tell a soul.

GOLUBKOV. Roman! Think again, for God's sake. You can't do that.

SERAFIMA. It's no use, I tried to tell him, but you won't stop him.

KHLUDOV. I know what, Charnota – come with me. Why not, eh?

CHARNOTA. Wait a minute! I've just realised where you're going! You can't be serious. Or have you got some brilliant new plan up your sleeve? After all you're clever enough – you weren't on the general staff for nothing. Or are you going to give yourself up and answer for what you did? Are you? Well if you are, Roman, I hope you realise that you'll only live long enough for them to get you off the boat and march you to the nearest wall! And under a strong escort so that the people don't tear you to pieces on the way! They remember you. And you think I'm going to go and face it with you . . . There's a lot chalked up against my name too, you know . . . though at least I didn't do any hangings.

SERAFIMA. Charnota! How can you – he's a sick man.

CHARNOTA. I'm trying to stop him from going.

GOLUBKOV. Stay here, Roman, you can't go!

KHLUDOV. You're going to miss Russia, Charnota.

CHARNOTA. Don't tell me. I miss it already. I miss Kiev, I miss the Dnieper, I miss the fighting . . . I've never run away from death, but you won't find me running back to certain death with the Bolsheviks either. For pity's sake, Roman – don't go.

KHLUDOV. I'm going. Goodbye. (*Exit.*)

CHARNOTA. Serafima, stop him! He'll regret it!

SERAFIMA. I can't stop him.

GOLUBKOV. No, I know him, you won't stop him now.

CHARNOTA. Well, if he wants to face the music, that's his affair. What about you two?

SERAFIMA. Let's go back and ask permission to return, Sergei. I've thought it over – let's go home tonight!

GOLUBKOV. All right, we'll go! I can't spend the rest of my life like this.

CHARNOTA. You're all right, they'll probably let you in. Let's divide up the money.

SERAFIMA. Money? What money? I suppose you blackmailed Korzukhin for it.

GOLUBKOV. He won twenty thousand dollars from Korzukhin.

SERAFIMA. In that case he can keep it.

GOLUBKOV. I don't need it either. I've come back here and that's all I care about. We'll get to Russia somehow or other. What you've given me already will be enough for us.

CHARNOTA. For the last time – do you want it? You don't? Doing the decent thing? All right, done. Our ways part, fate divides us. One of us heads straight for a noose, the others want to go home to Petersburg – but what about me? What am I now? I'm the Wandering Jew! I'm the Flying Dutchman! I'm – nothing!

A clock strikes five. The flag is hoisted over YANKO's *booth, the sound of an accordion drifts across and a Russian choir singing* 'The twelve robbers' . . .

Aha! D'you hear that? The cockroach races have started again! (*Throws open the french windows on to the balcony.*)

The sound of the choir swells.

I'm coming, Yanko! And if I don't win this time I'm going to buy you and all your filthy cockroaches as well! (*Exit.*)

GOLUBKOV. I can't bear to see this terrible city any longer!

SERAFIMA. What has happened these past six months, Sergei? Were we dreaming? Tell me the answer. Where were we running away to and what for? Lampposts on the platform, dangling men in black hoods . . . then this heat and stink and despair . . . I want to see the Nevsky again, I want to see the snow! I want to forget it all as though it had never happened!

The sound of the choir rises in a crescendo.
The distant voice of the muezzin begins to chant: 'La illah illa illah . . .'

GOLUBKOV. None of it happened, we imagined it all. Forget it. In a month we'll be home, then it will start snowing and the snow will cover our tracks . . . Come on – we're going!

SERAFIMA. We're going! No more dreams.

Both run out. Constantinople starts to fade and vanishes for ever.

The End Of The Last Dream.

Molière
(The League of Hypocrites)

A Play in Four Acts

Translated by Michael Glenny

Molière
(*The League of Hypocrites*)

Rien ne manque à sa gloire;
Il manquait à la nôtre.

Characters

JEAN-BAPTISTE POQUELIN DE MOLIERE	famous playwright and actor
MADELINE BEJART ARMANDE BEJART DE MOLIERE MARIETTE RIVALE	} actresses
CHARLES VARLET DE LAGRANGE	actor, nicknamed 'The Scribbler'
ZACHARIE MOIRRON	romantic actor
PHILIBERT DU CROISY	actor
JEAN-JACQUES BOUTON	candle-snuffer and Molière's servant
LOUIS XIV, surnamed The Great	King of France
MARQUIS D'ORSIGNY	duellist, nicknamed 'One-Eye'
MARQUIS DE CHARRON	Archbishop of Paris
MARQUIS DE LESSAC	gambler
THE JUST SHOEMAKER	king's jester
CHARLATAN	with a harpsichord
UNKNOWN WOMAN	in a mask
FATHER BARTHOLOMEW	itinerant preacher
BROTHER STRENGTH BROTHER FAITH	} members of the League of Holy Writ.
PROMPTER	

Members of the League of Holy Writ in masks and black capes.
Courtiers, musketeers and others.

ACT ONE

Heavily muffled sound of laughter from a thousand-odd people is heard from behind the curtain. The curtain rises to reveal the Théâtre du Palais-Royal. Heavy drapes. A green poster adorned with coats-of-arms and arabesques. Written on it in bold capitals: LES COMEDIENS DE MONSIEUR, followed by smaller print. A mirror. Armchairs. Costumes. Near the curtain separating two dressing rooms stands an enormous harpsichord. In the second dressing room hangs a large crucifix with a veilleuse burning in front of it.

In the first dressing-room there is a door stage left; numerous tallow candles. On the table in the second dressing room there is only a lantern with coloured glass panes.

Everything and everyone (except LAGRANGE) have the air of being keyed up for a special occasion; there is tension and anxiety. LAGRANGE, who has no part in the play being performed, is sitting in his dressing room deep in thought. He wears a dark cape. He is young, handsome, imposing. The lantern casts a mysterious light on to his face.

In the other dressing-room BOUTON is standing with his back to the audience and looking through a gap in the curtains. His back alone betrays his avid curiosity at what he sees. CHARLATAN puts his head round the door, cups his hand to his ear and listens.

Gusts of laughter can be heard, then a final burst of laughter and applause. A moment later MOLIERE appears between a gap in the curtains and runs down the steps into his dressing room. CHARLATAN withdraws discreetly.

MOLIERE is wearing a vast wig and grotesque helmet, and he holds a property sword. He is comically made up as Sganarelle: a mauve nose with a wart on it. He presses his left hand to his breast as though suffering from heart trouble. Make-up is running down his face.

MOLIERE (*throws off cloak, gasps for breath*). Water!

BOUTON. At once. (*Gives him a glass.*)

MOLIERE. Ah! (*Drinks, listening anxiously.*)

The door bursts open. DU CROISY, *made up as Polchinelle, runs in.*

DU CROISY. The king is applauding! (*Exit.*)

PROMPTER (*through a gap in the curtains*). The king is applauding!

MOLIERE (*to* BOUTON). Towel! (*Nervously mops his forehead.*)

MADELEINE (*in make-up, enters between the curtains*). Quick! The king is applauding!

MOLIERE (*excitedly*). Yes, yes I can hear. I'm coming. (*To* BOUTON.) Open up the stage! Holy Virgin! (*Crosses himself before passing through the curtain.*)

BOUTON *first opens the curtains dividing the dressing rooms from the stage, then raises the huge main curtain between the stage and the auditorium. The stage is seen through the wings. It is raised above the level of the dressing rooms and is empty. Chandeliers gleam with countless wax candles. The auditorium is invisible, except for a gilded box which is empty, but the mysterious, expectant presence of the people can be felt in the half-darkened hall.*

CHARLATAN's *face appears for a second in the doorway.* MOLIERE *advances on to the stage and turns so that we see him in profile. He pads up to the footlights like a cat, almost furtively. He bows, the feathers of his helmet sweeping the floor. As he does so, one invisible person in the auditorium starts to clap, followed by a crescendo of applause from the rest of the audience. Then silence.*

MOLIERE. Your . . . M–Majesty . . . your majesty . . . Most illustrious sovereign . . . (*He speaks the first words with a slight stutter – he has a trace of a stutter when speaking normally offstage – but then his speech becomes steadier and as soon as he is under way it is obvious that he is a great actor. He has an infinite wealth of intonation, facial expression and movement. His smile is very infectious.*) The actors of the Company of Monsieur, your most loyal and most devoted servants, have asked me to thank you for the unprecedented honour you have shown us by attending our theatre . . . Therefore, sire . . . I can say no more.

A slight titter breaks out among the audience and fades.

> O muse, o muse, my cunning Thalia!
> Each night, in answer to your call,
> At risk of ridicule and . . . failure
> I play at Sganarelle within this hall!

> Gauging my bow according to the prices –
> Tonight it's thirty sous a person in the stalls –
> I entertain by showing men their vices,
> In verse that's often little more than . . . rubbish!

A burst of laughter from the audience.

> Tonight, though, fairest muse of comedy,
> I beg thee – fire me with thy glance:
> How else my meagre gifts to remedy
> And raise a smile upon the Sun of France?

Thunderous applause.

BOUTON. Ah, what talent! 'The Sun' – that was a brilliant stroke!

CHARLATAN (*enviously*). When did he write that?

BOUTON (*haughtily*). He didn't. Made it up on the spot.

CHARLATAN. Incredible.

BOUTON. You couldn't do it.

MOLIERE (*abruptly changes his tone*).
> For us thou bear'st the burden of a crown;
> Compared with thee an actor's but a paltry thing,
> Louis the Great, nay (*raises his voice.*) France's
> > > greatest (*shouts.*) King!!

MOLIERE throws his hat into the air. The audience goes mad. There is a roar of 'Long live the King!' The candle flames wave and flicker. BOUTON and CHARLATAN wave their hats and shout, though they cannot be heard against the noise. A trumpet fanfare from the Royal Guard resounds above the roar. LAGRANGE has taken off his hat and stands motionless. The ovation dies down. Silence falls.

VOICE OF LOUIS. We thank you, Monsieur de Molière.

MOLIERE. Your Majesty's most humble servants beg you to watch one more comic interlude – but only if we have not tired you.

VOICE OF LOUIS. Oh, with pleasure, Monsieur de Molière.

MOLIERE (*shouts*). Curtain!

The main curtain falls and shuts off the auditorium, where the orchestra at once strikes up. BOUTON *then closes the backstage curtain, shutting off our view of the stage.* CHARLATAN *disappears.*

MOLIERE (*muttering as he enters dressing room*). That does it! I'll murder him!

BOUTON. Who should he want to murder in his hour of triumph!

MOLIERE (*grabs* BOUTON *by the throat*). You!

BOUTON (*screams*). You're strangling me . . . at a royal performance!

LAGRANGE *makes a move, but stops. Hearing the cry,* MADELEINE *and* MARIETTE RIVALE – *in the midst of changing and all but naked – rush in. The two actresses seize* MOLIERE *by his breeches to pull him away from* BOUTON, *whereupon* MOLIERE *kicks out at them. Eventually* MOLIERE *is torn away, clutching a piece of* BOUTON*'s coat. They manage to push* MOLIERE *into an armchair.*

MADELEINE. You're mad! The audience can hear everything!

MOLIERE. Let me go!

MARIETTE RIVALE. Monsieur Molière! (*Claps her hand over* MOLIERE*'s mouth.*)

BOUTON (*looking into mirror, feels his torn coat*). Well done. You move fast, I must say. (*To* MOLIERE.) What's the matter?

MOLIERE. You scoundrel . . . Why do I keep you on in the company when you try me so? We've played it forty times if we've played it once and everything was perfect – then just when the king comes a candle has to fall out of the chandelier and drip wax all over the stage.

BOUTON. Maître, it was your fault – when you did your little jig you knocked the candle off with your sword.

MOLIERE. You lying good-for-nothing!

LAGRANGE *puts his head in his hands and quietly weeps.*

MARIETTE RIVALE. He's right. You hit the candle with your sword.

MOLIERE. The audience is laughing. The king is shocked . . .

BOUTON. The king is the best-mannered man in France and he hasn't noticed a thing.

MOLIERE. So I knocked it off, did I? H'mm . . . in that case why was I shouting at you?

BOUTON. It is not for me to say, sir.

MOLIERE. I seem to have torn your coat.

BOUTON *laughs convulsively.*

MARIETTE RIVALE. Oh my God – look at me! (*Grabs a coat, wraps herself in it and rushes out.*)

DU CROISY (*appears in a gap in the curtains holding a lantern*). Madeleine Béjart – on stage please, on stage . . . (*Exit.*)

. MADELEINE. Coming! (*Exit.*)

MOLIERE (*to* BOUTON). Take this coat.

BOUTON. Thank you. (*Takes off his own coat and breeches, hastily dons a pair of* MOLIERE's *breeches with lace ruffles at the knee.*)

MOLIERE. Just a moment . . . why the breeches too?

BOUTON. You must agree, maître, it would be the height of bad taste to wear such a gorgeous coat with these shabby breeches. Look at them – these breeches are a disgrace. (*Puts on the coat.*) Maître, I have found two silver coins of trifling value in the pocket. What would you have me do with them?

MOLIERE. Damn me! Give them to a museum, you rascal. (*Freshens his make-up.*)

BOUTON. Agreed. I shall do as you say. (*Pockets the money.*) Well, I'm off to trim the wicks. (*Picks up his candle-snuffer.*)

MOLIERE. And kindly don't stare at the king from the stage.

BOUTON. No need to say that to me, maître – I'm as good a Frenchman as you are.

MOLIERE. Yes, a Frenchman by birth and a blockhead by profession.

BOUTON. And you are a great actor by profession and a boor by character. (*Exit.*)

MOLIERE. I must have committed some sin and God sent him to me from Limoges as a punishment.

CHARLATAN. Monsieur le directeur! Monsieur le directeur!

MOLIERE. Ah – you still here? Yours is a second-rate kind of act, monsieur, if you'll forgive my frankness, but the pit will like it. You can have the interval for a week. How *do* you do it, though?

CHARLATAN. A secret, monsieur.

MOLIERE. Well, I'll find out. Play a few chords – quietly, mind.

With an enigmatic smile CHARLATAN goes over to the harpsichord, sits on a stool a short distance away from the keyboard and makes motions in the air as though he were playing. The keys move and the instrument plays softly.

MOLIERE. The devil! (*Rushes to the harpsichord and snatches at what he imagines to be invisible strings.*)

CHARLATAN *smiles mysteriously.*

Very well, here's your advance. There's a spring somewhere, isn't there?

CHARLATAN. Will the harpsichord be staying in the theatre overnight?

MOLIERE. Of course. You can't drag it home by yourself.

DU CROISY (*looks in with his lantern and book*). Monsieur de Molière – on stage please. (*Exit.*)

MOLIERE. Yes, coming. (*Exit. As soon as he goes a muffled roat of laughter is heard.*)

The curtain over the entrance into the other dressing room is pushed aside and ARMANDE appears. She is seventeen, pretty, and her features are reminiscent of MADELEINE. She tries to slip past LAGRANGE.

LAGRANGE. Stop!

ARMANDE. Ah, it's you, Scribbler. Why do you hide yourself away here like a mouse? I've been looking at the king. I must hurry now.

LAGRANGE. There's plenty of time. He's on stage. Why do you call me 'Scribbler'? I'm not sure that I like it.

ARMANDE. Dear Monsieur Lagrange! The whole company has the greatest respect for you and your chronicle. But I'll stop calling you that if you don't like it.

LAGRANGE. I was waiting for you.

ARMANDE. Why?

LAGRANGE. Today is the seventeenth – look, I've put a black cross against the date in the chronicle.

ARMANDE. But what happened? Has someone in the company died?

LAGRANGE. I have marked this evening with a black cross as a sign of ill-omen. You must refuse him.

ARMANDE. Monsieur de Lagrange, who gave you the right to meddle in my affairs?

LAGRANGE. Harsh words. Don't marry him. I implore you!

ARMANDE. Oh, so you're in love with me, are you?

Faint music heard from behind the curtain.

LAGRANGE. No. I don't even like you.

ARMANDE. Let me go, sir.

LAGRANGE. No. You have no right to marry him. You're so young! I appeal to your better feelings.

ARMANDE. Truly, everyone in the company has taken leave of their senses. What is it to do with you?

LAGRANGE. I can't tell you, but it would be a great sin.

ARMANDE. Oh, you mean the gossip about my sister? I've heard that – pure nonsense. And even if they did have an affair once, what's that to me? (*She tries to push* LAGRANGE *out of the way and pass by.*)

LAGRANGE. Stop! You must refuse him. You won't? Well then – I shall kill you. (*Draws his sword.*)

ARMANDE. Madman . . . Murderer!

LAGRANGE. Why do you have to do this? It will be fatal. You know you don't love him. You're a young girl and he . . .

ARMANDE. No, I do love him.

LAGRANGE. Refuse him.

ARMANDE. Scribbler, I cannot. We are already lovers and . . . (*She whispers into* LAGRANGE's *ear.*)

LAGRANGE (*sheathes his sword*). Very well, go. I won't keep you any longer.

ARMANDE (*sidles past him*). Brute. You threatened me and for that I hate you.

LAGRANGE (*anxiously*). Forgive me. I only wanted to save you. (*Wraps himself in his cape and walks off holding his lantern.*)

ARMANDE (*in* MOLIERE's *dressing-room*). It's monstrous, monstrous . . .

MOLIERE (*entering*). Aha!

ARMANDE. Maître, the whole world is up in arms against me!

MOLIERE (*embraces her. At that moment* BOUTON *appears*). Devil take it. (*To* BOUTON.) Listen, go and see to the candles in the pit.

BOUTON. I've just done so.

MOLIERE. Very well, then, go along to the steward and bring me a carafe of wine.

BOUTON. I've already brought one. There it is.

MOLIERE (*in a low voice*). In that case just get out of here and go to the devil.

BOUTON. You should have said that in the first place. (*Starts to go.*) Ha, ha, ha . . . (*From the doorway.*) Tell me, maître, how old are you?

MOLIERE. Why?

BOUTON. Some men of the Horse Guards were asking me.

MOLIERE. Get out!

Exit BOUTON. MOLIERE *locks the door behind him.*

Kiss me.

ARMANDE (*puts her arms round his neck*). That nose! I can't get under it . . .

MOLIERE *removes his nose and wig. Kisses* ARMANDE.

You know I . . . (*Whispers something in his ear.*)

MOLIERE. My little girl . . . (*Reflects.*) That no longer frightens me, I have decided. (*Leads her to the crucifix.*) Vow that you love me.

ARMANDE. I love you, I love you, I love you.

MOLIERE. You won't deceive me? Look, I'm already getting wrinkles and I'm starting to turn grey. I am surrounded by enemies and the shame would kill me.

ARMANDE. No, no! How could I?

MOLIERE. I want to start a new life with you! But I'll pay the price for it, never fear. I shall make you! You are going to be a great actress, the first lady of my company. That is my dream and therefore it will come true. But remember – if you break your vow, you rob me of everything.

ARMANDE. I can see no wrinkles on your face. You are so brave and so great that you can never be wrinkled. You're Jean . . .

MOLIERE. Baptiste . . .

ARMANDE. . . . Molière. (*She kisses him.*)

MOLIERE (*laughs, then assumes dignified tone*). Tomorrow we shall be married. Of course it will bring me many cares . . .

Distant roar of applause. Knock at the door.

Ah, this life!

Another knock.

We cannot meet at Madeleine's house tonight, so instead when all the lights are out in the theatre come to the stage door, wait for me there in the garden and I will bring you here. There's no moon tonight.

The knock becomes a loud hammering.

BOUTON (*shouts from behind the door*). Maître . . .

MOLIERE *opens the door. Enter* BOUTON, LAGRANGE *and* ONE-EYE, *wearing the uniform of the Company of Black Musketeers and a black eyepatch.*

ONE-EYE. Monsieur de Molière?

MOLIERE. Your most obedient servant, sir.

ONE-EYE. The king has commanded me to hand you the cost of

his seat in the theatre – thirty sous. (*Gives him the coins on a cushion.*)

MOLIERE *kisses the coins.*

ONE-EYE. But since you performed some extra items, and in thanks for the poem which you composed and recited to him, his majesty bids me add something to the price of his ticket – here are five thousand livres. (*Gives him a bag.*)

MOLIERE. The king is gracious. (*To* LAGRANGE.) Put aside five hundred livres of this for me, and divide the rest equally among all the members of the company. Give it to them personally.

LAGRANGE. Thank you on behalf of all the actors. (*Takes bag and exit.*)

Distant sound of a fanfare.

MOLIERE. Excuse me, monsieur, the king is leaving. (*Exit.*)

ONE-EYE (*to* ARMANDE). Delighted to have this opportunity, mademoiselle . . . (*Sniggers.*) . . . Allow me to present myself – d'Orsigny, captain of musketeers.

ARMANDE (*curtseys*). Armande Béjart. Are you the famous swordsman who beats every opponent?

ONE-EYE (*sniggers*). And you, mademoiselle, are an actress in this company?

BOUTON. It's started. Oh, mon maître, how could you be so careless?

ONE-EYE (*staring in astonishment at the lace on* BOUTON's *breeches*). Did you say something to me, my dear sir?

BOUTON. No, sir.

ONE-EYE. Then are you in the habit of talking to yourself?

BOUTON. Just so, sir. I once used to talk in my sleep.

ONE-EYE. Indeed?

BOUTON. On my honour. And would you believe it . . .

ONE-EYE. Curious fellow . . . (*To* ARMANDE.) Your face, mademoiselle . . .

BOUTON (*edges between them*). . . . I even shouted aloud in my sleep. Eight of the best doctors in Limoges treated me . . .

ONE-EYE. And they cured you, I hope?

BOUTON. No, sir. They bled me eight times in three days, after which I lay motionless and was given the sacrament.

ONE-EYE (*bored*). What an eccentric fellow you are to be sure. (*To* ARMANDE.) I flatter myself, mademoiselle . . . Who is he?

ARMANDE. That is our candle-snuffer, monsieur – Jean-Jacques Bouton.

ONE-EYE (*reproachfully*). Some other time, my good man, I shall be delighted to hear how you roared in your sleep.

Enter MOLIERE.

Allow me to take my leave. I must join the king.

MOLIERE. Au revoir, monsieur.

Exit ONE-EYE.

ARMANDE. Au revoir, maître.

MOLIERE (*sees her out*). There is no moon. I shall be waiting for you. (*To* BOUTON.) Ask Madame Béjart to come and see me. Then put out the lights and go home.

Exit BOUTON, MOLIERE *changes out of his costume. Enter* MADELEINE, *her make-up removed.*

MOLIERE. Madeleine, I have something very important to tell you.

MADELEINE *clutches at her heart, sits down.*

I intend to get married.

MADELEINE (*in a lifeless voice*). Who to?

MOLIERE. Your sister.

MADELEINE. Please – tell me you're joking.

MOLIERE. Not at all.

The lights in the theatre start to go out.

MADELEINE. And what about me?

MOLIERE. Madeleine, you and I are old, firm friends, you are my true companion, but you know there was been no love between us for a long time now . . .

MADELEINE. Do you remember when you were in prison twenty years ago? Who used to bring you food?

MOLIERE. You did.

MADELEINE. And who has looked after you for twenty years?

MOLIERE. You, you have.

MADELEINE. No one would chase away a dog who has guarded a house for twenty years. But you would, Molière. You are a terrible man. You frighten me, Molière.

MOLIERE. Don't torture me. Passion has seized hold of me.

MADELEINE (*suddenly falls on her knees, crawls towards* MOLIERE). Couldn't you change your mind, Molière? We'll pretend you never said those words just now. Shall we? We'll go home. You'll light the candles, I'll come to you . . . you can read me the third act of 'Tartuffe'. (*Flatteringly.*) I think it's a work of genius . . . and if you need advice, whom will you ask, Molière? She's only a little girl . . . You know you've aged, Jean–Baptiste, your temples are turning grey. You like your hot–waterbottle . . . I'll do everything for you . . . Just think – the candle's burning . . . We'll light the fire and all will be well. And if . . . you can't do without . . . oh, I know you . . . Look at Rivale . . . she's not bad, is she? What a body! Well? I won't say a word . . .

MOLIERE. Think what you're saying! What's come over you? (*Miserably wipes the sweat from his brow.*)

MADELEINE (*gets up, dazed*). Marry anyone you like, only not Armande! Oh curse the day that I brought her to Paris!

MOLIERE. Please, Madeleine, be quiet. (*Whispers.*) I must marry her . . . it's too late. I must, don't you understand?

MADELEINE. I *see*. My God! (*Pause.*) I can't fight any more, I've no more strength left. Do what you want. (*Pause.*) I feel sorry for you, Molière.

MOLIERE. Let us still be friends . . .

MADELEINE. Don't come near me, I implore you! (*Pause.*) Well, I shall leave the company.

MOLIERE. Out of spite?

MADELEINE. Not out of spite, as God's my witness. Today was my last time on stage. I'm tired . . . (*Smiles.*) I shall go to church.

MOLIERE. I see your mind's made up. The theatre will give you a pension. You've earned it.

MADELEINE. Yes . . .

MOLIERE. When the shock has passed I believe you will feel more kindly about me and you will be my friend again.

MADELEINE. No.

MOLIERE. Don't you want to see Armande again either?

MADELEINE. I shall see Armande. She must know nothing of this, do you understand, nothing.

MOLIERE. Yes . . .

All the lights are out.

(*Lights a lantern.*) Come, it's late. I'll see you home.

MADELEINE. No thank you, there's no need. Just let me sit here for a few minutes.

MOLIERE. But you . . .

MADELEINE. I'm going soon, don't worry. You go.

MOLIERE (*wraps himself in his cape*). Farewell. (*Exit.*)

Muttering occasionally, MADELEINE *sits deep in thought by the crucifix. A light is seen through the curtain. Enter* LAGRANGE.

LAGRANGE (*gravely*). Who's still in the theatre? Who is it? Is that you, Madame Béjart? Has it happened, then? I know.

MADELEINE. I think so, Scribbler. (*Pause.*)

LAGRANGE. And you didn't have the strength to tell him?

MADELEINE. It's too late. I can't tell him now. It's better for me alone to be unhappy and not all three. (*Pause.*) You are a man of honour, Lagrange, and you're the only one I've told the secret to.

LAGRANGE. I am proud that you trust me, Madame Béjart, I

tried to stop you telling me, but I failed. No one will ever find out. Come, I'll see you home.

MADELEINE. No thank you. I want to think alone. (*Gets up.*) I gave up acting today, Lagrange. Farewell. (*Starts to go.*)

LAGRANGE. Shan't I see you home all the same?

MADELEINE. No, you must continue your round. (*Exit.*)

LAGRANGE (*puts the lantern on the table and sits down at his previous place. Lit by the green glow, he opens a folio, speaks as he writes*). 'The seventeenth of February. A royal performance. In the king's honour I shall draw a fleur de lys. Afterwards, when the lights were out, I came upon Madame Madeleine Béjart in distress. She has given up acting.' (*Puts down his pen.*) The reason? A terrible thing has happened in the theatre – Jean-Baptiste Poquelin de Molière is going to marry Armande without knowing that she is not Madeline Béjart's sister but her daughter. I cannot write that down, but to show my horror I shall put a black cross. And none of those who come after us will ever guess. The seventeenth – the end. (*Takes the lamp and leaves.*)

Darkness and silence for some time, then a light appears through the cracks in the casing of the harpsichord and a jangling sound is heard from within it. The lid is raised and MOIRRON steps out of the instrument, looking stealthily around. He is a boy of about fifteen with an unusually handsome, depraved and tormented face. He is ragged and dirty.

MOIRRON. They've gone. Satan take them all . . . (*Whimpering.*) I'm a miserable, filthy creature . . . I haven't slept for two days . . . I never sleep. (*Sobs, puts down his lamp, drops to the floor and falls asleep.*)

Pause, then there is a flicker of light from a small torch and MOLIERE stealthily leads ARMANDE in. She is wearing a dark cape. ARMANDE shrieks. MOIRRON immediately wakes up, shaking and terrified.

MOLIERE (*threateningly*). Who are you?

MOIRRON. Oh, monsieur, don't hit me. I'm not a thief, I'm Zacharie, the wretched Zacharie Moirron.

MOLIERE (*bursts out laughing*). I see! The wicked old trickster!

Curtain

ACT TWO

Scene One

Versailles.

The king's ante-chamber, brilliantly lit. A white staircase leads to unknown regions.

The MARQUIS DE LESSAC *and* LOUIS *are at a table playing cards. A cluster of courtiers, sumptuously dressed, is watching* LESSAC. *In front of him is a pile of gold coins, some spilling over on to the floor. Sweat is pouring down* LESSAC's *face.*

LOUIS *is the only person seated; all the others are standing and hatless.* LOUIS *wears the uniform of a White Musketeer, a plumed hat set rakishly on his head, the star of an order on his breast, gold spurs on his heels and a sword at his side.*

ONE-EYE *hovers behind the king's chair, advising him on his game. Nearby stands an armed* MUSKETEER, *who never lets the king out of his sight.*

LESSAC. Three knaves and three kings.

ONE-EYE (*suddenly*). Your pardon, sire, but the cards are marked, devil take it.

The courtiers are appalled. Pause.

LOUIS. Did you come to play with me with marked cards?

LESSAC. It is true, your majesty. The impoverishment of my estate . . .

LOUIS (*to* ONE-EYE). Tell me, monsieur le marquis, what do the rules of the game say that I should do in such an extraordinary case as this?

ONE-EYE. Sire, you should strike him across the face with the candleholder. That is to begin with . . .

LOUIS. What a disagreeable rule! (*Grasps candleholder.*) This candleholder weighs about fifteen pounds . . . I suggest we use lighter ones.

ONE-EYE. Allow me.

LOUIS. No, do not trouble yourself. And what do we do next?

COURTIERS (*indignant chorus*). Scold him like a dog!

LOUIS. Excellent. Kindly send for him. Where is he?

The COURTIERS *rush in various directions. Cries of* 'The Shoemaker!' 'The king wishes to see The Just Shoemaker!'

(*To* LESSAC.) But tell me, how is it done?

LESSAC. With the fingernail, your majesty. For example, I mark the queens with noughts.

LOUIS (*interested*). And the knaves?

LESSAC. With crosses, sire.

LOUIS. Most interesting. And how does the law regard these actions?

LESSAC (*thinks awhile*). With disapproval, your majesty.

LOUIS (*sympathetically*). And what can they do to you for this?

LESSAC. I can be put in prison.

JUST SHOEMAKER (*enters noisily*). I come, I run, I fly, I enter. Here I am. Greetings, your majesty. What has happened, great monarch? Whom must I scold?

LOUIS. You see, my dear Just Shoemaker, the marquis here has been playing with me and using marked cards.

JUST SHOEMAKER (*nonplussed; to* LESSAC). You . . . You . . . what? Have you . . . gone out of your mind? If you did that playing 'spot the lady' in the market place you'd get a punch on the snout. Have I given him enough, your majesty?

LOUIS. Yes, thank you.

JUST SHOEMAKER. May I take an apple?

LOUIS. Please do. Marquis de Lessac, take your winnings.

DE LESSAC *fills his pockets with gold.*

JUST SHOEMAKER (*amazed*). But your majesty, what does this mean . . . surely you are joking!

LOUIS (*into the distance*). Monsieur le duc, if it is not too inconvenient, put the Marquis de Lessac into prison for one month. Give him a candle and a pack of cards and let him draw noughts and crosses on them. Then send him back to his estate, together with his money. (*To* DE LESSAC.) Put your estate in order. And another thing – play no more cards. I have a premonition that you will not be so lucky next time.

LESSAC. Oh, sire.

Voice calls: 'Guard'. DE LESSAC *is taken away*.

JUST SHOEMAKER. Get out of this palace at once!

ONE-EYE. You scum!

Attendants bustle in and a table set for one appears in front of LOUIS *as though materialising from the floor*.

CHARRON (*appears suddenly by the fireplace*). Your majesty, allow me to introduce to you an itinerant preacher, Father Bartholomew.

LOUIS (*starts eating*). I love all my subjects, even vagrants. Introduce him to me, archbishop.

A strange incantation is heard through the door. It opens and FATHER BARTHOLOMEW *enters. He is barefoot, shaggy-haired, and has a rope tied round his waist. He has the eyes of a madman.*

BARTHOLOMEW (*dancing and singing*). We are all fools in Christ.

Everyone is surprised except LOUIS. BROTHER FAITH *– a wan face with a long nose, wearing a dark habit – moves away from the crowd of courtiers and sidles over to* CHARRON.

ONE-EYE (*looks at* BARTHOLOMEW; *quietly*). Revolting fellow, devil take it.

BARTHOLOMEW. O most illustrious king in all the world, I have come to tell you that the Antichrist has appeared in your kingdom.

Courtiers are dumbfounded.

This godless, venomous serpent, which is gnawing at the foot of your throne, bears the name of Jean-Baptiste Molière. Let him be burned in the public square together with his blasphemous creation 'Tartuffe'. Every faithful son of the church demands it.

BROTHER FAITH *hears the word* 'demands' *and clasps his head.* CHARRON's *expression changes.*

LOUIS. Demand? Of whom do they *demand* it?

BARTHOLOMEW. Of you, your majesty.

LOUIS. Of me? Archbishop, someone is demanding something of me.

CHARRON. Forgive him, your majesty. He is obviously somewhat unhinged. I didn't know. It is my fault.

LOUIS (*into the distance*). Monsieur le duc, if it is not too inconvenient for you, put Father Bartholomew into prison for three months.

BARTHOLOMEW (*cries out*). I suffer because of the Antichrist!

A brisk movement and FATHER BARTHOLOMEW *disappears as if he had never been there.* LOUIS *continues to eat.*

LOUIS. Archbishop, come here, I wish to speak to you in private.

All the courtiers retire to the staircase, the MUSKETEER *steps back, leaving* LOUIS *alone with* CHARRON.

LOUIS. Is he weak in the head?

CHARRON (*firmly*). Yes, your majesty, he is weak in the head, but he has the heart of a true servant of God.

LOUIS. Tell me – do you think this man Molière is dangerous?

CHARRON (*firmly*). He is Satan himself, your majesty.

LOUIS. H'm. So you share Father Bartholomew's opinion of him?

CHARRON. I do, your majesty. And I beg you to hear me, sire. No shadow has yet darkened your unclouded and victorious reign, nor ever shall so long as you . . .

LOUIS. What?

CHARRON. Love God.

LOUIS (*takes off his hat*). I do love Him.

CHARRON (*raises his hand*). He is there, you are on earth and there is no one besides.

LOUIS. Yes.

CHARRON. There are no bounds to your might, sire, and there never will be so long as the light of the church shines upon your kingdom.

LOUIS. I love the church.

CHARRON. And so, your majesty, I join the blessed Bartholomew in begging you to intercede for the church.

LOUIS. You think Molière has insulted the church?

CHARRON. I do, your majesty.

LOUIS. He's a talented actor, though, despite his impudence. Very well, archbishop, I shall intercede for the church. But . . . (*Lowers his voice.*) I shall attempt to correct his ways, because he may yet be able to add to the glory of my reign. But if he gives us another example of his impudence I shall punish him. (*Pause.*) This blessed man of yours – does he love the king?

CHARRON. Yes, your majesty.

LOUIS. Then you may release the monk in three days, but make it plain to him that when speaking to the king of France he must never utter the word 'demand'.

CHARRON. May God bless your majesty, and may His hand punish the godless.

A VOICE. The servant of your majesty, Monsieur de Molière.

LOUIS. Show him in.

MOLIERE *enters, bows to* LOUIS *from a distance, crosses the stage to the extreme curiosity of the courtiers. He has aged considerably, his face looks ill and grey.*

MOLIERE. Sire!

LOUIS. Monsieur de Molière, you have no objection if I go on with my dinner?

MOLIERE. Oh, sire!

LOUIS. Perhaps you will join me? (*Calls out.*) A chair and another place at table.

MOLIERE (*turns pale*). Your majesty, I cannot accept this honour. It is too great.

A chair is brought on and MOLIERE *sits on the edge of it.*

LOUIS. Would you care for some chicken?

MOLIERE. My favourite dish, your majesty. (*Pleading.*) Allow me to stand.

LOUIS. Eat your dinner. How is my godson getting on?

MOLIERE. To my great sorrow the child has died, your majesty.

LOUIS. What, the second child as well?

MOLIERE. My children do not live long, your majesty.

LOUIS. You should not grieve over it.

MOLIERE. No one in France, sire, has ever had dinner with you before. I am overwhelmed, and therefore somewhat nervous.

LOUIS. France, Monsieur de Molière, is sitting before you. France is eating chicken and is not nervous.

MOLIERE. Sire, you are the only person in the world who can say that.

LOUIS. Tell me, what is your talented pen going to offer the king in the near future?

MOLIERE. Your majesty . . . something that may . . . serve . . .

LOUIS. Your pen is sharp, but you must remember that there are certain themes which you must treat with discretion. And you must admit that in 'Tartuffe' you have been indiscreet. One must respect men of the church. I hope that no writer of mine could be an atheist?

MOLIERE (*frightened*). God forbid, your majesty.

LOUIS. It is my firm belief that in future your plays will keep to the proper path and therefore I give you permission to perform 'Tartuffe' at the Palais-Royal.

MOLIERE (*a transformation comes over him*). I love you, my king! (*Anxiously.*) Where is Archbishop de Charron? Did you hear that? Did you?

LOUIS *gets up. A voice cries* 'The king's dinner is ended!'

LOUIS (*to* MOLIERE). Today you shall prepare my bed for me.

MOLIERE *picks up two candelabra from the table and walks on ahead.* LOUIS *follows him. Everyone makes way for them as if blown aside by the wind.*

MOLIERE (*intones loudly*). Make way for the king! Make way for the king! (*Shouts as he climbs the staircase.*) See, Archbishop, you cannot touch me! Make way for the king!

A fanfare above.

'Tartuffe' is allowed! (*Exit with* LOUIS.)

Exeunt all COURTIERS. *Only* CHARRON *and* BROTHER FAITH *remain on stage, both dressed in black.*

CHARRON (*by the staircase*). No. The king cannot mend your ways. Almighty God arm me and lead me in pursuit of the godless man that I may seize him. (*Pause.*) And he will fall down from those stairs. (*Pause.*) Come here, Brother Faith.

BROTHER FAITH *approaches* CHARRON.

Brother Faith, what do you mean by sending me that lunatic? I trusted you when you assured me that he would impress the king.

BROTHER FAITH. Who was to know that he would use the word 'demand'?

CHARRON. Demand!

BROTHER FAITH. Demand! (*Pause.*)

CHARRON. Have you found the woman?

BROTHER FAITH. Yes, my lord, everything is ready. She has sent him a note and will bring him.

CHARRON. Will he come?

BROTHER FAITH. For a woman? You can be sure of that.

ONE-EYE *appears at the top of the staircase. Exeunt* CHARRON *and* BROTHER FAITH.

ONE-EYE (*gloatingly*). The archbishop was fishing for the Antichrist and instead he caught three months in prison! Serve the bigot right . . .

JUST SHOEMAKER (*appears from under the staircase*). Is that you, One-Eye?

ONE-EYE. You could say so. You may call me simply Marquis d'Orsigny. What do you want?

JUST SHOEMAKER. A note for you.

ONE-EYE. Who sent it?

JUST SHOEMAKER. How should I know who she was? I met her in the park, but she was wearing a mask.

ONE-EYE (*reads the note*). H'm . . . what sort of woman was she?

JUST SHOEMAKER (*studies the note*). A woman of easy virtue, by all appearances.

ONE-EYE. Why?

JUST SHOEMAKER. Because she writes notes.

ONE-EYE. Fool.

JUST SHOEMAKER. What are you barking at me for?

ONE-EYE. Is she well built?

JUST SHOEMAKER. You can find that out for yourself.

ONE-EYE. You're right. (*Goes off thoughtfully.*)

The lights begin to dim and shadowy MUSKETEERS *appear at the door like ghosts. A voice from the top of the staircase intones:* 'The king sleeps!' *Another more distant voice:* 'The king sleeps!' *A third voice below ground:* 'The king sleeps!'

JUST SHOEMAKER. And I'm going to sleep too.

He lies down on the card table, wraps himself in a portière embroidered with coats of arms, so that only his monstrous shoes protrude.

The palace dissolves and disappears into darkness.

Scene Two

The lights go up on a room in Molière's house.

Daytime. The harpsichord is open. MOIRRON, *a handsome man of about twenty-two and magnificently dressed, is playing softly on it.* ARMANDE, *in an armchair, cannot take her eyes off him as she listens.* MOIRRON *stops playing.*

MOIRRON. What do you think of my playing, maman?

ARMANDE. Monsieur Moirron, I have already asked you not to call me maman.

MOIRRON. To begin with, madame, I am not Moirron, but Monsieur de Moirron. So there! Ha, ha!

ARMANDE. I suppose you acquired the title from sitting in the harpsichord!

MOIRRON. Let's forget about the harpsichord. It's covered in the dust of oblivion. That was a long time ago. Now I'm a famous actor applauded by the whole of Paris. Ha, ha, ha!

ARMANDE. And I advise you not to forget that you have my husband to thank for that. He dragged you out of that harpsichord by your filthy ears.

MOIRRON. Not by my ears but by my equally filthy legs. There's no doubt that father's an honourable man, but he has a terrible nature and he's as jealous as Satan.

ARMANDE. I must congratulate my husband on having adopted a thoroughly insolent young rogue.

MOIRRON. I am somewhat insolent, it's true . . . It's my character . . . but what an actor I am! There's no one to equal me in the whole of Paris.

ARMANDE. You impudent creature! And what about Molière?

MOIRRON. Well, I'll not deny it . . . there are three of us, the maître and myself . . .

ARMANDE. And who's the third one?

MOIRRON. You, maman. You, my famous actress. You, my Psyche. (*Declaims, accompanying himself on the harpsichord.*)

>   Tis springtime in the bosky grove,
>   In search of prey, the god of love . . .

ARMANDE (*huskily*). Go away . . .

MOIRRON (*embraces ARMANDE with his left arm, plays the accompaniment with his right hand*).

>   Young Cupid sees . . .
>   A tender heart . . .

ARMANDE.   His victim flees . . .
>   He aims his dart . . . (*Anxiously.*) Where's Bouton?

MOIRRON. Have no fear, the faithful servant has gone to market.

> Venus herself has sent this love:
> Draw near, my dove, your ardour prove . . .

MOIRRON lifts up her skirt and kisses her leg.

ARMANDE. You monster! (*Anxiously.*) Where is Renée?

MOIRRON. The old woman's in the kitchen. (*Kisses the other knee.*) Come to my room, maman.

ARMANDE. Never, I swear by the Holy Virgin!

MOIRRON. Come to me.

ARMANDE. You're the most dangerous man in Paris. Curse the hour when they dragged you out of the harpsichord.

MOIRRON. Come, maman . . .

ARMANDE. I swear by the Holy Virgin I will not. (*Stands up.*) I will not go. (*She goes, followed by MOIRRON, who locks the door after him. From behind the door.*) Why are you locking the door? You'll ruin me!

Pause. Enter BOUTON with a basket of vegetables, carrot-tops sticking out of it.

BOUTON (*listens, puts the basket on to the floor*). Strange. (*Takes off his shoes, creeps up to the door and listens.*) The thieving wretch! This is no place for me, ladies and gentlemen. I haven't seen or heard a thing and I know nothing . . . God in heaven, he's coming! (*Exits, leaving his basket and shoes on the floor.*)

Enter MOLIERE. Puts down his cane and hat, looks at the shoes in amazement.

MOLIERE. Armande!

At once the key turns in the lock. MOLIERE rushes through the door. A shriek is heard from ARMANDE, a crash, then MOIRRON comes running out, wig in hand, pursued by MOLIERE.

MOIRRON. How dare you!

MOLIERE (*runs after him*). You villain! (*Choking.*) I can't believe . . . I can't believe my eyes! (*Sinks into arm-chair. The key turns in the lock.*)

ARMANDE (*behind the door*). Come to your senses, Jean-Baptiste!

BOUTON *looks round the door and disappears.*

MOLIERE (*shakes his fist at the door*). So you eat my bread and dishonour me in return?

MOIRRON. You dared to strike me! En garde! (*Draws his sword.*)

MOLIERE. Drop your sword at once, you dog!

MOIRRON. I challenge you!

MOLIERE. Me? (*Pause.*) Get out of my house!

MOIRRON. You're mad, father. Just like Sganarelle.

MOLIERE. You good-for-nothing vagabond! I took you in, but now for this I shall throw you back on to the dung heap! The only acting you will ever do again will be in fair-booths, Zacharie Moirron. From today you are no longer a member of the Palais-Royal company. Go.

MOIRRON. You wouldn't dismiss me from the company?!

MOLIERE. Get out. I see I adopted a thief.

ARMANDE (*behind the door, in despair*). Molière!

MOIRRON (*dazed*). Father, it's all your imagination, we were just rehearsing Cupid and Psyche . . . Don't you recognise the script? You wrote it yourself . . . Why are you ruining my life like this?

MOLIERE. Get out, or I really shall run you through with my sword.

MOIRRON. Very well. (*Pause.*) It would be extremely interesting to know who is going to play Don Juan now. Surely not Lagrange? Ha, ha! (*Pause.*) But take care, Monsieur de Molière, that you don't regret this madness. (*Pause.*) I know your secret.

MOLIERE *bursts out laughing.*

Have you forgotten Madeleine Béjart? Have you? She's ill and dying . . . She prays night and day . . . and by the way, monsieur, there is still a *king* in France.

MOLIERE. What are you babbling about, you despicable liar?

MOIRRON. Babbling? I'm going straight from here to the archbishop.

MOLIERE (*laughs*). Well, thank you for that piece of treachery. Now I know you for what you are. I tell you that though I might have relented before you said that, I shall never relent now. Get out, you miserable fool!

MOIRRON (*from the door*). Buffoon!

MOLIERE *seizes a pistol from the wall and* MOIRRON *disappears*.

MOLIERE (*rattles door, then speaks through the keyhole*). Whore!

ARMANDE *breaks into loud sobs behind the door*.

Bouton!

Enter BOUTON *in stockinged feet*.

BOUTON. Yes, monsieur?

MOLIERE. You pimp!

BOUTON. Monsieur . . .

MOLIERE. What are these shoes doing here, pray?

BOUTON. Monsieur, they're . . .

MOLIERE. You're lying, I can tell by your eyes that you're lying!

BOUTON. Monsieur, to tell a lie one at least has to say something. I haven't spoken a word. I took my shoes off because . . . Would you like to see the nails in them? These shoes are worn out, curse them . . . To tell you the truth I was clumping around while they were rehearsing and they locked the door on me.

ARMANDE (*behind the door*). Yes!

MOLIERE. What are the vegetables for?

BOUTON. Oh, the vegetables are nothing to do with it. Nothing at all. I've just brought them from the market. (*Puts on his shoes.*)

MOLIERE. Armande!

Silence.

(*Speaks through the key-hole.*) Do you want to kill me? I have a bad heart.

BOUTON (*through the key-hole*). Well, do you want to kill him? He has a bad heart . . .

MOLIERE. Get out. (*Kicks the basket.*)

Exit BOUTON.

Armande . . . (*Sits down on a stool by the door.*) Be patient a little longer and you'll soon be free. I just don't want to die alone . . . Armande . . .

ARMANDE *comes out with tear-stained eyes.*

Can you swear?

ARMANDE. I swear.

MOLIERE. Say something to me.

ARMANDE (*sniffs*). You're such a great man but at home . . . at home . . . I don't understand what comes over you. How could you? Think what you've done – you've started a scandal that will be all over Paris. Why did you chase Moirron out?

MOLIERE. You're right. It's a terrible disgrace. But you know, he is a snake and an out-and-out rogue . . . He's a spoilt, depraved boy and I fear for him. I struck him, and despair might drive him to spreading lying gossip all over Paris . . . He could cause trouble.

ARMANDE. Bring Moirron back, bring him back.

MOLIERE. I'll give him one day, then I'll fetch him back.

Curtain

ACT THREE

Scene One

A vaulted stone cellar lit by a candelabrum of three candles. A table covered with red cloth, on it a folio volume and some manuscripts.

Around the table sit members of the League of Holy Writ, who are masked; CHARRON, without a mask, is seated in an armchair to one side.

The door opens and two men of horrible aspect dressed in black lead in MOIRRON. He is blindfolded and his hands are bound. His hands are then freed and the blindfold removed.

MOIRRON. Where . . . what is this place?

CHARRON. That does not concern you, my son. Now repeat your denunciation before the assembly of these worthy brothers.

  MOIRRON *is silent.*

BROTHER STRENGTH. Are you dumb?

MOIRRON. Ah . . . I . . . my lord archbishop . . . I didn't quite catch what was said and . . . I think I had better not say anything.

CHARRON. I seem to remember, my son, that you told me something derogatory about Monsieur de Molière this morning.

  MOIRRON *is silent.*

BROTHER STRENGTH. Answer the archbishop, you tawdry coxcomb.

  Silence.

CHARRON. It appears that what you told me was mere slanderous gossip. This grieves me.

BROTHER STRENGTH. Lying can be dangerous, even for an actor. You could be sent to prison for perjury, my fine fellow, and feed the bed-bugs for a long time. We shall nevertheless pursue this investigation, whether you cooperate or not.

MOIRRON. I have never spread slander.

BROTHER STRENGTH. Kindly don't keep me in suspense, but get on with your story.

MOIRRON *says nothing*.

Ah, well. Enter!

Door opens and two men enter, even more fearsome in appearance than those who escorted MOIRRON.

(*Looks at* MOIRRON's *shoes*.) You have a fine pair of shoes, but we have some finer ones. (*To the* TORTURERS.) Bring me a Spanish boot.

MOIRRON. No, no. Several years ago when I was a boy I used to lie in a charlatan's harpsichord . . .

BROTHER STRENGTH. What has this to do with the matter in hand?

MOIRRON. I used to play on an internal keyboard. It was a trick, made to look as if the instrument was playing by itself.

BROTHER STRENGTH. And?

MOIRRON. Inside the harpsichord . . . No, I can't go on, holy father! I was drunk this morning, I've forgotten what I told you.

BROTHER STRENGTH. For the last time get on with it!

MOIRRON. And . . . one night I heard a voice which said that Monsieur de Molière . . . had married a woman who was not Madeleine Béjart's sister but her daughter . . .

BROTHER STRENGTH. Whose voice was it?

MOIRRON. I must have dreamed it.

BROTHER STRENGTH. Well, whose voice did you hear in your dream?

MOIRRON. Lagrange the actor's.

CHARRON. That will do. Thank you, my friend. You have done your duty. Do not distress yourself. A subject of the king and son of the church must always regard it as an honour to denounce any crime of which he may have knowledge.

BROTHER STRENGTH. Decent enough, this young fellow. At first I didn't care for him, but now I see he is a good Catholic.

CHARRON (*to* MOIRRON). Now my friend, you will spend a day or two in a place where you will be well treated and fed, and then you and I will go and see the king.

MOIRRON *is blindfolded, his hands are tied and he is led out.*

Brothers, the next person to appear is a stranger to our company, but I shall ask Brother Strength to speak to him, as he knows my voice.

Knock at the door. CHARRON *pulls his hood over his face and disappears into the shadows.* BROTHER STRENGTH *goes to open the door. A strange woman in a mask enters leading* ONE-EYE *by the hand. He is blindfolded.*

ONE-EYE. My dear creature, when are you going to let me take this blindfold off? You might have trusted me. (*Shudders.*) Your house smells damp, devil take it.

MASKED WOMAN. Just one more step, monsieur le marquis. There . . . now take it off . . . (*Slips into the shadows.*)

ONE-EYE (*removes blindfold, looks around*). Damn you! (*With the skill and speed born of experience he leaps with his back to the nearest wall, drawn sword in his right hand, pistol in his left. Pause.*) Some of you have swords showing beneath your capes, I see. With the odds as they are you may get me, but I warn you that three of you will be carried out of this hole feet first. I am d'Orsigny. Don't move! Where's that hussy who lured me into this trap?

MASKED WOMAN (*from the shadows*). I am here, monsieur le marquis, but I'm no hussy.

BROTHER STRENGTH. Fie, monsieur le marquis, that is no way to speak to a lady . . .

BROTHER FAITH. Please calm yourself, no one here is going to attack you.

BROTHER STRENGTH. Put your pistol away – it's staring at us like the evil eye and spoiling the conversation.

ONE-EYE. Where am I?

BROTHER FAITH. In the crypt of a church.

ONE-EYE. I demand to be released.

BROTHER FAITH. The door will be opened for you whenever you wish.

ONE-EYE. In that case, why lure me here, devil take you? Tell me first – is this a plot on the king's life?

BROTHER FAITH. God will forgive you for that thought, monsieur le marquis. We are the king's most loyal subjects. You are at a secret meeting of the League of Holy Writ.

ONE-EYE. League of holy fiddlesticks! I never believed that any such league existed. Why does it need me?

Puts away his pistol.

BROTHER FAITH. Please be seated, monsieur le marquis.

ONE-EYE. Thank you. (*Sits down.*)

BROTHER FAITH. We grieve for you, monsieur le marquis.

MEMBERS OF THE LEAGUE (*in chorus*). We grieve!

ONE-EYE. I would hate to be the cause of anyone's grief. Tell me what the matter is.

BROTHER FAITH. We wish to warn you that you are being made fun of in court circles.

ONE-EYE. You must be mistaken. With my reputation no one makes fun of me.

BROTHER FAITH. Everyone in France knows of your remarkable . . . talents. It is because of this that they take care to whisper behind your back.

ONE-EYE (*strikes the table with the flat of his sword*). Tell me their names!

The members of the league cross themselves nervously.

BROTHER STRENGTH. Please try not to make so much noise, monsieur le marquis.

BROTHER FAITH. The whole court is whispering about you.

ONE-EYE. Tell me, or I shall lose my patience.

BROTHER FAITH. Do you happen to know that infamous play by a certain Jean-Baptiste Molière called 'Tartuffe'?

ONE-EYE. I don't go to the Palais-Royal, but I've heard of it.

BROTHER FAITH. The godless author has made fun of religion and the servants of the church in this play.

ONE-EYE. The scoundrel!

BROTHER FAITH. But this Molière has not only mocked religion. He has also poured scorn upon the nobility, whom he detests. Perhaps you know his 'Don Juan'?

ONE-EYE. Yes, I have heard of it too. But what has the Marquis d'Orsigny to do with this buffoon at the Palais-Royal?

BROTHER FAITH. We have absolutely reliable information that this scribbler has portrayed you, monsieur le marquis, in the person of his hero Don Juan.

ONE-EYE (*sheathing his sword*). What sort of a man is this Don Juan?

BROTHER STRENGTH. An atheist, a rogue, a murderer and, if you'll forgive me, sir, a seducer of women.

ONE-EYE (*abruptly changing his expression*). I see. Thank you.

BROTHER FAITH (*picks up a manuscript from the table*). Perhaps you would care to acquaint yourself with the evidence?

ONE-EYE. No thank you, I'm not interested. Tell me, is there perhaps anyone among those present who thinks there are any grounds for making d'Orsigny out to be such a depraved character?

BROTHER FAITH. Is there anyone, brothers?

The members of the League indicate total negation.

There is no one. You see, therefore, what has prompted us to invite you in this strange fashion to our secret assembly. There are people of your own circle here, monsieur le marquis, so you will understand how unpleasant it could be for us to . . .

ONE-EYE. Quite. Thank you.

BROTHER FAITH. Monsieur le marquis, we trust that what has been said today will remain between ourselves, also that no one will be told that we were obliged to trouble you in this matter.

ONE-EYE. Have no fear, monsieur. Where is the lady who brought me here?

MASKED WOMAN (*comes forward*). I am here.

ONE-EYE (*sullenly*). I offer you my apologies, madame.

MASKED WOMAN. God will forgive you, monsieur le marquis, as I forgive you. Please come with me and I will take you to the place where we met. You must allow me to blindfold you once more because our honourable society forbids strangers to know the way to its meeting place.

ONE-EYE. Well, if you must . . .

ONE-EYE *is led out blindfolded.*

CHARRON (*removes his hood and comes out of the shadows*). I declare this meeting of the League of Holy Writ closed. Let us pray, brethren.

MEMBERS OF THE LEAGUE (*stand and intone*). Laudamus tibi, Domine, rex aeternae gloriae . . .

Curtain

Scene Two

A vast cathedral, drifting clouds of incense. Darkness, relieved by flickering, moving lights.

The archbishop's confessional, lit by a single candle. Two dark figures walk by. Hoarse whispers of 'Have you seen "Tartuffe"?' 'Have you seen "Tartuffe"?'

ARMANDE *and* LAGRANGE *enter, supporting* MADELEINE *by both arms. She is grey and ill.*

An organ begins to peal.

MADELEINE. Thank you, Armande. And you too Charles, my devoted friend.

LAGRANGE. We'll wait for you here. Here is the confessional.

MADELEINE *crosses herself, knocks gently and enters the confessional.* ARMANDE *and* LAGRANGE *wrap themselves in their black capes and sit down on a bench, where they are swallowed up by the darkness.*

CHARRON (*appears in the confessional*). Come nearer, my daughter. Are you Madeleine Béjart?

The organ stops playing.

I have learned that you are one of the most pious daughters of the church and you are dear to my heart. I have decided to hear your confession myself.

MADELEINE. You do a great honour to me, a sinner. (*Kisses* CHARRON's *hands*.)

CHARRON (*blesses* MADELEINE, *places the end of his stole on her head*). Are you ill, my poor child?

MADELEINE. I am, my lord.

CHARRON (*in a martyred voice*). Do you wish to leave this world?

MADELEINE. I do.

Organ starts playing.

CHARRON. What is your sickness?

MADELEINE. The doctors say that my blood is infected. I see the devil and I am afraid of him.

CHARRON. Poor woman! How do you ward off the devil?

MADELEINE. I pray.

The organ stops.

CHARRON. For that the Lord will raise you up and will love you.

MADELEINE. He will not forsake me?

CHARRON. No. How have you sinned? Tell me.

MADELEINE. I have sinned all my life, father. I was a wanton woman, I lied, for a long time I was an actress and so aroused the lusts of many men.

CHARRON. Do you remember any particularly grievous sin?

MADELEINE. No, my lord.

CHARRON. Ah, the folly of it! You come with a sin that is lodged like a red-hot nail in your heart and you will not let me take it out for you. It is now or never, my child. Do you understand the meaning of that word 'never'?

MADELEINE (*pauses*). I do. (*Terrified.*) Oh, how afraid I am!

CHARRON (*transformed into the devil*). You see the fires of hell and between them . . .

MADELEINE. . . . . a sentinel walks up and down . . .

CHARRON. . . . . and whispers . . . 'Why didn't you leave your sin behind, why have you brought it with you?'

MADELEINE. And I shall wring my hands and cry out.

The organ begins again.

CHARRON. And then the Lord will hear you no more. And you will hang in chains with your legs in the fire . . . and there you will remain for ever. Do you understand the meaning of the words 'for ever'?

MADELEINE. I am afraid to admit it to myself. If I did, I would die of fear. (*Cries out weakly.*) I do understand. And what if I leave my sin here?

CHARRON. Then you shall hear the heavenly mass, which is sung into all eternity.

A procession with candles passes near by. Children's voices burst into song, then the procession disappears.

MADELEINE (*groping as though in the darkness*). Where are you, holy father?

CHARRON (*in a low voice*). I am here . . . I am here . . .

MADELEINE. I want to hear the eternal mass . . . (*Whispers passionately.*) A long time ago I lived with two men at the same time and conceived my daughter Armande. All my life I have been in agony because I never knew whose child she was . . .

CHARRON. Ah, wretched woman.

MADELEINE. She was born in the provinces. When she grew up I brought her to Paris and gave it out that she was my sister. But he was blinded by passion for her and married her. I said nothing to him, to spare his feelings. So it may be that because of it he has committed mortal sin and I am cast into damnation. Oh, how I long to pass on to where I may hear the eternal mass.

CHARRON. Et ego, archiepiscopus, absolvo te in nomine Patris et Filii et Spiritus Sancti.

MADELEINE (*crying with ecstasy*). Now may I pass on in peace?

The organ starts to play loudly.

CHARRON (*exultantly*). Pass on, my child, pass on!

The organ stops.

Is your daughter here? Call her over here and I shall forgive her for her unwitting sin as well.

MADELEINE (*comes out of the confessional*). Armande, Armande, come here! The archbishop will bless you too. Oh, the happiness . . . at last!

LAGRANGE. I shall take you to the carriage.

MADELEINE. And Armande?

LAGRANGE. I shall come back for her. (*Leads* MADELEINE *off into the dark.*)

ARMANDE *enters the confessional,* CHARRON *appears. In his horned mitre he looks fearsome and diabolical. He makes the sign of the cross over* ARMANDE *several times, using the devil's reversed cross. The organ starts playing.*

CHARRON. Tell me, do you know who was with me just now?

ARMANDE (*suddenly realises everything, horrified*). No, no . . . She is my sister, my sister . . .

CHARRON. She is your mother. I absolve you. But you must flee from here today, flee I tell you!

ARMANDE *gives a weak cry, falls down on her face and lies motionless at the entrance to the confessional.* CHARRON *disappears. The organ plays softly.*

LAGRANGE (*emerges from the gloom*). Armande, are you unwell?

Darkness.

Scene Three

Daylight. The king's audience-chamber. LOUIS, *in a gold-embroidered black coat, is seated at a table. Before him stands the grim, dark figure of* CHARRON. *The* JUST SHOEMAKER *is sitting on the floor mending his shoe.*

CHARRON. She confirmed it to me at her deathbed confession. At the time I did not even consider it necessary, your majesty, to question the actor Lagrange, not wishing to exaggerate the unsavoury affair. So I stopped the proceedings. But it is beyond doubt that Molière has committed the most dreadful of crimes. However, I leave the case to your majesty's own judgment.

LOUIS. Thank you, archbishop. You have acted rightly. I regard the evidence as complete. (*Rings a bell, says into the distance.*) Summon the director of the Palais-Royal Theatre, Monsieur de Molière, immediately. Remove the guards from these rooms, I shall speak to him alone. (*To* CHARRON.) Archbishop, send me this man Moirron.

CHARRON. At once, sire.

JUST SHOEMAKER. It seems, great monarch, that your kingdom cannot keep in being without informers.

LOUIS. Be quiet, fool, and mend your shoe. Don't you like informers?

JUST SHOEMAKER. What's there to like about them? They are treacherous dogs, your majesty.

Enter MOIRRON. *His eyes look hunted and he appears to have slept in his clothes.* LOUIS, *whom he is obviously seeing for the first time at such close quarters, makes a great impression on him.*

LOUIS (*politely*). Zacharie Moirron?

MOIRRON. Yes, your majesty.

LOUIS. Was it you who used to sit in the harpsichord?

MOIRRON. Yes, sire.

LOUIS. Did Monsieur de Molière adopt you?

MOIRRON *is silent.*

I asked you a question.

MOIRRON. Yes.

LOUIS. Did he teach you how to act?

MOIRRON *starts to cry.*

I asked you a question.

MOIRRON. Yes.

LOUIS. What was your motive in denouncing him in the king's name? You wrote in your statement: 'desiring to serve justice'.

MOIRRON (*dully*). Yes, desiring to . . .

LOUIS. Is it true that he hit you in the face?

MOIRRON. It is true.

LOUIS. What for?

MOIRRON. His wife was unfaithful to him with me.

LOUIS. I see. You are not obliged to state that when you are cross-examined. We can say 'for personal reasons'. How old are you?

MOIRRON. Twenty-three.

LOUIS. I have some good news for you. Your denunciation has been confirmed by the investigator. What kind of reward do you want from the king? Would you like money?

MOIRRON (*shudders, pause*). Your majesty, allow me to join your theatre company at the Hotel de Bourgogne.

LOUIS. No. I hear that you are a bad actor. Impossible.

MOIRRON. I am a bad actor? (*Naively.*) Well, then, the Theatre du Marais?

LOUIS. That is also impossible.

MOIRRON. Well what am I to do?

LOUIS. Why must you follow the dubious calling of an actor? You have an unstained record. If you wish, you could enter the royal service and work in the secret police. Submit your application to the king in person. It will be granted. You may go.

Exit MOIRRON.

JUST SHOEMAKER. Off to the gallows, off to the gallows . . .

LOUIS. Fool. (*Rings.*) Monsieur de Molière!

Hardly has one door shut behind MOIRRON *when* LAGRANGE *enters by another. He leads* MOLIERE *in and at once goes out again.* MOLIERE *is in a strange state. His collar is awry, his wig untidy, his face leaden, his hands are shaking and his sword hangs crookedly.*

MOLIERE. Sire . . .

LOUIS. Why have you come with someone else, when you were invited alone? Who accompanied you?

MOLIERE (*with a frightened smile*). My faithful pupil, the actor de

Lagrange . . . brought me here. Forgive me, I have had a heart attack and could not come alone. I hope I have not angered your majesty. (*Pause.*) You see . . . I had an accident . . . forgive my untidy appearance. Madeleine Béjart died yesterday and my wife Armande left the house at the same time . . . She left everything – can you imagine it? – her wardrobe, her rings . . . and she left me an insane note . . . (*Takes a scrap of paper from his pocket and smiles ingratiatingly.*)

LOUIS. My lord archbishop was right. You are not only a filthy blasphemer in your plays – you are also a criminal and an atheist.

MOLIERE *is dumbfounded.*

I hereby pass sentence upon you in the matter of your marriage: I forbid you to appear at court and forbid you to perform 'Tartuffe'. Merely in order to save your company from starving I allow you to perform your comedies at the Palais-Royal, but nothing else . . . and from this day onward take care not to let me hear from you again. I deprive you of the king's patronage.

MOLIERE. But your majesty, this is a catastrophe . . . worse than hanging . . . (*Pause.*) Why?

LOUIS. For the shadow that your scandalous marriage has cast upon the royal name.

MOLIERE (*sinks into an armchair*). Forgive me, I cannot get up . . .

LOUIS. You may go. The audience is ended. (*Exit.*)

LAGRANGE (*glances in at the door*). Well?

MOLIERE. The carriage . . . call it . . . take me home . . .

Exit LAGRANGE.

I should talk it over with Madeleine, but she's dead. What does it all mean?

JUST SHOEMAKER (*sympathetically*). What's the matter with you? You don't believe in God, is that it? Oh, you've had a hard time of it . . . Here, take this apple . . .

MOLIERE (*takes apple mechanically*). Thank you.

CHARRON *enters and stares at* MOLIERE *for some time, his eyes glistening with satisfaction.*

On seeing CHARRON, MOLIERE *revives. Before this he had been slumped forward on the table. He raises himself. His eyes light up.*

Ah, the holy father! Satisfied? This is for 'Tartuffe', isn't it? I know why you are up in arms for the church. You're a clever man and you saw what was behind it, didn't you, reverend father? No doubt of it. Some friends once said to me 'You should write a play about a hypocritical, evil priest'. And so I described you. Where else could I find a greater hypocrite than you?

CHARRON. I grieve for you, for whoever treads this path will surely end his days on the gallows, my son.

MOLIERE. Don't call me your son. I am not the devil's son. (*Draws his sword.*)

JUST SHOEMAKER. Now – what's this, what's this?

CHARRON (*with a gleam in his eyes*). Though you won't even get as far as the gallows. (*Looks round ominously.*)

Enter ONE-EYE, *with a cane.*

ONE-EYE (*walks up to* MOLIERE *in silence and kicks his leg*). Monsieur, you jostled me and you have not apologised. You are an ignorant boor.

MOLIERE (*automatically*). I beg your pardon. (*Suddenly aware.*) You kicked me!

ONE-EYE. You liar!

MOLIERE. How dare you! What do you want from me?

Enter LAGRANGE.

LAGRANGE (*horrified*). Maître, come away from here at once, come away! (*Nervously.*) Monsieur le marquis, Monsieur de Molière is unwell.

ONE-EYE. I found him with a drawn sword. He is well. (*To* MOLIERE.) My name is d'Orsigny. You, my dear sir, are a blackguard.

MOLIERE. I challenge you.

LAGRANGE (*anxiously*). Come away! Don't you know who he is?

CHARRON. Gentlemen, what are you doing? In the king's audience-chamber . . . !

MOLIERE. I challenge you!

ONE-EYE. Good, the matter's settled. I shall not insult you any
longer. (*Smirks.*) God is my judge, even if the king puts me into
the Bastille for this! (*To* LAGRANGE.) You, sir, are witness.
(*To* MOLIERE.) Give him your instructions to dispose of your
property. (*Draws his sword, tests the tip.*) No instructions? (*Gives a
whoop.*) En garde! (*Makes a cross in the air with his sword.*)

CHARRON. Gentlemen, come to your senses! Gentlemen! (*Runs
up the staircase and surveys the duel from there.*)

LAGRANGE. This is cold-blooded murder!

JUST SHOEMAKER. They're fighting in the king's audience-
chamber!

ONE-EYE *seizes the* JUST SHOEMAKER *by the scruff of the
neck and silences him.* ONE-EYE *lunges at* MOLIERE, *who parries
the attack and then cowers behind the table.* ONE-EYE *jumps up on to
the table.*

LAGRANGE. Maître, throw away your sword!

MOLIERE *throws it away and collapses on the floor.*

ONE-EYE. Take his sword!

LAGRANGE (*to* ONE-EYE.) You can't run through an unarmed
man!

ONE-EYE. I'm not going to. (*To* MOLIERE.) Pick up your
sword, you cowardly wretch!

MOLIERE. Don't insult me and don't hit me. There's something I
don't understand. You see, I have a weak heart . . . my wife has
left me . . . her diamond rings are scattered all over the floor . . .
she didn't even take a clean shift with her . . . I am
overwhelmed . . .

ONE-EYE. What are you talking about?

MOLIERE. I can't understand why you wanted to attack me. I've
only seen you a couple of times in my life. You brought me the
money once, didn't you? But that was a long time ago. I am ill,
so please don't touch me.

ONE-EYE. I shall kill you after your next performance! (*Sheathes
sword.*)

MOLIERE. Very well, if you like . . . I don't care . . .

The JUST SHOEMAKER *suddenly jumps up and disappears.*
LAGRANGE *raises* MOLIERE, *picks up his sword and leads him*
out. ONE-EYE *watches him as he goes.*

CHARRON (*comes down the stairs, livid with fury*). Why didn't you
kill him?

ONE-EYE. What business is it of yours? He threw down his
sword, devil take it.

CHARRON. You clown!

ONE-EYE. What?! Devil's priest!

CHARRON *suddenly spits in* ONE-EYE's *face.* ONE-EYE *is so*
dumbfounded that he spits back at CHARRON. *The door opens and*
the JUST SHOEMAKER *rushes in, greatly alarmed, followed by*
LOUIS. *The others are so engrossed in their quarrel that they continue*
to spit at each other.

LOUIS. Excuse me for disturbing you. (*Exit, shutting the door.*)

Curtain

ACT FOUR

Scene One

MOLIERE's house. Evening. Candles in sconces make mysterious shadows on the walls. Disorder; manuscripts scattered about. MOLIERE dressed in nightcap, underclothes and dressing gown, is seated in an enormous armchair, BOUTON in another one. On one table are two swords and a pistol. On another is the evening meal and some wine, from which BOUTON takes occasional sips.

LAGRANGE in a dark cape is walking up and down, half muttering to himself, half humming. Behind him on the wall marches his dark shadow.

LAGRANGE. He was in the harpsichord . . . and he overheard me . . .

MOLIERE. Stop it, Lagrange. It was none of your doing. Fate has visited my house and has robbed me of everything, that is all.

BOUTON. It's the truth. I have a tragic fate too. Once I used to sell pies in Limoges . . . No one bought the pies, of course. Then I wanted to be an actor and came to you . . .

MOLIERE. Be quiet, Bouton.

BOUTON. Very well.

A bitter pause; then a squeak on the staircase is heard. The door opens and MOIRRON enters. Instead of a coat he is wearing a filthy jerkin, unkempt, unshaven and half drunk, he carries a lantern. The people in the room shade their eyes with their hands. They recognise MOIRRON and LAGRANGE seizes the pistol from the table. MOLIERE knocks LAGRANGE's hand upward, LAGRANGE shoots and hits the ceiling. MOIRRON is not in the least taken aback and stares dully at the spot hit by the bullet. LAGRANGE, grabbing the first thing to hand, shatters a jug, rushes at MOIRRON, throws him to the ground and starts to strangle him.

LAGRANGE. Let the king punish me for this if he likes . . . (*Roars.*) Judas!

MOLIERE (*in an agonised voice*). Bouton . . . Bouton . . .
(MOLIERE *and* BOUTON *drag* LAGRANGE *and* MOIRRON *apart. To* LAGRANGE.) You'll ruin me, you . . . with all this shooting and noise . . . What more do you want? Do you want to make things worse by committing a murder in my own house?

Pause.

LAGRANGE. Zacharie Moirron, do you know me, you dog?

MOIRRON *nods.*

Go where you like tonight, death will be waiting for you. You won't live to see the morning. (*Wraps himself in his cloak and falls silent.*)

MOIRRON *nods to* LAGRANGE, *kneels down in front of* MOLIERE *and bows his head to the ground.*

MOLIERE. Why did you come, my son? The crime has been revealed, so what more do you expect to uncover in my house? What will you write in your report to the king? Or do you suspect me of being a forger as well? Go on, look through my cupboards and chests if you like.

MOIRRON *bows down again.*

Say what you want without grovelling.

MOIRRON. My most beloved, respected teacher, you think I have come to ask forgiveness. You are wrong. I have come to set your mind at rest: by midnight tonight at the latest I shall hang myself outside your house, because I cannot go on living. Here is the rope. (*Takes a rope from his pocket.*) And here is a note saying 'I am going to hell'.

MOLIERE (*bitterly*). Thank you for setting my mind at rest.

BOUTON (*gulps down some wine*). Yes, a very hard case. A certain philosopher once said . . .

MOLIERE. Be quiet, Bouton.

BOUTON. I'll say no more.

MOIRRON. I came to be near you. And if I were to stay alive beyond tonight I would never once look at Madame Molière again.

MOLIERE. You won't be able to, my son, because she has left me and I shall be alone for ever. I have an impetuous nature and am prone to do a thing first and only think about it afterwards. Now that I've had time to think and have grown wiser after what has happened, I forgive you and take you back again into my house. Come back.

MOIRRON *bursts into tears.*

LAGRANGE (*opens his cloak*). You are not a man. You invite people to treat you like a floorcloth.

MOLIERE (*to* LAGRANGE). You impudent puppy! Don't talk about things you don't understand. (*Pause. To* MOIRRON.) Get up, or you'll tear your breeches.

Pause. MOIRRON *gets up. Pause.*

Where's your coat?

MOIRRON. I pawned it in a tavern.

MOLIERE. How much for?

MOIRRON *makes a gesture of despair.*

(*Shouts.*) What lunacy – to go and leave a satin coat in a tavern. (*To* BOUTON.) Go and redeem the coat. (*To* MOIRRON.) They say you've been on the loose and that you've even wandered as far as the king?

MOIRRON (*beating his breast*). And the king said I ought to become a police spy . . . He told me I was a bad actor . . .

MOLIERE. Oh, the folly! The king was wrong, you're an actor of the first rank and you would be useless as a police spy, you haven't the temperament for it. My only regret is that I shan't be able to act with you much longer. They've set their one-eyed dog on me – the musketeer. The king has withdrawn his patronage and so I shall probably be murdered. I shall have to flee.

MOIRRON. Mon maître, for as long as I am alive he shall not murder you, believe me! You know how I can handle a sword.

LAGRANGE. It's true, you're an excellent swordsman . . . But before you take on One-Eye make sure you buy yourself a requiem mass at Notre Dame.

MOIRRON. I'll get him from behind.

LAGRANGE. Just your style.

MOIRRON (*to* MOLIERE). I shall stay beside you wherever you are, at home, in the street, day and night. That's why I came.

LAGRANGE. Like a police spy.

MOLIERE (*to* LAGRANGE). Stop your mouth with that lace at your throat.

MOIRRON. My dear Scribbler, don't insult me. Why insult someone who can't answer back? Leave me alone – I am a marked man. And don't attack me tonight. If you kill me, you'll be hanged and the League will have our defenceless Molière murdered.

MOLIERE. You have grown much wiser since you left my house.

MOIRRON (*to* LAGRANGE). Don't forget that the maître has been declared an atheist for 'Tartuffe'. I was with the League in the cellar . . . They take no account of the law, so we must be prepared for anything.

MOLIERE. I know. (*Shudders.*) Was that a knock?

MOIRRON. No. (*To* LAGRANGE.) Take the pistol and the lantern, you and I must go outside and keep watch.

LAGRANGE *and* MOIRRON *take their weapons and the lantern and go. Pause.*

MOLIERE. The tyrant, the tyrant . . .

BOUTON. What are you saying? Who do you mean?

MOLIERE. The king of France . . .

BOUTON. Quiet, for God's sake!

MOLIERE. Louis the Great! Louis the tyrant!

BOUTON. All's lost now. We'll both be hanged.

MOLIERE. Oh Bouton, I almost died of fear today. There he sat like a golden idol and his eyes were like emeralds – can you imagine it? My hands were bathed in a cold sweat. Everything swam before me, everything turned upside down. I only knew one thing – that the idol was crushing the life out of me.

BOUTON. We'll both be hanged, me as well, side by side in the square. There you'll swing, and I'll be next to you – I, Jean-Jacques Bouton, an innocent victim. Where am I? In the kingdom of heaven. I don't recognise the place.

MOLIERE. All my life I've licked his spurs and only thought of one thing – don't crush me. And now he has crushed me all the same. The tyrant!

BOUTON. There'll be a roll of drums in the square. Who stuck his tongue out at the wrong time? It'll hang out down to your waist.

MOLIERE. Why did he do it? What for? I asked him this morning – what for? I don't understand it . . . I said to him: 'How can you do this, your Majesty, I protest. I am insulted, I haven't flattered you enough? Your Majesty, where will you find another plate-licker like Molière? . . . Why did it happen, Bouton? Because of 'Tartuffe'. That's why I've been humiliated . . . I thought I'd found an ally. And what an ally he proved to be. Never let yourself be humiliated, Bouton. I hate this royal tyranny!

BOUTON. One day, maître, they'll put up a monument to you. A girl by a fountain with a stream of water running out of her mouth. You're a great man, but if only you could keep silent . . . I just wish your tongue would dry up . . . If we're overheard it'll be the death of me too.

MOLIERE. What more must I do to prove I'm a worm? But I'm a writer, your Majesty, I have a brain, I have thought this over coolly and carefully and I protest to you – she is not my daughter! (To BOUTON.) Ask Madeleine Béjart to come to me, I want her advice.

BOUTON. What are you saying, maître?

MOLIERE. Oh, yes, she's dead. Why didn't you tell me the whole truth, my dear? Or no, why didn't you teach me a lesson and hit me and beat me until I came to my senses? . . . You see, she said 'We'll light the candles . . . and I'll come to you . . .' (Painfully.) The candles are lit, but she's not here . . . And I've torn your coat . . . here's a louis d'or for your coat. Show me where it's torn.

BOUTON. Maître, for God's sake go to bed and lie down! What coat?

MOLIERE *suddenly pulls the blanket over his head and disappears beneath it.*

Almighty God, please see to it that no one heard what he was saying. Let's use a trick. (*Speaks unnaturally loudly and artifically as though continuing the conversation.*) What was that you were saying, my dear sir? That our king was the best, the most brilliant king in all the world? I quite agree with you, sir.

MOLIERE (*under the blanket*). You'll never make an actor.

BOUTON. Be quiet! (*In artificial voice.*) Yes, I shall always be the first to shout 'Long live the king!' . . .

A knock at the window, MOLIERE *anxiously pokes his head out from under the blanket.* BOUTON *carefully opens the window and the frightened* MOIRRON *appears, holding a lantern.*

MOIRRON. Who was that shouting? What's happened?

BOUTON. Nothing has happened. Why should anything happen? I was having a talk with Monsieur de Molière and I simply happened to shout 'Long live the king!' Surely Bouton has the right to shout if he wants to? Indeed he does, so he shouts: 'Long live the king!'

MOLIERE. God, what a talentless fool!

Curtain

Scene Two

The actors' dressing-room at the Théâtre du Palais-Royal. The old green poster is hanging there as before, the lamp is still burning beneath the crucifix and the green-glassed lantern in LAGRANGE's *dressing-room. But the noises from behind the curtain are boos and whistles.*

MOLIERE *is sitting in his armchair in dressing-gown and night-cap, made up with a grotesque nose. He is nervous and light-headed, rather as though drunk.*

Beside MOLIERE *stand* LAGRANGE *and* DU CROISY, *in black doctors' robes but without make-up. Grotesque doctors' masks are lying about. The door opens and* BOUTON *rushes in. At the start of the scene* MOIRRON *stands motionless to one side, in a black cloak.*

MOLIERE. Well, is he dead?

BOUTON (*to* LAGRANGE). Killed by a sword-thrust . . .

MOLIERE. Kindly speak to the director of the Palais-Royal and not to the actors. This may be my last performance but I am still in charge!

BOUTON (*to* MOLIERE). Yes, he's dead. He was run through with a sword.

MOLIERE. God rest his soul. What can we do – we're helpless.

PROMPTER (*looks in at the door*). What's happening?

LAGRANGE (*in a purposely loud voice*). What's happening? The musketeers have broken into the theatre and killed the doorkeeper.

PROMPTER. Oh! (*Exit.*)

LAGRANGE. As secretary of the theatre, I have to report that the theatre is full of musketeers who have forced their way in without paying, and other persons unknown. I have no power to arrest them, but I hereby cancel the performance.

MOLIERE. But . . . but . . . but! He cancels the performance! Don't you forget who you are! Compared with me you are a mere boy and I am a grey old man.

LAGRANGE (*whispers to* BOUTON). Has he been drinking?

BOUTON. Not a drop.

MOLIERE. What else was I going to say?

BOUTON. My dear Monsieur de Molière . . .

MOLIERE. Bouton! . . .

BOUTON. . . . get out! I know that's what you were going to say. I've been with you for twenty years and that's the only thing you ever *have* said to me, apart from 'Be quiet, Bouton!' I've got used to it by now. But you love me, maître, and for my sake I beg you on bended knee not to finish the performance but to flee. The carriage is ready.

MOLIERE. What makes you think I love you, you empty-headed chatterbox? No one loves me. People harry me and persecute me. And the archbishop has given orders that I'm not to be buried in consecrated ground. So everyone will rest in peace while I rot outside the fence in purgatory. But I don't need their cemetery. I despise all that. You've been hunting me down all my life, you're all my enemies.

DU CROISY. We! In God's name, maître . . .

LAGRANGE (*to* BOUTON). How is he going to act when he's in this state?

Roars and booing from behind the curtain.

There! Listen to it.

MOLIERE. It's Shrove Tuesday! They've often broken the chandeliers at the Palais-Royal in carnival time before now. The pit is enjoying itself, that's all.

BOUTON (*ominously*). One-Eye is in the theatre.

Pause.

MOLIERE (*calmly*). Oh. (*Suddenly terrified.*) Where's Moirron? (*Rushes over to* MOIRRON *and hides in his cloak.* MOIRRON *bares his teeth and silently puts his arms around* MOLIERE.)

DU CROISY (*whispers*). We must fetch a doctor.

MOLIERE (*looks timidly out from under the cloak*). He can't touch me on stage, can he?

Silence. The door opens and RIVALE *runs in. She is wearing practically nothing except a doctor's hat and pair of enormous cartwheel spectacles.*

RIVALE. We can't make the interval last any longer. Either we start or . . .

LAGRANGE. He insists on going on, so what can we do?

RIVALE (*looks at* MOLIERE *for a long time*). We'll go on.

MOLIERE (*emerging from the cloak*). Well said! Come here and let me give you a kiss, my dear old friend. You can't start the last performance and not finish it. She understands. You've been acting with me for twelve years, and do you know, I haven't once seen you properly dressed, you're always naked.

RIVALE (*kisses* MOLIERE). Oh, Jean-Baptiste, the king will forgive you, he must . . .

MOLIERE (*vaguely*). He . . . yes . . .

RIVALE. Will you listen to me?

MOLIERE (*thoughtfully*). I will. But not to them. (*Stumbles.*) They are fools. (*Gives a sudden shudder and his mood changes completely.*) Forgive me, gentlemen, I have been unpardonably rude to you. I don't understand how it could have slipped out. I must be on edge. I hope you will make allowances for me. Monsieur du Croisy . . .

DU CROISY ⎫
LAGRANGE ⎬ (*in chorus*). Not at all! Think nothing of it! No
BOUTON ⎭ apologies needed!

RIVALE. Now listen carefully. As soon as you've said your last lines we will let you down through the trap–door and hide you in my dressing-room until morning. You will leave Paris at dawn. Agreed?

MOLIERE. Agreed. On stage for the last scene, everyone.

DU CROISY, LAGRANGE *and* MOIRRON *grab their masks and go*. MOLIERE *embraces* RIVALE; *she goes*. MOLIERE *takes off his dressing-gown*. BOUTON *opens the curtain shutting off the dressing rooms from the wings. On the stage are an enormous bed, a white statue, a portrait on the wall and a table with a little bell. The lights have green shades, giving an intimate, domestic feel to the set. The* PROMPTER *enters his box and lights his candle behind the main curtain, the front of the house is noisy. Malicious whistles are heard occasionally.* MOLIERE, *quite his old self, hops nimbly into bed, gets under the bedclothes and pulls them over his head.*

(*Whispers to the* PROMPTER.) Right!

The gong is struck and the auditorium falls silent. The music strikes up and MOLIERE *starts snoring in time to it. The huge curtain opens with a rustle. One senses that the theatre is packed. Several vague faces are just visible in the gilded stage box. A loud roll on the kettle-drums, and* LAGRANGE *rises out of the floor wearing a ridiculous nose and a black nightcap. He stares into* MOLIERE's *face.*

(*Starting up in fright.*)

Devil take it! Who's this here?
I'm sleeping – kindly go away!

LAGRANGE. 'Tis Doctor Purgon, have no fear:
A doctor shall you be today?

MOLIERE. A doctor? I? Ye Gods, what's that?

The portrait on the wall bursts open and from it leaps DU CROISY *with a huge red nose, vast pair of spectacles and doctor's cap.*

Another? Lord, what demonology!

DU CROISY. Know by my gown, sir, and my hat
        I'm doctor of venereology.

MOLIERE. Am I awake or am I dreaming?

The statue falls apart to disclose RIVALE *in robes and spectacles.*

God save us! 'Tis another spectre!

RIVALE. Greatest am I in wit and learning:
        The faculty of med'cine's rector!

MOLIERE. Welcome, learned doctors all.

The pillows are flung aside and MOIRRON *rises up from them in doctor's rig, clutching a vast scroll with a dangling seal.*

One more! And pray who might you be?

MOIRRON. I come in answer to the call
        To grant a medical degree.

Curtain rises upstage to reveal a chorus of grotesque masked doctors and apothecaries, brandishing huge syringes, knives, etc.

RIVALE (*addresses the assembled 'DOCTORS'*).
        Doctores! Convocati estis,
        Et credo quod trovabitis
        Dignam materiam medici
        In savanti homine that here you see:
        Whom in things omnibus
        Dono ad interrogandum,
        Et to the bottom examinandum
        Vestris capacitatibus.

LAGRANGE.
            Cum permissione domini praesidis,
            Doctissimae facultatis,
            Et totius his nostrils actis
            Companiae assistentis,
            Domandabo assistentis,
            Domandabo tibi, docte bacheliere
            Quae sunt remedia,
            Quae in maladia

Called hydropisia
Convenit facere?

MOLIERE.

Clisterium donare,
Postea bleedare,
Afterwards purgare.

CHORUS.

Bene, bene bene respondere,
Dignus est intrare
In nostro corpore.

DU CROISY.

If bonum semblatur domine praesidi
Doctissimae facultati
Et compania praesenti,
Domandabo tibi, docte bacheliere,
Quae remedia eticis,
Pulmonicis atque asmaticis
Do you think à propos facere?

ONE-EYE *suddenly emerges from the darkened interior of the stage box, swings his legs over the edge and sits poised.*

MOLIERE.

Clisterium donare,
Postea bleedare,
Afterwards purgare.

CHORUS.

Bene, bene, bene respondere:
Dignus, dignus est intrare
In nostro docto corpore.

MOLIERE (*suddenly falls awkwardly*). Madeleine . . . Send Madeleine to me . . . I must speak to her. Help me!

A roar of laughter from the audience.

You there in the pit, don't laugh, wait a moment, wait . . . (*Falls silent.*)

The music goes on playing for a few more moments, then breaks off raggedly. Confusion on stage.

LAGRANGE (*pulls off his mask, walks up to the footlights*). Gentlemen, while playing the role of Argan Monsieur de Molière has collapsed . . . (*With emotion.*) The performance cannot be completed.

Silence. Then a cry from the stage box: 'Give us our money back!' Whistles, boos.

MOIRRON (*removing his mask*). Who was that who shouted for his money back? (*Draws his sword, tests its point.*)

BOUTON (*on stage, in a strangled voice*). Who was it?

MOIRRON (*points to the box*). Was it you . . . or you?

Silence.

(*To* ONE-EYE.) You filthy brute!

ONE-EYE *draws his sword and climbs down on to the stage.*

(*Lopes towards* ONE-EYE *with sword ready.*) Come on, come here . . . (*As he passes* MOLIERE *he glances down at him, stops, straightens up, rams his sword-point into the boards, turns round and walks off stage.*)

The PROMPTER *suddenly bursts into tears . . .* ONE-EYE *looks at* MOLIERE, *sheathes his sword and leaves the stage.*

LAGRANGE (*to* BOUTON). Bring down the curtain, for God's sake!

The CHORUS *comes to life,* 'DOCTORS' *and* 'APOTHECARIES' *rush to* MOLIERE *and crowd around, hiding him from view.* BOUTON *at last lowers the curtain, causing a loud roar from the audience.* BOUTON *runs after the* CHORUS *as they carry* MOLIERE *off.*

LAGRANGE. Gentlemen, help me! (*Addresses the audience through a gap in the curtain.*) Gentlemen, I beg you – go home . . . there has been an accident.

RIVALE (*through another gap*). Gentlemen, please . . . Gentlemen, gentlemen . . .

The curtain bulges and sways as people try to climb on to the stage out of curiosity.

DU CROISY (*through a third gap*). Gentlemen, gentlemen . . .

LAGRANGE. Put the lights out!

DU CROISY *extinguishes the chandeliers by slashing the candles with his sword. The din in the auditorium subsides a little.*

RIVALE (*through a gap in the curtain*). Have some consideration, please, gentlemen! Go home, please . . . the show is over . . .

The last lights are put out and the stage grows dark. Everything fades, except for the lamp by the crucifix. The stage is sombre and empty. Not far from MOLIERE's mirror sits a dark, hunched figure. A lantern appears on stage, carried by LAGRANGE.

LAGRANGE (*in a solemn voice*). Who is still here? Who is here?

BOUTON. I am, Bouton.

LAGRANGE. Why don't you go to him?

BOUTON. I don't want to.

LAGRANGE (*walks over to his dressing room, sits down in the light of the lantern, opens his book, speaks to himself as he writes*). 'The seventeenth of February. The comedy of 'Le Malade Imaginaire', written by Monsieur de Molière, was performed for the fourth time. At 10 o'clock in the evening, Monsieur de Molière, while playing the role of Argan, collapsed on stage and was at once taken, unshriven, by the relentless hand of death'. (*Pause.*) For this I mark the day with a black cross. (*Ponders.*) What was the cause of it? Why did it happen? How shall I put it? The reason for this was the king's disfavour and the evil work of the black LEAGUE! . . .

The scene slowly darkens.

Curtain

Adam and Eve

A Play in Four Acts

Translated by Michael Glenny

Adam and Eve was premièred at the Gate Theatre, London by Theatre at Large on 22 November 1989, with the following cast:

ÉVA VOIKÉVICH,
 a student of foreign languages; 23   Sarah Keyzor
ADÁM KRASÓVSKY,
 a civil engineer; 28   David Drysdale
PROFESSOR YEFROSÍMOV,
 a scientist; 41   Colin R. Campbell
DARAGÁN, *an aviator; 37*   Howard Belgard
PÓNCHIK–NEPOBÉDA, *a writer; 35* Jeremy Minns
ZAKHÁR MARKÍZOV,
 an ex-member of a trade union; 32 David Glennie
ÁNYA, *a housemaid; 23*   Daniele Sanderson
TÚLLER 1 ⎱ *cousins*   Chris Hawley
TÚLLER 2 ⎰   Eleanor Creed-Miles

Directed by Stuart Wood
Designed by Jane Frere
Lighting by David Lawrence
Sound by Martin Coster

The following characters were cut from the Theatre at Large production:

KLÁVDIA PETRÓVNA, *a psychiatrist; 35*
MARIA VIRUES, *a Spanish aviatrix; 28*
DE TIMONEDA, *a Spanish aviator*
SEEWALD, *a German aviator*
PÁVLOV, *a Russian aviator*

ACT ONE

Leningrad in May.

A ground-floor room; one window opens on to a courtyard. The most remarkable item in the set is a large, heavily shaded lamp hanging above a table. Also noticeable is a loudspeaker, from which flows the melodious strains of Gounod's Faust, *broadcast from the Mariinsky Theatre. Now and again snatches of accordion music can be heard coming from the courtyard.*

EVA VOIKEVICH *and* ADAM KRASOVSKY *are listening to* Faust.

ADAM (*kissing* EVA). What a lovely opera *Faust* is. And do you love me?

EVA. Yes, I do.

ADAM. *Faust* today, and tomorrow evening we go to the Crimea! What bliss! When I was queuing for the tickets, I broke out in a hot sweat because I realized how wonderful life is!

ANYA *enters suddenly.*

ANYA. Oh, sorry . . .

ADAM. Anya! You might at least . . . you know . . . knock . . .

ANYA. I thought you were in the kitchen.

ADAM. In the kitchen? In the kitchen? Why should I be in the kitchen when *Faust* is playing on the wireless?

ANYA *starts laying the table.*

ADAM. And tomorrow we're off to the Crimea for six weeks! (*He juggles with a glass and drops it; the glass breaks.*)

EVA. Doesn't matter – that means good luck.

ANYA. Now look what you've done. That was Daragan's glass.

ADAM. I'll buy him another one. I'll buy Daragan five glasses.

ANYA. Oh, and where will you buy one? There aren't any glasses to be had.

ADAM. Don't panic! There'll be glasses galore at the end of the five-year plan . . . You're right, though, Anya. I really should be in the kitchen now, because I was going to clean my brown shoes.

He exits.

ANYA. Oh, how I envy you, Eva. He's handsome, he's an engineer and he's a communist.

EVA. You know, Anya, I really think I *am* happy. Although . . . and yet . . . oh, I don't know! . . . Yes, Anya – why don't you get married, if you like the idea so much?

ANYA. All the men I meet are no good. Everyone else manages to get a decent one, but all I ever end up with is some kind of golliwog, like the booby-prize in a lottery! And the wretch drinks, too!

EVA. He drinks?

ANYA. Sits around in his vest and pants and blue specs reading *The Count of Monte-Cristo* and drinking with his friend Kubik.

EVA. He's a bit of a tearaway, your young man, but he's great fun.

ANYA. Fun! He's nothing but a hooligan with an accordion. No, I'm not going to marry him. Last week he beat up that little man in number ten and was thrown out of his trade union for it. And he left his wife, so he has to pay her alimony. Catch me living with *him*!

EVA. Yes, I've been looking at myself and I've come to the conclusion I really am happy.

ANYA. But Daragan is unhappy.

EVA. Does he know already?

ANYA. I told him.

EVA. Now that was rotten of you, Anya!

ANYA. Why? He's bound to find out. He asked me today: 'Is Eva coming to see Adam this evening?' So I said: 'She's coming – and she'll be staying.' – 'What d'you mean?' says he. 'What I say – they got married today!' 'Wha–at?!' . . . Aha, you're blushing, Eva! All the men in this flat have fallen for you, you know!

EVA. What?! Who's fallen for me?

ANYA. You'll soon see, when Ponchik comes. He's in love with you too.

EVA. I'm off to the Crimea! Tomorrow evening sharp at six in the first-class sleeper – and to hell with all Ponchiks!

ANYA sweeps up the broken glass and exits.

ADAM rushes in.

ADAM. Do you like my room?

EVA. I think so. Yes, I do . . .

ADAM kisses EVA.

EVA. Don't . . . wait . . . Anya will come in again at any moment . . .

ADAM. No one's going to come in. (*He kisses EVA.*)

Voices can be heard outside the window.

MARKIZOV'S VOICE. Bourgeois!

YEFROSIMOV'S VOICE. You're behaving like a hooligan!

MARKIZOV'S VOICE. Who are you calling a hooligan?

YEFROSIMOV jumps up from the courtyard on to the window-sill, twitching with indignation. YEFROSIMOV is thin and clean-shaven. From his immaculate, well-cut suit it is obvious that he has recently been abroad on a government-sponsored trip. From his impeccable white shirt it is obvious that he is a bachelor who does not have to look after his own clothes; this is done for him by an old lady who, convinced that YEFROSIMOV is a demigod, washes and irons for him, reminds him of what to wear and lays it out for him every morning. Slung on a leather strap across his shoulder is some kind of apparatus that is clearly not a camera. YEFROSIMOV startles all those who meet him by his curious tone of voice and gestures.

YEFROSIMOV. Please forgive me . . .

ADAM. What the hell are you up to?

YEFROSIMOV. I'm being chased by a gang of drunken louts! (*He jumps down from the window-sill into the room.*)

MARKIZOV *appears on the window-sill. As* ANYA *described him, he is wearing vest, pants, socks with suspenders, blue spectacles and, despite the warm weather, an overcoat with a fur collar.*

MARKIZOV. Who's a hooligan? (*Out of the window.*) Comrades! Did you hear that? He called me a hooligan. (*To* YEFROSIMOV.) Any more out of you and I'll fetch you one round the ear, then you'll see who's a hooligan!

ADAM. Markizov! Get out of my room this minute!

MARKIZOV. I could tell he's a bourgeois 'cos he was wearing a hat.

YEFROSIMOV. For God's sake, stop him somebody! He'll smash my apparatus!

EVA. Get out of this room! (*To* ADAM.) Go and phone for the police at once.

ANYA *runs in.*

ANYA. Are you at it again, Zakhar?

MARKIZOV. I'm sorry, Anya, but I've been insulted. (*To* EVA.) You're not going to bother the police at this hour, are you?

ANYA. Get out, Zakhar!

MARKIZOV. All right, I'm going. (*He shouts out of the window.*) Hey, Vasya! Kubik! I want you to be my seconds! Go round and stand by the front door, there's good lads, and wait for this poof in a mauve suit to come out. He's an alcoholic with a camera. I'm going to fight a duel with him. But I advise you, Mr Foreign Bourgeois, Count Dracula or whoever you are, not to try leaving this building! In fact, if I were you I'd put up a camp-bed in this flat and settle in here. See you later. (*Exit through window.*)

Exit ANYA.

YEFROSIMOV. My only regret is that all the members of the Soviet government aren't here to witness this scene, so that I could show them the sort of raw material they're using to build an ideal, classless society . . .

A brick flies through the window.

ADAM. Markizov! I'll have you up for assault and you'll be sent to Siberia!

EVA. Ugh, what a horrible man.

YEFROSIMOV (*still twitching*). I am calm! I am calm! I'm only upset because I've disturbed you. How long do you suppose we shall be besieged in here?

ADAM. Oh, don't worry about them. Those 'seconds' of his will soon get bored and disappear. If the worst comes to the worst I shall take steps to deal with them.

YEFROSIMOV. You don't happen to have some of that . . . what's it called . . . water, do you?

EVA. Of course. (*She pours out a glass of water from a jug on the table.*) Here you are.

YEFROSIMOV. Thank you. (*He drinks.*) Allow me to introduce myself. My name is . . . h'm . . . Alexander Ippolitovich . . . My God, I've forgotten my surname!

ADAM. You've forgotten your surname?

YEFROSIMOV. Oh Lord, this is terrible! . . . What *is* my surname? It's very well known . . . begins with 'R', I think . . . R . . . Let me see: hydrocyanic acid . . . phenoldichloroarsenate . . . Ah yes! Yefrosimov. That's it. Yefrosimov.

ADAM. I see . . . Are you *the* Yefrosimov?

YEFROSIMOV. Yes, yes, I am. (*He drinks some more water.*) In short, I am Academician Yefrosimov, professor of chemistry. You don't object?

EVA. We're delighted.

YEFROSIMOV. And you? Whose window did I climb through?

ADAM. I am Adam Krasovsky.

YEFROSIMOV. Are you a Communist Party member?

ADAM. Yes.

YEFROSIMOV. Very good. (*To* EVA.) And you?

EVA. I'm Eva Voikevich.

YEFROSIMOV. Communist?

EVA. No, I don't belong to the Party.

YEFROSIMOV. Excellent. Excuse me . . . what did you say your name was?

EVA. Eva Voikevich.

YEFROSIMOV. Can't be!

EVA. Why not?

YEFROSIMOV. And you? . . . Er . . .

EVA. This is my husband. We were married today. Yes, yes, yes . . . Adam and Eve!

YEFROSIMOV. Aha! I spotted that at once. And you say I'm mad.

EVA. No one has said anything of the sort!

YEFROSIMOV. I can see you think I am. But no, I'm not. Don't worry, I'm quite normal. I admit I do look rather . . . When I was walking along the street, those . . . Oh, I've forgotten again . . . you know: small people . . . go to school . . .

EVA. Children?

YEFROSIMOV. That's it! Boys! They whistled at me, and those . . . reddish-brown, furry . . . they bite . . .

ADAM. Dogs?

YEFROSIMOV. Yes. They went for me. And at street corners those . . . er . . .

ADAM. }
EVA. } Policemen!

YEFROSIMOV. Gave me some funny looks. Perhaps I was walking in zigzags. I came into your house because I wanted to see Professor Buslov, but he wasn't at home. He had gone to the opera, to hear *Faust*. Would you mind if I rest a little? I'm exhausted.

EVA. Please do. Stay here and wait till Buslov comes back.

ADAM. We were just about to have something to eat . . .

YEFROSIMOV. Oh, thank you! You are quite charming!

ADAM. Is that a camera?

YEFROSIMOV. No. Ah . . . I mean, yes. Of course, it's a camera. And since fate has brought me into your home, you must let me photograph you!

EVA. Well, really . . .

ADAM. I don't know . . .

YEFROSIMOV. Sit down, sit down . . . (*To* ADAM.) Is your wife a person of good character?

ADAM. To me, she's perfect.

YEFROSIMOV. Excellent! I shall photograph her. She must live.

ADAM (*aside to* EVA, *quietly*). To hell with him . . . I don't want my photo taken.

YEFROSIMOV. Tell me, Eva, do you love life?

EVA. Oh, I do. Very much.

YEFROSIMOV. Good for you! Splendid. Sit down, please.

ADAM (*aside*). Dammit, I don't want him to photograph me, he's mad!

EVA (*whispers to* ADAM). He's just eccentric, like all chemists. Shut up! (*Aloud.*) Come on, Adam – sit down and smile!

Grim-faced, ADAM *sits down beside* EVA. *There is a knock at the door, but* YEFROSIMOV *is busy with his apparatus and* ADAM *and* EVA *are absorbed in their pose.* PONCHIK-NEPOBEDA *opens the door and stands on the threshold, while* MARKIZOV *cautiously clambers up on to the window-sill.*

YEFROSIMOV. Attention, please! (*A blinding ray of light is projected out of the front of the apparatus.*)

PONCHIK. Oh! (*Exit, dazzled.*)

MARKIZOV. Christ! (*He shields his eyes and falls back off the window-sill.*)

EVA. Goodness – that was some magnesium!

PONCHIK (*knocks twice*). Adam, can I come in?

ADAM. Yes, of course. Come in Pavel.

Enter PONCHIK, *a short man in horn-rimmed spectacles, wearing shorts and checked stockings.*

PONCHIK. Hello, old man. You and Eva here? Having your picture taken together, eh? He, he, he! I see! Hang on a moment – I'll just go and smarten myself up. (*Exit.*)

EVA. Will you give us your card?

YEFROSIMOV. Of course, of course. Only not just now – a little later.

ADAM. What a strange camera. Is it foreign? I've never seen one like that before . . .

A dog's plaintive howl is heard in the distance.

YEFROSIMOV (*alarmed*). Why is that dog howling? H'mm . . . What is your job, Eva?

EVA. I'm studying foreign languages.

YEFROSIMOV. And you, Adam?

ADAM. I'm an engineer – a civil engineer.

YEFROSIMOV. Can you tell me some simple chemical formula – the formula for chloroform, for instance?

ADAM. Chloroform? . . . Chloroform . . . Eva, can you remember the chemical formula for chloroform?

EVA. I never knew it!

ADAM. I'm afraid chemistry's not up my street. My job is building bridges.

YEFROSIMOV. But there's no point . . . There's no point in building bridges now. Give it up! Who on earth can think about building bridges *now*? The idea's laughable . . . You spend two years building a bridge and I'm proposing to blow it up in three minutes. What's the point of wasting time and materials? . . . God, it's stifling! And why are the dogs howling out there? The fact is, I've been sitting in my laboratory for two solid months and this is my first breath of fresh air. That's why I'm behaving so oddly and forget the simplest words. (*He laughs.*) But I can't help imagining the look on their faces in Western Europe. Adam, have you ever thought there might be a war?

ADAM. Of course I have. It's highly likely, because the capitalist world hates socialism so much.

YEFROSIMOV. The capitalist world is filled with hatred for the socialist world and the socialist world seethes with hatred for the capitalist, my dear bridge-builder – and the formula for chloroform is $CHCl_3$! There *will* be a war because it's so close and stifling today. There *will* be a war because every day in the tramcar people say to me: 'Look at him – wearing a hat!' There'll be a war because when you read the newspapers (*He takes two newspapers out of his pocket.*) your hair stands on end and you think you're having a nightmare. (*He points at one of the newspapers.*) What are they saying? 'Capitalism must be destroyed'. And what are they saying over there? (*He points into the distance.*) What are they printing in *their* newspapers? 'Communism must be destroyed'. It's a nightmare. Look: 'A black man is executed in the electric chair.' Somewhere else, God knows where, in Rangoon for instance, someone has cut the telephone wires; Albanians are being killed in Yugoslavia; Basques are shooting Spaniards in Spain, Afghans are shooting each other in Kandahar. Tomorrow they'll be doing it in Pennsylvania. I tell you it's a nightmare. Girls with rifles – girls! – are marching down the street past my window and singing: 'Red rifles shooting – bang, bang, bang! Bourgeois capitalists – go hang, hang, hang!' And this happens every day! The fire's crackling under the cauldron, bubbles are rising in the water – you've got to be blind not to see that any minute now it's going to come to the boil.

ADAM. I'm sorry, professor, but I must object. Electrocuting blacks is one thing, but Red rifles shooting – that's legitimate defence. You can't be against that song, professor.

YEFROSIMOV. No, I'm against singing in the streets on principle.

ADAM. Ha, ha, ha! . . . As I see it, there's going to be a terrible explosion, but it will be the last, great, cleansing explosion that will solve all those problems, because the USSR has a *great idea* on its side, so it's bound to win.

YEFROSIMOV. It may well be a great idea, but the fact is there are a lot of people in the world who have another idea – and *their* idea is to destroy you and your idea.

ADAM. Well, we'll see about that!

YEFROSIMOV. I'm very much afraid that most people won't have the opportunity to 'see about it'. It's all to do with the little old men . . .

EVA. What little old men?

YEFROSIMOV (*mysteriously*). Nice little old men, with clean collars and well-pressed trousers . . . Essentially, little old men don't care a damn about any ideas except one – that their housekeeper serves them their coffee at the right time every morning . . . And they're not squeamish – oh no! One of them, you see, used to sit in his laboratory and, impelled by nothing more than childish curiosity, amused himself by mixing various smelly things in a test tube – perhaps some of that chloroform, for instance, a bit of sulphuric acid and so on, and then he heated it up just to see what would happen. What happened was that before he'd even had time to finish his coffee thousands of people were lying around in heaps; first they turned dark blue, then other people loaded them on to lorries and drove them away to be buried in a pit. But most interesting of all, Adam, was the fact that they were all young men and absolutely innocent of any ideas . . . I'm frightened of ideas! Any one of them may be all right in itself, but only until some old professor uses technology to arm it and make it lethal. You may have a perfectly innocent idea, but one day a scientist will come along and add arsenic to it . . .

EVA (*miserably*). I'm frightened too. You'll be poisoned, my Adam!

ADAM. Don't be afraid, Eva, don't be afraid! I'll put on a gas-mask and we'll beat them!

YEFROSIMOV. You might just as well pull a hat over your face. Oh, my dear engineer – there is only one word to fear, and that word is 'super'. Let's imagine that there's a man in this room: a hero, even an idiot if you like. But a super-idiot? What does he look like? How does he drink his tea? What acts will he perform? Or a super-hero? The mind boggles. But it no longer matters what he or anyone else does: the only thing that matters is – what *it* will smell like. However hard the little old man tried, it always smelled of something – either mustard, or bitter almonds, or rotting cabbage, and finally it smelled rather nicely of geraniums. That was a sinister smell, my friends, but it still wasn't the 'super-gas'. It will be 'super' when the scientist makes one that doesn't smell, doesn't explode and works quickly. Then the little old man will mark that test tube with a black cross, so as not to confuse it with the others, and he'll say: 'I have done my best. The rest is up to you. Now let the ideas fight it out!' (*In a whisper.*) And the fact is, Adam, it now *has* no smell, it *doesn't* explode – and it works quickly.

EVA. I don't want to die! What are we going to do?

YEFROSIMOV. Go underground! Down into the nether regions, Eve, oh primal mother of mankind! Instead of building bridges, Adam, burrow down, build a subterranean city and take refuge in it!

EVA. I don't want any of that! Adam, let's get away to the Crimea – as quickly as possible.

YEFROSIMOV. Oh, my child, have I upset you? Calm down, don't worry. Forget everything I've been saying: there's not going to be a war. And this is why: finally someone will come along who will say, 'If the flow of ideas can't be stopped, then we must curb and restrain these dreadful old men.' But you won't catch them by wearing gas-masks! Something radical is needed. Look – (*He puts one hand across the back of his other hand, with the fingers of both hands spread open.*) – this is a cell of the human body . . . Now (*He closes the fingers of both hands.*) what has happened? The same cell as before, but the gaps between its constituent particles have been closed up. Now when those gaps were open, Adam, it was through them that the old man's gas penetrated! You don't understand? Doesn't matter! Off you go and catch the train for the Crimea! You have my blessing, Adam and Eve!

DARAGAN *has appeared silently in the open doorway. He is clad from head to foot in black leather, except for a silver bird, with wings outstretched in flight, that is embroidered right across his chest.*

Now if someone invents the means to close up those fingers, then, Adam, there will be no more chemical warfare, and consequently there will be no more war at all. But the only question will be – who to give this invention to . . .

DARAGAN (*suddenly*). That is the easiest question of all, Professor. If that invention exists, it must immediately be given to the Revolutionary Military Council of the Soviet Republic . . .

ADAM. Ah, Daragan! Let me introduce you: Professor, this is Andrei Daragan.

DARAGAN. I know the Professor already. Pleased to meet you.

ADAM. Look, Daragan, I have a confession to make – Eva and I got married today.

DARAGAN. I know that too. Ah well, congratulations, Eva. So have you moved in with us? We'll be neighbours. I've heard you speak, Professor: you once gave a lecture to our officers. It was entitled 'The Detection of Arsenical Gas in Chemical Warfare'. It was brilliant!

YEFROSIMOV. Ah yes, I remember . . .

DARAGAN. It's good to know there are scientists in our workers' republic who have such colossal knowledge as yours.

YEFROSIMOV. Thank you. And what, if I may ask, is your profession?

DARAGAN. I serve the republic as commander of a fighter squadron.

YEFROSIMOV. I see, I see . . .

DARAGAN. You were saying just now, Professor, that it might be possible to invent something that would put an end to chemical warfare.

YEFROSIMOV. Yes, I was.

DARAGAN. Amazing! And you also wondered, didn't you, about who to give it to?

YEFROSIMOV (*frowning*). Oh, yes. That is an agonizing question. I suppose, in order to save mankind from disaster, an invention like that should be given to every country simultaneously.

DARAGAN (*looking grim*). What? (*Pause.*) Every country? Do you mean that, Professor? You'd give an invention of unique military importance to capitalist countries?

YEFROSIMOV. Well, what else do *you* propose?

DARAGAN. I'm amazed at you. In my opinion . . . Forgive me, Professor, but I advise you not to breathe a word of your ideas anywhere outside this room . . .

Behind YEFROSIMOV's *back* ADAM *makes signals to* DARAGAN *which obviously mean: 'Yefrosimov is off his rocker'.*

DARAGAN (*staring at* YEFROSIMOV's *apparatus*). Of course, I do realize the whole matter is a very complex one . . . And is this invention simple to put into effect?

YEFROSIMOV. I imagine it will be simple . . . comparatively . . .

PONCHIK (*enters noisily*). Greetings, comrades, greetings! Here I am! Ah, Eva! (*He kisses EVA's hand.*)

EVA. Meet the Professor . . .

PONCHIK. How d'you do. Pavel Ponchik-Nepobeda – writer.

YEFROSIMOV. Yefrosimov.

They shake hands.

All sit down at the table.

PONCHIK. Congratulate me, my friends! A great literary event has taken place in Leningrad . . .

EVA. What's that?

PONCHIK. My novel has been accepted for publication . . . Six hundred pages. And so . . .

ADAM. Read it to us . . .

EVA. But we're just going to have supper . . .

PONCHIK. I can read during a meal, you know.

ADAM. We have some literary news too: Eva and I were married today.

PONCHIK. Where?

ADAM. Where? . . . At the register office, of course.

PONCHIK. I see . . . (*Pause.*) Congratulations.

DARAGAN. Where do you live, Professor?

YEFROSIMOV. I live . . . it's number sixteen . . . a brown house . . . I'm sorry, er . . . (*He takes out a notebook*). Aha. Yes, that's it: Zhukovsky Street . . . Dear me, I must fight this problem.

DARAGAN. Have you only just moved there?

YEFROSIMOV. Oh, no. I've been living there for the last three years. I just forgot the name of the street.

EVA. It can happen to anybody.

DARAGAN. H'mm . . .

PONCHIK *stares wildly at* YEFROSIMOV.

ADAM. Come on – the novel, the novel!

PONCHIK (*produces a thick manuscript*). But perhaps it'll bore you to listen?

EVA. No, no! We want to!

DARAGAN. Go on – read away!

PONCHIK (*lays the MS in front of him on the table; he reads*). 'Red Greenery'. A novel. Chapter one. '. . . Where once the earthly faces of Prince Baratynsky's serfs furrowed the thin, poor soil, there are now to be seen the fresh, pink cheeks of collectivised peasant women. "Oh Vanya, Vanya!" rang out from the edge of the field . . .'

YEFROSIMOV. I do beg your pardon . . . I must just ask you one question: this was published in yesterday's *Evening News*, wasn't it?

PONCHIK. I beg your pardon! What d'you mean – in the *Evening News*? I'm reading from my manuscript – it's not been published yet!

YEFROSIMOV. Forgive me. (*He takes out a newspaper and shows it to* PONCHIK.)

PONCHIK. Well I'm damned! The bastard!

ADAM. Who's a bastard?

PONCHIK. Marin-Roshchin, that's who! Listen to this: (*He reads from the newspaper.*) 'Where once the hungry serfs of Count Sheremetiev tilled the poor soil . . .' Bloody scoundrel! (*He reads.*) '. . . collective-farm peasant women now toil happily in their red headscarves. 'Igor!' came the cry from the edge of the field . . .' The son of a bitch!

EVA. You mean he just cribbed it from your novel?

PONCHIK. How could he have done? No, we were in the same party of writers that went out to visit this collective farm. He followed me around like my shadow and we both saw exactly the same things.

DARAGAN. But who *did* the estate once belong to? Was it Sheremetiev – or Baratynsky?

PONCHIK. It used to be the Rimsky-Korsakov estate.

YEFROSIMOV. Really! Well, now the public only has to decide one thing: which of these two wrote a better description of what he saw . . .

PONCHIK. Yes . . . I see . . . who wrote a better description of what he saw . . . Was it that plagiarist who varnished the truth and painted everything in absurdly rosy colours, or was it Ponchik-Nepobeda?

YEFROSIMOV (*ingenuously*). The plagiarist made a better job of it, I think.

ADAM *hastily pours* PONCHIK *a glass of vodka.*

PONCHIK. Thank you, Adam. (*To* YEFROSIMOV.) Apollon Akimovich personally said to me in Moscow: 'Well done! A powerful novel!'

YEFROSIMOV. And who is Apollon Akimovich?

PONCHIK. Good God! . . . (*Accepting another glass of vodka.*) Thank you, Adam . . . I suppose you don't know who Savely Savelievich is either? Perhaps you've never read *War and Peace*? You've never even been inside the censor's office but you criticize my work!

EVA. Ponchik!

DARAGAN. Fill your glasses! Another vodka all round!

The telephone rings in the hall. DARAGAN *runs out and pulls a curtain over the doorway into the room.*

Hello, yes . . . Yes, it's me. (*Pause. He turns pale and clutches his forehead.*) Has the car left already? (*Pause.*) Right – at once! (*He replaces the receiver and calls in a low voice.*) Ponchik! Come here!

PONCHIK (*goes out into the hall*). Who is that fool?

DARAGAN. It's Professor Yefrosimov, the famous biochemist.

PONCHIK. Well, to hell with him. He may know a lot about chemistry, but . . .

DARAGAN. Shut up, Ponchik, and listen. I'm now going to drive out to the airfield on an urgent matter. *You* will do the following: without using the telephone and having first told Adam that the Professor is on no account to leave this flat, go straight to You-Know-Where and tell them, firstly – that I suspect Professor Yefrosimov has made a discovery that is of the greatest possible military importance; that he is carrying his invention on him in the guise of a camera, and that he is here. Secondly – that I suspect he is mentally unstable and may do something idiotic, by which I mean take his invention abroad . . . Thirdly – tell You-Know-Who to come here at once and check out my suspicions. That's all. But, Ponchik, if the Professor and his apparatus leave this flat, you will be responsible and you may have to face a charge of high treason.

PONCHIK. Comrade Daragan – for God's sake . . . but if I . . .

There is a sharp knock at the front door.

DARAGAN. That's my driver. (*He opens the door.*) No ifs and buts. I'm going. (*Exit, leaving his peaked cap behind.*)

PONCHIK. Comrade Daragan, you've forgotten your cap.

DARAGAN (*from outside*). To hell with it!

PONCHIK. God, what have I got myself into?! (*Quietly.*) Adam!

ADAM (*coming out into the hall*). What is it?

PONCHIK. Listen, Adam – make sure that bloody chemist and his apparatus don't leave this flat until I get back.

ADAM. What's this all about?

PONCHIK. Daragan and I have come to the conclusion that his apparatus is a secret military invention that rightly belongs to the state.

ADAM. But it's a camera!

PONCHIK. Camera my foot!

ADAM (*pause*). Aha . . . I see . . .

PONCHIK. When I come back, I shall not be alone. And remember: *you're* responsible for keeping the Professor here. (*Exit through the front door.*)

ADAM (*calls to* PONCHIK *through the doorway*). Where's Daragan?

PONCHIK (*from the landing*). I don't know.

ADAM (*shuts the front door*). What a ghastly evening this has turned out to be. (*Shaken and bewildered, he returns to the room.*)

EVA. Where are Ponchik and Daragan?

ADAM. They've gone out to the shop.

EVA. What on earth for? There's everything here . . .

ADAM. They won't be long . . .

Pause.

YEFROSIMOV (*suddenly*). My God! Jack! Jack! . . . What a fool I am! I forgot to photograph Jack . . . And I should have taken him first of all. Oh Lord, this is appalling. But surely it couldn't happen all at once and so quickly? Eva, tell me – is *Faust* still playing? Oh, God . . . (*He goes over to the window and peers out.*)

ADAM (*quietly to* EVA). Do you think he's normal?

EVA. I think he's absolutely normal.

YEFROSIMOV. Is *Faust* still playing?

EVA. Just a moment. (*She switches on the radio, from which are heard the last bars of the scene in the cathedral, after which comes the March.*) Yes, it's still on.

YEFROSIMOV. Why should Buslov, a physiologist, want to go and hear *Faust?*

EVA. My dear Professor, what's the matter? Calm down! Have a drink!

YEFROSIMOV. Wait, wait! . . . Do you hear? There it is again . . .

ADAM (*nervously*). What? It's only a dog howling.

YEFROSIMOV. But they've been howling all day. If only you knew how that worries me. I'm torn between two desires: to wait for Buslov or to abandon him and run and find Jack . . .

ADAM. Who is Jack?

YEFROSIMOV. Ah, if it weren't for Jack I'd be quite alone in this world, because I don't count my aunt, who irons my shirts . . . Jack brightens my whole life . . . (*Pause.*) Jack is my dog. You see, I once saw four people walking along, carrying a puppy and laughing. It turned out they were going to drown it! And I paid them twelve roubles not to drown it. Now he's full-grown and I'm never parted from him. On the days when I'm not using toxic materials he sits in the laboratory and watches me working. Why should anyone want to drown a dog?

EVA. What you need, Professor, is to get married!

YEFROSIMOV. Oh, I can never get married until I've found out why the dogs have started howling. So please tell me – should I wait for Buslov or go home to Jack? What do you advise?

EVA. But Professor – you mustn't go on like this! What on earth can happen to Jack? You're just being neurotic! Obviously, what you must do is wait for Buslov, talk to him, then go home and go to bed.

The front doorbell rings. ADAM *goes to open it, admitting* TULLER 1, TULLER 2 *and* KLAVDIA PETROVNA. *Last of all to enter is a worried* PONCHIK.

TULLER 1. Hello, Adam! We heard about your wedding, old man, and decided to drop in and congratulate you! Good to see you ... .

ADAM *is nonplussed; he has never seen* TULLER *before in his life.*

ADAM. Er . . . good to see you too . . . Come in, come in!

All five go into the room.

TULLER 1. Introduce me to your wife.

ADAM. This is Eva . . . Eva, this is . . . er . . .

TULLER 1. Tuller, friend of Adam's. I suppose he hasn't told you about me, has he?

EVA. Well, no, he hasn't . . .

TULLER 1. The old so-and-so! Let me introduce my cousin – he's Tuller too!

TULLER 2. Pleased to meet you.

TULLER 1. Eva, we've brought Klavdia along with us too. I was sure you wouldn't mind. She's a very clever lady – a doctor. Psychiatrist, actually. Adam hasn't told you about her, either? Some friend, eh? Oh, Adam! (*To* EVA.) You don't mind some uninvited guests dropping in out of the blue?

EVA. No, no, of course not – why should we? Adam always has such nice friends. Anya! Anya!

TULLER 1. You mustn't put yourself to any trouble. My cousin Tuller has taken care of everything . . .

TULLER 2. Tuller's right – I have . . . (*He unwraps a large parcel containing several cardboard boxes.*)

EVA. Oh, you shouldn't have done that. We have plenty here.

Enter ANYA, *who takes the boxes and exit.*

Ponchik – sit down. But where's Daragan? Do sit down, comrades.

KLAVDIA. God, the heat!

EVA. Adam! Do the introductions . . .

TULLER 1. You mean – introduce us to Professor Yefrosimov? No need. We know each other.

TULLER 2. Tuller, the Professor obviously doesn't recognize you.

TULLER 1. Impossible!

YEFROSIMOV. Do forgive me . . . I confess I'm a little confused . . . I'm afraid I *don't* recognize you . . .

TULLER 1. Oh, come now . . .

KLAVDIA. Oh, shut up Tuller! I couldn't recognize my own brother in this heat. My brain literally starts to melt in August. Oh, this August!

YEFROSIMOV. Excuse me, but it's not August.

KLAVDIA. Not August? Then what month *is* it?

TULLER 1. There you go! It's so hot and so close that Klavdia's had a brainstorm. For heaven's sake, Professor, tell her which month it is.

YEFROSIMOV. At all events it's not August. It's . . . you know . . . what d'you call it . . . (*Pause.*)

TULLER 1 (*quietly and meaningfully*). Here in the USSR it is May, Professor – May! . . . (*He changes his tone.*) Well now, this time last year . . . in Sestroretsk, at the seaside, you were renting a room from a widow, Maria Pavlovna Ofitserskaya, and I was staying next door, with the Kozlovs. You and Jack would go off to the beach every day, and once I even took a snap of your Jack.

Pause.

YEFROSIMOV. What a coincidence . . . You're quite right: I was staying in Maria Pavlovna's dacha . . . Obviously my memory has failed me yet again.

TULLER 2 (*to* TULLER 1). Call yourself a photographer! Obviously you're not a very memorable personality. By the way, have you seen that remarkable camera the Professor's got?

TULLER 1. Oh really, Tuller! That's not a camera.

TULLER 2. Tell me another! That's a foreign camera.

TULLER 1. Now, Tuller . . .

TULLER 2. It's a camera!

TULLER 1. And I say it's not!

TULLER 2. It is a camera!

YEFROSIMOV. You see, comrade Tuller, it . . .

TULLER 1. No, no, Professor, he needs to be taught a lesson. (*To* TULLER 2.) Want a bet? Fifteen roubles?

TULLER 2. Done!

TULLER 1. Well now, Professor, what is that apparatus of yours? Is it a camera?

YEFROSIMOV. You see . . . no, it's not a camera . . .

EVA. What?!!

ANYA *enters and starts to clear the table. From the radio comes the strains of the 'Internationale', performed by massed choirs and orchestra.*

TULLER 1. Right! Hand over your fifteen roubles! And let that be a lesson to you.

TULLER 2. But look here . . . I mean, anyone can see . . . it's a 'Pixie'!

TULLER 1. Pixie yourself! Come on – pay up.

From outside comes the howl of a dog, followed by a woman's short, bloodcurdling scream.

ANYA (*drops the crockery*). Oh, I feel sick . . . (*She falls dead.*)

> Several brief, agonized cries are heard from the courtyard. An accordion stops playing in mid-phrase.

TULLER 1. Aaaah! (*He falls dead.*)

TULLER 2. Bogdanov! Get that apparatus . . . (*He falls dead.*)

KLAVDIA. Oh God, I'm going . . . (*She falls dead.*)

PONCHIK. Christ! What's happening?! (*He staggers, then runs headlong out of the flat, slamming the front door behind him.*)

> The music on the radio drops in pitch as it slows down and stops. A second or two of confused voices, then the radio goes dead.

> Total silence reigns everywhere.

YEFROSIMOV. My premonition! I knew it! Jack! (*Despairingly.*) Oh, Jack!

> ADAM *runs over to the body of* KLAVDIA, *examines her face intently, then stands up and slowly walks towards* YEFROSIMOV; *he has a grim look.*

ADAM. So what *is* that apparatus of yours? You've killed them, haven't you! (*In a frenzy.*) Help! Help! Seize this man and his machine! (*He lunges at* YEFROSIMOV.)

EVA. Adam! What are you doing?

YEFROSIMOV. Stop! You're mad! Don't you understand? Eva, get this wild beast off me!

EVA (*glancing out of the window*). Oh, what's happening? Adam, look out of the window! The children are all lying on the ground . . .

ADAM (*leaves* YEFROSIMOV, *runs over to the window*). Explain this!

YEFROSIMOV. That? That – is your ideas in action! . . . It's the black man in the electric chair! It means I've failed! It's 'Red rifles shooting!' It's war! It's . . . solar gas! . . .

ADAM. What? I can't hear you properly . . . What? Gas?! (*He grabs* EVA *by the hand.*) Come on – down into the cellar! Hurry! (*He pulls* EVA *towards the door.*)

EVA. Adam, save me!

YEFROSIMOV. Stop! You don't have to run anywhere. You're in no danger. Don't you understand? This apparatus protects you from the gas! I invented it! Yes, I did! I – Yefrosimov! You're both safe! Hold your wife tightly, Adam, or she'll go out of her mind.

ADAM. And are the others dead?

YEFROSIMOV. Yes!

EVA. Adam! Adam! (*Pointing to* YEFROSIMOV.) He's a genius! He foresaw it all!

YEFROSIMOV. Say that again! Genius, did you say? Genius? If there's anyone else left alive, let him repeat her words!

EVA (*in a paroxysm of fear and revulsion*). I hate dead bodies! I'm afraid of them! Oh quick – let's go down to the cellar. (*Exit, followed by* ADAM.)

YEFROSIMOV (*alone*). They're dead . . . And those children? They would have grown up, ideas would have got at them . . . What sort of ideas? The idea of drowning a puppy? . . . And you too, my friend. You hadn't an idea in your head, except a few innocent ones – to do harm to no one, to lie at my feet, to look into my eyes, and to have enough to eat! . . . why, oh why drown a dog?

The light slowly fades until Leningrad is in darkness.

ACT TWO

A large department store in Leningrad; a grand staircase leads up to the first floor. The huge plate-glass windows on the ground floor are all smashed, and a tramcar protrudes into the store where it went off the rails and crashed through a large display-window. The woman tram-driver half-hangs out of the broken windscreen. On a ladder half-way up a stack of shelves a dead salesman is still holding a shirt. A dead woman lies collapsed across a counter; by the entrance, a man who died standing up leans against a doorpost. The floor is littered with abandoned purchases. Through the huge, gaping window-frames heaven and hell can be seen: heaven at the top, in the shape of the rays of the early morning sun; hell lower down – the glow of innumerable huge fires. Between them there is a swirl of smoke, through which can just be seen a distant quadriga of four bronze horses on top of a monument, still standing amid blazing ruins. Everywhere there is a (literally) deathly silence.

EVA enters from the street, picking her way through the broken glass. Her dress is in shreds, and she is clearly suffering from mental trauma. Turning back towards the street, she talks to someone who is still outside.

EVA. But I warn you – I'm not staying here alone for any longer than a quarter of an hour. Listen – I'm just as much in need of comfort and attention as Jack! I'm a young woman, and what's more I'm a weak and cowardly woman . . . All right, then, I'll do all I can, but don't go so far away that I can't sense your presence. All right? . . . What? . . . They've gone . . . (*She sits down on the staircase.*) Must have a cigarette . . . matches . . . (*She looks up at the dead salesman.*) Matches! (*She goes through his pockets, finds a box of matches in one of them and lights a cigarette.*) Were you having an argument with the customer? Did you have children, I wonder? Oh well, doesn't matter . . . (*She climbs up the ladder and starts to take the shirts off a shelf.*)

The sound of a heavy fall is heard from above, a shower of broken glass tumbles down the staircase, followed by DARAGAN. He is encased up to his neck in a leather flying-suit; it is torn and stained with oil and blood. A lighted electric torch is clipped to his chest. His hair is grey, his face covered in ulcers. DARAGAN *walks uncertainly down the stairs, feeling his way with his hands held out: he is blind.*

DARAGAN. Help! Help me! Hey, comrades . . . is anyone there? Help me! (*He misses his footing and falls to the bottom of the staircase.*)

EVA (*comes to her senses and gives a piercing scream*). He's alive! (*She covers her face with her hands.*) He's alive! (*She shouts towards the street.*) Hey, you men! Come back! . . . Adam! There's someone alive here! An airman! (*To* DARAGAN.) They'll be here in a moment to help you. Are you injured?

DARAGAN. Is that a woman? A woman? Speak louder, I can't hear you – I've gone deaf.

EVA. Yes – I'm a woman.

DARAGAN. Don't come near me! Don't touch me! You'll die if you do!

EVA. I'm safe – the gas can't harm me.

DARAGAN. Keep back, or I'll shoot! Where am I?

EVA. You're in a department store.

DARAGAN. In Leningrad?

EVA. Yes, yes.

DARAGAN. Fetch an officer – quickly! Hey, you, woman – fetch me an army officer!

EVA. There's no one here – they're all dead!

DARAGAN. Then get a pencil and paper . . .

EVA. I haven't got any . . .

DARAGAN. Hell! Is there no one here but an illiterate cleaning-woman?

EVA. Can't you see me? Can't you see?

DARAGAN. Silly bitch – I'm blind. I fell and was blinded. I can't see a thing . . .

EVA (*recognizing him*). Daragan! You're Daragan!

DARAGAN. Oh God, the pain! (*He collapses.*) I'm a mass of ulcers . . .

EVA. You're Daragan!

DARAGAN. What? . . . Perhaps I am . . . I told you not to come near me . . . Listen, woman: I'm poisoned, I'm going mad and I'm dying . . . (*He groans.*) Get hold of paper and pencil . . . Can you write?

EVA. Let me take off your flying-suit. You're covered in blood!

DARAGAN (*furiously*). Don't you understand Russian? Get back! I'm dangerous!

EVA. What are you talking about? . . . Adam! Adam! . . . Don't you recognize my voice?

DARAGAN. What? Speak louder, I've gone deaf . . . Write down what I say: Report. We penetrated the enemy's balloon barrage and our bombers went through, but every pilot in the squadron was killed except me. The city was set on fire and the fascist wasps'-nest was a mass of flames. Furthermore, the dangerous Ace of Clubs has been destroyed. I, Daragan, shot him down. But I was blinded by a toxic vapour and crashed in Leningrad. Being blind I can no longer serve the Soviets. As I am a bachelor, I give my pension to the state, and request that my medals be placed in my coffin. I further request . . . request . . . inform . . . locate . . . oh, I forget what it was . . . Inform Eva that Daragan is the world's champion fighter pilot. Date, time. Dispatch, top priority, to General Headquarters. (*He shouts.*) Oh, oh . . . comrades . . . (*He jumps up and walks about, clutching his stomach.*) Someone! For pity's sake! Shoot me! For pity's sake! I can't stand the pain! Give me a revolver! Water! Give me something to drink!

EVA. I won't give you your revolver! Here, drink! (*She hands him the waterbottle that is clipped to the back of his belt.*)

DARAGAN (*tries to drink from the waterbottle, but cannot swallow*). My revolver! (*He fumbles for it, but is too weak.*) It's in the holster!

EVA. I won't give it to you! Wait – put up with it for a few more minutes. Some men will be here very soon.

DARAGAN. I'm burning inside! I'm on fire!

A trumpet fanfare suddenly blares out from a loudspeaker.

EVA. That signal again! (*She shouts.*) Where is it coming from? Where?

The loudspeaker falls silent.

DARAGAN. Don't let any doctors come near me! I'll shoot the swine! Why doesn't anyone take pity on a blind man? Call someone! Or perhaps I've been taken prisoner?

EVA. You remember me – I'm Eva! Eva! You know me! Oh, Daragan, I can't bear to see you suffering like this! I'm Eva!

DARAGAN. I don't remember anything! I know nobody! Help me! Help . . .

From outside, a car is heard approaching. It stops.

EVA. It's them! Oh, thank God! Adam! Adam! Here, here! There's a man here – alive!

ADAM *and* YEFROSIMOV *rush in.*

YEFROSIMOV. God Almighty!

ADAM. It's Daragan! How did he get here?

EVA. He fell here out of his aeroplane.

DARAGAN. Keep back! Keep back, everyone! I'm lethal – I'm still covered in the liquid.

YEFROSIMOV. Which gas poisoned you? Which gas? Did it have a smell?

EVA. Louder – he's deaf.

YEFROSIMOV. Deaf, is he? (*He turns a knob on his apparatus.*)

DARAGAN. Comrade! I have to report that I saw countless columns of smoke.

EVA. He's out of his mind, Adam. He doesn't recognize anyone. Dear, dear Adam – do something quickly, or he'll die.

YEFROSIMOV *aims the beam from his apparatus at* DARAGAN, *who lies motionless for a while, groaning; suddenly he revives, and the ulcers on his face are seen to have healed. Slowly,* DARAGAN *sits up.*

(*Weeping, she embraces* YEFROSIMOV.) Dear, great, beloved, wonderful man! Let me kiss you! (*She strokes his hair, kisses him.*) You're a genius!

YEFROSIMOV. Aha! Now let me try it on another one. (*He swings the apparatus around until the ray falls on the dead salesman.*)

No, that one's well and truly dead . . . No, I'll never see Jack
again . . . never . . . (*He sobs.*)

ADAM. Professor! What's the matter with you? Calm yourself!

YEFROSIMOV. Yes, yes, thank you . . . you're quite right . . .
(*He sits down.*)

DARAGAN. I can see again. I don't know how it was done, but
. . . (*He looks at the others in perplexity.*) Who are you? (*Pause.
Slowly his expression changes.*) Eva?! Is it you?

EVA. Yes – it's me! Me!

DARAGAN. Don't come too close. I'll take off my flying-suit
myself. (*He takes it off.*) Aren't you . . . Adam?

ADAM. Yes, I am.

DARAGAN. But don't come near me! You'll be poisoned! . . .
How did you all get here? Oh yes, I see . . . I fell into this
building when my plane crashed and you happened to be here
. . . Oh, the ringing in my ears! . . . So you came here and . . .

ADAM. No, Daragan, it wasn't like that.

YEFROSIMOV. Don't tell him all the truth at once, or you won't
be able to control him.

ADAM. Yes, you're right.

DARAGAN. No, I must admit it's not all clear to me . . . (*He
drinks from the water-bottle offered to him by* EVA.)

ADAM. Where have you come from?

DARAGAN. When I returned from . . . well, in short, when I had
completed the mission of escorting our bombers, I met the
champion fascist fighter-pilot who's known as the Ace of Clubs:
he came at me out of a cloud, and in the roundels on his wings I
could see his emblem – the ace of clubs.

A military march blares out from the loudspeaker.

What's that music?

EVA (*bursting into tears*). It's playing again! Again! It's death – death
floating in the air. Sometimes we hear it shouting in unknown
languages, sometimes it sounds like music!

ADAM. Eva, stop it at once!! (*He shakes her by the shoulders.*) Shut up! Don't give way! If you go mad, who's going to cure you?

EVA. Yes, yes. (*She calms down.*)

DARAGAN. Switching on his smoke-generator, he manoeuvred his plane to write the word 'commun', then he used his machine-gun in Morse code to rap out the word 'land' and finished by using smoke again to draw an ace of clubs in the sky. I understood his signal – it meant: 'Communist – drop out of the sky, I am the Ace of Clubs', and I felt a cold stab in the pit of my stomach. One of us wouldn't be flying back home. I knew what a good engine he had and his machine-gun could fire at forty rounds per second. He did a double-corkscrew, an Immelmann turn and a barrel-roll – all the manoeuvres that make an airman's heart shrivel with fear when he meets the Ace of Clubs. But mine didn't shrivel – on the contrary, it seemed to swell and get heavier. He had come up and over behind me, and I realized he had been able to spray me with poison gas. I don't remember how I managed to turn away, but we disengaged. I laughed, knowing that I would never fly again, and I took a long-range shot at him. Then I suddenly saw the Ace of Clubs burst into flames and start pouring out smoke. He stalled and began spiralling downwards. Then he plummeted like a bundle of burning straw, and now he's lying at the bottom of the Neva or the Gulf of Finland. All my guts seemed to be on fire, I was blind – and crashed here . . . Is he – Yefrosimov?

The music from the radio stops.

ADAM. Yes.

DARAGAN. Of course . . . He invented that apparatus, didn't he? . . . I suppose you know there's a war on, by the way? (*He looks around, sees the wrecked tramcar.*) What does this mean? (*He stands up, walks over to the tramcar and looks at the dead driver.*) Dead, is she? Went off the rails. A bomb, I suppose. Take me to General Headquarters.

ADAM. Look, Daragan – no one else is left alive.

DARAGAN. What do you mean? . . . Hell, I still can't think straight . . . But I get the general picture . . . When did I take off on that mission? . . . Yes, it must have been yesterday evening, when that writer-fellow was reading about some prince's serfs . . . Look – do you realize? The whole world is at war!

EVA. Daragan, there is no one in Leningrad except us. Now keep a grip on yourself, or you may go out of your mind.

DARAGAN (*inertly*). Where have they all gone?

EVA. Yesterday evening, just after you left us, the gas came and poisoned everyone.

YEFROSIMOV. The only ones left alive are Adam and Eve and myself.

DARAGAN. Adam . . . and Eve! By the way, I already thought you were behaving oddly yesterday evening. I'd say you were mentally ill.

YEFROSIMOV. No, no, my nerves were upset, but I am most certainly not mentally unbalanced. *You're* the one who needs to take care of himself, mentally and physically. Lie down and wrap yourself up.

DARAGAN (*with a twisted grin*). There are two million inhabitants in Leningrad . . . They can't all be done for! I know more about air-raids than you do . . . What kind of gas is needed to asphyxiate the whole of Leningrad?

EVA. We know . . . we know . . . (*She makes a cross with her two index fingers.*) The test tube marked with a black cross . . . (*She weeps.*)

DARAGAN *looks around anxiously, reflects for a moment, then goes over to the windows. His gait is that of a sick man. For a while he stares out, then clasps his head.*

ADAM (*worried*). Look, Daragan . . . Daragan, stop it . . .

DARAGAN (*shouts*). My plane! Comrades! A plane for the squadron commander! (*He fumbles in his pockets, takes out a small round tin and shows it* YEFROSIMOV.) Ever seen one of these before? Oh, they thought we Russians were a lot of bumpkins, did they? That we still went around in clogs with straws in our hair, did they? . . . Two million? . . . Factories? . . . Children? . . . See that? See the black cross on it? The regulation says: 'Not to be thrown without an order from the Military Council of the Soviet Republic', doesn't it? Well, now *I'm* giving the order: unscrew the lid to prime it – and throw it!

ADAM. Throw it? But where? Where?

DARAGAN. Straight at the target. And I know where that is! I know where to deliver this little package!

EVA. Adam, Adam – stop him!

DARAGAN (*puts the tin away; his legs weaken, and he sits down. In a stern voice*). Why is the city burning?

ADAM. The tramcars continued running for an hour or so after all the drivers were killed. They crashed into each other and into cars and lorries whose drivers were also dead. Blazing petrol spilled out of the tanks and set the buildings on fire, gas mains blew up . . .

DARAGAN. How did you survive?

ADAM. The Professor irradiated us with the beam from his apparatus; after that the human organism doesn't absorb any toxic gas.

DARAGAN (*sitting up and pointing at* YEFROSIMOV.) You are a traitor to the Soviet State!

EVA. Daragan – what are you saying?

DARAGAN. Give me my revolver!

ADAM. I won't!

DARAGAN. What? (*From a pocket he produces a hand-grenade.*) Professor Yefrosimov must be called to account! I guessed, yesterday evening, what he had invented. And now, no matter whether or not anyone else is left alive in Leningrad, you two will be witnesses to how Professor Yefrosimov answers Daragan's questions. I swear to you he is a dangerous traitor.

YEFROSIMOV (*indignantly*). What is this?

DARAGAN. No need to take offence! We shall find out the truth in a moment or two. But if I discover anything wrong, my grenade will see to it that you leave this store in a hurry – and in small pieces. Now – why didn't you hand over your apparatus to the state in time?

YEFROSIMOV. I don't understand the question. What do you mean – 'in time'?

DARAGAN. Answer!

Pause.

EVA. Adam! Adam! Why are you just sitting there and watching?
. . . Professor, why don't you say something?

ADAM. Daragan, I forbid this absurd and dangerous performance.
I order you to put that hand-grenade away.

DARAGAN. Who are you to forbid me?

ADAM. I, Adam Krasovsky, am the senior Party member to have
survived in Leningrad. I have therefore assumed power in this
city, and I have already decided this case to my own satisfaction.
I forbid you to harass Yefrosimov or to attack him. And you,
Professor, tell him the facts. That will shut him up.

YEFROSIMOV. He . . . what's the word . . . he frightened me.

EVA (*accusingly, to* DARAGAN). You frightened him.

YEFROSIMOV. I completed my research and made the discovery
on the first of May, and I realized that I had made all toxic
substances useless for military purposes; they could all be thrown
on the rubbish-heap. Not only would the living cell cease to
absorb any toxic matter after it had been irradiated, but
furthermore, even if the organism had already been poisoned,
any living creature could be saved, provided it was not dead. It
was obvious, therefore, that there would be no more chemical
warfare. I irradiated myself. But it was not until the morning of
the fifteenth that my mechanic brought me the framework and
controls of the apparatus into which I could install the hollow
lenses containing a solution of potassium permanganate and the
cell which generated the polarizing ray. I went out to see Buslov,
and that evening I ended up in Adam's flat. An hour after my
arrival there, the entire population of Leningrad was poisoned by
the gas.

DARAGAN. But were you intending to take your ray abroad and
give it to a foreign power?

YEFROSIMOV. I may 'intend' to do whatever I like.

DARAGAN (*lying down*). Listen to what he's saying, Adam. I feel
weaker, and I'm shivering all over . . . But how did the gas
attack happen? We met the enemy squadron over Kronstadt and
dispersed it before it reached Leningrad . . .

ADAM (*bending over* DARAGAN). Those weren't the planes that
dropped the gas. The ones that did flew much higher, in the
stratosphere.

DARAGAN. I see . . . I must be ready to fly again, when I feel a bit stronger . . . in case they come again . . .

YEFROSIMOV. You're not going to be flying again. Anyway, there's no point in flying any more: it's all over.

DARAGAN. It's all over?! How do you know?

YEFROSIMOV. Not only will you not fly any more, you won't even be able to sit up. You're going to be lying down for a long time, if you don't want to die.

DARAGAN. I've never had a woman to care for me, and now I'd like to be lying in a clean bed with a glass of lemon tea on the bedside table . . . I'm ill . . . Then when I've recovered, I'll climb up to six thousand metres, to the very ceiling, and at sunset I'll . . . (*To* ADAM.) What about Moscow?

ADAM. Silence. No word from Moscow.

EVA. All we hear is snatches of music and incomprehensible babble in different languages. There's fighting in every country.

ADAM. At dawn this morning we travelled fifty kilometres by car and saw nothing but corpses and fragments of glass bombs. Yefrosimov said they contained the bacillus of bubonic plague . . .

DARAGAN. I don't want to hear any more. You've told me enough. (*Pause. He points to* ADAM.) Let him give the orders, and I'll obey.

ADAM. Eva, help me to lift him up.

They lift up DARAGAN. EVA *picks up the small holdall that she brought with her.*

DARAGAN. Where are we going?

ADAM. Out to the forest, where there's a store of petrol.

DARAGAN. And we must look for an aeroplane.

ADAM. All right, let's go. We may even get through to the airfield. We'll come back here to collect a few essentials, and then – away! Otherwise we'll never get out of this graveyard!

Exeunt.

A car is heard starting up and driving away. After a while,

PONCHIK-NEPOBEDA *comes stumbling through the entrance of the store. His clothes are torn and he is filthy.*

PONCHIK (*nearly hysterical*). I must . . . I must hang on to my sanity and not think, not rack my brains wondering why I'm the only one to be left alive. Oh Lord! Oh Lord! (*He falls to his knees and crosses himself.*) Dear God, please forgive me for writing for the *Atheist Monthly*. Forgive me, dear Lord! To people I might be able to deny it, because I wrote under a pseudonym, but I can't lie to you – it was me! I worked for the *Atheist Monthly* out of thoughtlessness. I'll tell nobody but you, O Lord, but I'm a Christian believer to the marrow of my bones and I hate communism. And I promise you, as all these dead souls are my witnesses, that if you will show me how to get out of this and stay alive, I'll . . . (*He takes out the manuscript of his novel.*) But Lord, you don't have any objection to collective farms, do you? Well, what's so very wrong about them? The peasants used to live and work apart, now they'll be together. So what's the difference, O Lord? They'll be all right, damn them – they haven't been gassed . . . Look down in mercy, O Lord, on your servant Ponchik-Nepobeda, whose life is in peril, and save him. I'm an Orthodox believer and my grandfather was a bellringer. (*He gets up.*) What's happening to me? I seem to be going crazy with terror. (*He clutches his head.*) Don't send me mad! What am I looking for? If only I could find just one man who would teach me . . .

MARKIZOV'*s voice is heard in the distance, crying weakly:* '*Help!*'

It can't be! I must be hearing things! There's nobody else left alive in Leningrad!

MARKIZOV *crawls into the store. On his back is a knapsack, one of his legs is bare and the foot and ankle are covered with ulcers.*

MARKIZOV. I've made it. I can die here now. God, the pain! I'm soaked in my own tears, but there's no one to help me and my foot is rotting! Everybody else was killed at once, but I'm being killed slowly and in agony, and what for? I'll just have to keep on shouting like a wretched prisoner, until I die of exhaustion. (*He shouts weakly.*) Help!

PONCHIK. A man! And he's alive! So my prayer was heard! (*He rushes over to* MARKIZOV *and embraces him.*) You're Markizov!

MARKIZOV. Yes, I'm Markizov. And I'm dying as you can see. (*He embraces* PONCHIK *and bursts into tears.*)

PONCHIK. No, I can't be mad after all – I recognized you. Don't you recognize me?

MARKIZOV. Who are you?

PONCHIK. My God, surely you recognize me! Recognize me, I implore you! Then I'll feel better . . .

MARKIZOV. I'm sorry, but I can't see too well, comrade.

PONCHIK. I'm Ponchik-Nepobeda, the famous writer. Oh God, try and remember – you and I lived in the same apartment house. I remember you well – you were expelled from your trade union for hooliganism . . . You're Markizov!

MARKIZOV. Why did they expel me from the union? Why? Because I beat up that little bureaucrat? Well, who wouldn't have beaten him up? Was it because I drank? But how can a baker not drink? All my family were drinkers – grandfather and great-grandfather. Perhaps because I read books? But who's going to teach a baker anything, unless he reads for himself? Oh, well, it doesn't matter now. Don't worry, you won't have to put up with me for long. It'll soon be dark and I'll soon be gone . . .

PONCHIK (*prays*). Just one more thing, O Lord: save Comrade Markizov's life. I'm not praying for myself, but for another.

MARKIZOV. Look out of the window, comrade, and you'll see that God can't exist – that's for sure.

PONCHIK. But who except a terrible, just God can have punished a sinful world like this?

MARKIZOV (*weakly*). No, it was *them* – they let loose that gas poisoned the whole USSR for being communist . . . I can't see anything any more . . .

PONCHIK. Don't give way! Stand up, dear man. Oh, the cruelty of it – for him to appear and then die on me!

Enter YEFROSIMOV *carrying a suitcase, and with a haversack slung over one shoulder and his apparatus over the other. Catching sight of* PONCHIK *and* MARKIZOV, *he stops in amazement. On seeing* YEFROSIMOV, PONCHIK *bursts into tears of joy.*

YEFROSIMOV. Where on earth have you two come from? How do you happen to be in Leningrad?

PONCHIK. Professor . . . Yefrosimov? . . .

YEFROSIMOV (*to* PONCHIK). Weren't you at Adam's flat yesterday evening? Wasn't it you who wrote the novel about the collective farm?

PONCHIK. Yes, it was . . . it was me! I'm Ponchik-Nepobeda!

YEFROSIMOV (*bending over to look at* MARKIZOV). And this person? What's the matter with him? . . . Ah yes, he's the one who attacked me! . . . That means you were both in Leningrad when the catastrophe happened. How did you survive?

MARKIZOV (*dully*). I ran along the street, then I sat in a cellar, ate some fish and now I'm dying.

YEFROSIMOV. Ah . . . now I think I remember . . . the door slammed . . . (*To* PONCHIK.) Tell me, when I was photographing Eva and Adam, did you come into the room?

PONCHIK. Yes, your apparatus dazzled me.

YEFROSIMOV. I see. (*To* MARKIZOV.) But you, I don't understand why . . . How could the ray have reached you? You weren't in the room.

MARKIZOV (*weakly*). Ray? Oh, yes. I'd climbed up on to the window-sill.

YEFROSIMOV. Aha . . . so *that's* how it happened.

He points his apparatus at MARKIZOV, *and switches on the ray.* MARKIZOV *stirs, shivers, opens his eyes and sits up.*

Can you see me?

MARKIZOV. Yes, I can see now.

YEFROSIMOV. What about your leg?

MARKIZOV. It's better. And I can breathe properly, too.

YEFROSIMOV. Aha. You can see now . . . Yesterday you swore at me and called me a bourgeois. But I am most certainly not a bourgeois. And this is not a camera. I am not a photographer – and I am not an alcoholic, either!

Music starts to come from the loudspeaker.

MARKIZOV. You're a scientist, comrade, so how could you be an alcoholic? Let me kiss your hand . . . and I'll recite poetry for you . . . The gas hit Leningrad like an invisible hailstorm . . . but this scientist saved me . . . Give me your hand! If I can't kiss you – have a drink. (*He proffers a flask.*)

YEFROSIMOV. Go to hell! I never drink. I only smoke . . .

MARKIZOV. Why are you so angry? . . . Want a cigarette? Go ahead, have a smoke . . .

YEFROSIMOV (*hysterically*). What right have you to call me an alcoholic? How dare you push your fist in my face?! I've spent all my life in a laboratory and I wasn't even married, and you, no doubt, have had three wives . . . You're an alcoholic yourself! I charge you with it in front of all those present and will take you to court. I shall bring a civil action against you!

PONCHIK. Professor – what are you talking about?

MARKIZOV. Comrade, dear man, don't go on like that – calm down . . . I've been in court before, and they threw the book at me . . . But you are a great man! I can breathe . . . Here, have a swig.

YEFROSIMOV. I don't drink.

MARKIZOV. How can anyone not drink? Your nerves'll kill you:

The music from the loudspeaker stops.

I know how you feel. I jumped into a tramcar . . . but the conductress was dead. And I still offered her ten kopecks . . . (*He pours vodka into* YEFROSIMOV's *mouth.*)

YEFROSIMOV. Can you breathe freely?

MARKIZOV. Yes, I can. (*He breathes.*) Quite freely. And can you believe it, I wanted to kill myself . . .

YEFROSIMOV (*pointing to* MARKIZOV's *foot*). You have gangrene.

MARKIZOV. 'Course I have. I can see it's gangrene all right. Expect I'll survive.

YEFROSIMOV. Don't you realize? It's *gangrene*! Who's going to amputate your leg now? I should do it, but I'm no surgeon.

MARKIZOV. I trust you – chop it off!

YEFROSIMOV. You fool! You should have stood with both feet on the window-sill! The ray didn't touch that foot . . .

MARKIZOV. Well, to hell with that foot . . . I'll manage with one. (*He declaims.*) Oh great and learned man. You've helped us all you can!

YEFROSIMOV. I shouldn't shout, if I were you. Take a grip on yourself, or you'll go completely off your head. Follow my example and . . .

PONCHIK (*suddenly, in an access of frenzy*). I demand that you irradiate me with that beam of yours too! Why did you forget me!

YEFROSIMOV. But you must be crazy! You already have been irradiated! Pull yourself together . . . and take your hands off the apparatus.

MARKIZOV. Leave the machine alone, you fool! You'll break it!

PONCHIK. Will you at least tell me what that miraculous thing is?

YEFROSIMOV. There's nothing miraculous about it. Permanganate and a polarizing beam . . . Ordinary potassium permanganate.

MARKIZOV. I see, permanganate . . . And don't you lay your hands on his apparatus! Don't touch what you don't understand. Ah, I can breathe, I can breathe . . .

YEFROSIMOV. Please don't stare at me like that! You both have a look of hysteria, and it worries me . . . Now – paper and pencil, otherwise I'll forget what I should collect and take with me from this shop. What's that in your pocket?

PONCHIK. It's the manuscript of my novel.

YEFROSIMOV. Oh, you don't need that any more . . . Your Apollon Akimovich is frying in hell now.

MARKIZOV. There's no other paper. Hand it over! (*He snatches the manuscript from* PONCHIK.)

YEFROSIMOV. Got a pencil? Good. Now write this down: first we need – Oh, God . . . what d'you call 'em . . . the things you chop wood with . . .

PONCHIK. Axes?

MARKIZOV. Axes!

YEFROSIMOV. Axes. Medicines . . . Collect everything you can
lay your hands on which will help to support life . . .

From outside comes the sound of an approaching lorry.

There they are! They've found a lorry and brought it here. (*He
runs to the entrance and shouts.*) Eva! Adam! I've found two more
people who are alive!

ADAM *shouts back an indistinct reply.*

YEFROSIMOV. Yes – two more alive! Here they are!

PONCHIK (*runs over to* YEFROSIMOV *and clings on to him*). It's
us! (*Exit, following* YEFROSIMOV.)

MARKIZOV. It's us – we're here! (*He tries to run, but cannot.*)
Don't forget me – I'm alive too! . . . No, Markizov, it seems
your running days are over . . . (*He shouts.*) Don't leave me
behind. Don't leave me . . . Hey, wait for me!

*Through the windows, a whole block of houses can be seen collapsing
noiselessly, revealing a colonnade and some bronze horses, lit by a
strange light.*

Comrades – look at that! Look!

Curtain

ACT THREE

The interior of a large tent at the edge of a forest. The tent is full of a great variety of objects: short lengths of tree-trunk for sitting on; a table; a radio receiver; crockery; a piano-accordion; a machine-gun and, for some reason, a large and richly gilded ceremonial chair or throne taken from a palace. The tent is made of whatever materials came to hand: canvas, brocade, silk, chequered oil-cloth. One side of the tent is open, and a rainbow can be seen beyond the trees of the forest.

Noon. MARKIZOV, *with crutches beside him and wearing blue spectacles, is sitting in the gilded armchair, holding a tattered and somewhat charred book.*

MARKIZOV (*reads*). '. . . And the Lord God said, It is not good that the man should be alone; I will make him an helpmeet for him . . .' Good idea, but where does he find this helpmeet? There's a hole in the page after that. (*He reads.*) '. . . And they were both naked, the man and his wife, and they were not ashamed . . .' Damn, the book's burned at the most interesting bit. (*He reads.*) '. . . Now the serpent was more subtle than any beast of the field which the Lord God had made.' Full stop. The rest of the page has been torn out.

Enter PONCHIK-NEPOBEDA. *Like* MARKIZOV *he has grown a beard and is dressed in rags, wet from the rain. He unslings a shotgun from his shoulder and throws a dead bird into a corner of the tent.*

There's a bit about you here: 'Now the serpent was more subtle than any beast of the field . . .'

PONCHIK. Like hell it's about me – what makes you think I'm a serpent? Is lunch ready?

MARKIZOV. In half an hour, Your Highness.

PONCHIK. Just time for a glass or two before we eat . . .

MARKIZOV. You know Adam checks the levels in all the bottles of spirit . . .

PONCHIK. Huh! It's none of his business. Each one of us is boss in his own department. I'm surprised at you – you shouldn't let yourself be sat upon. You're in charge of food and drink, aren't you? You are. So you can run that department as you please. I'm in the habit of having a drink before meals, and I work just as hard as the others, if not harder . . .

MARKIZOV. Quite right, Comrade Serpent! (*He takes off his spectacles; pours out a drink for* PONCHIK *and himself. They clink glasses and drink.*)

PONCHIK (*suddenly*). Wait a moment . . . (*He runs over to the radio, switches it on and twiddles the knobs.*)

MARKIZOV. There's nothing to be heard – I was listening out all morning. The airwaves are empty, brother Serpent.

PONCHIK. Will you kindly stop calling me a serpent?

They fill up and drink again.

MARKIZOV. I have to admit I get bored without something to read . . . Lord, what a fool I was to let my *Count of Monte-Cristo* get ruined. Look, I picked it up in that cellar – and this is all that was left of it . . . By the way, in *this* book there's a whole lot about our Adam and Eva.

PONCHIK (*glancing at the Bible*). Lot of mystical rubbish!

MARKIZOV. But I must read something – it's so boring in this empty world!

PONCHIK. I've been delighted to notice that you're a changed man since the catastrophe, and whatever people may say, I think it's been due to my influence. Literature is a great and powerful force!

MARKIZOV. What made me change wasn't literature – it was my foot. It made me lame, I couldn't fight people, so what was there to do but read – read anything I happened to lay my hands on? But I haven't been able to find anything except this burnt and torn book.

PONCHIK. So let's read my novel again!

MARKIZOV. We've read it twice already . . .

PONCHIK. So listen to it again. I promise you it won't make your ears drop off! (*He picks up his manuscript and reads.*) '. . . Chapter

One. Where once the earthy, emaciated faces . . .' You see, I'm gradually improving it as we go along. I've put in the word 'emaciated'. How does it sound?

MARKIZOV. Sound? . . . Sounds all right.

PONCHIK. Yes, I thought so too. '. . . emaciated faces of Prince Volkonsky's serfs.' After a lot of thought I changed 'Prince Baratynsky' to 'Prince Volkonsky . . .' I hope you noticed?

MARKIZOV. Yes, I noticed.

PONCHIK. You can learn a lot from listening to me '. . . Prince Volkonsky's serfs furrowed the thin, poor soil, we now see the fresh, pink cheeks of collective-farm peasants . . . 'Hey, Vanya, Vanya', the cry rang out from the edge of the field . . .'

MARKIZOV. Stop! I now realize that you are a great man. You write well, in fact you're a genius. Will you therefore please explain to me why good literature is always so boring?

PONCHIK. Because you're a fool, that's why!

MARKIZOV. I'm not talking about real, printed books. I always like reading them; but when it's 'good literature', like yours, it's nothing but 'Hey, Vanya, Vanya', nothing but collective farms and tractor-drivers working overtime for no pay.

PONCHIK. God, the rubbish in this man's head, however hard I try to educate him! So you really think all 'literature' is hand-written manuscripts? And why should it always be about collective farms and tractor-drivers? You can't have read much.

MARKIZOV. I've read a lot.

PONCHIK. What – when you were playing the hooligan in Leningrad? I somehow don't think they slung you out of your union for reading too much . . .

MARKIZOV. Why are you always trying to needle me? That book was right about you – you're a serpent. But that other book was talking about me when it said . . . let me see . . . yes: 'My past, monsieur le comte, is dead.'

PONCHIK. Oh, how right the late Apollon Akimovich was when he said 'Do not' – he said – 'do not cast your pearls before swine, comrades!' Historic remark! (*He throws his manuscript aside. He tosses back a glass of vodka. Pause.*)

MARKIZOV. She doesn't love him.

PONCHIK. Who doesn't love whom?

MARKIZOV (*mysteriously*). Eva doesn't love Adam.

PONCHIK. And what's that to you?

MARKIZOV. And I predict that she will fall in love with me.

PONCHIK. What?!

MARKIZOV (*whispers*). She doesn't love Adam. I was walking past their tent last night and I heard her crying. She doesn't love Daragan either, she doesn't love you, and as for the great Yefrosimov . . . Anyway, since he's such a great man he doesn't come into it. Therefore – *I* am going to be the lucky one . . .

PONCHIK. But . . . I see . . . Listen: when the fires were blazing in Leningrad, I went into the bank where I have a foreign-currency account and I took this out of my safe-deposit box . . . (*He produces a wad of banknotes.*) These are dollars. I'll give you a thousand dollars if you'll give up any thoughts of having Eva.

MARKIZOV. What use are dollars to me, for God's sake?

PONCHIK. Don't believe Adam or Daragan when they try to tell you that foreign currency is now worthless anywhere in the world. The Soviet rouble – I'm telling you this in secret – won't be worth a damn, that's for sure. But don't worry – out there (*He points into the distance.*) plenty of people are left alive. And as long as two people survive, dollars will have a value until all life on earth finally comes to an end. See that old man's face printed on that dollar bill? That's George Washington, and he's immortal. When Daragan manages to make contact with the outside world, with those dollars you'll be able to marry a woman who'll make everyone's mouth drop open. And none of your Anya's – you'll be far out of the housemaid league! . . . But what will Eva want with a cripple like you? No, there are two forces left in this world: dollars and literature, and I've got 'em both!

MARKIZOV. Buy me off, gag me with money, would you? . . . Oh well, cheap at the price, I suppose. (*He pockets the dollars, plays a fast little waltz on the accordion, then puts the instrument down.*) Go on reading your novel.

PONCHIK. All right. (*He reads.*) '. . . fresh, pink cheeks of collective-farm peasants. "Hey, Vanya, Vanya . . ."

EVA *enters suddenly.*

EVA. '. . . rang out from the edge of the field!' I seem to have heard that line before. But how can you sit there reading at a moment like this? Listen – doesn't that make your heart stand still?

The distant sound of an aeroplane engine can be heard.

Can you hear it?

The noise of the engine rises to a crescendo, then cuts out. EVA goes over to the radio, switches it on, twirls the knobs and listens.

Nothing, not a sound.

MARKIZOV. I've been listening out since this morning, and there hasn't been a squeak. (*He offers a bunch of flowers to* EVA.) I picked these for you, Eva.

EVA. You shouldn't have bothered. My tent is full of flowers – there are so many, I haven't the time to put them in water or throw them out.

PONCHIK. Exactly. For a start, that bunch of yours looks dead, and secondly, it's pointless to fill up a person's tent with weeds . . . (*He snatches the bouquet from* MARKIZOV's *hand and throws it out of the tent. He quietly hisses to* MARKIZOV.) You cheat! You took my money, didn't you? That's simply amoral . . .

EVA. What are you two whispering about?

MARKIZOV. Nothing, nothing. I shan't say another word. He has bought my silence.

EVA. To hell with both of you, then. All those tricks you've been playing lately and your stupid remarks bore me to death. Is lunch ready?

MARKIZOV. I'll just see how the soup's getting on.

PONCHIK. Yes, take a look at the soup, cock – we're all hungry!

EVA. If you want to help this man, who's trying to educate himself, don't confuse him. The word is 'cook', not 'cock'.

PONCHIK. There are different ways of pronouncing it.

EVA. Don't talk rubbish.

MARKIZOV. 'Cook'? I'll write that down. (*He makes a note in an exercise book.*) In which language?

EVA. English.

MARKIZOV. I see. Thanks. Back in a moment. (*Exit.*)

PONCHIK. Eva, I must have a talk with you.

EVA. But I don't want to . . .

PONCHIK. Please hear me out!

EVA. Well?

PONCHIK. Who talks to you in the depths of the forest? Who? Before the catastrophe, I held a certain position in Soviet literature, and now, if Moscow has been destroyed as completely as Leningrad, I am the *only Soviet writer left*! Who knows – it may be that fate has chosen me to record the story of this great disaster for furture generations. Are you listening?

EVA. I'm listening with great interest. I thought you were going to tell me you loved me – but this is really interesting.

PONCHIK (*quietly and confidentially*). I know your secret.

EVA. My secret? What secret?

PONCHIK. You're unhappy with Adam.

EVA. What business is that of yours? . . . And by the way, how did you find out?

PONCHIK. I often don't sleep at night. And do you know why? Because I'm obsessed by one thought. You can guess what it is . . . Anyway, a few nights ago I heard the sound of a woman crying. Who else can have been weeping in this awful forest, since there's no other woman here but you?

EVA. Unfortunately . . .

PONCHIK. And what can that dear, that one and only woman have been crying about, oh my Eva?

EVA. I want to see a city full of live people again! Where are they?

PONCHIK. You're suffering – and you don't love Adam. (*He tries to embrace* EVA.)

EVA (*limply*). No – go away.

PONCHIK. I don't understand you.

EVA. Go away.

PONCHIK. What are they doing with that aeroplane out there? (*Exit.*)

EVA (*puts on a pair of earphones; listens*). Nothing!

MARKIZOV *enters.*

MARKIZOV. Lunch will be ready soon. Where's Ponchik?

EVA. I chased him out.

MARKIZOV. Tell me, please . . . Or rather, I have something to tell you. A most important piece of news.

EVA. I know all the news here.

MARKIZOV. No, you don't. It's a secret. (*Quietly.*) I want to tell you that I'm a rich man.

EVA. I'd understand it if the heat had made you delirious, but it's been raining. Oh – you smell of vodka!

MARKIZOV. Vodka? Nonsense. I took some valerian drops because my pains have started again. Listen. Money will keep its value. Don't believe what Adam or Daragan say. As long as two people are left alive on this earth . . . money will be needed for trade. You can't dispute that – it's an economic theory, so it must be true. And I've been reading in a book – no idea what it's called – that there were once only two people on earth: Adam and Eve. And they loved each other very much. I'm not quite sure what happened after that, because the book was all torn. Do you see?

EVA. No, I don't.

MARKIZOV. But that story doesn't apply here, because you don't love your Adam. And you need another Adam . . . No, don't shout at me. You think I've got something indecent in mind, don't you? No. I am a man of mystery and extremely rich. I lay these thousand dollars at your feet. Put them away.

EVA. Zakhar, where did you get these dollars?

MARKIZOV. I saved them in my previous life, before the catastrophe.

EVA. Zakhar – *where* did you get these dollars? You stole them in Leningrad, didn't you? Take care Adam doesn't find out! You know how strict he is about looting. Oh, Zakhar!

MARKIZOV. You may say what you like, but I didn't pinch them.

EVA. Aha! Then Ponchik gave them to you – am I right?

MARKIZOV. Yes, he did.

EVA. What for?

MARKIZOV *does not reply*.

Come on – out with it!

MARKIZOV. So that I wouldn't make up to you.

EVA. And you offered them to me. You're a fine pair. Now listen: do you realize that you two are making my life a misery by behaving like this? Every night I dream the same dream: a black horse with a black mane carries me away and out of this forest! Why is fate so cruel? Why was only one woman saved? Why didn't poor Anya get irradiated too? Then you could have married her and been happy . . .

MARKIZOV *suddenly starts to sob*.

What's the matter with you? Zakhar, please – stop it.

MARKIZOV. Poor Anya was killed!

EVA. Forget it, forget it, Zakhar! Please don't remind me of it, or I'll burst into tears too, and then we'll both be miserable. So that's enough! (*Pause.*) The horse carries me away, and I am not alone . . .

MARKIZOV. Who are you with?

EVA. No, no, I was joking . . . Forget about it . . . At all events, Markizov, you're not a bad man, so let's make a pact – you won't pursue me any more. If you all go on dogging my footsteps, you'll drive me to suicide, and you wouldn't want that, would you?

MARKIZOV. No, of course not, Eva . . . I agree to your pact.

EVA. By the way, Zakhar, why do you wear those simply awful blue spectacles?

MARKIZOV. I have weak eyesight, and apart from that it makes me look like an intellectual.

EVA. That's all nonsense about your eyesight. And they don't make you look like an intellectual – you look more like some petty crook. Let me give you some honest advice – get rid of them!

MARKIZOV. Is that honest advice?

EVA. It is.

MARKIZOV. All right. (*He hands her his spectacles.*)

   EVA *throws the spectacles away.*

   The noise of the aeroplane engine is heard again.

EVA. That noise makes me shiver with excitement . . . Zakhar! In memory of this great day – there's a flower for you! I want to see people again! So, shall we be friends?

MARKIZOV. Oh yes, yes!

EVA. Sound the trumpet, Zakhar. It's time for lunch.

MARKIZOV (*picks up the trumpet*). Oh, there's no need . . . they're coming.

   Enter DARAGAN and ADAM. ADAM has grown a beard, and he has changed: he seems older than the others. He is sunburnt and has a serious look. DARAGAN is clean-shaven, his face permanently scarred where the ulcers have healed. They are followed by PONCHIK, carrying a large tureen of soup.

EVA. Well, don't keep me in suspense. Tell me – is it ready?

DARAGAN. Yes.

EVA (*embracing DARAGAN*). Oh Daragan, it's thrilling! Professor! Where are you? Come and have lunch.

ADAM. I propose that in view of the importance of the occasion we might all have a glass of vodka – except Daragan, that is. Zakhar, what's the state of our alcohol supply?

MARKIZOV. Why should it have changed? Minimum.

YEFROSIMOV (*from outside the tent*). Zakhar! What do you mean by that? A little or a lot?

MARKIZOV. I mean . . . a lot!

YEFROSIMOV. In that case, it's 'maximum'.

Enter YEFROSIMOV, wiping his hands on a towel. He is wearing a dirty white shirt and torn trousers. He is clean-shaven.

EVA. Sit down everybody.

ALL sit down at table; they eat and drink.

PONCHIK. I must say, this soup's not bad. What's for the second course?

MARKIZOV. Roast pigeon.

ADAM stands up.

ADAM. Attention, please! It is midday. I declare this session of the colony's assembly open. Ponchik, take the minutes . . . (*He sits down.*) The item for today is the matter of Daragan flying out to find out what is happening in the rest of the world. Any questions?

EVA. Daragan, show me your hands.

DARAGAN. Comrades, on my word of honour, I am absolutely fit.

EVA. Hold out your hands!

DARAGAN. Look, comrades, you're not doctors, when all's said and done . . . Well, all right. (*He holds out his hands; all examine them.*)

EVA. No, they're not shaking . . . (*To* YEFROSIMOV.) Alexander, look carefully: are they shaking or not?

YEFROSIMOV. No, they're not shaking . . . he can fly.

PONCHIK. Hurrah!

EVA. Daragan's going to fly! Daragan's going to fly!

ADAM. Right then – he will fly. What action will you take, Daragan, if the war is still going on?

DARAGAN. If the war is still in progress, I will engage the enemy forces at the first place I meet them.

ADAM. That's reasonable. There can be no objections, I take it.

DARAGAN. Why don't you say something, professor? Well? Don't you realize that the USSR is bound to win? You know from the scraps of information we've picked up on the radio that the war has become a civil war all over the world, and do you still not understand who has right on their side? . . . Ah, Professor, you sit there in silence without moving a muscle of your face, yet even at a distance I sense that you are an alien presence. What would you call that – instinct? Very well, then . . .

DARAGAN *stands up and puts on his oil-spattered flying-suit, binoculars and Mauser automatic. He tests the electric lamp clipped to his chest.*

Professor, you are a pacifist! Ah, if only I had had your education, then I might be able to understand how it is, with your keen mind and colossal talents, you can't sense what your attitude *should* be . . . However, that's irrelevant now. In honour of pacifism, I too want to make a peaceful demonstration. Quietly and modestly, I will show the world that the Soviet Republic is appropriately armed for its own defence . . . and that no more Soviet cities can be attacked. So, Professor, give me your apparatus.

YEFROSIMOV. Certainly. (*He unslings the apparatus from his shoulder and hands it to* DARAGAN.)

DARAGAN. And those containers from your laboratory marked with a black cross.

YEFROSIMOV. You're not going to take a gas bomb with you!

DARAGAN. And why not?

YEFROSIMOV. Because I have destroyed them. (*Pause.*)

ADAM. You don't mean it!

DARAGAN. If that's a joke, Professor, I don't think it's funny.

YEFROSIMOV. No, it's not a joke . . . I caused the gas to break down into its constituent elements . . . Look: these are just empty containers now . . . I'm not joking. (*He throws several small, hollow, bright metal spheres on to the table.*)

DARAGAN. Wha-a-at? (*He draws his Mauser automatic.*)

PONCHIK. Hey! Hey! What's going on?

EVA. Daragan – don't you dare!! Adam!

DARAGAN *raises his automatic and points it at* YEFROSIMOV.

Instantly, MARKIZOV *hits the automatic with his crutch and grapples with* DARAGAN. DARAGAN *fires, and hits the radio set; the glowing external valves of the radio are extinguished.*)

DARAGAN. Adam, hit this mad cripple over the head with his other crutch! Zakhar – let go of me, or I'll kill you!

MARKIZOV (*panting*). You'll have a job to kill me!

PONCHIK. For God's sake look out, Daragan, or you'll kill *me*!

EVA (*standing in front of* YEFROSIMOV *to shield him*). Go on – kill both of us at once! (*She draws a Browning automatic; shouts.*) Take care, or I'll shoot!

Pause.

DARAGAN. What is this?!

ADAM (*to* EVA). You were given that pistol to defend yourself in case you met a dangerous animal in the forest, and now you're using it to protect a criminal . . .

EVA. There's murder in the colony! Help! Help!

DARAGAN (*to* MARKIZOV). Let go, you devil! Let go! (*He wrenches himself out of* MARKIZOV's *grasp.*) No, this is not murder! Adam, write out an order sentencing him to be shot. There is an enemy in our midst!

YEFROSIMOV. In an access of madness the peoples of the world are asphyxiating each other with poison gas, and this man, burning for revenge, wants to reduce the world's population by one more unit. Will somebody please explain to him how absurdly he's behaving?

DARAGAN. Don't shield him, Eva! He won't escape his punishment – a minute or two either way will make no difference.

YEFROSIMOV. I am not hiding behind a woman. I simply demand to be given a fair trial before there's any talk of shooting me.

DARAGAN. Adam! You're our leader. Set up a court and try him.

ADAM. Yes, I have only now realized the implications of what he's done . . . He . . . Ponchik, Markizov – sit down there at the table. You will try this traitor!

PONCHIK. Wait, comrades – forgive me, but I feel rather unwell . . .

MARKIZOV *gulps down a tumbler of vodka.*

ADAM. Comrades! All listen to me! The rotten capitalist world, the world of loathsome exploitation and repression, has attacked the workers' state . . . Why did this happen? . . . Why?! Answer me! . . . Eva, I'm telling you, as my wife, to move away from that man.

EVA. I shall not move away from Yefrosimov until Daragan puts away that Mauser.

ADAM. Put it away, Daragan, for the time being – be a friend and do as I say.

DARAGAN *replaces the automatic in its holster.*

ADAM. I repeat: Why? Because they knew that the workers' state is destined to bring liberation to all mankind. We had begun to move towards our goal, and soon – very soon – we would have achieved it . . . And the capitalists knew this meant the end for them. Then, in literally one minute, Leningrad was wiped off the face of the earth, and very possibly not only Leningrad . . . Think – two million rotting bodies! And now, when Daragan, a man who has given his all in the service of the only just and rightful cause in the world – our cause! – is going to fly to do battle with the brutes that are destroying us – now, this traitor, this anarchist, this political illiterate, this dreamer has treacherously destroyed our one, priceless weapon of defence! There can be no mercy for him. The only adequate punishment is the death penalty!

DARAGAN. No, no, Adam! He's not an anarchist, he's not a dreamer! He is a conscious enemy – a fascist! You think that's a face, don't you? No – look more closely: it's a cardboard mask. I can clearly see the features of fascism behind the mask!

YEFROSIMOV. Anger has clouded your vision. I am equally indifferent to both communism and fascism. Apart from that, I saved your life with the aid of that very apparatus – unique in the world and invented by myself – which you are carrying over your shoulder.

DARAGAN. Your apparatus belongs to the USSR! And who

saved my life is irrelevant. I am alive, and therefore I am doing my duty, which is to defend the Soviet Union!

ADAM. I, Adam, say that we will now take a vote. Who is in favour of the death penalty for this saboteur? (*He raises his hand.*) Ponchik, Markizov – raise your hands!

PONCHIK. Comrades! I'm having a heart attack!

EVA. Adam! Let me speak!

ADAM. You'd do better to keep quiet. Oh, Eva, I'm afraid I shall have to teach you a lesson or two!

EVA. You're a phantom.

ADAM. What? . . . Eva, what *are* you talking about?

EVA. A ghost. And all the rest of you, too. You don't really exist. Not one of you here ought to be alive. But by pure chance this great scientist came along and, effectively, summoned you back from the other world – yet now you're going for him like a pack of snarling wolves to kill him . . .

Pause.

PONCHIK. This is terrible, comrades. (*To* YEFROSIMOV.) Why did you empty those canisters of gas?

EVA. I now have to tell you – Adam, my husband, and the whole gathering – that Daragan, this man of death, had decided that, under the pretext of those gas-canisters, he would kill Yefrosimov in order to eliminate a rival. And that is the truth of the matter.

Silence.

ADAM. You must be out of your mind, Eva.

EVA. I am not. Tell me, Daragan, in front of these witnesses, did you confess to me you were in love with me three days ago?

Shattered, PONCHIK *stands up;* MARKIZOV *downs a glass of vodka.*

DARAGAN. I protest! This is irrelevant to the case of Yefrosimov!

EVA. No. It is most relevant. Are you afraid to repeat to these people what you said to me? Does that mean that you said something indecent, or shameful, or insulting?

DARAGAN. I'm not afraid of anything!

EVA. Very well, then: when we were down by the river, did you not ask me: 'Eva – do you love Adam?'

Silence.

ADAM (*in a strangled voice*). And what did you reply?

EVA. I told him to mind his own business. Next question, Daragan: did you not whisper to me that you offered your heart to me for ever?

ADAM. And what did you say to that?

EVA. I told him that I didn't love him. And who, Daragan, gripped me by the wrist, twisted my arm behind my back and asked me whether I loved Yefrosimov? Who whispered: 'Ah, that Yefrosimov!' That's why he tried to shoot him! I tell you all sincerely that he (*Pointing to* YEFROSIMOV.) is a good, lovely man. He doesn't shout, he doesn't give orders or make scenes. I don't know why, but I sew your buttons on for all of you, but he never asks me to, and his trousers are in permanent danger of falling down! And anyway – the rest of you make my life a misery! As far as I'm concerned you can all shoot each other dead. Or better still, I'll shoot myself. Yesterday morning, Adam, you asked me whether I had fallen for Daragan, and last night, when I was trying to get to sleep, you started pestering me with questions about my feelings for Yefrosimov . . . And then today that creep, Ponchik . . .

ADAM. What did Ponchik do today?

EVA. He read me his bloody novel *three* times. That novel makes my head ache. My life's not worth living . . .

Long pause.

YEFROSIMOV. Right now the sun is shining over the world's oceans and somewhere a fleet of battleships is floating bottom-up. There is no more war – anywhere. You can tell it from the way the birds are singing. And there's no more need to poison anyone any more.

MARKIZOV. The bird with the broken leg – a bird of unusual intelligence – is no longer alarmed and no longer stares anxiously up into the sky. That means the war is over.

DARAGAN. Who believed this woman, when she said that I wanted to kill Yefrosimov for personal reasons?

Pause.

YEFROSIMOV. No one.

DARAGAN. The anti–gas apparatus, five incendiary bombs and a machine–gun – we can at least be thankful for those. I can manage without the gas–canisters, Professor! When normal life is restored in the Soviet Union, you will be rewarded for your invention. (*He points to the apparatus.*) But after that, you will be tried for destroying the gas bombs and the court will sentence you to be shot. We shall meet again, you and I. And the court will decide which of us was right. (*He looks at his watch.*) One o'clock.

ADAM. Has anyone any further business? Quickly. And make it brief. It's time for Daragan to go.

MARKIZOV. I have a request. (*He takes out a piece of paper and reads from it.*) I wish to be allowed to change my first name from Zakhar to Henry.

Silence.

ADAM. On what grounds?

MARKIZOV. I don't want to live in a new world with an idiotic name like 'Zakhar'.

ADAM (*perplexed*). Any objections? No? Permission granted.

MARKIZOV. Please sign and date this resolution.

MARKIZOV *hands the piece of paper to* ADAM, *who signs it and gives it back.* MARKIZOV *puts the paper in his pocket.*

DARAGAN. Well, goodbye comrades. In three hours time I'll be in Moscow . . .

EVA. As far as I'm concerned, you can stay there!

DARAGAN. Adam! (*Pause.*) If I come back alive, I will not pursue Eva any longer. She was telling the truth when she said I loved her, but I will no longer – and once I've made a promise, I keep it. Shall we forget the whole thing?

ADAM. You have promised and will keep your word. We'll forget it. (*He embraces* DARAGAN.)

DARAGAN (*looks at the radio set*). I'm afraid you won't get any more news by radio.

PONCHIK. That's what happens when people start shooting . . .

DARAGAN. You can expect me or news of me daily, at the latest in three weeks' time, by the first of August. But light a bonfire on the landing-ground every day, a bonfire that throws up a tall column of smoke. Then on the first, and let's say on the second and third of August as well, if necessary, light some big bonfires. But if I haven't returned by the third of August at the very latest, then don't expect either me or news of me. Listen out for a burst of machine-gun fire or a trumpet-call and watch out for an Immelmann turn! (*Exit.*)

ADAM *and* PONCHIK *follow him out.*

YEFROSIMOV. Eva! Eva!

EVA. Sasha!

YEFROSIMOV. I shall leave today!

EVA. Say that again. Are you really leaving? Aren't you afraid of forgetting something and leaving it behind? No, you won't leave. But if you do – then to hell with you! (*Exit.*)

YEFROSIMOV *follows her out.*

MARKIZOV (*alone*). So *that's* what it's all about! (*Pause.*) And that fool gave me all those dollars! (*Pause.*) Henry Markizov. Sounds good.

Outside, an aeroplane engine starts up and roars to a crescendo. A trumpet-call is heard.

He's taking off. (*He looks out of the tent.*) Oh, well, he's gone.

A burst of machine-gunfire is heard from above.

Let's hope he gets to Moscow . . . (*He picks up the accordion.*)

One after another, two signal-rockets are fired off from the landing-ground.

He's gone, he's gone, he's gone . . . happy landings! (*He plays a cheerful march on the accordion.*)

Curtain

ACT FOUR

The time is just before dawn on the morning of 10th August.

A tent in the forest clearing; a bonfire is burning in front of the tent. Two or three large bonfires can be seen in the middle distance, on the edge of the landing-ground.

Holding a lantern in one hand, MARKIZOV climbs awkwardly down a rope-ladder suspended from the large, horizontal limb of an oak tree.

MARKIZOV (*sits down beside the bonfire, takes an exercise book from his pocket and starts to write, reading the words aloud as he does so*). In vain did Henry the watchman strain his eyes to scan the darkened heavens. For other than the darkness he could see nothing, except owls perched in the trees. Thus is must be assumed that the bold aviator has perished somewhere amid this world's vast open spaces, and the little band of survivors is doomed to be marooned in the forest for ever. (*He closes his exercise book.*) I can't stand the boredom and monotony of life in the forest. We should all leave this place and try our luck somewhere else in this ruined world. (*He glances into the tent.*) Hey there, friend! Wakey, wakey! Show a leg!

PONCHIK (*from inside the tent*). Who's that?

MARKIZOV. It's me, Henry. Wake up!

PONCHIK. Henry? What Henry? I've only just got to sleep, and now all these Henrys! (*He comes out of the tent wearing a blanket, in which holes have been cut for the head and arms.*) It's very early. Why did you disturb my sleep?

MARKIZOV. It's your turn to keep the bonfires burning.

PONCHIK. I don't want to. (*Pause.*) I most definitely don't want to. This is the tenth night since the first of August that we haven't had a proper night's sleep, because we have to keep ·. awake and burn pine-branches at all four corners of the landing-ground. It's torture . . .

MARKIZOV. I agree. And in the daytime it means burning damp, green wood so as to make thick smoke, and it hurts your eyes . . .

PONCHIK. It's like a bloody dictatorship. What's the date today?

MARKIZOV. As far as I know, it's Sunday the ninth of August.

PONCHIK. Rubbish. You're wrong. Look at the sky.

MARKIZOV. Well, so what? It's lightening. Nearly dawn.

PONCHIK. It's been the tenth of August for the past hour. I'm fed up with this performance. Daragan said quite clearly that if he wasn't back in three weeks – in other words, by the third of August – he wouldn't be coming back at all. And now it's the tenth! Thanks to Adam, we've been going through this all-night agony for a whole extra week to no purpose. And the amount of tree-felling and wood-chopping we've had to do! I tell you I'm not going to do it any more.

MARKIZOV. He'll force you to. He's the leader.

PONCHIK. No! I've had enough! To hell with him – he's not going to force *me*. Later this morning I'm going to demand an assembly and have a resolution passed that we shall pull up sticks and set out for the open spaces . . . Look, what's that?

MARKIZOV. That? It's a spider's web, that's all.

PONCHIK. Correct. Spider's webs are appearing all over the forest. And that means – autumn. In about three weeks' time it will start raining, it will get misty, and soon after that the cold weather will begin. Living like Red Indians is all very well in summer, but as soon as it gets cold I'm getting out of this God-forsaken place.

MARKIZOV. Surely you haven't forgotten? We were driven here by the plague and the contaminated water.

PONCHIK. We should have headed west, towards Europe, where there are cities and civilization and central heating!

MARKIZOV. Cities? Central heating? As far as we know, there's only plague, famine and heaps of corpses there too . . .

PONCHIK (*looking around*). 'As far as we know' – my foot! The fact is, we know absolutely nothing whatsoever. (*Pause.*) That story is just communist eyewash . . . a blind belief that the

USSR is bound to win. Personally, I'm in no doubt at all that Daragan is dead because he, completely on his own, ran into enemy forces – West European forces! – and, being the blockhead that he is, he took them on in a fight. He's a fanatic! In fact, they're all fanatics. Communism's got nothing to do with it: in his case it's pure vanity. He shot down the Ace of Clubs – so he's the world champion. And our champion is now lying dead somewhere, in the wreckage of his aeroplane . . . (*Pause.*) God, my nerves are giving me hell!

MARKIZOV. So let's have a brandy.

PONCHIK. Good idea! Brrr . . . It's chilly . . . Morning's on the way . . . and a gloomy, cheerless morning it is, too.

MARKIZOV *pours out two glasses of brandy and they drink.*

MARKIZOV. Well, how are your nerves now?

PONCHIK. I'll tell you what's upsetting my nerves . . . Just look what communism has brought us to! We annoyed and frightened and provoked the rest of the world – of course by 'we' I don't mean us, the intellectuals, but '*Them*'. *They* just went on grinding out our propaganda, proclaiming the destruction of all the values that civilization rested on . . . And Europe and America put up with it . . . they went on putting up with this endless stream of hostile threats until suddenly their patience snapped: drop dead, you barbarians, you half-Mongol hordes! . . . Daragan was cock of the walk, or so he thought. Now where is he? Face down in the shit – for good . . . And Zakhar Markizov, ex-trade union member, is now sitting on a tree-stump in the forest, looking like an owl with a belly-ache, and staring up into the sky.

MARKIZOV. I'm not Zakhar – I'm Henry! That's all been signed and sealed, and I asked everyone not to call me Zakhar.

PONCHIK. Why are you getting so wound up? What does it matter? Really, as if it made any difference to anything: Henry . . . Oh, all right . . . But we seem to have got ourselves into such a state of nervous tension that someone only has to say one word and the other person goes straight for his throat!

MARKIZOV. I am any man's equal now – I'm the same as the rest of you. There are no more bourgeois now . . .

PONCHIK. Oh, stop frothing at the mouth! Have a brandy,

Henry the Fourth! Listen: there used to be something called the USSR and it has ceased to exist. The whole country was hit by chemical warfare and has been cordoned off and a notice put up: 'Plague. Keep out'. That is the result of provoking a clash with the civilized world. Do you imagine I believe for one moment that the same has happened to the rest of Europe? Over there, brother Henry, electric lights are burning and cars are driving along the asphalt. And we are sitting round a camp-fire, gnawing bones like dogs and afraid to go anywhere because on the other side of the stream there is bubonic plague . . . To hell with bloody communism.

MARKIZOV. And who wrote all that garbage about the fresh, pink faces of collectivized peasants? I thought you were *for* communism.

PONCHIK. Shut up, you don't understand these things.

MARKIZOV. You're right, I don't . . . '. . . the serpent was more subtle than all the beasts of the field.' And you, Comrade Serpent, have found a nice refuge inside Adam's shirt, where you're warm and safe, waiting for the right moment to sink your fangs into him.

PONCHIK. Serpent, indeed! You, you blockhead, can never understand the agony of a poet's tortured soul!

MARKIZOV. I admit it, my head's in a complete muddle now. So where *do* you stand now: are you for communism or against it?

PONCHIK. Your communism is finished now, *kaputt* – and glory be to God for that! But even after its death it has left us in the hands of an immature fantasist in a gendarme's uniform . . .

MARKIZOV. Who are you talking about? Come on, explain . . . Who is it?

PONCHIK. Adam . . .

Pause. From the distance come sounds of revolver shots.

PONCHIK *and* MARKIZOV *leap to their feet.*

MARKIZOV. Hey! What was that?

They listen intently.

PONCHIK. Don't worry, that was just someone doing some target practice. Or it was a spiritual seance: Adam, father of mankind, was shooting into the empty air to summon up the spirits of the dead. He wants to ask their advice, because he doesn't know what to do next. (*He shouts.*) Go on! Summon them up! Daragan is no more! This is the dawn of the tenth of August! Stop this bloody farce!

Silence.

MARKIZOV. By the way, Serpent, I've written a novel.

PONCHIK. Read it to me.

MARKIZOV (*takes out a thick exercise book and reads*). 'Chapter One. When all the people on earth died, and Adam and Eve were left, the only other person left alive was Henry, and he fell in love with Eve. Madly in love. And every day Henry would go to the bird with the broken leg to talk about Eve, because there was no one else to talk to.'

PONCHIK. Go on.

MARKIZOV. That's all. That's the end of Chapter One.

PONCHIK. Well, what comes next?

MARKIZOV. Next comes Chapter Two.

PONCHIK. Read it!

MARKIZOV (*reads*). 'Chapter Two. "Eve! Eve!" a voice rang out at the edge of the field . . .'

PONCHIK. What's this?! Cross that out at once!

MARKIZOV. But you said I should learn from you!

PONCHIK. I said 'learn', not steal! Anyway, what's all this about Henry falling in love with Eve? What about the thousand dollars? . . . (*He stops, cocks his head and listens.*) Wait! Listen!

MARKIZOV (*jumps to his feet*). By God! It's a humming noise in the sky . . .

PONCHIK. Rubbish. There's a humming in your head, that's all . . .

MARKIZOV. Who's that?

PONCHIK. Who goes there?

It has been gradually getting lighter in the forest. From a distance comes ADAM's voice: 'Who's that by the campfire?'

MARKIZOV. It's us.'

Enter ADAM.

ADAM. Well now, Comrade Ponchik – isn't it time you relieved the Professor on fire duty at the landing-ground?

PONCHIK. I'm not going.

ADAM. You're setting a bad example, Ponchik.

PONCHIK. I'm not your serf, Adam.

ADAM. I'm the leader of this colony and I demand obedience.

PONCHIK. Henry – you're my witness. I want you to hear this. When the leader starts to behave irrationally, I have the right to question whether he should be obeyed. You're exhausting us all with this pointless work of keeping the bonfires alight.

ADAM. I represent the Party, and the Party demands . . .

PONCHIK. I don't know where or what your 'Party' is. It's more than likely that it doesn't exist any longer.

ADAM (*draws his revolver*). Just you dare repeat that remark and . . .

PONCHIK (*hides behind a tree*). Henry! You heard him threaten me! He's got a revolver. I will no longer tolerate the use of force.

ADAM. Ponchik, you're an intelligent man, a Soviet writer. Don't provoke me, I'm tired. Go and keep the bonfires burning.

PONCHIK (*coming out from behind the tree*). Me – a Soviet writer? Watch this! (*He picks up his manuscript and tears it into small pieces.*) So much for those earthy faces, so much for those fresh pink cheeks, and so much for Prince Volkonsky-Baratinsky! Look, everyone – look at Ponchik-Nepobeda, who once had real talent but destroyed it, and himself, by writing just the sort of trashy, arse-licking novel that the Soviet cultural policemen wanted him to write! (*To* MARKIZOV.) You can have 'rang out from the edge of the field'! I give it to you as a present! Write away – you're welcome to every feeble cliché in the whole lousy novel! . . . I will now submit to brute force. (*Exit.*)

ADAM. Henry, Henry . . .

MARKIZOV. You'd better go and get some sleep, or you will have been up for two nights running.

ADAM. Would you mind going up the tree again?

MARKIZOV. I'll go *up* – but I'll go up to the top of that hill over there.

ADAM. What do you think, Henry – do you think Daragan will come back?

MARKIZOV. Theoretically . . . he might. (*Exit.*)

Exit ADAM.

It grows lighter in the forest.

After a while YEFROSIMOV *enters, in rags and covered in soot. He goes into the tent. Through the striped side of the tent we see the glow of a lamp that he has lit. Pause.*

Enter EVA, *furtively. She is wrapped, head and shoulders, in a woollen shawl. There is a knapsack on her back and she carries a wicker basket.*

EVA. Sasha . . .

YEFROSIMOV *unbuttons the window of the tent and looks out.*

YEFROSIMOV (*stretching out his arms*). Eva! You're not asleep.

EVA. Sasha, put that light out. It's daylight.

YEFROSIMOV (*puts out the light*). Aren't you afraid that Adam will be angry because we are together so often?

EVA. No, I'm not afraid. Haven't you washed yet?

YEFROSIMOV. No. There's no water in the tent.

EVA. Let me at least wipe your face. (*She tenderly wipes the soot from his face.*) Sasha, you're in rags and you've got all black in this terrible forest . . . (*Pause.*) What were you thinking about last night? Tell me.

YEFROSIMOV. I was staring into the fire and I could quite clearly see Jack. I was thinking that I am the unhappiest of all the survivors. No one else has really lost anything, except perhaps Markizov, who lost his foot, but I am utterly bereft. I've been crushed by all that I've seen and been through, but worst of all was losing Jack.

EVA. Dear Sasha! Is it possible, is it natural to be so attached to a dog? After all, it's rather insulting when there's a human being who's very attached to *you*.

Enter ADAM *quietly. Catching sight of the two people talking, he shudders, then sits down on a tree-stump and listens to them. He cannot be seen by* EVA *and* YEFROSIMOV.

The poor dog is dead, and there's nothing to be done about it. And here, in this awful, gloomy forest, there is a woman – possibly the only woman left in the world – who, instead of sleeping, comes to your window and looks into your eyes, and you can find nothing better to say than to reminisce about a dead dog! What misery for me!

YEFROSIMOV (*suddenly embraces* EVA.) Eva! Eva!

EVA. At last! At last he's thought of the right thing to do!

ADAM *covers his eyes with his hand and shakes his head.*

Am I any worse than Jack? The man leans out of the window and dazzles me with the light shining from his eyes! And now I know and adore the formula for chloroform, and what's more, I long to wash his shirts. I hate war . . . It turns out we're absolutely alike, he and I, we are one soul that has been split in two until now, and just imagine – I saved his life, gun in hand! No, really, it's too unfair to prefer a dumb animal to me!

YEFROSIMOV. Oh Eva. I've loved you for a long time!

EVA. Then why didn't you say so?

YEFROSIMOV. I didn't realize it myself. Or perhaps I'm hopelessly unfitted for normal, warm-blooded human life . . . But Adam – what about Adam? . . . Do I feel guilty about him? Or do I feel sorry for him?

EVA. You're a genius, but you're a silly genius. I don't love Adam. Why did I marry him? God alone knows, I don't. Mind you, I liked him *then* . . . But suddenly the catastrophe happened, and I saw that my husband was a man with a stone jaw, a fighter and an organizer. All I hear is – war, gas, plague, mankind, we'll build new cities . . . we'll find 'the human material' . . . But I don't want 'human material': I simply want *people*. Most of all I want one man in particular. And after that, a little house in Switzerland and – to hell with ideas, wars, classes, ideologies, strikes . . . I love you and I adore chemistry . . .

YEFROSIMOV. Then you are my wife! I'll go and tell everything to Adam – now . . . But what do we do then?

EVA. There's food in my knapsack and the bird with the broken leg is in this basket. I made sure you would have an animal to look after, so that you wouldn't madden me by moaning about Jack all the time! . . . We can reach the cars in an hour and you can drive us away.

YEFROSIMOV. Light has now dawned in my rather stupid brain and I realize that I can't live without you. I adore you.

EVA. I am Eve, but he is not my Adam. *You* will be Adam, and we'll live in the mountains. (*She kisses him.*)

YEFROSIMOV. I'll go and look for Adam . . .

ADAM (*appearing from behind a tree*). No need to look for me – I'm here.

EVA. You shouldn't eavesdrop, Adam! That is my firm conviction. We have no state secrets. This is a private conversation between a man and a woman, and no one else should dare to listen. Besides, you're holding a revolver and you frighten me. Go away!

YEFROSIMOV. Don't worry, Eva . . . People here are in the habit of drawing revolvers now and again, and once they even shot at me. So it no longer has any effect.

EVA. Go away, Adam!

ADAM. I wasn't eavesdropping, I was listening, and what I heard was what both of you wanted to tell me. I always carry a revolver, and just now I was firing a salute in memory of a dead airman who will never fly back here any more. He won't come, and your fire-watching chores are over. You said I had a stone jaw, didn't you? What nonsense. Everybody's jaws are the same, but you think you're the only two real people because you and he care for that injured bird. Some of us, though, think about bigger, more important things than a cockerel with a broken leg. Anyway, my concerns are not important to you, but they mattered to poor Daragan. And he's a hero, no less! (*Pause.*) Do you remember that evening, Eva, when Anya and the Tullers and all the others died? I had our tickets for the night express to the Crimea – coach number seven – in my pocket . . . what matters now is not that cockerel, but the fact that, no matter what my jaw may be made of, my wife is leaving me alone in this empty world . . . What is there to be done about it? Nothing. There – take the tickets to the Crimea and get out of here! You're free.

EVA (*sobbing*). Adam, I'm terribly sorry for you, but I don't love you . . . Goodbye!

ADAM. Professor! You've taken my wife, and I give you my name too. You are Adam. Just do me one favour: leave at once. I'll feel very uncomfortable if Ponchik and Markizov appear now. But when you get to the cars, wait for an hour. I think they'll want to catch you up. Please go.

YEFROSIMOV. Adam – goodbye! (*Exit with* EVA.)

ADAM *picks up the trumpet and sounds a call.*

Enter MARKIZOV *and* PONCHIK.

ADAM. Comrades! I have to announce that to judge by all the available facts that gallant and trusty officer, Daragan, must be presumed dead. The Soviet Republic will honour his memory. At all events, you are free from your obligations here. Anyone who wants to can leave the forest, provided he's not afraid of the plague lurking out there. If not, he can stay here with me for a while . . . (*He points to the tent.*)

PONCHIK. Why aren't you telling this to Yefrosimov too?

ADAM. Yefrosimov and my wife Eva – she and I are divorced – have already gone. They went along the wolf-track to the cars . . .

PONCHIK *makes a nervous movement.*

. . . No, no, don't worry. They'll wait for you at the cars.

PONCHIK. I'm going after them . . . (*He hurriedly prepares to go, collecting his shotgun and stuffing things into a knapsack.*)

ADAM. What about you?

MARKIZOV. Me?

PONCHIK. Come on, Henry! Don't let yourself be fooled by any of his stupid arguments. Do you want to turn into a wild man of the woods?

MARKIZOV. Come with us, Adam. You can't stay in this forest alone.

ADAM. Why not?

MARKIZOV. You'll be so miserable, you'll drink yourself to death . . . Don't you want to go with Eva?

PONCHIK. No – his satanic pride won't let him admit he's beaten! He still believes that Daragan will come down to him out of the sky. Well, stay here in your little socialist paradise in the forest until it starts snowing! Goodbye . . . Come on, Henry!

MARKIZOV. Come with us!

ADAM. Goodbye! . . . Off you go . . .

MARKIZOV *and* PONCHIK *exeunt.*

Sunrise. It's pointless to try and deceive myself any longer. There's no one to keep the fires going for . . . But right now I don't want to think about anything . . . I'm only human, and I want to do nothing but sleep. (*He goes into the tent.*)

Pause; then the sound of an aeroplane engine is heard, growing louder, then fading away before coming closer again, followed by a burst of machine-gun fire.

At this, ADAM comes running out of the tent; he stumbles, clutches at his heart and sits down on a tree-stump, unable to run . . .

A trumpet-call, followed by distant voices, are heard, soon followed by the entry of VIRUES, wearing a flying-suit. She takes off her leather helmet. Her face is disfigured by a single large scar.

VIRUES. ¡Adam! ¡Yefrosimov! (*Seeing* ADAM.) ¡Holá! ¡Buenos días!

ADAM (*hoarsely*). I don't understand . . . Who are you?

VIRUES. ¡Escucha! (*Pointing up into the sky.*) ¡El gobierno mundiál mi ha mandado! Estoy aviador español . . . ¿No entiende? ¿Habla frances? . . . Où est-ce que se trouve Adam?

A second aeroplane is heard to approach and land.

ADAM *draws his revolver and starts to move away backwards.*

VIRUES. Non, non! Je ne suis pas une ennemie fasciste! Je suis votre amie! Êtes-vous Adam?

ADAM. Moi – Adam. Où est Daragan?

VIRUES. Daragan viendra! Il viendra vite!

Enter DE TIMONEDA, *who removes his flying-helmet and clasps* ADAM *by the hand. He makes drinking motions;* ADAM *hands him a water-bottle and* DE TIMONEDA *drinks greedily.*

Enter DARAGAN.

ADAM (*shouts*). Daragan! (*He clutches at his heart.*)

Another aeroplane lands, another trumpet-call sounds.

DARAGAN. So the leader's still alive, is he?

ADAM (*embraces* DARAGAN). Daragan! . . . We'd given you up!

DARAGAN. I was late because I got into a dog-fight over Cape Finisterre.

SEEWALD (*enters at a run; shouts*). Sind Sie Russen? Gott sei dank! (*To* DARAGAN.) Ist das Professor Jefrossimov?

DARAGAN. Nein, nein – das ist Adam!

SEEWALD. Ach, Adam! Freut mich sehr! (*He shakes* ADAM *by the hand.*)

DARAGAN. Where's Eva? Where's Markizov?

ADAM. You were so late in returning that none of them could bear staying here, and I'm the only one left.

DARAGAN. And Yefrosimov?

ADAM. Yefrosimov left with Eva. She's not my wife any more. I'm alone.

DARAGAN. Which way did they go?

ADAM. Along the wolf-tracks, to the cars.

DARAGAN. Comrade Pavlov!

Enter PAVLOV.

PAVLOV. Here!

DARAGAN. There are four people on that path. Bring them back. One of them is Yefrosimov.

PAVLOV *exits.*

DARAGAN *suddenly embraces* ADAM.

DARAGAN. Don't grieve. Look, this is my wife. My dear Spanish *señora* was dying from the effects of the gas, covered in ulcers, far away from here. (*To* VIRUES.) Maria! This is Adam. Give him a kiss.

VIRUES. ¿Abrazar? ¡Con mucho gusto! (*She embraces* ADAM.)

ADAM *suddenly bursts into tears in* VIRUES's *arms.*

DARAGAN. There, there Adam . . . don't give way . . .

SEEWALD. Nimm das und trinke! (*He hands* ADAM *his water-bottle.*)

ADAM (*sits down on a tree-trunk and drinks*). Oh, the human race! . . . Come over here, Daragan . . . What's the news from Moscow?

DARAGAN. They're coming back in droves. Most of the population was evacuated to the Urals.

ADAM. Was the city burnt?

DARAGAN. Only some districts . . . it was attacked by incendiary bombs.

ADAM. And were many people asphyxiated by the gas?

SEEWALD. Nein, nein.

DARAGAN. No, the enemy didn't use solar gas on Moscow, only conventional gas. About 300,000 people died.

ADAM (*shakes his head*) I see . . .

Enter MARKIZOV *and* PONCHIK.

MARKIZOV (*excitedly*). People! Foreigners! (*He strikes a pose; declaims.*) 'The great hour has struck . . .'

DARAGAN. Well done, Henry! It has indeed!

PONCHIK. Victory! Victory! We've won!

A low powerful noise of aircraft engines is heard in the distance.

DARAGAN. That means he's coming. (*He shouts.*) Back to the planes!

SEEWALD. Zu den Flugzeugen!

SEEWALD *and* DE TIMONEDA *run off.*

ADAM. Oh, Ponchik!

PONCHIK. Comrade Adam! I had a momentary attack of moral weakness. Cowardice, if you like. I am intoxicated at meeting some fellow human beings again! Oh why, oh why, did I destroy my manuscript! Apollon will call for me again! Let's hope the printing presses are still working in Moscow!

MARKIZOV. Apollon Akimovich? But I thought you . . .

PONCHIK. Shut up, cripple!

Enter EVA and YEFROSIMOV, arm in arm. YEFROSIMOV is carrying the wicker basket containing the injured cockerel. They stay in the shadows, away from the others.

ADAM. I can't bear to see them!

DARAGAN. Go to the landing-ground . . .

Exit ADAM.

Silence.

DARAGAN is standing in sunlight, his airman's insignia glittering.

YEFROSIMOV remains in the shadows.

Good morning, Professor.

YEFROSIMOV. Good morning, destroyer of men. (*He frowns.*)

DARAGAN. I am not a destroyer. I am the commander of the escort of the World Government and I am accompanying it to Leningrad. There's no one to destroy any more. We have no more enemies. I have some good news for you, Professor: I shot the man who invented solar gas.

YEFROSIMOV (*shivers*). I'm not glad at your shooting anyone.

VIRUES. Yefrosimoff?

DARAGAN. Yes, that's Vefrosimov. Look at him. He saved your life. (*He points to the apparatus slung over his shoulder.*)

VIRUES. ¿Que hombre geniál? (*She points to her scar.*)

EVA. Sasha! I beg you – don't argue with him, don't annoy him! Why? You don't argue with the victor! (*To DARAGAN.*) Why are you still trying to settle old scores with him? We are peaceful people, we cause harm to no one. Let us go free! . . . (*Suddenly to*

VIRUES.) A woman! A woman! At last – another woman! (*She weeps.*)

DARAGAN. Calm her. Give her a drink of water. I'm not settling any scores. (*To* YEFROSIMOV.) Professor, you're going to fly out of here with us. Yes, I forgot to mention . . . you distracted me . . . I apologize for having shot at you and, of course, I'm very glad that I dïdn't kill you. (*To* MARKIZOV.) Thank you, Henry!

MARKIZOV. Lucky for you that I was so quick off the mark with my crutch . . . Tell me, Daragan, what are dollars going to be worth now?

PONCHIK. Cretin! (*Exit hastily.*)

DARAGAN. Dollars? Why do you ask?

MARKIZOV. Oh, you know . . . just idle curiosity . . . Serpent! (*Exit, following* PONCHIK.)

DARAGAN (*to* YEFROSIMOV). Are you longing for rest and peace? Well, you shall have it! But please make one final effort. There is a squadron of seaplanes on the Neva. Tomorrow we want to start disinfecting and cauterizing the city of Leningrad, using your method of burning oxygen, and we can't do it without your help. Then you may go and live where you please. The whole world is open to you, and you won't need a visa.

YEFROSIMOV. I want only one thing – for you to stop dropping bombs. Then I shall leave for Switzerland.

A trumpet-call is heard, followed by the approach of the shadow of an enormous airship.

DARAGAN. The airship has come for you, Professor. Time to go aboard.

YEFROSIMOV. Are they taking me away to try me for having destroyed those gas–canisters?

DARAGAN. Oh, Professor! . . . You never will understand the people who organize and govern mankind. Still, no matter . . . At least lend us your genius to do us this last service. Come with me – the Secretary-General wants to see you.

Curtain

The Last Days
(Pushkin)

A Play in Four Acts

'And kept safe by fate
Perhaps these lines of mine
Will not in Lethe sink . . .'

Yevgeni Onegin

Translated by William Powell and Michael Earley

Characters

PÚSHKINA
GONCHARÓVA
VORONTSÓVA
SALTYKÓVA
STATION MASTER'S WIFE
MAIDSERVANT
BITKÓV
NIKÍTA
D'ANTHES
SHÍSHKIN
BENEDÍKTOV
KÚKOLNIK
DOLGORÚKOV
BOGOMÁZOV
SALTYKÓV
NIKOLAI 1
ZHUKÓVSKY
HECKEREN
DÚBELT
BÉNCKENDORF
RAKÉEV
PONOMARÉV
STRÓGANOV

DANZÁS
DAL
STUDENT
OFFICER
STATION MASTER
TURGÉNEV
VORONTSÓV
FILÁT
AGAFÓN
FIRST PREOBRAZHENSKY
  OFFICER
SECOND
  PREOBRAZHENSKY
  OFFICER
NÉGRO
KAMMERJUNKER
VASILY MAXÍMOVICH
SERVANT
POLICE OFFICER
GENDARME OFFICERS
POLICEMEN
STUDENTS
CROWD

Pronunciation note

e after consonant/vowel or in initial position in Russian names
sounds ye (as in yet). The e in Ponomarev is pronounced yo (as in
yacht) and stressed.
Stressed i sounds ee (as in leek); otherwise, it sounds like i(t)
Stressed o sounds like o in or; otherwise h(o)t

ACT ONE

Evening. The drawing room of ALEXANDER SERGEEVICH PUSHKIN's *apartment in St Petersburg. Candles in the corner beside the grandfather clock and two burning candles on an old piano. A fireplace and part of the bookshelves in the study are visible through the door. Coals burn in the study fireplace and in the drawing-room fireplace.*

ALEXANDRA NIKOLAEVNA GONCHAROVA *sits playing the piano, and the clock-repairman* BITKOV *stands at the clock with his tools. Under* BITKOV's *hands the clock sounds the hour and chimes. A blizzard is heard outside.* GONCHAROVA *quietly plays the piano and sings.*

GONCHAROVA (*sings*). . . . The blizzard blinds the sky with darkness, spinning snowy whirlwinds wild . . . Now it's howling like a beast, now it's wailing like a child . . .

BITKOV. What a marvellous song! I was repairing a clock near Launderers' Bridge today, I'm going across the bridge and, good Lord, it really *does* spin and whirl! Right into your eyes and ears! (*Pause.*) Permit me to ask who was it who composed that song?

GONCHAROVA. Alexander Sergeevich.

BITKOV. Really! How clever. It *does* wail in the chimney, by God, just like a child. A beautiful composition.

The door-bell rings. Enter NIKITA.

NIKITA. Alexandra Nikolaevna, Colonel Shishkin requests to be received.

GONCHAROVA. Who is this Shishkin?

NIKITA. Shishkin, the colonel.

GONCHAROVA. At this hour? Tell him I cannot possibly receive him.

NIKITA. But what do you mean, Alexandra Nikolaevna, not receive him?

GONCHAROVA. Oh, my dear Lord, I remember now! . . . Ask him in here.

NIKITA. Right, madam. (*Goes to the doors.*) Oh, despair . . . Oh, ruination . . . (*Exits.*)

A pause.

SHISHKIN (*enters*). I beg a thousand pardons, my glasses are misted over. It is an honour to introduce myself: Alexei Petrov Shishkín, retired Colonel. I beg your indulgence for disturbing you. What weather, eh? A master wouldn't drive his dog out into the street in weather such as this. But what can you do? With whom do I have the honour of speaking?

GONCHAROVA. I am Natalya Nikolaevna's sister.

SHISHKIN. Ah, yes, I've heard about you. Extremely glad to meet you, mademoiselle.

GONCHAROVA. Veuillez-vous vous asseoir, monsieur.

SHISHKIN. Parlez russe, mademoiselle. Thank you. (*Sits down.*) I say, what weather, eh?

GONCHAROVA. Yes, a real blizzard.

SHISHKIN. May I see the Kammerjunker?

GONCHAROVA. I am very sorry, but Alexander Sergeevich is out.

SHISHKIN. And his wife?

GONCHAROVA. Natalya Nikolaevna is out visiting too.

SHISHKIN. Oh, what beastly bad luck! It's just impossible to catch him in.

GONCHAROVA. Please don't get upset. I can talk to you.

SHISHKIN. I ought to speak to the kammerjunker himself. But, as you like, as you like. It's a simple little matter. At various times Mr Pushkin has pawned to me Turkish shawls, pearls and silver valued at about twelve and a half thousand paper roubles.

GONCHAROVA. I know . . .

SHISHKIN. Twelve and a half thousand if it's a kopek.

GONCHAROVA. Couldn't you wait just a little longer?

SHISHKIN, I would, patiently, with the greatest pleasure, madam. Christ, too, was patient and bid us be also. But you must put yourself in my position. One has to eat. And I have sons, I dare to mention, in the navy. I have to support them. I came to warn you, madam, that tomorrow I sell the goods. I've found a suitable gentleman, a Persian.

GONCHAROVA. I implore you to wait a bit longer. Alexander Sergeevich will pay the interest.

SHISHKIN. Believe me, I can't. I've been waiting since November; other people would have sold long ago. I'm afraid to let the Persian go.

GONCHAROVA. I have a little necklace and some silver. Perhaps you would care to have a look.

SHISHKIN. Excuse me, madam, your silver is worthless compared to what the Persian . . .

GONCHAROVA. But please, how can you do without things! Perhaps you'd care to have a look. Come to my room, please.

SHISHKIN. Very well, if you insist. (*Follows* GONCHAROVA.) Lovely flat you have here. How much do you pay?

GONCHAROVA. Four thousand three hundred.

SHISHKIN. Bit dear. (*Exits with* GONCHAROVA *to the inner rooms.*)

Left alone, BITKOV *listens for a moment, runs up to the piano with a candle, examines the music, hesitates for a moment, enters the study. He reads the titles of books, then, crossing himself in fright, disappears into the depths of the study. After a short time he returns to his place at the clock in the drawing room.* GONCHAROVA *enters, behind her* SHISHKIN *with a small bundle in his hands.*

GONCHAROVA. I will tell him.

SHISHKIN. And so we'll re-write the promissory note. Only, you must ask Alexander Sergeevich to come around himself, because cabs are terribly expensive now. The Fourth Izmailov Company, in Borshchov's house, at the rear of the courtyard, little window . . . He knows . . . (*At the door.*) Au revoir, mademoiselle.

GONCHAROVA. Au revoir, monsieur.

SHISHKIN *exits.*

BITKOV (*shutting the clock case, puts his tools in a bag*). All fixed, ma'am, it's alive again. But in the study . . . Well, I'll stop by tomorrow.

GONCHAROVA. Good.

BITKOV. Excuse me. (*Exits.*)

GONCHAROVA *by the fireplace.* NIKITA *appears in the doorway.*

NIKITA. Oh, oh, Alexandra Nikolaevna!

GONCHAROVA. Well, what's wrong with you?

NIKITA. Oh, Alexandra Nikolaevna! (*Pause.*) Now all your goods are gone.

GONCHAROVA. We'll redeem them.

NIKITA. With what? We won't, Alexandra Nikolaevna.

GONCHAROVA. Why are you cawing at me today?

NIKITA. I'm not a crow, I don't caw. Raoul gets four hundred roubles for the Lafitte, why it's horrible just thinking about it! Then there's the coachmaker, the apothecary . . . On Thursday Karadygin needs to be paid for the bureau. And the IOUs? The dunning letters are bad enough, but on top of that we even owe the milkwoman! No matter what money we get, nothing's left in our pockets, everything goes out for debts. Alexandra Nikolaevna implore him, let's go to the country. No good will come of staying in St Petersburg, mark my words. We could take the children, it will be quiet, more space . . . It's a den of thieves here, Alexandra Nikolaevna, and everything is three times more expensive, three times. And just you look, the master and everyone, why, they've turned all yellowish, and the insomnia . . .

GONCHAROVA. Tell Alexander Sergeevich yourself.

NIKITA. I've told him often enough, ma'am. And he answers: 'You old bore – my head's spinning like a whirlwind as it is.' After thirty years of course I bore him!

GONCHAROVA. Well, tell Natalya Nikolaevna.

NIKITA. I won't tell Natalya Nikolaevna, she won't go. (*Pause.*) But without her? You, he, and the children could go.

GONCHAROVA. Have you gone mad, Nikita?

NIKITA. He could go pistol-shooting in the morning and then go riding . . . There'd be space and comfort for the children.

GONCHAROVA. Stop tormenting me, Nikita, go away.

NIKITA exits. After sitting by the fireplace for a while, GONCHAROVA exits into the inner rooms. A bell rings. NIKITA enters the study which is half-dark – not through the drawing room but from the anteroom – and behind him flits a man who goes with him to the back of the study. They put on a light at the back of the study.

NIKITA (*barely audible, at the back of the room*). Yes, sir, yes, sir, very good. (*Enters the drawing room.*) Alexandra Nikolaevna, he's come home sick, he's asking for you.

GONCHAROVA (*entering*). Oh all right, coming.

NIKITA exits into the dining room.

(*Knocks at the door of the study.*) On entre? (*Enters the study. His voice is heard, muffled.*) Alexandre, êtes-vous indisposé? Lie down, lie down. Perhaps we should call for the doctor? (*Enters the dining room, speaks to NIKITA who enters with a cup in his hands.*) Undress the master. (*Goes out to the fireplace, waits.*)

NIKITA stays in the study for a while, and then exits into the anteroom, closing the door behind him.

(*Enters the study. Her words are muffled.*) Everything is all right . . . No, no . . .

The bell rings. NIKITA enters the drawing room. GONCHAROVA immediately runs to meet him.

NIKITA (*handing her a letter*). A letter for Alex . . .

GONCHAROVA (*threatens NIKITA, takes the letter*). Ah, from the dressmaker? All right. Say I'll be there tomorrow afternoon. Well, what are you standing there for, get moving . . . (*Quietly.*) You've been told not to deliver letters.

NIKITA exits.

(*Returns to the study. Her voice is muffled.*) For goodness sake, Alexander, it's from the dressmaker. Of course, I'll send for a doctor. Here, let me cross you . . . What? . . . All right . . . Don't get alarmed, I beseech you.

The light in the study goes out. GONCHAROVA *returns to the drawing room, closes the door to the study, pulls the curtain across it.*

(*Reads the letter. Hides it*). Who are these scoundrels? Once again. Good Lord! (*Pause.*) We must go to the country. He's right.

A knock is heard. NIKITA's *voice muffled.* NATALYA NIKOLAEVNA PUSHKINA *appears. She undoes the ties of the bonnet, throws it on the piano, squints shortsightedly.*

PUSHKINA. You're not asleep? Alone? Is Pushkin home?

GONCHAROVA. He came home quite sick, went to bed, and asked not to be disturbed.

PUSHKINA. Oh, the poor man! But it's not surprising – what a storm, good Lord! The snow whipped into our faces.

GONCHAROVA. Who did you come home with?

PUSHKINA. D'Anthès brought me home. Well, why are you looking at me like that?

GONCHAROVA. So you're still inviting trouble?

PUSHKINA. Oh, for the sake of all that's holy, stop moralizing. . .

GONCHAROVA. Tasha, what are you doing? Why are you just courting disaster?

PUSHKINA. Ah, mon Dieu! Azya, that's ridiculous. Why, what's wrong with my beau-frère escorting me home?

GONCHAROVA *gives the letter to* PUSHKINA.

(*She reads it, whispers.*) Did he see it?

GONCHAROVA. No, God forbid. Nikita was going to give it to him.

PUSHKINA. Oh, the old nitwit! (*Throws the letter into the fireplace.*) Intolerable people! Who's doing this?

GONCHAROVA. That won't do any good. That one will burn, but tomorrow another one will come. He'll find out anyway.

PUSHKINA. I'm not accountable for anonymous slander. He'll understand that this is all lies.

GONCHAROVA. Why are you speaking to me like this. No one can hear us.

PUSHKINA. Oh all right, all right. I confess that I *did* see him once at Idaliya's but it happened accidentally. I didn't even suspect that he would come there.

GONCHAROVA. Tasha, let's go to the country.

PUSHKINA. Run away from Petersburg? To hide in the country? Just because of some pack of low life . . . A contemptible anonymous person . . . He really will think then that I am guilty. There's nothing between us . . . To leave the capital? For no reason? I have absolutely no wish to go mad in the country, thank you very much.

GONCHAROVA. You mustn't see D'Anthès. Don't you see how hard it is for him? And besides, our financial affairs are in such a state . . .

PUSHKINA. Just what are you telling me to do? Naturally if one is going to live in the capital one must have sufficient means.

GONCHAROVA. I don't understand you.

PUSHKINA. Don't vex yourself, Azya, go to bed.

GONCHAROVA. Good-night. (*Exits.*)

Alone, PUSHKINA *smiles, obviously remembering something. Quietly* D'ANTHES *appears in the doorway leading to the dining room. He is wearing a military helmet and a greatcoat dusted with snow; he is holding ladies' gloves in his hand.*

PUSHKINA (*whispers*). How could you dare? How did you get in here? Leave my house this instant. Sheer effrontery! I'm ordering you!

D'ANTHES (*with a strong French accent*). You left your gloves in the sleigh. I was afraid that your hands might freeze tomorrow, so I returned. (*Puts the gloves on the piano, touches his helmet with his hand in salute and turns around to go.*)

PUSHKINA. Do you realize what danger you're exposing me to? He's just behind those doors. (*Runs to the study doors, listens.*) Just what were you expecting when you came in? And what if he had been in the drawing room? He has forbidden them to allow you to cross this threshold! Why, it's death!

D'ANTHES. Chaque instant de la vie est un pas vers la mort. The servant told me that he was asleep, so I came in.

PUSHKINA. He won't stand for that, he'll kill me!

D'ANTHES. Of all the Africans, I imagine, he is the most bloodthirsty. But don't worry – he'll kill me, not you.

PUSHKINA. I'm feeling dizzy, what's going to happen to me!

D'ANTHES. Calm down, nothing will happen to you. They'll put me on a gun-carriage and take me to the cemetery. And the storm will go on just like now, and nothing in the world will change.

PUSHKINA. I beg you by everything that is dear to you, leave my house.

D'ANTHES. Nothing on earth is dear to me except you, don't beg me.

PUSHKINA. Go away.

D'ANTHES. Oh, no. You're the cause of all this madness. You never want to hear me out. But in fact there is a matter of the greatest importance. You must listen to me. There . . . Yes? Other countries. Say just one word to me – and we'll run away.

PUSHKINA. And you say this to me after one month of marriage to Ekaterina, my sister? You are both a criminal and insane! Your actions do you no honour, baron.

D'ANTHES. I married her because of you, with just one aim, to be closer to you. Yes, I committed a crime. Let's run away.

PUSHKINA. I have children.

D'ANTHES. Forget them.

PUSHKINA. Oh, not for anything.

D'ANTHES. I'll knock on his door.

PUSHKINA. Don't you dare! Do you really want to destroy me?

D'ANTHES kisses PUSHKINA.

Oh, cruel torture! Why, why did our paths cross! You've made me lie and tremble constantly . . . Sleepless nights . . . Restless days . . .

The clock strikes.

My God, leave!

D'ANTHES. Come to Idaliya's once again. We must talk.

PUSHKINA. Meet me in the Winter Garden tomorrow at
Vorontsova's ball.

D'ANTHES *turns around and leaves.*

(*Listens.*) Will Nikita tell him or not? No, he won't tell him, he
won't talk for anything. (*Runs up to the window, looks out.*) Oh,
bitter poison! (*Goes to the study doors, puts her ear to them.*) He's
asleep. (*Crosses herself, blows out the candles, exits to the inner rooms.*)

*Darkness. Then out of the darkness – a winter day emerges. The dining
room in the apartment of* SERGEI VASILIEVICH SALTYKOV. *A
well-stocked library nearby. Part of the drawing room is visible from the
library. Breakfast is laid on the table in the dining room.* FILAT *is
standing at the doors.*

KUKOLNIK. Allow me, Alexandra Sergeevna, to present our
finest national poet, Vladimir Grigorievich Benediktov. He has
true, luminous talent! (*To the* OFFICERS.) Back me up on this.
You value his work highly, don't you!

The two PREOBAZHENSKY OFFICERS (SALTYKOV's sons)
smile.

SALTYKOVA. Enchantée de vous voir. Delighted to see you, Mr
Benediktov. And Sergei Vasilievich loves our literati.

Following BENEDIKTOV, *a modest man in a civil service uniform,
the lame* PRINCE PETER DOLGORUKOV *kisses*
SALTYKOVA's *hand.*

Delighted to see you, Prince Peter Vladimirovich.

IVAN VARFOLOMEEVICH BOGOMAZOV *appears in the
dining room.*

BOGOMAZOV. Alexandra Sergeevna. (*Goes up to kiss*
SALTYKOVA's *hand.*) But I see the most honourable Sergei
Vasilievich is not here yet.

SALTYKOVA. He'll be here right away, he asked me to beg your
pardon. He has probably been detained at the bookshop.

BOGOMAZOV (*to* DOLGORUKOV). Greetings, Prince.

DOLGORUKOV. Greetings.

BOGOMAZOV (*to* KUKOLNIK). I was at the theatre yesterday, I saw your play. A sheer delight! And packed out! You couldn't even fit a sheet of paper between them! Allow me to congratulate and embrace you. May you live many, many years, Nestor Vasilievich!

FILAT. Sergei Vasilievich has arrived.

KUKOLNIK (*softly, to* BENEDIKTOV). Well, brother, now you'll be able to feast your eyes.

SALTYKOV enters. He is wearing a top-hat and fur coat, has a cane and a large volume under his arm. He follows FILAT without looking at anyone. BENEDIKTOV bows to SALTYKOV, but he bows to mid air. DOLGORUKOV, BOGOMAZOV, and KUKOLNIK look at the ceiling, pretending that they do not notice SALTYKOV. FILAT pours a jigger of vodka, SALTYKOV casts an unseeing glance at the group of guests, drinking up, eats a piece of black bread, screws up his eyes. The PREOBRAZHENSKY OFFICERS smile.

SALTYKOV (*to himself*). Yes, sir, isn't that nice. Secundus pars. Secundus. (*Laughs a satanic laugh and exits.*)

BENEDIKTOV turns pale.

SALTYKOVA. Mon mari . . .

KUKOLNIK. Alexandra Sergeevna, please don't fret. We know, we know. Speak your native tongue, Alexandra Sergeevna. You will hear how our language sounds on the lips of a poet.

SALTYKOVA (*to* BENEDIKTOV.) My husband is the most terrible eccentric. I hope you will feel free to make yourself at home here.

SALTYKOV returns. He is without his top-hat, fur coat, and cane, but carrying the large volume as before. Everyone turns to give him their undivided attention.

SALTYKOV. Ah! Delighted to see you! (*Pounds the book.*) Secundus pars. Secundus. A malicious misprint! Corpus juris romani! Elsevier the publishers! (*To the* OFFICERS.) Greetings, my sons.

They smile.

BOGOMAZOV. May I take a look, Sergei Vasilievich?

SALTYKOV. Get back!

SALTYKOVA. Sergei, what's wrong with you? Really!

SALTYKOV. Books are not printed to be touched by hands. (*Puts the book on the mantlepiece. To* SALTYKOVA.) If you so much as touch it . . .

SALTYKOVA. I wouldn't think of it, and there's no need for me to . . .

SALTYKOV. Filat, some vodka! Please take your places.

SALTYKOVA. Please be seated.

They take their places. FILAT *serves them.*

SALTYKOVA (*looking at* KUKOLNIK's *hand*). May I congratulate you.

KUKOLNIK. Yes, sir. The Emperor awarded it.

DOLGORUKOV. The hand of His Highness rewarded you, Mr Kukolnik.

SALTYKOV. Not much of ring!

KUKOLNIK. Sergei Vasilievich!

SALTYKOV. This ring reminds me of – Filat! What is that on the mantlepiece?

FILAT. A book, sir.

SALTYKOV. Don't go near it.

FILAT. No, sir.

SALTYKOV. Yes, this reminds me . . . In my time as a young man, Emperor Pavel awarded me a star studded with diamonds of extraordinary magnitude.

The OFFICERS *look askance at* SALTYKOV.

But I could buy a ring like that for 200 roubles, or 150.

SALTYKOVA. Sergei, what are you saying!

BENEDIKTOV *is crushed.*

The whole thing is a lie; you don't have any star.

SALTYKOV. You don't know about it. I've been hiding it from everyone along with the snuffboxes for thirty-seven years now.

SALTYKOVA. You're delirious.

SALTYKOV. Don't listen to her, gentlemen. Women understand

nothing about the awards which are given out by the Russian emperors . . . I just saw . . . He was driving along the Nevsky . . . le grand bourgeois . . . in a small sleigh . . . Antip was the driver . . . ,

BOGOMAZOV. You mean to say that you saw His Majesty the Emperor, Sergei Vasilievich?

SALTYKOV. Yes, him.

BOGOMAZOV. The Emperor's driver is called Peter.

DOLGORUKOV. If I am not mistaken, Sergei Vasilievich, the incident with the star happened at the same time as the one with the horse?

SALTYKOV. No, prince, you are mistaken. This event happened later, during the reign of Emperor Alexander. (*To* BENEDIKTOV.) And so, sir, you write poetry?

BENEDIKTOV. Yes, sir.

SALTYKOV. A dangerous occupation. Not long ago your confrère Pushkin got a good going over from the Third Section of His Majesty's own chancellery, you know.

SALTYKOVA. It's just impossible to sit at the same table with you! Your conversation is so unpleasant!

SALTYKOV. Please eat, gentlemen. (*To* SALTYKOVA.) You are wrong to treat it so lightly, they can give you a going over too.

SALTYKOVA. Stop it, I beg you.

DOLGORUKOV. However, they say it *is* true. I also heard that it was a long time ago.

SALTYKOV. No, I heard it just recently. I was driving along past Chain Bridge, and suddenly I heard a man screaming. 'What's that?' I ask. 'They're flogging Pushkin, sir,' they said.

BOGOMAZOV. Oh come now. Sergei Vasilievich, that's just Petersburg fables.

SALTYKOV. What do you mean, fables? They almost gave me a going over once. Emperor Alexander wanted to buy my horse and offered a good price – ten thousand roubles. And to avoid selling her, I shot her with a pistol. I held the pistol to her ear and fired. (*To* BENEDIKTOV.) I have your poems in my library. Bookcase Z. Have you written anything new?

KUKOLNIK. Come now, Sergei Vasilievich. (*To* BENEDIKTOV.) Recite *Remember*. Officers, you love poetry, do beg him to do it.

The PREOBRAZHENSKY OFFICERS *smile.*

SALTYKOVA. Ah, yes, yes we're all asking. Really, it's all so pleasant after these miserable stories about floggings.

BENEDIKTOV. Really, I . . . I know things poorly by heart . . .

SALTYKOVA. Filat, stop banging the crockery.

BENEDIKTOV.
> Do you now remember, Nina
> How your minstrel, all aglow
> With a passion burning keenly
> Utterly bewitched by you
> In the noisy ballroom . . .

Oh really, I've forgotten . . . How . . . how . . .

> Led you through the madly turning
> Throng, before its envious gaze;
> And your hip, with pleasure burning
> Made my palm in its turn blaze.
> And my hand, o'ercome with languor
> Separated from the fire
> Of your waist so full of wonder
> And everlasting desire.

> And when you had grown quite weary
> And had sat down for a rest,
> Like an ocean were before me
> Tender ripples of your chest.
> And upon this very ocean
> In the foam of milk-white spray
> Through the haze as in a vision
> Was a pair of waves portrayed.

The PREOBRAZHENSKY OFFICERS, *winking at each other, drink up.*

> Listening to me, friendly, smiling,
> Then – a caprice of your head
> Sent an ash-blond tress fall, sliding
> Full across my cheek. I said:
> Do you now remember, Nina,

> Or has time's flood swept away
> To the sea of cold oblivion
> All I hoped for on that day?

KUKOLNIK. Bravo! Bravo! How about that! Give him a hand, officers.

They all applaud.

SALTYKOVA. A brilliant work.

BOGOMAZOV. A charming poem.

SALTYKOV. Well, perhaps they won't flog *you*.

FILAT (*to* SALTYKOVA.) Countess Alexandra Kirilovna Vorontsova to see you.

SALTYKOVA. Ask her into the drawing room. (*Standing up.*) Excuse me, gentlemen, I am leaving you. Do smoke, if you wish. (*Disappears into the living room.*)

SALTYKOV and the guests move to the library. FILAT serves champagne and pipes.

KUKOLNIK. To the health of our foremost national poet!

BOGOMAZOV. Encore! Encore!

SALTYKOV. The foremost poet?

KUKOLNIK. I stake my life on it, Sergei Vasilievich!

SALTYKOV. Agafon!

AGAFON appears.

Agafon, move Benediktov out of room two, bookcase Z, shelf thirteen and put him in this bookcase, and move Mr Pushkin into that one. (*To* BENEDIKTOV.) I keep the best things in this bookcase. (*To* AGAFON.) Don't even think of dropping it on the floor.

AGAFON. Yes, sir, Sergei Vasilievich. (*Exits.*)

BENEDIKTOV is overwhelmed.

DOLGORUKOV. I share your opinion completely. Mr Kukolnik, but I have heard, if you can imagine it, that our foremost poet is Pushkin.

KUKOLNIK. Society chimeras!

AGAFON *appears with a small volume, mounts the step ladder by the bookcase.*

SALTYKOV. You say that Pushkin is foremost? Agafon, hold on a minute!

AGAFON *remains on the step ladder.*

KUKOLNIK. He has not written anything for a long time now.

DOLGORUKOV. I beg your pardon, what do you mean he is not writing? Why, just recently I was given a manuscript copy of his latest poem. Not a complete one unfortunately.

BOGOMAZOV, BENEDIKTOV, KUKOLNIK *examine the piece of paper. The* OFFICERS *drink.*

KUKOLNIK. My God, my God! And it is a Russian who writes that! Officers, don't go near this sheet of paper.

BOGOMAZOV. Ay-yay-yay! (*To* DOLGORUKOV.) Allow me to copy it. I love forbidden literature, sinner that I am.

DOLGORUKOV. Please, do.

BOGOMAZOV (*sitting down at the table*). But not a word to anyone, Prince! Sh . . . (*Writes.*)

KUKOLNIK. If this poetry enjoys the favour of our contemporaries, then take heed: don't write in Russian! You will not be understood! Leave for that world where the *terza rima* of the divine Alighieri is heard to this day! Hold out your hand to the great Francesco! His *canzone* will inspire you! Write in Italian, Vladimir.

SALTYKOVA (*coming out of the living room*). Still arguing, gentlemen! (*Disappears through the dining room.*)

BOGOMAZOV. Bravo, bravo, Nestor Vasilievich!

BENEDIKTOV. Nestor, what are you so worked up about?

KUKOLNIK. My soul cannot allow injustices! Pushkin was talented, that is unquestionable. Shallow, superficial, but there was talent. But he abused it and squandered it! He quenched his small flame! He became barren, like the fig tree! And he writes nothing but shameful lines like these. The only thing which he has preserved is his conceit! His tone is so arrogant, his judgements so harsh! I feel sorry for him!

BOGOMAZOV. Bravo, bravo! Tribune!

KUKOLNIK. I drink to the health of our foremost national poet – Benediktov.

VORONTSOVA (*on the threshold to the library*). Everything that you have said is untrue. (*Pause.*) Ah, if only more understood that there are extraordinary people superior to them . . . How marvellously Pushkin combines genius and enlightenment! Alas, there are many who envy him; he has many enemies. And, forgive me, but I think that I have just been listening to venomous envy speaking with the lips of man. Really, Benediktov is a horrible poet. Hollow and unnatural . . .

KUKOLNIK. Please, Countess!

DOLGORUKOV *giggles with delight, falling on* BOGOMAZOV's *back.*

SALTYKOV (*returning to the library*). Ah, Alexandra Kirilovna. Allow me to present two literary men – Nestor Vasilievich Kukolnik and Vladimir Grigorievich Benediktov.

DOLGORUKOV *is convulsed with delight. The* OFFICERS *quietly retreat to the dining room and disappear.*

VORONTSOVA. Ah, my God . . . Be magnanimous and forgiving, I got carried away . . . Forgive me . . . Dear Alexandra Sergeevna, I must run. (*Disappears into the drawing room.*)

SALTYKOV *follows* VORONTSOVA. *With a contorted face* BENEDIKTOV *exits into the dining room.* KUKOLNIK *follows him.*

BENEDIKTOV. Why did you bring me to this breakfast? I was sitting quietly at home . . . And you're always, you are forever . . .

KUKOLNIK. You don't mean you can take the ravings of a society lady seriously?

SALTYKOV. Agafon! Remove them both – Pushkin and Benediktov too – to the other room, case thirteen!

Curtain

ACT TWO

Night. VORONTSOVA's palace. The Winter Garden. A fountain. Lights through the greenery. Startled birds flutter between the nets. A colonnade at the back, beyond it an empty drawing room. The groan of an orchestra and rustle of a crowd in the distance. By the colonnade, motionless, a NEGRO wearing a turban. In the grove of trees itself, hidden from the glances of society, DOLGORUKOV sits on a small couch in formal evening dress. Champagne in front of him. He is eavesdropping on the conversations in the Winter Garden. Not far from the colonnade sits PUSHKINA, and beside her – NIKOLAI I.

NIKOLAI I. I am riven by great sadness when I hear the splash of the fountain and the fluttering of feathered creatures in this grove of trees.

PUSHKINA. But why?

NIKOLAI I. This artificial nature reminds me of the real nature – the quiet babbling of brooks and the shadow of the oak groves . . . If only it were possible for me to cast off this weighty attire and retreat to the solitude of the forests, to peaceful valleys! Only there, at one with the earth, can a tormented heart find rest . . .

PUSHKINA. You are very tired.

NIKOLAI I. No one knows, no one will ever understand, what a heavy burden I am doomed to bear!

PUSHKINA. Don't distress us all with such sad words.

NIKOLAI I. Are you being sincere? Oh yes, oh yes. Could such clear eyes lie? I value your words, you alone have found them for me. I want to believe that you are a good woman. But one thing always frightens me, all I have to do is glance at you . . .

PUSHKINA. What is it?

NIKOLAI I. Your beauty. Oh, how dangerous it is! Be careful, be careful! That is friendly advice, believe me.

PUSHKINA. Your interest does me great honour!

NIKOLAI I. Oh, believe me, I am speaking with an open heart, with a pure soul. I often think about you.

PUSHKINA. Do I deserve this honour?

NIKOLAI I. I drove past your house today, but your curtains were closed.

PUSHKINA. I don't like the daylight, the winter twilight soothes me.

NIKOLAI I. I know what you mean. I don't know why, but every time I go out driving, some unknown force draws me to your house, and my head turns involuntarily and I wait for a glimpse of your face in the window . . .

PUSHKINA. Don't say such things.

NIKOLAI I. Why?

PUSHKINA. It upsets me.

A KAMMERJUNKER *comes out of the living room and approaches* NIKOLAI I.

KAMMERJUNKER. Your Imperial Majesty, Her Imperial Majesty commands me to report that she departs with Grand Duchess Maria in ten minutes.

PUSHKINA *stands up, curtsies, exits to the dining room, disappears.*

NIKOLAI I. One should say: with Her Imperial Highness, the Grand Duchess Maria Nikolaevna. Further: when I am talking with someone you must not interrupt. Blockhead! Report to Her Majesty that I will be there within ten minutes, and ask Zhukovsky to come to me.

The KAMMERJUNKER *exits.* NIKOLAI I *is alone for a while. He looks into the distance with a heavy gaze. Wearing a star and ribbon,* ZHUKOVSKY *enters, bowing.*

ZHUKOVSKY. Your Imperial Majesty wishes to see me?

NIKOLAI I. Vasily Andreevich, I can't see very well from here, who is that black man standing by the colonnade?

ZHUKOVSKY *stares hard. He is crushed.*

Perhaps you could explain to him that it is improper.

ZHUKOVSKY *sighs.*

What is he wearing? He apparently does not understand the utter foolishness of his behaviour. Perhaps he was intending to go to the *Convention Nationale* along with the other liberals, and ended up at this ball by mistake. Perhaps he supposes that he will do me too great an honour if he put on the uniform which was conferred upon him? So, tell him that I do not hold anyone in the service by force. Why are you silent, Vasily Andreevich?

ZHUKOVSKY. Your Imperial Majesty, don't be angry with him and don't punish him.

NIKOLAI I. That's bad, Vasily Andreevich, we have known each other some time now. You well know that I never punish anyone. The law punishes.

ZHUKOVSKY. I will make so bold as to say this: first, a false system of education, the society in which he spent his youth . . .

NIKOLAI I. Society! I don't know any more whether society influenced him or vice-versa. It's enough to remember the verses with which he delighted our 'friends of December 14th'.

ZHUKOVSKY. Your Majesty, that was so long ago.

NIKOLAI I. He hasn't changed a bit.

ZHUKOVSKY. Your Majesty, he has become your most fervent admirer . . .

NIKOLAI I. Dear Vasily Andreevich, I know your kindness. You believe that, but I do not.

ZHUKOVSKY. Your Majesty, be condescending to a poet called to bring glory to his fatherland . . .

NIKOLAI I. No, no, you can't bring glory to the fatherland with poems such as those. Not long ago he gave us another treat. *The History of Pugachov.* Hardly appropriate . . . A villain *has* no history. He has an altogether strange partiality for Pugachov. He wrote a novel, compared him to an eagle! And what can you say about that? I don't trust him. He has no heart. Let us go to the Empress, she wanted to see you. (*Exits to the colonnade.*)

The NEGRO *leaves his place and follows* NIKOLAI I.
ZHUKOVSKY *walks up to the colonnade, looks into the distance, threatens someone secretly with his fist. He leaves.*

VORONTSOVA *and* VORONTSOV *come out to meet* NIKOLAI I, *they bow.*

VORONTSOVA. Sire!

VORONTSOV. Votre Majesté Impérial! . . .

Exeuent. Wearing a uniform and orders BOGOMAZOV *comes into the Winter Garden, not from the colonnade, but from the side. He heads straight for the grove.*

DOLGORUKOV. Careful there, this place is taken.

BOGOMAZOV. Bah! Prince! You look like a recluse.

DOLGORUKOV. You do too. Well, so what, have a seat. Not much happening, but the champagne's good.

BOGOMAZOV. And the ball, how is it? Semiramis, eh? Do you like balls, prince?

DOLGORUKOV. Adore them. You see so much riff-raff.

BOGOMAZOV. Now, now, little Petey, mind.

DOLGORUKOV. I'm not Petey to you.

BOGOMAZOV. Well, so he's not Petey? My dear little Prince, not so long ago you were soiling your nappies, while I am an Actual State Councillor to the Emperor.

DOLGORUKOV. I am obliged, your excellency, to request you not to express yourself in such trivial terms.

BOGOMAZOV. The flower of the artistocracy is at this ball, prince!

DOLGORUKOV. You could count the aristocrats at this ball on the fingers of one hand and the only genuine one among them is me.

BOGOMAZOV. You don't say! How is that? I would be curious to know.

DOLGORUKOV. Because I am descended from a saint. Yes, sir, from the great prince Mikhail Vsevolodovich of Chernigov, a martyr who was canonized.

BOGOMAZOV. One only has to look at you to see that you're descended from a saint. (*Points into the distance.*) And in your opinion the man who walked by just now is not an aristocrat.

DOLGORUKOV. Oh much better than that. He bought the rank

of steward from the mistress of a Minister. In spite of his base physiognomy, he made his fortune.

BOGOMAZOV. All right, Petey! And that one? That's Princess Anna Vasilievna, of course.

DOLGORUKOV. That's it, that's it. A lively old woman! It's time the old witch was dead and buried, but she goes cantering around from ball to ball.

BOGOMAZOV. My, my, what a tongue! Is that Ivan Kirillovich with her?

DOLGORUKOV. No, his brother Grigory, a well-known boor.

BOGOMAZOV. Look out now, Prince, someone will hear you – then there'll be trouble.

DOLGORUKOV. And maybe nothing will happen. I hate them all! Peasants! Sycophants! I can't even decide which of them is the most disgusting.

BOGOMAZOV. Well, of course, how can they match up to Saint Petey, the Martyr

DOLGORUKOV. I'll thank you not to make jokes. (*Drinks.*) He himself was here.

BOGOMAZOV. His Majesty?

DOLGORUKOV. Himself.

BOGOMAZOV. Who was he talking with?

DOLGORUKOV. With the Moor's wife. What an item! You came too late.

BOGOMAZOV. And what happened?

DOLGORUKOV. He stroked her hand. Our poet will soon be decorated again.

BOGOMAZOV. I see you hate Pushkin too, then.

DOLGORUKOV. I despise him. It's ridiculous! The cuckold. They're here tête-à-tête, and he stands by the colonnade wearing a wretched frock-coat, his hair all over the place, a wolfish gleam in his eye. That frock-coat will cost him dearly!

BOGOMAZOV. There's a minor bit of gossip circulating, Prince Peter, that he has written an epigram about you.

DOLGORUKOV. A lot I care for his verses! Shsh . . . Quiet.

HECKEREN enters the garden, and after some time so does PUSHKINA.

HECKEREN. I was watching you and I realize why you are called Psyche of the North. You are so beautiful.

PUSHKINA. Ah, baron, baron . . .

HECKEREN. But I understand: You must be bored by this swarm of admirers buzzing around you with their compliments. Do sit down, Natalya Nikolaevna; I'm not boring you?

PUSHKINA. Oh no, I'd love to.

Pause.

HECKEREN. He's coming just now.

PUSHKINA. I don't understand. What's going on?

HECKEREN. Why do you answer me like that? I am your friend, not a traitor. Oh, how much evil your beauty is yet to cause! Release my son. Look what you have done to him. He loves you.

PUSHKINA. Baron, I do not wish to hear such speeches.

HECKEREN. No, no, don't leave, he'll be here any moment. I came here on purpose, so that you could exchange a few words.

D'ANTHES enters the garden, HECKEREN goes off to the side.

D'ANTHES. This damned ball! It's impossible to get close to you. Were you and the Emperor talking alone?

PUSHKINA. For God's sake, what are you doing? Don't talk with that look on your face, we can be seen from the drawing room.

D'ANTHES. Your hand was in his. You have hurled reproaches in my face, but you are perfidious.

PUSHKINA. I'll come, I'll come. Wednesday at three o'clock. Leave me now, for the sake of all that's holy.

GONCHAROVA comes out from the colonnade.

GONCHAROVA. We are getting ready to leave. Alexander is looking for you.

PUSHKINA. Yes, yes. Au revoir, monsieur le baron.

HECKEREN. Au revoir, madame. Au revoir, mademoiselle.

D'ANTHES. Au revoir, mademoiselle. Au revoir, madame.

The music thunders triumphantly. PUSHKINA *and*
GONCHAROVA *leave.*

HECKEREN. Remember all the sacrifices I have made for you.
(*Leaves with* D'ANTHES.)

VORONTSOVA *has appeared in the drawing room; guests come up
to her saying good-bye. The music suddenly breaks off, and immediately
silence.*

DOLGORUKOV. I love balls, I love them.

BOGOMAZOV. Listen to him!

Into the garden, from the place where BOGOMAZOV *exited,*
VORONTSOVA *enters. Very tired, she sits down on the small
couch.*

DOLGORUKOV. The ambassador's a fine fellow! We've seen
what kind of things are going on. Pushkin will have enough
horns for a crown. The Tsar's horns behind and D'Anthès' in
front! Three cheers for the loving god-father!

BOGOMAZOV. You really hate him with a passion, Prince! Well
I swear, I'll tell no one, a friend to the grave – who sent him that
anonymous lampoon? That was the spark that set the forest
ablaze. A most effective joke, I'll say that quite frankly. Why
they've been ferreting about for two months, but no one can
figure out who it was. It was neatly done! Tell me, Prince,
frankly, who did it?

DOLGORUKOV. Who? How would I know? Why ask me? But
whoever sent it, it had to be done. He won't forget it!

BOGOMAZOV. He won't, he won't! Well, good-bye, Prince,
before they start putting out the lamps!

DOLGORUKOV. Good-bye.

BOGOMAZOV. But I must say, Petey, as a friend, do watch
what you say.

DOLGORUKOV *finishes his champagne, goes out of the grove.*

VORONTSOVA. Prince?

DOLGORUKOV. Countess . . .

VORONTSOVA. Why are you alone? You haven't been bored, have you?

DOLGORUKOV. My goodness, Countess is it possible to be bored in your house? An entrancing ball!

VORONTSOVA. But I feel sad, somehow.

DOLGORUKOV. Countess, you distress me. But that's just nerves, I assure you.

VORONTSOVA. No, an inescapable sadness. There is so much that is base in the world! Have you never pondered that?

DOLGORUKOV. Every day, Countess. One who has a sensitive heart cannot avoid understanding that. Morals have collapsed – such is the age, Countess! But why these gloomy thoughts?

VORONTSOVA. *Pénard*! Hangman! Scoundrel!

DOLGORUKOV. You are ill, Countess! I will call your servants.

VORONTSOVA. I heard you sneering . . . You were pleased because some wretch had sent a lampoon to a man being victimized . . . You did it yourself! And if I were not afraid of dealing him yet another blow, I would expose you to him! You should be killed like a dog! I hope you die on the scaffold. Get out of my house! Get out! Get out! (*Disappears.*)

DOLGORUKOV (*alone*). She overheard. The wildcat! She's probably his lover too. Someone was listening behind the colonnade. Yes, they heard everything. And it's him again! Everything because of him! Well, all right, you won't forget me, you won't forget me, I swear it! (*Limping, he goes to the colonnade.*)

Darkness. Then from the darkness – candles behind green screens. Night. A government office. LEONTY VASILIEVICH DUBELT *sits at the desk.*

The door opens slightly, RAKEEV, *a police captain, appears.*

RAKEEV. Your excellency, Bitkov wants to see you.

DUBELT. Show him in.

RAKEEV *disappears and* BITKOV *enters.*

BITKOV. How do you do, your excellency?

DUBELT. And my greetings to you. How are you, my dear fellow?

BITKOV. With your prayers, fine, your excellency.

DUBELT. Let's suppose it never occurred to me to pray for you. But you're well? Why come here at night?

BITKOV. In so much as I find myself in constant worry as to . . .

DUBELT. His Majesty is not in need to your worrying. What task were you assigned? Secret surveillance which you should carry out to the best of your ability. And less of the rhetoric, you're not in the pulpit.

BITKOV. Yes, sir. While holding Kammerjunker Pushkin under secret surveillance I actually infiltrated his apartment.

DUBELT. Nice! And you didn't catch it in the neck?

BITKOV. No, thank God.

DUBELT. What's his valet's name? Frol, isn't it?

BITKOV. Nikita.

DUBELT. Nikita the Credulous. Go on.

BITKOV. The first room, your excellency, is the dining room . . .

DUBELT. Never mind that.

BITKOV. The second is the drawing room. The kammerjunker's works lie on the piano in the drawing room.

DUBELT. On the piano? What kind of works?

BITKOV. 'The blizzard blinds the sky with darkness, spinning snowy whirlwinds wild. Now it's howling like a beast, now it's wailing like a child. Now it rustles in the rooftops jerking at the ragged straw . . . Now like some belated traveller it comes knocking on our door . . . The blizzard blinds the sky with darkness, spinning snowy whirlwinds wild. Now it's howling like a beast, now it's wailing like a child.'

DUBELT. Well, what a memory you have! Go on.

BITKOV. In the greatest danger I once penetrated the study, which study is entirely full of books.

DUBELT. What books?

BITKOV. What I managed to see, I memorized, your excellency. On the left hand from the fireplace: *The Owl: Bird of Night, The Cavalry Officer Maid, The History of the Glorious Thief Vanka-Cain* . . . and on alcoholism and how to cure it as a lesson for all . . . from the university printing house . . .

DUBELT. I recommend that you read the last book. You drink?

BITKOV. Never touch the stuff.

DUBELT. Let's forget the books. Go on.

BITKOV. Today I uncovered a note of extreme importance lying on the floor: 'Come to see me immediately, otherwise there will be trouble'. Signed – William Duke.

DUBELT *rings.* RAKEEV *enters.*

DUBELT. Send Vasily Maksimovich in.

RAKEEV *exits.* VASILY MAKSIMOVICH *enters, a clerk in civilian uniform.*

William Duke.

VASILY MAKSIMOVICH. We've already gone through everything, your excellency, there is no such person in St Petersburg.

DUBELT. Wonders will never cease! An Englishman has disappeared in Petersburg.

RAKEEV (*enters*). Your excellency, Ivan Varfolomeevich Bogomazov is here about this same case.

DUBELT. Show him in.

RAKEEV *exits.* BOGOMAZOV *enters.*

BOGOMAZOV. I beg your pardon, your excellency. Is Third Section looking for Duke? That's Zhukovsky, he likes using joke signatures.

DUBELT (*waving his hand at* VASILY MAKSIMOVICH). Good . . . (*To* BOGOMAZOV.) Wait outside if you will, Ivan Varfolomeevich, I'll see you in just a moment.

VASILY MAKSIMOVICH *and* BOGOMAZOV *exeunt.*

Well, you son of a bitch! Parasite! Vasily Andreevich Zhukovsky, an Actual State Councillor, the tutor of the heir to the throne, the Tsarevich! You should know his handwriting by now!

BITKOV. Oh, what a cock-up! I do apologize, your excellency!

DUBELT. You got the whole Section worked up over that. You should be punched squarely in the mouth, Bitkov! Go on.

BITKOV. Today, towards evening, a letter appeared on the table, addressed to a foreigner.

DUBELT. To a foreigner again?

BITKOV. To a foreigner, your excellency. To the Dutch embassy, to Monsieur Baron Heckeren, Nevsky Avenue.

DUBELT. Bitkov! (*Holds out his hand.*) The letter, give me the letter. Let me have it for half an hour.

BITKOV. Your excellency, what do you mean, the letter? Judge for yourself – you pop into the study for a moment, hands shaking. He'll come at any moment and grab the letter. It's risky business.

DUBELT. Your hands don't shake when you're getting your salary. Find out exactly when the letter will be delivered, by whom it will be received in the embassy, and by whom the answer will be delivered. Get going.

BITKOV. Yes sir. Your excellency, have my fee paid.

DUBELT. Fee? For that Duke business you should be paying us. Go to Vasily Maksimovich, say that I ordered 30 roubles paid you.

BITKOV. What, 30 roubles, your excellency? I have young children . . .

DUBELT. 'Judas Iscariot went unto the chief priests, and they covenanted to give him pieces of silver . . .' And there were thirty of these pieces of silver, my dear friend. In his memory I pay everyone likewise.

BITKOV. Your excellency, grant me at least 35.

DUBELT. That sum is too large for me. Go and ask Ivan Varfolomeevich Bogomazov in to see me.

BITKOV *exits*. BOGOMAZOV *enters*.

BOGOMAZOV. Your excellency, guess what these papers are.

DUBELT. Guesswork is not good enough. You are holding a copy of the letter to Heckeren.

BOGOMAZOV. Leonty Vasilievich, you are a magician. (*Gives him the paper.*)

DUBELT. No, you are the magician. How did you manage it so cleverly?

BOGOMAZOV. The rough draft was lying in the waste paper basket, incomplete, sadly.

DUBELT. Thank you. Has it been sent off?

BOGOMAZOV. The valet will take it tomorrow.

DUBELT. What else, Ivan Varfolomeevich?

BOGOMAZOV. I was at a literary breakfast at Saltykov's.

DUBELT. What does the old fibber say?

BOGOMAZOV. It's terrible! He calls His Majesty the Emperor le grand bourgeois . . . (*Takes out a paper.*) And then Petey Dolgorukov let me copy this . . .

DUBELT. The cripple?

BOGOMAZOV. The same.

DUBELT. So. Anything else, Ivan Varfolomeevich?

BOGOMAZOV. Vorontsov's ball. (*Gives him a paper.*)

DUBELT. Thank you.

BOGOMAZOV. Leonty Vasilievich, you must watch that cripple Petey. No one can handle the damage he's unleashed. He calls everyone a sycophant. It won't be enough to break his other leg. He says he's descended from a martyr.

DUBELT. He'll soon be a martyr himself.

BOGOMAZOV. Allow me to take my leave of you, your excellency.

DUBELT. You have been of extraordinary assistance, Ivan Varfolomeevich. I will have the pleasure of informing the Count about you.

BOGOMAZOV. Leonty Vasilievich, I am deeply touched. I just do my duty.

DUBELT. I understand, I understand. Do you need a small sum, Ivan Varfolomeevich?

BOGOMAZOV. Well, 200 roubles, say, would not come amiss.

DUBELT. But I'll have 300 paid to you to make it a round number, thirty ten-rouble notes. Please tell Vasily Maksimovich.

BOGOMAZOV *bows, exits.*

(*Reads the paper brought by* BOGOMAZOV.) 'The blizzard blinds the sky with darkness . . . spinning snowy whirlwinds wild . . .' (*Hears something, looks out of the window, straightening his epaulettes.*)

The door opens, the gendarme PONOMAREV *appears, after him* NIKOLAI I *walks in the door, wearing a Cuirassier's helmet and a greatcoat, and after* NIKOLAI – BENCKENDORF.

Greetings, Your Imperial Majesty. Everything is in order in the Headquarters of the Corps of Gendarmerie, your Imperial Highness.

NIKOLAI I. I was driving with the Count when I noticed you had a light burning. Are you busy? Have I disturbed you?

DUBELT. Ponomarev, the overcoats. (PONOMAREV *takes the overcoats from* NIKOLAI I *and* BENCKENDORF.)

NIKOLAI I (*sitting down*). Sit down, Count. Sit down, Leonty Vasilievich.

DUBELT (*standing*). Yes, Your Majesty.

NIKOLAI I. What are you working on?

DUBELT. I am reading poetry, Your Majesty. I intended to report to His Eminence.

NIKOLAI I. Report away, don't let me stop you. (*Picks up some book or other, examines it.*)

DUBELT. Your Eminence, some frivolous fools are spreading around copies of Pushkin's poem on Bryulov's *Crucifixion*. Remember, you ordered the picture put under guard? Excerpts only, unfortunately. (*Reads.*)

Now at the foot of the one true cross
As if in front of the town mayor's house
There, where the holy women should be

> Stand two threatening sentries with guns
> Tell me the point of having a guard:
> Is then the painting owned by the state?
> And you're afraid of robbers and mice? . . .

Then there's a gap.

> Or do you fear the rabble will mock
> Him who was killed to redeem mankind?
> And thus the simple people are barred
> So their masters may stroll at their ease?

BENCKENDORF. What is the title?

DUBELT. *Worldly Power.*

NIKOLAI I. That man is capable of anything, except good. Neither awe for divinity, nor love for the fatherland . . . Ah, Zhukovsky! He is always playing the advocate . . . What a way he has with words! I'm sorry for the family, sorry for his wife, a good woman. Continue, Leonty Vasilievich.

DUBELT. Besides this, we found a short poem in manuscript on the person of Andrei Sitnikov, a student, during a search. Signed: A. Pushkin.

BENCKENDORF. Read it, please.

DUBELT. Let me report, your eminence, that it is not favourable.

NIKOLAI I (*leafing through the book*). Read it.

DUBELT (*reads*).
> In Russia all we have that's legal
> Is a pillar 'neath an eagle.

NIKOLAI I. He wrote that?

DUBELT. The copy is signed: A. Pushkin.

BENCKENDORF. It is remarkably curious that no matter who writes such vile things, they are always ascribed to Mr Pushkin. Such is his repute.

NIKOLAI I. You're right. (*To* DUBELT.) Investigate.

BENCKENDORF. Is there anything urgent?

DUBELT. What do you mean, your eminence: I expect there to be a duel in the capital not later than the day after tomorrow.

BENCKENDORF. Between whom?

DUBELT. Between His Majesty's court Kammerjunker Alexander Sergeevich Pushkin and Cavalry Guard Regiment Lieutenant Baron Egor Osipovich Heckeren-D'Anthès. I have a copy of the rough draft of an insulting letter from Pushkin to Baron Heckeren, the father.

NIKOLAI I. Read the letter.

DUBELT (*reads*). '. . . Like an old pimp, you lie in wait for my wife in every corner to tell her of the love of your bastard son. And when he, suffering from a vile disease, stayed at home, you said . . .' a blank . . . 'don't wish that my wife should continue to hear your parental counsels . . .' Blank. 'Your son had the effrontery to speak with her, since he is a coward and a blackguard. I have the honour to be . . .

NIKOLAI I. He will end badly. I tell you, Alexander Khristoforovich, he will end badly. Now I see it.

BENCKENDORF. He is an incorrigible duellist, Your Majesty.

NIKOLAI I. Is it true that Heckeren has been whispering to Pushkin's wife?

DUBELT (*glancing at the paper*). It is true, Your Majesty. Yesterday at Vorontsova's ball.

NIKOLAI I. The ambassador . . . Forgive me, Alexander Khristoforovich, for placing such a burden on you. A veritable martyrdom!

BENCKENDORF. Such is my duty, Your Majesty.

NIKOLAI I. He is a man who has led a shameful life. He will never be able to absolve his sins in the eyes of his descendants. But time will take revenge on him for these verses, for directing his talent not towards glorifying our national pride, but insulting it. And he will not die like a Christian. Treat duellists according to the law. (*Gets up.*) Good night. Don't trouble to see me out, Leonty Vasilievich. I've sat here too long, it's time for sleep. (*Exit accompanied by* BENCKENDORF.)

After a little time BENCKENDORF *returns.*

BENCKENDORF. The emperor has a kind heart.

DUBELT. A heart of gold.

Pause.

BENCKENDORF. So how will the duel be handled?

DUBELT. As you command, your eminence.

Pause.

BENCKENDORF. Please send men to lie in wait at the place of the duel so that they may catch them with their pistols and try them. Take into consideration the fact that the appointed place of the duel may be changed.

DUBELT. I understand, your eminence.

Pause.

BENCKENDORF. How good a shot is D'Anthès?

DUBELT. He can hit an ace at ten paces.

Pause.

BENCKENDORF. I feel sorry for the emperor.

DUBELT. Indeed!

Pause.

BENCKENDORF (*rising*). Leonty Vasilievich, make sure that your men do not make a mistake, otherwise they'll go to the wrong place.

DUBELT. Yes, your eminence.

BENCKENDORF. Good night, Leonty Vasilievich. (*Exit.*)

DUBELT (*alone*). 'The blizzard blinds the sky with darkness, spinning snowy whirlwinds wild . . .' 'To the wrong place!' . . . It's all right for you to say that . . . 'The blizzard blinds the sky with darkness . . .' To the wrong place? (*Rings.*)

The door opens a little.

Send Captain Rakeev to me.

Darkness.

Curtain

ACT THREE

HECKEREN's *apartment. Carpets, paintings, collections of weapons.*
HECKEREN *sits listening to a music box.* D'ANTHES *enters.*

D'ANTHES. Good day, father.

HECKEREN. Ah, hello my dear boy. Well, come here, sit down.
I haven't seen you for a long time, I've missed you. What are
you looking so unhappy about? You can talk to me. You pain
me with your silence.

D'ANTHES. J'étais très fatigué ces jours-ci. I am out of sorts. This
snowstorm has been going on for three days now. Even if I lived
here for a hundred years, I doubt I would get used to such a
climate. The snow flies every which way and everything is
white.

HECKEREN. You're being a hypochondriac. And that's bad!

D'ANTHES. Snow, snow, snow . . . How dreary it is! I wouldn't
be surprised to see wolves on the streets.

HECKEREN. But I have grown accustomed to it these fourteen
years. Il n'y a pas d'autre endroit au monde, qui me donne
comme Petersbourg, le sentiment d'être à la maison. When I get
bored, I lock myself up away from people. I amuse myself, and
boredom vanishes. Listen, isn't it charming! I bought it today.

The box plays.

D'ANTHES. I don't understand your passion for such rubbish.

HECKEREN. Oh no, this is not rubbish. I love gadgets the way
women love clothes. But what's wrong with you?

D'ANTHES. I'm depressed, father.

HECKEREN. Why did you do it, Georges? We were living so nice
and peacefully together.

D'ANTHES. It's ridiculous to talk about it. You know yourself
that I couldn't not marry Ekaterina.

HECKEREN. That's just what I'm saying: your passions will kill·
me. Why did you destroy our home? As soon as the woman
appeared in our house, I got uneasy; I felt as if I were being
driven out of my nook. I lost you, and in came pregnancy, noise,
the street. I hate women.

D'ANTHES. Ne croyez pas de grâce que j'aie oublié cela . . . I
know that all too well.

HECKEREN. You ingrate, you trampled underfoot peace and
quiet.

D'ANTHES. This is unbearable. Look, it all got muddled and then
vanished.

HECKEREN. Well and what can you possibly have to complain
about now? Don't you see her? Your desires are fulfilled; no one
thinks about mine. No, anyone else would have turned his back
on you long ago.

D'ANTHES. I want to take Natalya away to Paris.

HECKEREN. What! Oh my God! That I didn't even suspect.
Have you thought about what you are saying? Not happy with
merely depriving me of peace and quiet, now you want to smash
my life completely. He abandons his pregnant wife here and
abducts her sister! It's monstrous! What are you doing to me?
My whole career, everything is over! Everything will perish! But
no, I don't believe it. What callousness! What selfishness! And
finally, what madness!

A knock.

Yes, yes.

A SERVANT (*hands him a letter*). For your excellency. (*Exits.*)

HECKEREN. One minute, will you allow me?

D'ANTHES. Please.

HECKEREN *reads the letter, drops it.*

D'ANTHES. What's wrong?

HECKEREN. I warned you. Read it.

D'ANTHES (*reads*). So . . . So . . .

Pause.

HECKEREN. How dare he! He has forgotten who he is dealing with! I will destroy him! To me?!

Pause.

Disaster. A disaster is upon us. What have you done to me?

D'ANTHES. You reproach me for another man's foulness?

HECKEREN. He's a mad animal! Georges, you've put me in the hands of a desperate duellist.

D'ANTHES. Don't be hasty. (*Goes away to the window.*) Everything is covered up, buried . . . This is not about you. His style is deplorable. I don't understand where he got the idea that he was a writer. His style is deplorable. I've always maintained that.

HECKEREN. Don't pretend. Why did you insinuate yourself into his household? What role have you forced me to play? He has already attacked us once. I can still remember his face with its bared teeth. Why do you want to seduce her?

D'ANTHES. I love her.

HECKEREN. Don't say that again! You don't love anybody, you are just out for pleasure! Don't contradict me! What am I to do now? Challenge him? How will I be able to look the king in the face? And even if by some miracle I managed to kill him . . . What is to be done?

A knock. The SERVANT *leads in* STROGANOV, *who is blind. The* SERVANT *exits.*

STROGANOV. *Mille excuses* . . . Forgive me, dear Baron, for being late for dinner, but just listen to it . . . I don't remember such a snowstorm.

HECKEREN. You are a welcome guest at any time, Count.

STROGANOV (*feels* D'ANTHES's *hand*). It's the young Baron Heckeren. I recognize your hand. But it's like ice. Has something disturbed you?

HECKEREN. Count, we have had a catastrophe. Please give us your advice. I just received a letter from a man who hates Georges and me.

D'ANTHES. I am against publicizing this letter.

HECKEREN. Oh no. Do not interfere, the letter is addressed to me. And the count is my friend. The letter was written by Pushkin.

STROGANOV. Alexander?

HECKEREN. Yes. Our enemies have spread a malicious rumour and that is the reason for this vile attack. The jealous madman imagined that Baron D'Anthès had designs on his wife. In order to aggravate the insult, he writes an abusive letter to me.

STROGANOV. My niece promised to be a beauty. Now, unfortunately, I cannot judge whether these hopes were justified.

HECKEREN. I beg you in advance to forgive me for what you are about to hear. (*Reads.*) 'You acted paternally as a pimp for your son . . . like an old procurer, you lie in wait for my wife at every turn, to tell her of the love of your bastard son . . .' In his malice he drags the pure name of a mother through the mud! . . . I don't know who whispered to the madman that I was supposedly inciting Georges! Further, he writes that Georges is sick with a vile disease. He showers gutter abuse on him and threatens him. No, I cannot read any more.

STROGANOV. One can hardly believe that it was written by a Russian nobleman. Ah, what an age! What wantonness! Dear Baron, he is throwing the gauntlet not only to you. If he writes like that to the representative of a crowned head, he is challenging society. He is a *carbonari*. Yes, Baron, it's bad. It is a dangerous letter.

HECKEREN. What? Am I, a royal plenipotentiary representative, supposed to challenge him? Count, I am lost. Advise me. Am I to challenge him?

STROGANOV. Oh no.

HECKEREN. He attacks like a poisonous beast! Baron D'Anthès has given him no cause.

STROGANOV. After this letter, Baron, it no longer makes any difference whether Baron D'Anthès gave him cause or not. But it is impossible for you to fight with him. It could be said that Baron D'Anthès sent his father . . .

D'ANTHES. What can they say about me?

STROGANOV. But they won't say it, I suppose. (*To*

HECKEREN.) You must write to him that Baron D'Anthès challenges him. And add only one thing about yourself – that you will teach him to respect your office.

D'ANTHES. So be it.

HECKEREN. Yes, so be it. I am eternally grateful to you, Count, we have imposed excessively upon your attention. But I implore you, consider the full magnitude of the insult they have given. Let us go, Count, the table is set. (*Leads* STROGANOV *away*.)

D'ANTHES *alone. Suddenly he throws the music box onto the floor. It answers with a groan. He takes a pistol, shoots at a painting without aiming.*

HECKEREN. What are you doing? Ah, my heart!

D'ANTHES *turns silently and walks out.*

It is dark.

Outside. From the darkness – a crimson winter dawn. A stream in the snowdrifts. A hump-backed bridge. Quiet and deserted. After a while HECKEREN *walks onto the bridge, upset. He looks for something in the distance, about to move further. At that moment a pistol shot, not loud, is heard.* HECKEREN *stops, grips the railings. A pause. Then another shot, not loud, far away.* HECKEREN *lowers his head. A pause.*

D'ANTHES *comes onto the bridge. His greatcoat is thrown over one shoulder and is dragging. His frock-coat is covered in blood and snow. The sleeve of his frock-coat is cut open. His arm is bandaged with a bloodied handkerchief.*

HECKEREN. Heaven! Oh heaven! Thank you! (*Crosses himself.*) Lean on me. The handkerchief, here, take this handkerchief.

D'ANTHES. No. (*Clutches the railing, spits blood.*)

HECKEREN. Your chest, is your chest all right?

D'ANTHES. His aim was good. But he was unlucky . . .

DANZAS *walks up onto the bridge.*

DANZAS. Is that your carriage?

HECKEREN. Yes, yes.

DANZAS. Will you be so kind as to give it up to the other opponent.

HECKEREN. Oh yes, oh yes.

DANZAS. Driver! You in the carriage! Drive around below, there is a road there! What are you gawping at, you fool! Drive around below, where it's flat! (*Runs off the bridge.*)

HECKEREN (*softly*). And he?

D'ANTHES. He won't write anything else.

It is dark.

From the darkness – the winter day coming to its end. NIKITA, *wearing glasses, holding a notebook, is sitting in an armchair by the study fireplace in Pushkin's apartment.*

NIKITA (*reads*). 'There is no happiness on earth . . .' Yes, that's right, there's no bliss here . . . 'There's peace and freedom, though . . .' And that's something else we don't have . . . No sleep at night, what kind of peace is that? 'A weary slave, I've thought of flight . . .' Flight to where? What's that he's thought of?

BITKOV *enters.*

'A weary slave, I've thought of flight . . .' I can't make it out.

BITKOV. 'To distant labours and delight.' Hello, Nikita Andreevich.

NIKITA. How do you know that?

BITKOV. I was at Mr Zhukovsky's in the Shepelev palace yesterday, fixing the telescope. He read the guests these same lines.

NIKITA. Oh. Well?

BITKOV. They voiced their approval. Profound, they said.

NIKITA. Yes, profound, quite profound . . .

BITKOV. And where is he?

NIKITA. He went for a ride with Danzas, to the hills probably.

BITKOV. Why with Danzas? Do you mean the colonel? Why isn't he back yet?

NIKITA. What's up with you today? Had too much to drink or something?

BITKOV. I meant that it's late. It's suppertime.

NIKITA. Why should that matter to you? Did he invite you to supper? You'd do better to look at the clock in the study. What were you mending? It says one o'clock and strikes thirteen.

BITKOV. We'll have a look. We'll have the whole thing sorted out. (*Goes away to the back of the study.*)

The bell. ZHUKOVSKY *enters the living room from the dining room.*

NIKITA. Your excellency, please come in.

ZHUKOVSKY. How's that – he's gone riding? He's not in?

NIKITA. Only Alexandra Nikolaevna. And the children went with nanny to see the princess . . .

ZHUKOVSKY. But what's going on, I ask you?

GONCHAROVA *enters.*

GONCHAROVA. My dearest friend! Hello, Vasily Andreevich!

ZHUKOVSKY. Hello, Alexandra Nikolaevna. Permit me to ask what is going on? I'm not a child, Alexandra Nikolaevna.

GONCHAROVA. What has upset you. Vasily Andreevich? Sit down . . . How are you?

ZHUKOVSKY. Ma santé est gâtée par les attaques de nerfs . . . And all because of him.

GONCHAROVA. And what's wrong?

ZHUKOVSKY. I ask you! Yesterday he was galloping along like one possessed in a cab. He calls out of the cab to me that he can't wait in to see me and asks me to call on him today. I put off my business matters, drive over here, and he, if you please, has gone for a ride!

GONCHAROVA. I do beg you to forgive him, there's been some mix-up here. I should really give you a big kiss for the trouble you put yourself to for Alexander's sake.

ZHUKOVSKY. Ah, I don't need any kisses . . . Forgive me, I forgot myself . . . I renounce such things forever! Why do I put myself to such trouble, I wonder? No sooner do I sort one thing out than he immediately wrecks it! Nature obviously did not stint on intelligence, and if he's grown stupid now, he ought to be flogged!

GONCHAROVA. But what happened, Vasily Andreevich?

ZHUKOVSKY. This – the Tsar is angry with him, that's what, mademoiselle! Please! The day before yesterday at a ball, the Emperor . . . What can one say? Well, what can one say? I just burned with shame . . . Picture it – standing there, by the colonnade, in a frock-coat and black trousers . . . Excuse me, Alexandra Nikolaevna. Nikita!

NIKITA *enters*.

What did you set out for your master for the ball the day before yesterday?

NIKITA. A frock-coat.

ZHUKOVSKY. A uniform! You should have given him a uniform!

NIKITA. He ordered it, he doesn't like the uniform.

ZHUKOVSKY. It doesn't matter what he likes. Suppose he orders you to give him his dressing gown? This is your business, Nikita. Go on, go on.

NIKITA. Oh, misery . . . (*Exit.*)

ZHUKOVSKY. A scandal. The Emperor doesn't like frock-coats, the Emperor cannot stand frock-coats. And besides, he has no right! The uniform goes with his job. It's not proper, it's not decorous! But it's not just the frock-coat. He's started talking about retirement again. What a time to pick! He's not doing any work, Alexandra Nikolaevna! Where's the history he promised? And now they've started talking about some poems of his again. Do you remember what happened before? . . . And he has a multitude of well-wishers! Believe me, they'll make sure everyone hears!

GONCHAROVA. It's horrible what you say, Vasily Andreevich! But he's been so upset, so sick lately . . . Sometimes when I close my eyes I feel like we're flying into an abyss . . . Everything has got all tangled up . . .

ZHUKOVSKY. It must be untangled, it's sheer folly. The Emperor is very kind-hearted but you must not provoke him . . . You must not provoke him! Look, Alexandra Nikolaevna, tell Natalya Nikolaevna – if she crosses the Tsar there'll be no chance of saving it.

GONCHAROVA. How can we thank you, Vasily Andreevich?

ZHUKOVSKY. What are thanks? I'm not his nanny! If he wants to do damage, let him, let him, it's only himself he harms! . . . Good-bye Alexandra Nikolaevna.

GONCHAROVA. Oh, no, no . . . How can you leave like this . . . Stop, wait, he'll be here soon, he'll be here soon . . .

ZHUKOVSKY. I don't intend to see him; and besides I have no time.

GONCHAROVA. Temper your anger with mercy, he'll mend his ways . . .

ZHUKOVSKY. Enough, Alexandra Nikolaevna. En cette dernière chose je ne compte guère. (*Goes to the doors, sees a stack of books on the piano.*) I haven't seen that one yet. The new *Onegin*? Ah, good!

GONCHAROVA. They came from the printer's today.

ZHUKOVSKY. Ah, good. Very good.

GONCHAROVA. I've done some fortune-telling today using this book.

ZHUKOVSKY. How can you do that using a book? Do it for me.

GONCHAROVA. Name a page.

ZHUKOVSKY. 144.

GONCHAROVA. And a line.

ZHUKOVSKY. Well, fifteen.

   BITKOV *appears by the fireplace in the study.*

GONCHAROVA (*reads*). 'I learned the voice of other wishes . . .'

ZHUKOVSKY. For me? True . . .

GONCHAROVA. 'I learned a sadness new . . .'

ZHUKOVSKY. True, true.

GONCHAROVA. 'I have no rapture for the first . . .'

BITKOV (*in a whisper*). 'And the old grief makes me sad.'
(*Disappears into the study.*)

ZHUKOVSKY. Eh?

GONCHAROVA. 'And the old grief makes me sad.'

ZHUKOVSKY. Ah, ah . . . How he draws the thought out of himself! And how easily he finds an actual word to match the mental one! He soars, he soars! Oh hot blood! . . . The ungrateful fool. Whip him! Give him a good thrashing!

The apartment darkens in the twilight.

GONCHAROVA. And now you do it for me.

ZHUKOVSKY. Page?

GONCHAROVA. 139.

ZHUKOVSKY. And the line?

GONCHAROVA. Fifteen too.

ZHUKOVSKY (*reads*). 'It's pleasant, with rapier wit
　　　　　　　　To madden a blundering fool.

PUSHKINA *stands in the doorway.*

No, something's wrong . . . 'It's pleasant with rapier wit
　　　　　　　　To madden a blundering fool.
　　　　　　　　But better in silence to dig
　　　　　　　　A grave he can decently fill . . .'

No, you've missed, Alexandra Nikolaevna. Oh, forgive me, Natalya Nikolaevna! All this noise we're making, reading poetry . . .

PUSHKINA. Good day, Vasily Andreevich, I'm glad to see you. Read as much as you like, I never listen to poetry. Except yours . . .

ZHUKOVSKY. Natalya Nikolaevna, for heaven's sake!

PUSHKINA. Except yours, Vasily Andreevich. Votre dernière ballade m'a fait un plaisir infini . . .

ZHUKOVSKY. I'm not listening, I'm not listening!

The clock chimes in the study.

Oh goodness! I have to see the Tsarevich! . . . Au revoir, chère
madame, je m'aperçois que je suis trop bavard . . .

PUSHKINA. Have supper with us.

ZHUKOVSKY. Thank you, but I really cannot. Au revoir,
mademoiselle. Be so good as to tell him! Please don't bother to
see me out. (*Exits.*)

Twilight.

GONCHAROVA. Tasha, Vasily Andreevich came to talk about
the unpleasantness at the ball over the frock-coat.

PUSHKINA. How tiresome it all is! I warned him.

GONCHAROVA. What's the matter with you?

PUSHKINA. Leave me alone.

GONCHAROVA. I cannot understand you. Don't you see that all
these unpleasant episodes are because he is unhappy? And you are
completely indifferent to what might cause calamity for the
entire family.

PUSHKINA. Why has nobody ever asked me if I am happy? All
they can do is make demands on me. But has anyone ever felt
pity for me? What else does he want from me? I bore his
children, and all my life I've been listening to poems, nothing
but poems . . . Well, read some poems! Zhukovsky's happy, and
Nikita's happy, and you're happy . . . leave me alone.

GONCHAROVA. Your soul is opposed to doing good, quite
opposed. I see. You don't love him.

PUSHKINA. More love I cannot give.

GONCHAROVA. Alas, I can read your thoughts. And I pity the
entire family.

PUSHKINA. Well then you might as well know. (*Pause.*) Know
that I was supposed to see him today, but he did not come. And
I'm depressed.

GONCHAROVA. So that's the path you've taken!

PUSHKINA. Well what's bothering you? Is he really lonely? You
take such pains for him, and this is how I see it . . . (*Puts her
fingers over her eyes.*)

GONCHAROVA. You've gone mad! Don't you dare talk to me

like that, don't you dare, don't dare! I pity him, everyone has abandoned him!

PUSHKINA. Look me in the eyes.

NIKITA (*in the doorway*). Colonel Danzas asks you to receive him.

PUSHKINA. Say no. I cannot possibly receive him.

DANZAS (*enters wearing a greatcoat*). My apologies. You must receive me. I have brought Alexander Sergeevich. He is wounded. (*To* NIKITA.) Don't just stand there! Help carry him in! Only be careful. Don't jolt him!

NIKITA. Heavenly Mother! Alexandra Nikolaevna, oh disaster!

DANZAS. Don't shout. Don't jolt him!

NIKITA *runs out.*

Get some light in here.

PUSHKINA *sits motionless.*

GONCHAROVA. Light! Light!

BITKOV *appears in the doorway of the study with a lighted candelabra.*

DANZAS. Run. Help carry him in.

BITKOV *runs out with the candelabra. The* MAIDSERVANT *has appeared from the inner rooms with a candle.* BITKOV *runs out of the anteroom into the study with the candelabra and hides in the back, and after him, in the twilight, a group of people carries someone past into the back of the study.* DANZAS *immediately closes the door to the study.*

PUSHKINA. Pushkin, what's happened to you?

DANZAS. No, no, don't go in, I beg you. He ordered that no one be admitted until he is bandaged. And don't shout. You will disturb him. (*To* GONCHAROVA.) Take her to her room, that's an order.

PUSHKINA (*falling on her knees in front of* DANZAS). I'm not to blame! I swear it, I'm not to blame!

DANZAS. Quiet, quiet. Take her.

GONCHAROVA *and the* MAIDSERVANT *lead* PUSHKINA

into the inner rooms. BITKOV *runs out of the study shutting the door behind him.*

(*Taking out some money.*) Fly to Million Street, don't haggle with the cabbie, go to Doctor Arendt, you know him? And bring him here immediately. If he's not there, get any doctor you can, whoever, and bring him here.

BITKOV. Yes, sir, I understand, your excellency.

Military music is heard outside.

(*Rushes to the window.*) Oh Lord! The Guard is marching. They won't let me through. I'll go by the back way, through the yard. (*Runs out.*)

GONCHAROVA *appears.*

GONCHAROVA. D'Anthès? Tell the truth, how is he?

DANZAS. He is fatally wounded.

Darkness.

Curtain

ACT FOUR

Night. Pushkin's drawing room. The mirrors are curtained. Some kind of box, straw. A small couch. On it DANZAS is sleeping, fully dressed. All the doors are shut. From time to time the muffled sound of the crowd from the street.

ZHUKOVSKY appears quietly out of the study with a candle, sealing-wax, and a seal. He puts the candle on the piano, walks up to the window, looks out.

ZHUKOVSKY. Ay, ay, ay . . .

DANZAS. What? (*Sits up.*) I dreamt that I was in the guard-house. Well, that's only natural, the dream is about to come true.

ZHUKOVSKY. Konstantin Karlovich, I will intercede for you with the Tsar.

DANZAS. Thank you, but please don't bother. We will have to answer for this duel according to the law. (*Feels his epaulettes.*) Farewell. Ah well, exile to front-line battalions, Caucasian mountains.

ZHUKOVSKY. Look at what's going on in the street. The crowds are growing and growing. Who would have thought it!

DANZAS. I've already seen enough.

Through the doors from the inner rooms comes PUSHKINA, and with her a MAID.

MAID. Please ma'am, come to your room. Please, ma'am.

PUSHKINA (*to the MAID*). Go away.

The MAID leaves.

(*At the doors to the study.*) Pushkin, can I come in?

DANZAS. Now, how do you like that?

ZHUKOVSKY (*barring PUSHKINA's way*). Come to your senses, Natalya Nikolaevna.

PUSHKINA. What stupidity! The wound isn't dangerous . . . He will live. But you must give him some more opium to stop his suffering . . . And then the whole family must go to Polotnyany at once, at once. Why haven't they finished packing yet? 'It's pleasant with rapier wit to madden a blundering fool.' Pleasant. Pleasant? In silence . . . I've forgotten, forgotten everything . . . Pushkin, order them to let me see you.

ZHUKOVSKY. Natalya Nikolaevna.

DANZAS (*through the dining room door*). Vladimir Ivanovich . . . Doctor Dal . . .

DAL *enters.*

Help us.

DAL. Natalya Nikolaevna, there's nothing you can do here . . . (*Takes a flask from the piano, pours medicine into a small glass.*) Please, drink this.

PUSHKINA *pushes the glass away.*

Don't do that. You'll feel better if you take it.

PUSHKINA. No one listens to me. I want to talk to you.

DAL. Go ahead.

PUSHKINA. Is he suffering?

DAL. No, he's not suffering any more.

PUSHKINA. Don't you dare frighten me. That's cowardly . . . You are a doctor. Please help. But you aren't a doctor, you're a fabulist, you write fairy tales . . . And I don't need fairy tales. Save the man. (*To* DANZAS.). And you are the one who brought him here . . .

DAL. Let's go, I will help you.

The MAID *takes* PUSHKINA *under the arm.*

PUSHKINA. 'It's pleasant with rapier wit . . .' I've forgotten it all . . . I don't believe Alexandrina.

DAL *and the* MAID *lead* PUSHKINA *away.*

DANZAS. What is she saying to me?

ZHUKOVSKY. Konstantin Karlovich, you mustn't pay attention

to her! She is a terribly sad woman . . . They'll tear her to shreds now, absolutely.

DANZAS. But he wouldn't have escaped me. Believe me, I would have challenged him. But he ordered me not to. And how can I challenge him when I'll be locked up tomorrow?

ZHUKOVSKY. What are you saying! You want to increase your misery? It's all over, Konstantin Karlovich.

From behind the doors a soft, harmonious chorus is heard, barely audible. DANZAS leaves through the dining room and shuts the door behind him. GONCHAROVA enters from the inner rooms and goes to the window.

GONCHAROVA. And he cannot see this.

ZHUKOVSKY. Yes, he can, Alexandra Nikolaevna.

GONCHAROVA. Vasily Andreevich, I am not going to her room again. I'm going to put on my coat now and go outside. It's too painful for me, I cannot stay here any longer.

ZHUKOVSKY. Don't surrender to that voice: it is a dismal voice, Alexandra Nikolaevna. Can you really abandon her? She is to be pitied; people will start ripping into her now.

GONCHAROVA. Why are you tormenting me?

ZHUKOVSKY. Go, I command you – go.

GONCHAROVA *exits.*

(*Listens to the chorus*). What have you done . . . Yes, earth and ashes . . . (*Sits down, takes out a notebook, takes a pen from the piano, writes something down.*) There were no rays from his sharp mind . . . (*Composes, mutters.*) Then, as in a dream it came . . . I wished to ask you what you see . . .

DUBELT *enters quietly.*

DUBELT. Greetings, Vasily Andreevich.

ZHUKOVSKY. Greetings, General.

DUBELT. Do you intend to seal the study?

ZHUKOVSKY. Yes.

DUBELT. I will request that you stay a moment. I will go into the study, and then we will put the police seal on it too.

ZHUKOVSKY. What do you mean, General? It pleased the Tsar to entrust me with sealing it and examining the papers . . . I don't understand. I must examine the papers alone . . . For goodness' sake, why another seal?

DUBELT. Do you object, Vasily Andreevich, if the police seal is stamped next to yours?

ZHUKOVSKY. For goodness' sake, but . . .

DUBELT. The papers must be presented to Count Benckendorf for examination.

ZHUKOVSKY. What? There are personal letters there among them. For goodness' sake, I could be called an informer. You are encroaching on the one valuable thing I have – my good name. I will report to His Majesty the Emperor.

DUBELT. You permit yourself to suppose that the police can contradict the instructions of His Majesty the Emperor. Do you suppose that people will dare call you an informer? Ah, Vasily Andreevich . . . Can you really think that the government would take such a measure to hurt someone? This isn't to do harm, Vasily Andreevich. Come on, we're wasting time.

ZHUKOVSKY. As you wish.

DUBELT *goes into the study with a candelabra, then returns, offers the sealing wax to* ZHUKOVSKY. ZHUKOVSKY *applies the seal. Sound of breaking glass and a roar from the street.*

DUBELT (*softly*). Hey.

The portière of the inner doors moves aside and BITKOV *appears.*

Who are you, dear fellow?

BITKOV. I am the clock repairman, your excellency.

DUBELT. Run outside, my friend, and find out what happened.

BITKOV. Yes sir. (*Disappears.*)

DUBELT *starts to seal the door.*

ZHUKOVSKY. Who would have thought his death would attract such crowds . . . Universal sadness . . . I'd guess there are about ten thousand here today.

DUBELT. Police estimates put the figure at forty-seven thousand.

Pause.

BITKOV (*enters*). Your excellency, two men began shouting that it was deliberate that foreign doctors were treating Mr Pushkin, and then the doctor came out and someone threw a brick, breaking a streetlight.

DUBELT. Aha.

BITKOV disappears.

Ah, rabble, rabble.

The chorus behind the doors suddenly grows louder.

(*At the doors to the inner rooms.*) Please, gentlemen.

The inner doors open and ten POLICE OFFICERS enter the drawing room, single file, wearing greatcoats and holding their helmets.

It's time to bear the coffin out, gentlemen, please. Captain, Rakeev, trouble yourself to lead the procession. And I ask you, Colonel, to stay here. Ensure that every assistance be rendered to Madame Pushkin with all necessary dispatch.

The OFFICERS begin to follow RAKEEV into the dining room, except for one who returns to the inner rooms.

And you, Vasily Andreevich, will stay with Natalya Nikolaevna, isn't that right? The wretched woman needs comforting . . .

ZHUKOVSKY. No, I want to carry him. (*Exits.*)

DUBELT is alone. He straightens his epaulettes and aiguilletes, goes to the dining room doors.

It is dark.

Night on the Moika. The dim and flickering glow of streetlights. Behind the curtains the windows of Pushkin's apartment are flooded with light.

The entrygate. It is quieter by the gateway, but the crowd howls with excitement. The police restrain the crowd. Suddenly a group of students appears and tries to make its way through to the gateway.

POLICE SERGEANT. Students are not permitted. Get back. No entry.

Shouts from the students: 'What's this? Why can't Russians pay their respects to their dead poet?'

Back! Bar them, Ivanenko! It's against the law. Against the law to admit students.

Suddenly one of the students separates from the group and climbs up a streetlight.

STUDENT (*waving his hat*). Fellow citizens, listen! (*Takes out a sheet of paper, glances at it.*) 'The poet's soul could not survive the shame of petty sneers . . .

The rumbling of the crowd quiets down. The police freeze in surprise.

'Against convention he rebelled; alone, and he was killed.'

Shouts in the group of students: 'Hats off!'

POLICE SERGEANT. Sir! What are you doing there?

STUDENT. 'Killed. What is the point of wailing now, the useless choir of tears . . .'

POLICE SERGEANT. Pull him down from the streetlight!

Agitation in the crowd. A woman's voice from the crowd: 'Murdered!'

STUDENT. 'And was it you who from the first his persecution willed?'

A whistle. The police rush to the streetlight. The crowd starts to roar. Shouts from the crowd: 'Run!'

POLICE SERGEANT. What're you staring at? Take him!

STUDENT. 'The wondrous genius expired, extinguished like a lamp . . .' (*The student's words drown in the roar of the crowd.*) '. . . His murderer struck him in cold blood . . . Salvation there is none.' (*He disappears.*)

A shout: 'Hold him!' *The police chase the student. Lights in Pushkin's apartment go off. At the same time an officer in an army uniform climbs up another streetlight.*

OFFICER. Fellow citizens! What we have just heard is the truth. Pushkin's murder was premeditated, planned. This disgusting murder insults the whole nation.

POLICE SERGEANT. Silence!

OFFICER. The death of the great citizen occurred because in this country unbridled power rests with unworthy men who treat the people like slaves . . .

Police whistles pierce the air everywhere. RAKEEV appears in the gateway.

RAKEEV. Aha! Arrest him!

GENDARMES appear. The OFFICER disappears. At the same moment the clatter of horses' hooves is heard. A shout in the crowd: 'They'll trample us!' The crowd rushes to the side and starts to roar.

RAKEEV. Press the crowd back!

A space is cleared in front of the gateway. The windows of Pushkin's apartment have gone dark, but light starts flooding the gateway. It becomes quiet. And at this moment from the gateway flows soft, sad singing; gendarme OFFICERS appear first, then the first candles appear.

It is dark.

The singing gradually mingles with the whistling of the snowstorm. Night. An out-of-the-way post station. A candle. A fire in the stove. The STATION MASTER'S WIFE has gone to the window and is trying to make out something in the snowstorm. The light of lanterns flashes outside the window, low voices are heard. The STATION MASTER enters the room first with a lantern and lets RAKEEV and ALEXANDER TURGENEV go ahead of him. His wife bows.

RAKEEV. Who is at the station?

TURGENEV *rushes to the fire, warms his hands.*

STATION MASTER. There's no one, your excellency, no one.

RAKEEV. And who's this?

STATION MASTER. My wife, my spouse, your excellency.

TURGENEV. What's this, tea? Pour me a glass, for God's sake.

RAKEEV. And one for me, only make it quick. You'll have the horse ready within the hour, a troika for the cart, and for *that* . . . a pair.

TURGENEV *drinks tea, scaling his lips.*

STATION MASTER. But the troika, your . . .

RAKEEV. The troika within the hour. (*Takes the glass and drinks.*)

STATION MASTER. Yes, sir. Yes, sir.

RAKEEV. We'll lie down for an hour. In exactly one hour . . .

You have a clock? Wake us in an hour. Alexander Ivanovich, is it all right with you if we sleep for an hour?

TURGENEV. Oh yes, yes. My hands and feet are numb.

RAKEEV. If any traveller arrives, wake us up earlier and let the gendarme know.

STATION MASTER. I understand, I understand, yes sir.

RAKEEV (*to the* STATION MASTER'S WIFE). And you, old lady, there's nothing to see out of that window, there's nothing of interest.

STATION MASTER. There's nothing, nothing . . . Yes sir. Please come into the tidy part of the station.

His WIFE *opens the door, goes into the other room, lights a candle there, returns.* RAKEEV *goes into the other room,* TURGENEV *follows him.*

TURGENEV. My God!

The door closes behind RAKEEV *and* TURGENEV.

WIFE. Who are they, who's that they've got?

STATION MASTER. If you look outside I'll give you such a thrashing. Things will go badly for you. What a burden this is. And they had to come along this route . . . You look outside, and I'll give it to you . . . Don't you mess about with him!

WIFE. What did I see out there . . .

The STATION MASTER *exits. She immediately presses herself against the window. The outer door opens.* PONOMAREV *looks in cautiously, then enters.*

PONOMAREV. Have they bedded down?

WIFE. They have.

PONOMAREV. Give me five kopecks' worth, my bones are frozen.

She pours a glass of vodka, gives him some gherkins.

(*Drains the glass, eats, rubs his hands.*) Give me another.

WIFE (*pouring*). What are you doing that for? You should sit down and warm yourself.

PONOMAREV. I'll get warmed up there.

WIFE. And where are you travelling to?

PONOMAREV. Oh you misery of women. Just like Eve . . .
(*Drinks, gives her money, and goes out.*)

> *She throws a scarf over her head and is already getting ready to go outside when BITKOV appears in the doorway. He's wearing a short fur coat, his ears are wrapped by a scarf under his cap.*

BITKOV. Have they fallen asleep? (*Sighs, walks up to the fire.*)

WIFE. Frozen?

BITKOV. Just take a look out of the window, what kind of question is that? (*Sits down, unwinds the scarf.*) You the station master's wife? Yes, that's obvious enough. What's your name?

WIFE. Anna Petrovna.

BITKOV. Give me a quart, Petrovna!

> *She gives him a quart, bread, gherkins.*

> (*Drinks greedily, takes off his coat.*) What a thing is this? Eh? Holy Mother of God! . . . Fifty-five versts . . . And I've been saddled with it . . .

WIFE. Who saddled you with it?

BITKOV. Fate. (*Drinks.*) This is absurd; it's completely unthinkable.

WIFE. Well, I won't tell a soul, not a soul, may my tongue perish, I won't tell! Who are you carrying?

BITKOV. None of your business, it's a state matter.

WIFE. And why is it then you don't stop and rest anywhere? Why you'll freeze to death!

BITKOV. They won't waste any tears over us, and he doesn't feel the cold any more. (*Goes up to the inner doors on tiptoe and listens.*) They're snoring now; that's a shame. They have to be woken soon!

WIFE. Where are you taking him?

BITKOV. Well now, trying to make me talk. None of your business, woman, it's our job. (*Pause.*) To Sacred Hills. As soon as he's buried, it will be time at last for my soul to repent. Going on leave. He's going to distant labours and delights, and I'm going on leave. Ah, how many poems I've learned, damn them all!

WIFE. Why are you tormenting me, with all this stuff I can't understand?

BITKOV (*drains the glass*). Yes, he wrote poetry . . . And because of this poetry there's no rest for anyone . . . not him, not the masters, not me, slave of God Stepan Ilyich . . . Why I followed him everywhere . . . But he was unlucky. Whatever he wrote, it was always wide of the mark, never quite what . . .

WIFE. And they executed him for that?

BITKOV. Well now . . . What am I doing talking to this old woman? Fool!

WIFE. Why are you so rude?

BITKOV. How could I not be rude to you? . . . But maybe you aren't a fool. I bore him no ill-will, cross my heart. He was a real man. Just one flaw – that poetry . . . And I followed him everywhere, I even chased after him in cabs. He'd be in one and I'd jump on the one behind. He didn't even suspect. What fun it was!

WIFE. But now he's dead. So why are you still following him?

BITKOV. Just in case. He's dead . . . Yes, he's dead, and now you see it's night, a storm, utter chaos, and we're covering fifty versts at a time, fifty versts . . . And now he's dead . . . I'm afraid of this too – we'll bury him and will there be any point . . . ? Maybe there still won't be any peace and quiet . . .

WIFE. Is he a werewolf?

BITKOV. Perhaps, a werewolf. (*Pause.*) What's this ache inside me? Pour me some more . . . What's that sucking my blood? . . . Yes, it was a hard death. What agony he suffered! He was shot in the stomach . . .

WIFE. Ay, ay, ay . . .

BITKOV. Yes, he chewed his hands to stop himself from screaming, so his wife wouldn't hear. And then . . . silence. (*Pause.*) Only, honest to God, what business was it of mine? I'm a slave, a nobody . . . Why they never let him go anywhere alone – where he went, I went too. Not one step, no, no, no . . .

But on *that* day, on that Wednesday, I was sent somewhere else . . . I immediately sensed something was up – he was alone so that . . . They're clever. They knew he'd have to go there. Because his time had come. So he went straight to the rendez-vous and they were already waiting for him there. (*Pause.*) I wasn't there. (*Pause.*) And now I'll never go to his house again. Now his apartment there is cleaned out, empty.

WIFE. Who's that gentleman with you?

BITKOV. Alexander Ivanovich. Mr Turgenev, accompanying the coffin. No one else was allowed. Only he was given the order, Mr Turgenev.

WIFE. And that old man?

BITKOV. His valet.

WIFE. Isn't he going to warm himself up?

BITKOV. Doesn't want to. We've already argued and argued with him and gave up. He's guarding it – won't leave it. I'll take some out for him. (*Gets up.*) Oh, the storm . . . He wrote the best poetry: 'The blizzard blinds the sky with darkness, spinning snowy whirlwinds wild. Now it's howling like a beast, now it's wailing like a child . . .' Do you hear, he was right, just like a child. How much for a quart?

WIFE. Don't be silly.

BITKOV (*tosses money on the table with a grand gesture*). 'Now it rustles in the rooftops jerking at the ragged straw, now like some belated traveller it comes knocking on our door.'

The STATION MASTER *enters. Runs up to the inner doors, knocks.*

STATION MASTER. Your excellency, time to go, time to go.

RAKEEV *immediately appears at the inner doors.*

RAKEEV. Time to go.

Curtain

Methuen Modern Plays
include work by

Jean Anouilh
John Arden
Margaretta D'Arcy
Peter Barnes
Sebastian Barry
Brendan Behan
Edward Bond
Bertolt Brecht
Howard Brenton
Simon Burke
Jim Cartwright
Caryl Churchill
Noël Coward
Sarah Daniels
Nick Dear
Shelagh Delaney
David Edgar
Dario Fo
Michael Frayn
John Godber
Paul Godfrey
David Greig
John Guare
Peter Handke
Jonathan Harvey
Iain Heggie
Declan Hughes
Terry Johnson
Sarah Kane
Charlotte Keatley
Barrie Keeffe
Robert Lepage
Stephen Lowe

Doug Lucie
Martin McDonagh
John McGrath
David Mamet
Patrick Marber
Arthur Miller
Mtwa, Ngema & Simon
Tom Murphy
Phyllis Nagy
Peter Nichols
Joseph O'Connor
Joe Orton
Louise Page
Joe Penhall
Luigi Pirandello
Stephen Poliakoff
Franca Rame
Mark Ravenhill
Philip Ridley
Reginald Rose
David Rudkin
Willy Russell
Jean-Paul Sartre
Sam Shepard
Wole Soyinka
C. P. Taylor
Theatre de Complicite
Theatre Workshop
Sue Townsend
Judy Upton
Timberlake Wertenbaker
Victoria Wood

Methuen Student Editions